D0301602

A HISTORY OF IRISH THEATRE
1601–2000

While most accounts of Irish theatre begin with the Abbey Theatre, Christopher Morash's comprehensive study goes back three centuries earlier to Ireland's first theatre. Written in an accessible style, yet drawing extensively on unpublished sources, it traces an often forgotten history leading up to the Irish Literary Revival, and then follows that history to the present. The main chapters are each followed by short sections, focusing on a single night at the theatre that give the reader a sense of what it was like to be in an Irish theatre in 1663, 1822 or at the first Irish production of Samuel Beckett's *Waiting for Godot* in 1955. Morash creates a remarkably clear picture of the cultural contexts which produced the playwrights who have been responsible for making Irish theatre's worldwide historical and contemporary reputation: Farquhar, Sheridan, Boucicault, Wilde, Yeats, Synge, Shaw, O'Casey, Beckett, Brian Friel, Frank McGuinness and Martin McDonagh. Morash also deals with aspects of Irish theatre often ignored, including audiences, performance styles, theatre architecture, management and other aspects of Irish theatre culture. This book is an essential, entertaining and highly original guide to the history and performance of Irish theatre.

Christopher Morash is Senior Lecturer in English at the National University of Ireland, Maynooth. He has published extensively on Irish theatre and Irish cultural studies. He is the author of *Writing the Irish Famine* (1995), and consultant-editor for the theatre section of the *Encyclopaedia of Ireland*.

A HISTORY OF IRISH THEATRE
1601–2000

CHRISTOPHER MORASH

PUBLISHED BY THE PRESS SYNDICATE OF THE UNIVERSITY OF CAMBRIDGE
The Pitt Building, Trumpington Street, Cambridge, United Kingdom

CAMBRIDGE UNIVERSITY PRESS
The Edinburgh Building, Cambridge CB2 2RU, UK
40 West 20th Street, New York, NY 10011-4211, USA
477 Williamstown Road, Port Melbourne, VIC 3207, Australia
Ruiz de Alarcón 13, 28014 Madrid, Spain
Dock House, The Waterfront, Cape Town 8001, South Africa

http://www.cambridge.org

First published 2002

Printed in the United Kingdom at the University Press, Cambridge

Typeface Baskerville Monotype 11/12.5 pt. *System* LaTeX 2ε [TB]

A catalogue record for this book is available from the British Library.

Library of Congress Cataloguing in Publication data

Morash, Christopher, 1963–

A history of Irish theatre, 1601–2000 / Christopher Morash.

p. cm.

Includes bibliographical references and index.

ISBN 0 521 64117 9 (hardback)

1. Theater – Ireland – History. 2. Irish drama – History and criticism. I. Title.

PN2601 .M64 2002
792′.09415 – dc21 2001035894

ISBN 0 521 64117 9 hardback

Contents

Illustrations

Photographs

Maps

Plans

Acknowledgements

If I had not been aware of it before, working on this book made me conscious of how many people share my enthusiasm for Irish theatre history. Time after time, mention of the project brought forth suggestions, references, unpublished research or collections of theatre memorabilia. For all of those conversations beginning with the words 'you might be interested in this...', I would thus like to thank the following people: Charles Benson, Richard Bizot, Marie Boran, Conrad Brunström, Ophelia Byrne, Mary Clarke, Joe Cleary, Vincent Comerford, Allie Curran, Gerry Dawe, Seamus Deane, Mairead Delaney, John Devitt, Roger Doyle, Annette Fern, John Flood, Ray Gillespie, Stan Hickey, Eamonn Jordan, Margaret Kelleher, Tom Madden, Ann Matthews, Frank McGuinness, Emer Nolan, Colette O'Daly, Sunniva O'Flynn, Eoin O'Morain, Jim O'Shea, Stephen Rea, Shaun Richards, Marilyn Richtarik, Linzi Simpson, Bruce Stewart, Christopher Wheatley, Kevin Whelan, Penny Woods. Less directly, I would like to acknowledge the influence of Alan Andrews and Terence Brown, who taught me the craft.

Nicholas Grene of Trinity graciously gave me a chance to give part of the book a public airing in that most hospitable of environments, the Synge Summer School; that paper was subsequently published in *Interpreting Synge: Essays from the Synge Summer School, 1991–2000*, Nicholas Grene (ed.) (Dublin, 2000). I would also like to thank Brian Cosgrove of the English Department, National University of Ireland, Maynooth, for helping to fund this research; and Wojtek Kosinski of Berlitz GlobalNET, for donating computer equipment.

The maps and drawings in this book were paid for with the help of publications grants from the Publications Committees of NUIM, and of the National University of Ireland, and I am extremely grateful to both bodies. Jim Keenan, who drew the maps, and Kevin Weldon, who drew the architectural plans, both contributed enormously to this book.

For permission to quote from unpublished manuscript materials, I would like to acknowledge the following: Edward Beckett and the Estate of Samuel Beckett; Noel Carnduff; Druid Theatre Company; James Hardiman Library, National University of Ireland, Galway; Harvard Theatre Collection; Houghton Library, Harvard University; Linenhall Library; Council of Trustees, National Library of Ireland; Carolyn Swift; the Board of Trinity College Dublin. All published materials have been quoted in the spirit of fair dealing.

Finally, I would never have started writing this book had it not been for my editor at Cambridge, Ray Ryan, who turned a chance comment into a four-year project to which he gave his fullest support. I would never have completed the book were it not for my wife, Ann, who made it possible for me to write in more ways than I could list. In gratitude, I dedicate this *History of the Irish Theatre* to our children – Christopher, Dara and Aoife – in the hope that one day they will enjoy reading it as much as I enjoyed writing it.

Chronology

1601	7 Sept.	*Gorboduc*, Dublin Castle
	27 Sept.	Mountjoy arrives in Cork prior to Battle of Kinsale (Dec. 24)
1607	4 Sept.	Tyrone, Tyrconnell and other Gaelic earls flee Ireland
1633	25 July	Thomas Wentworth becomes Lord Deputy
1635		Probable date for building Werburgh Street Theatre
1638	1 Jan.	James Shirley, *The Royal Master* (Dublin Castle)
	28 Feb.	John Ogilby appointed Master of the Revels in Ireland
1639		Shirley, *St Patrick for Ireland* (Werburgh Street)
		Last recorded Corpus Christi play, Kilkenny
1640	17 Mar.	Henry Burnell, *Landgartha*; Werburgh Street closes shortly thereafter
1641	12 May	Wentworth executed
1642	Oct.	Catholic Confederation assembles in Kilkenny
1646		Henry Burkhead, *Cola's Furie* (published Kilkenny)
1649	30 Jan.	Execution of Charles I
1650	27 Mar.	Cromwell captures Kilkenny
1660	14 May	Charles II crowned
1661	8 May	Ogilby confirmed as Master of the Revels in Ireland
1662	18 Oct.	Fletcher's *Wit Without Money*; first play performed in Smock Alley
1663	10 Feb.	Katherine Philips, *Pompey* (Smock Alley)
	23 Feb.	Earl of Orrery, *The Generall* (Smock Alley)
		Hic et Ubique published
1670	Dec.	Galleries collapse in Smock Alley during Jonson's *Bartholomew Fair*

1677	9 July	Smock Alley company play Oxford; first Irish tour
1685	6 Feb.	James II crowned
1688	5 Nov.	William of Orange arrives in England; Smock Alley closes shortly thereafter
1689	18 Apr.	Siege of Derry begins (lifted 31 July)
1690	1 July	Battle of the Boyne; James goes into exile in France, July 4
1691	3 Oct.	Treaty of Limerick ends war, promising toleration to Catholics
	Dec.	Free performance of *Othello*, Smock Alley
1692	31 Mar.	Smock Alley re-opens to the public
1695	7 Sept.	First 'Penal Law' restricting Catholic rights passed
1698	Dec.	Farquhar's *Love and a Bottle* (Drury Lane)
1712	4 Nov.	*Tamerlane* riot at Smock Alley
1713		First Smock Alley tour to Cork
1720	7 April	Declaratory Act defines British Parliament's right to legislate for Ireland
		Charles Shadwell's *Rotherick O'Connor*
1722		William Philips, *Hibernia Freed*
1734	9 Mar.	Aungier Street Theatre opens
1735	11 Dec.	Smock Alley re-opens after renovations
1736		Theatre Royal, Cork, opens
1743	4 Feb.	Thomas Sheridan, *The Brave Irishman* (Smock Alley)
1745	Sept.	Sheridan becomes manager of Smock Alley
1747	19 Jan.	Kelly riot, Smock Alley
1754	2 Mar.	*Mahomet* riot, Smock Alley
1758	23 Oct.	Spranger Barry opens Crow Street Theatre, Dublin
1760	14 May	Charles Macklin, *The True-Born Irishman* (Crow Street)
1770		New theatres open in Belfast and Limerick
1775	17 Jan.	Richard Brinsley Sheridan, *The Rivals* (Covent Garden)
	2 May	Sheridan, *St Patrick's Day* (Covent Garden)
1779	4 Nov.	Volunteers demand free trade
1782	21 June	Declaratory Act repealed, giving power to Irish Parliament
		John O'Keeffe, *The Poor Soldier* (Crow Street)
1784	20 Dec.	Robert Owenson becomes manager of Fishamble Street Theatre

1786	1 June	Act for Regulating the Stage . . . of Dublin (26 Geo. III)
1791	14 Oct.	United Irishmen founded, Belfast
1795	Sept.–Oct.	Formation of Orange Order
1798	May/June	United Irish rebellion begins in Leinster and Ulster
1800	1 Aug.	Act of Union
1803	23 July	Robert Emmet leads unsuccessful rising
1804		Beginning of 'Familiar Epistles' pamphlet war
1811		James Sheridan Knowles, *Brian Boroimhe* (Belfast)
1814		Richard Lalor Sheil, *Adelaide* (Crow Street)
1821	18 Jan.	Theatre Royal, Hawkins Street, opens
1822	14 Dec.	'Bottle Riot', Hawkins Street
1829	13 Apr.	Catholic Emancipation Act allows Catholics to enter Parliament
1844	Oct.	Queen's Royal Theatre opens
1845	9 Sept.	First signs of potato blight; beginning of Famine
1848	July	Abortive Young Ireland rising
1859	April	Fenian Brotherhood established, USA
1861	April	Dion Boucicault, *The Colleen Bawn* (Hawkins Street; Irish première)
		Edmund Falconer, *Peep O' Day* (Drury Lane)
1867		Fenian attacks in England, Ireland and North America
1871	27 Nov.	Gaiety Theatre opens
1874	2 July	First Home Rule Bill defeated
		Dion Boucicault, *The Shaughraun* (Wallack's Theatre, NY)
1879		Star of Erin Music Hall (later Olympia Theatre) opens, Dublin
1880	9 Feb.	Theatre Royal, Hawkins Street, burns
1884	1 Nov.	Gaelic Athletic Association founded
		J. W. Whitbread becomes manager of Queen's Theatre
1885	14 Aug.	'Ashbourne' Land Act
1886	26 Apr.	Hubert O'Grady, *The Famine* (Queen's; Irish première)
1893	31 July	Gaelic League founded
1895		Grand Opera House, Belfast, opens

1898	12 Aug.	Irish Local Government Act (61 and 62 Vict.) changes regulation of theatre
	26 Dec.	J. W. Whitbread, *Wolfe Tone* (Queen's)
1899	8 May	W. B. Yeats's *Countess Cathleen*; Irish Literary Theatre first performance
1901	21 Oct.	Douglas Hyde, *Casadh an tSúgáin* (Irish Literary Theatre)
1902	2 Apr.	W. B. Yeats, *Cathleen ni Houlihan* (Irish National Dramatic Company)
1903	March	First National Theatre Society tour (London)
	14 Aug.	'Wyndham' Land Act
	17 Oct.	J. M. Synge, *In the Shadow of the Glen* (National Theatre Society)
1904	25 Feb.	J. M. Synge, *Riders to the Sea* (National Theatre Society)
	Nov.	Ulster Literary Theatre founded
	27 Dec.	Abbey Theatre opens; W. B. Yeats, *On Baile's Strand*, *Cathleen ni Houlihan*; Lady Gregory, *Spreading the News*
1906	24 Oct.	National Theatre Society Ltd registers as a company
1907	26 Jan.	J. M. Synge, *Playboy of the Western World* (Abbey); riots throughout week
	9 Mar.	Lady Gregory, *The Rising of the Moon*
		Queen's closes for renovations; reopens 1909
1908	Nov.	Cork Dramatic Society founded
1909	25 Aug.	G. B. Shaw, *The Shewing-Up of Blanco Posnet* (Abbey)
1910	27 Oct.	T. C. Murray, *Birthright* (Abbey)
		Annie Horniman withdraws subsidy from Abbey
1911	30 March	St John Ervine, *Mixed Marriage* (Abbey)
	Sept.	First Abbey tour of America
		Three film versions of *Colleen Bawn* released in America and Australia.
1912	4 March	P. J. Bourke, *When Wexford Rose* (Queen's)
1913	16 Jan.	Third Home Rule Bill defeated in House of Lords
	26 Aug.	Irish Transport and General Workers Union strike
1916	24 Apr.	Easter Rising begins; rebels surrender, 29 April; leaders executed, May.

	25 Sept.	Irish première of G. B. Shaw's *John Bull's Other Island* (Abbey)
	13 Dec.	Lennox Robinson, *The Whiteheaded Boy* (Abbey)
		Queen's introduces almost exclusively Irish repertoire
1919	21 Jan.	Soloheadbeg Ambush begins Anglo-Irish War
	1 Apr.	First meeting of Dáil Éireann; declared illegal, 12 Sept.
1921	9 July	Truce opens negotiations for Anglo-Irish Treaty (signed 6 Dec.)
1922	14 Apr.	Anti-Treaty forces seize Four Courts, Dublin
1923	12 Apr.	Sean O'Casey, *The Shadow of a Gunman* (Abbey)
	27 Apr.	Suspension of campaign by Anti-Treaty forces
		W. B. Yeats, Nobel Prize
1924	3 March	Sean O'Casey, *Juno and the Paycock* (Abbey)
1925	14 Sept.	George Shiels, *Professor Tim* (Abbey)
	3 Dec.	Boundary Commission define border between Free State and Northern Ireland
		G. B. Shaw, Nobel Prize
1926	11 Feb.	*Plough and the Stars* riots (Abbey)
	16 May	Fianna Fáil founded; wins general election, 1932
1928	28 Aug.	An Taibhdhearc opens with *Diarmuid agus Gráinne*
	14 Oct.	First Gate production, *Peer Gynt* (in Peacock Theatre)
	12 Dec.	Oscar Wilde, *Salomé* (Gate; in Peacock)
1929	3 July	Denis Johnston, *The Old Lady Says 'No!'* (Gate; in Peacock)
	16 July	Censorship of Publications Act
1930	17 Feb.	Gate Theatre opens with Goethe's *Faust*
1932	13 Oct.	Thomas Carnduff, *Workers* (Belfast Repertory Theatre)
		Amateur Dramatic Association founded
1935	29 Apr.	Teresa Deevy, *The King of Spain's Daughter* (Abbey)
1937	14 June	Irish Constitution enacted
1938	10 Aug.	W. B. Yeats, *Purgatory* (Abbey)
1940		Ulster Group Theatre founded
1943	1 Feb.	Committee for Encouragement of Music and the Arts (CEMA) created, Northern Ireland

1948	21 Dec.	Republic of Ireland Act (effective 1949)
1951	18 July	Abbey Theatre burns
		Arts Council established, Republic of Ireland
		Lyric Theatre founded, Belfast
1952	3 July	Bord Fáilte (Irish Tourist Board) founded
1953		First All-Ireland Drama Festival, Athlone; first Tóstal Festival
	26 Jan.	M. J. Molloy, *The Wood of the Whispering* (Abbey)
	1 June	Louis D'Alton, *This Other Eden* (Abbey)
1954	19 Nov.	Brendan Behan, *The Quare Fellow* (Pike)
1955	28 Oct.	Samuel Beckett, *Waiting for Godot* (Pike; Irish première)
	21 Nov.	Walter Macken, *Twilight of the Warrior* (Abbey)
1957	April	First Dublin Theatre Festival
	12 May	Pike Theatre prosecuted for obscenity after production of Tennessee Williams' *The Rose Tattoo*
1958	2 July	Industrial Development Act, to encourage foreign investment
		Dublin Theatre Festival cancelled due to Episcopal opposition
1959	2 Feb.	John B. Keane, *Sive* (Listowel Drama Group)
1960	26 Jan.	Sam Thompson, *Over the Bridge* (Ulster Bridge Productions)
1961	11 Sept.	Tom Murphy, *A Whistle in the Dark* (Stratford East, London)
	31 Dec.	RTÉ television begins broadcasting
1962		CEMA becomes Arts Council of Northern Ireland
1963		Economic growth in Republic 23 per cent over four-year period
1964	2 Sept.	Eugene McCabe, *King of the Castle* (Gaiety)
	22 Sept.	Máiréad Ní Ghráda, *An Triail* (An Damer)
	28 Sept.	Brian Friel, *Philadelphia, Here I Come!* (Gaiety)
1965		Taoiseach Sean Lemass and Northern Ireland PM Terence O'Neill meet
1966	18 July	New Abbey Theatre opens
1968	5 Oct.	RUC baton Civil Rights marchers, Derry
	18 Mar.	Tom Murphy, *Famine* (Abbey: Peacock)
		Críostóir Ó Floinn, *Cóta Bán Chríost* (An Taibhdhearc)

1969	14–15 Aug.	Riots in Derry and Belfast, British troops enter Northern Ireland
		Samuel Beckett, Nobel Prize
1970	11 Jan.	Formation of Provisonal IRA
	16 Sept.	Protest over *A State of Chassis* (Peacock)
1971	March	Tom Murphy, *The Morning After Optimism* (Abbey); Hugh Leonard, *Patrick Pearse Motel* (Gaiety); John Boyd, *The Flats* (Lyric)
1972	22 Jan.	Republic signs Treaty of Accession to EEC
	30 Jan.	'Bloody Sunday'; British Army kill thirteen people in Derry
1973	20 Feb.	Brian Friel, *The Freedom of the City* (Abbey)
	8 Oct.	Hugh Leonard, *Da* (Olympia)
1974	14–29 May	Ulster Workers' Council strike shuts down Northern Ireland
	27 May	Car bombs in Dublin and Monaghan kill thirty-three people
1975	6 Oct.	Tom Murphy, *The Sanctuary Lamp* (Abbey)
		Druid Theatre Company founded, Galway
1976	22 Jan.	Unemployment in Irish Republic reaches 116,000
1977	13 Oct.	Tom Kilroy, *Talbot's Box* (Abbey)
1979	5 Apr.	Brian Friel, *Faith Healer* (Long Acre Theatre, Long Island)
1980	23 Sept.	Brian Friel, *Translations* (Guildhall, Derry; first Field Day production)
	27 Oct.	Republicans begin hunger strike in Long Kesh Prison (ends 3 Oct. 1981)
		Arts Councils begin funding regional theatres
1982		Neil Jordan's *Angel* marks resurgence of Irish film-making
1983	9 May	Tom Mac Intyre, *The Great Hunger* (Peacock)
	15 May	Charabanc Theatre Company founded; *Lay Up Your Ends*
	29 Sept.	Tom Murphy, *The Gigli Concert* (Abbey)
	9 Nov.	Christina Reid, *Tea in a China Cup* (Lyric)
1984		School of Drama and Theatre Studies founded, Trinity College Dublin
1985	18 Feb.	Frank McGuinness, *Observe the Sons of Ulster* (Peacock)

	15 Nov.	Anglo-Irish Agreement
	5 Dec.	Tom Murphy, *Bailegangaire*
1987	23 Sept.	Stewart Parker, *Pentecost* (Field Day)
	8 Nov.	IRA bomb kills eleven people in Enniskillen
1988	26 Sept.	Frank McGuinness, *Carthaginians* (Peacock)
1990	24 Apr.	Brian Friel, *Dancing at Lughnasa* (Abbey)
	9 Nov.	Mary Robinson becomes first female President of Ireland
1993	13 Apr.	Frank McGuinness, *Someone Who'll Watch Over Me* (Abbey; Irish première)
1994	31 Aug.	IRA cease-fire; Loyalist paramilitaries follow suit, 10 Oct.
	5 Oct.	Marina Carr, *The Mai* (Peacock)
1995	30 March	Sebastian Barry, *The Steward of Christendom* (Royal Court, London)
	24 Nov.	Referendum legalises divorce in Republic
1996	1 Feb.	Martin McDonagh, *The Beauty Queen of Leenane* (Town Hall, Galway)
1997	4 July	Conor McPherson, *The Weir* (Royal Court, London)
1998	10 Apr.	Good Friday Agreement
	10 Dec.	John Hume and David Trimble share Nobel Peace Prize
		Arts Council budget for theatre (Republic) reaches £8 million
1999		Exchequer surplus in Irish Republic exceeds £1 billion
	24 Mar.	*Angel/Babel* (Operating Theatre)
2000	May	£50 million promised for building new Abbey Theatre

INTRODUCTION

Please take your seats . . .

This is a book about going to the theatre in Ireland. It has been written for those of us who will always feel that little rush of excitement when the houselights begin to dim, the auditorium goes silent, and a room full of strangers turns into an audience waiting for something to happen.

This could have been a very different kind of book. The tradition of writing for the theatre in Ireland (or, indeed, of Irish people writing for the theatre – the two are by no means identical) is so impressive and sustained that it would have been possible to have focused squarely on a line of dramatic writing that begins (to take a convenient starting point) with Farquhar, moves through Sheridan and forgotten (but in their time hugely influential) figures such as John O'Keeffe and James Sheridan Knowles, continues to Boucicault and that astounding burst of Irish dramatic activity at the beginning of the twentieth century – Shaw, Yeats, Lady Gregory, Synge – followed by O'Casey, the towering presence of Beckett, and then concludes with the parallel explosion of writing at the end of the century: Murphy, Friel, McGuinness, and newer writers such as Marina Carr and Conor McPherson.

Of course, writers and their work play a role in a history of the theatre, as do the actors, directors, and designers who turn scripts into plays on the stage, the architects who build those stages, and the managers, entrepreneurs, and patrons who somehow find money to keep the whole unwieldy business going. At the same time, a history of the Irish theatre is a history of Irish audiences: who they were, how much they paid for their tickets, where they sat, whether they watched reverentially or threw oranges at the orchestra.

We can never fully know what it was like to sit in an Irish theatre in 1662 or 1754 or 1904. In some cases, however, we can reconstruct a reasonably accurate picture of what those vanished audiences expected, and of what they saw on those now-darkened stages. Through the imaginative leap that all attempts to respect the reality of past lives demand of us, we may at least glimpse the ways in which others have responded to the ephemeral – yet enduring – experience of a night at the theatre.

CHAPTER 1

Playing court, 1601–1692

7 September 1601. The Great Hall of Dublin Castle is alight with dozens of wax candles, mounted in candelabra around the room. Baron Mountjoy, the Lord Deputy of Ireland, is seated at one end of the chamber, surrounded by his court; from the other end, a group of wild men appear, dressed only in clusters of leaves. The wild men produce a thick bundle of sticks. They pull, twist and hit the bundle, trying to break it, but with no success. Then one of the wild men draws out a single twig and snaps it. Within minutes, the entire bundle is torn apart and every stick broken, thus presenting in dumbshow the argument of the play which is to follow: Thomas Sackville and Thomas Norton's *Gorboduc*, a verse tragedy in which a divided kingdom descends into fratricide, rebellion, and civil war, leaving 'the land for a long time almost desolate and miserably wasted'.

This production of *Gorboduc* is as good a place as any to start a history of the theatre in Ireland, even though *Gorboduc* is not an Irish play. Written for the 1561/2 Christmas festivities at London's Inner Temple, *Gorboduc* was already archaic when Mountjoy revived it in 1601; but this does not mean that he was ineptly aping London fashion. In 1601, Dublin Castle was supposed to be the administrative centre around which Ireland revolved; however, with Hugh O'Neill, the Earl of Tyrone, in open rebellion in Ulster, and Spanish forces only a fortnight away from landing in Kinsale, it might be more accurate to say that Dublin Castle provided a common arena of intrigue for a number of competing groups: the Gaelic aristocracy, the Old English whose ancestors had come to Ireland during the Norman invasions of the twelfth century, the New English of the Elizabethan plantations, and a constantly shifting cadre of English administrators and soldiers. These factions were capable of a variety of strategic and usually unstable alliances; and many of them would have been represented in Dublin Castle on that September evening. And so, when a character in *Gorboduc* warns that 'with fire and sword thy native folk shall perish . . . when noble men do fail in loyal troth, and subjects will be kings',[1] Mountjoy was doing more than entertaining his guests; he was using the theatre to define the terms of war.

Hovering somewhere near Mountjoy as he watched *Gorboduc* may well have been his 'Irish fool', Neale Moore, a traditional Gaelic clown, or *druth*, who had been in the service of the English nobleman since at least 1600. Moore's presence should remind us that while Ireland did not have any theatres in 1601, it had a long history of performance, extending back at least to the seventh century. Outside the Pale, it had long been common practice for Gaelic noblemen to retain the services of artists ranging from *filid*, who could compose verse in complex metres, to the *braigetóirí*, who amused their audiences by farting. In Dublin and Kilkenny, there was liturgical drama as early as the fourteenth century, and the script of one such play still exists: the *Visitatio Sepuleri* performed in the Church of St John the Evangelist, within a few paces of Dublin Castle. Equally, civic processions with theatrical elements passed the gates of the castle on feasts such as Corpus Christi. Meanwhile, throughout the period there are tantalising hints of strolling players, entertaining audiences with lost forms of performance.[2]

The Irish *druth* Neale Moore watching the English tragedy *Gorboduc* can stand as an emblem of the unexpected ways in which the competing cultures of early seventeenth-century Ireland were thrown together. Indeed, when the wild men first began to creep into the Great Hall at the beginning of *Gorboduc*, we can imagine a moment of *frisson*, as if Neale Moore's world from outside the Pale – at least as it was fantasised from inside the Pale – was invading the inner sanctum of the castle. Of course, this could not have lasted for more than a moment, for Mountjoy's audience would have recognised the wild men as conventional masque figures whose task was to present an allegorical tale. In this case, however, transferring the parable of the bundle of sticks from an English to an Irish context transformed its meaning: when first staged in London in 1561, the moral that a divided land was easily conquered would have been understood as an admonishment; in Dublin in 1601, it was a threat. Indeed, two days after he watched *Gorboduc*, Mountjoy set off once again to pursue a war in which, as his secretary, Fynes Moryson, observed, 'the common sort of the rebels were driven to extremities beyond the record of most histories I ever did read'. By the time the Battle of Kinsale had been fought on Christmas Eve, Gaelic Ireland – Neale Moore's Ireland – was in defeat, and 'the whole Countrie' was 'harried and wasted'.[3]

In the years that followed, plays continued to be produced privately in great houses around the island, but it was not until Thomas Wentworth, the Earl of Strafford, arrived as Lord Lieutenant in July of 1633 that the first attempt was made to build a theatre. From the beginning of his administration, Wentworth set about transforming Dublin into an image of royal power, rebuilding part of Dublin Castle, laying down strict codes of court etiquette, and planning a mint. The theatre was a major part of life at the court of Charles I in London; consequently, Wentworth set about building a theatre for his court in Dublin. By late 1635 (and possibly earlier) he had a 'gentleman of the household', John Ogilby, making, 'great preparations and disbursements in building a new theatre, stocking and bringing over a Company of Actors and Musicians, and settling them in Dublin'.[4] A few years later, Ogilby was made the first Master of the Revels in Ireland.

Ogilby's timing was propitious. The London theatres had been closed because of plague since 12 May 1636, and this enabled him to recruit a strong company of English actors: Edward Armiger and William Perry, who had connections with London's Red Bull theatre; William Cooke, who had been under the patronage of the young Prince Charles (later Charles II); almost certainly Thomas Jordan from Salisbury Court; and possibly members of Queen Henrietta's Men from the Cockpit, who had disbanded in 1636. Then, on 23 November 1636, he pulled off an even greater *coup* when he brought to Dublin a prestigious resident playwright, James Shirley. This core company are referred to on the title page of one play performed in Dublin as 'His Majesty's Company of Comedians', and while they probably arrived in small groups, by the late autumn of 1637 they were able to première Shirley's *The Royal Master* in the new theatre.[5]

There is still much that is not known about this first Irish theatre, including the exact date of its opening and its precise location. In 1749, the earliest historian of the Irish stage, W. R. Chetwood, claimed that the Werburgh Street Theatre opened in 1635, and this opinion was echoed by most historians up to the middle of the twentieth century, until W. S. Clark pushed the date ahead to 1637. However, a letter recently uncovered by Alan Fletcher in which Wentworth refers to 'a Playhouse lately sett up and allowed by me' clearly indicates that the theatre had been at least 'sett up' before June 1636 – although how long before is still a matter for speculation.[6] Similarly, no one is quite sure of its location, although we do know that it was located on or near Werburgh Street, only a few hundred metres from the castle precincts, and within the city walls.

Early seventeenth-century maps of Dublin show Werburgh Street (or 'St Warbers Stret', as John Speed's 1610 map calls it) closely lined with buildings, including the church that gives the street its name. Sir Adam Loftus, Lord Chancellor until 1638, lived there, and a company of sadlers, a surgeon and a letter-writer all had business premises on the street. This means that Ogilby's theatre was an indoor theatre squeezed into an already built-up streetscape, like the Blackfriars or Salisbury Court in London. The few existing written descriptions from the eighteenth century indicate that it was opposite Hoey's Court, and there was a nineteenth-century tradition that it was located in what later became Derby Square, on the west side of Werburgh Street. This latter view has been given added credence by recent archaeological work in the area, which has unearthed some unusual curved walls in early seventeenth-century buildings on the south side of the Square, across from Hoey's Court, and within the old city walls near what had been Pole Gate.[7]

While there are no eyewitness descriptions of the theatre, it is still possible to assemble a reasonably accurate picture of the building's interior. The eighteenth-century theatre historian Thomas Wilkes claims to have been told that Werburgh Street 'had a gallery and pit, but no boxes, except one on the Stage for the then Lord Deputy, the Earl of Strafford',[8] and this would accord with what is known of private indoor London theatres of the time. In terms of size, a good point of comparison here is probably the Blackfriars, where the pit was 30 feet (9 metres) deep, and 23 feet (6.9 metres) wide, according to one recent estimate, seating an audience of about three hundred, to which could be added another hundred in a balcony running around the three walls of the auditorium.[9] The stage was certainly smaller than that of the large outdoor London theatres, for when one of Shirley's Dublin plays, *The Doubtful Heir*, made its London debut at the Globe in 1640, a new prologue asked the audience to 'pardon our vast stage'.[10] Again, we might draw a comparison with Blackfriars stage, which was about the same size as its pit, while there is some evidence to suggest that Salisbury Court (with which Shirley was connected from 1629 to 1633, and in which several of his Dublin plays were staged after he returned to London) may have had a rounded forestage, shaped like half a hexagon.[11]

Whatever its shape, the Dublin stage, like its London counterparts, certainly had an upper acting area, for the opening scene of *The Politician* (written by Shirley for the theatre in 1639) begins with one character warning another to 'avoid the gallery', which we are told is lined with paintings; a later scene takes place on the city walls above the gates. Other plays written for the theatre require a small discovery space, probably behind a set of double doors, in the upstage wall, and stage directions for Henry Burnell's *Landgartha* (1640) – 'Enter Reyner musing at one doore, and Hubba to him at the other' – specify two further entrances, with doors, on either side of the stage. Finally, a scene in Shirley's *St Patrick for Ireland* (1639), in which a character is swallowed up by the ground, indicates at least one trap in the main stage.

This first Dublin theatre, then, was a versatile, intimate performing space, and in some respects it was a typical court theatre. One prologue written for the theatre addresses what was probably the largest group in the audience – courtiers and castle functionaries – when the poet observes that he 'did expect a session, and a train / So large, to make the benches crack again', just as the epilogue to *Landgartha* tells us that the play was commanded to appear 'fore the Court Break up'. At the same time, the Werburgh Street audience were not exclusively members of the court. A prologue to a lost play, *The Generall*, curses the 'dreadful word *vacation*', and pines for 'the term' to come, 'though law came with it', indicating that the theatre had patrons from the law courts, and possibly from Trinity College, founded in 1592. This same prologue goes on to note the presence in the audience of 'some soldiers' while in *Landgartha* there are a pair of clownish farmers who tell the audience that 'when in Towne, we doe / Nothing but runne from Taverne, to Taverne; . . . Now and then to see a Play'.[12] In short, while the audience of the Werburgh Street theatre was by no means a representative sample of the predominantly Irish-speaking population of the island as a whole, it did bring together the tight circle of courts, castle and college that would form the foundation of Irish theatre audiences for almost two centuries.

When this audience gathered by candlelight to watch Shirley's *The Royal Master*, probably in the late autumn of 1637, the little auditorium must have crackled with tension. Everyone in that room would have been aware that when Shirley had lived in London, he had been part of the group of courtiers who congregated around the Catholic wife of Charles I, Henrietta Maria. Rumours would have circulated that Shirley himself had converted to Catholicism, probably in 1624. Thomas Wentworth had almost certainly heard those same rumours, for he was a consummate court insider, and his letters show that while in Ireland he kept up with London's theatre gossip. Shirley did nothing to dispel these stories after he arrived in Dublin, for the 1638 Dublin edition of *The Royal Master* contains a commendatory verse by Richard Bellings, a prominent Catholic, later Secretary to the Supreme Council of the Catholic Confederation in the 1640s, and its envoy to Pope Innocent X.

Seated in his viceregal box on the side of the stage, Wentworth must have noted with some satisfaction the anxious swell of conversation, and the suspicious, sidelong glances. Sponsorship of an Irish theatre with a Catholic resident playwright in 1637 was precisely the sort of audacious move we might expect from a man who once told a correspondent: 'I am not afraid of any Man's complaint, being well assured in myself that whoever questions me shall work towards my greater Justification.' During the period in which the Werburgh Street theatre operated, Wentworth's strategy was, as he admitted to a friend, 'to bow and govern the native by the planter, and the planter by the native'.[13] Playing one faction against another, Wentworth embarked on a series of labyrinthine and increasingly perilous manoeuvres to raise money in Ireland for Charles I, dispossessing Catholic landowners while at the same time absolving Catholics from the need to take a special oath of loyalty forced upon Ulster Presbyterians.

Although Shirley was no wide-eyed innocent when it came to court intrigue, he would not have been in Dublin for long before he realised that he had become a player in a dangerous game. Back in London, he had gained admittance to Charles' court in 1634 after writing an admired masque, *The Triumph of Peace*, which uses theatrical spectacle to create a flattering image of harmony emanating from the monarch. In Dublin, he found himself writing for a court in which the cultivation of suspicion and discord – not harmony – was a basic strategy of survival, and he soon recognised that a few allegorical cherubs were not going to change the situation. As early as his first Dublin play, *The Royal Master*, a character dismisses a masque as a collection of 'pretty impossibilities . . . Some of the gods, that are good fellows, dancing, / Or goddesses; and now and then a song, / To fill a gap.'[14] From that point on, Shirley's plays for the Dublin theatre register an anxious awareness that he was not going to find an image of reconciliation for his divided audience, and this anxiety would eventually dominate his last Irish play, *St Patrick for Ireland*, staged in the autumn of 1639.

It may well have been Shirley himself who spoke the prologue with which the play begins, in which he claims to 'have no despair, that all here may, / Be friends, and come with candour to the play'. By the closing months of 1639, this was a slim hope. A few months earlier, in June, the position of Charles I had been weakened further by the Treaty of Berwick, in which he was forced to admit temporary defeat in his campaign to impose Anglican worship on the Scots (who, of course, were linked to their co-religionists in Ulster). For the soldiers, courtiers and lawyers sitting on the benches in Werburgh Street, this stalemated religious war would have been uppermost in their minds as they watched Patrick's crusade to evangelise the Irish. 'We are of Britain, Sir', the saint tells the Irish king, Leogarius, in act I, making Patrick initially appear to be a type of evangelising English colonist.[15] However, from that point on, any simple allegorical reading of the play becomes increasingly complicated.

Part of the problem is the figure of St Patrick, who was closely associated with Irish Catholicism. Indeed, *St Patrick for Ireland* may well have been a piece of special pleading on behalf of Shirley's former patron, Queen Henrietta Maria, who had requested Wentworth to reopen St Patrick's Purgatory, an Irish site of Catholic pilgrimage demolished in 1632 by zealous reformers. The audience of court insiders would, of course, have known this, and there must have been more than a few whispered comments when Shirley's Patrick makes his first entrance, trailing a procession of choristers who sing a sonorous, liturgical-sounding ode in bad (but suggestively Catholic) Latin. And yet, a few scenes later in Shirley's play, two native Irish noblemen attempt to hide by disguising themselves as Roman 'idols', standing on an altar bedecked with candles and incense, and uttering duplicitous prophecies. This must have looked like precisely the sort of exposure of superstition and religious imposture that would warm the heart of any Protestant missionary. 'We are but half-gods, demi-gods', they tell the audience, 'there's nothing beneath the navel.' In the end, *St Patrick for Ireland* is torn between the desire to create miraculous stage spectacles, and the conflicting urge to expose them, so that when an Irish magician, Archimagus, is swallowed up by the earth in the play's final moments, Patrick remains sceptical. 'I suspect him still', he tells the audience.

'Howe'er the dice run, gentlemen', Shirley boasted in the epilogue to *St Patrick for Ireland*, 'I am / The last man borne still at the Irish game.'[16] At that point, the game was nearly over. By the beginning of 1640, members of the Werburgh Street company were already beginning to slip away, and on 16 April Shirley would sail home to London. Before he left, however, he would have been able to watch the depleted company play Henry Burnell's *Landgartha*, the first Irish play by an Irish writer, staged on St Patrick's Day, 1640. 'A semi-maske . . . now't can be no more', Burnell apologises in his prologue, 'For want of fitting Actors here at Court. The Warre and want of Money, is the cause on't.' Indeed, 'the Warre' dominates Burnell's play, in which a female warrior, the Norwegian Landgartha helps the Danish king, Reyner, to defeat both the Swedish and German kings, even though Reyner has betrayed her. The play ends with Landgartha agreeing to live as Reyner's wife, and he in turn pledges his faithfulness; yet, she tells him 'my heart shall still receive you; But on my word, / Th' rest of my body you shall not enjoy, sir.' In terms of sexual allegory, this failed consummation is a tragic end, which Burnell tells us offended some ('but not of best judgements') who expected Landgartha to accept 'the Kings Kind night-embraces'. This could not be, Burnell insists, in a 'Tragie-Comedy', which 'sho'd neither end Comically or Tragically, but betwixt both'.[17]

Landgartha's place in the Irish cultural wars of the 1640s comes into focus with the character of Marfisa, who first appears 'in an Irish Gowne tuck'd up to mid-legge, with a broad basket-hilt Sword on, hanging in a great Belt, Broags on her feet, her hayre dishevell'd, and a payre of long neck'd big-rowll'd Spurs on her heels'. In performance, Marfisa's costume and speech mark her out either as Gaelic, or, more probably, as one of the Old English, who in many cases had adopted the speech and dress of the indigenous population. In case the audience miss the point, shortly after her entrance a character comments: 'The fashion / Of this Gowne, likes me well, too; I thinke you had / The patterne on't from . . . Ireland.'[18] Throughout the play, Marfisa and her foil Hubba (a conventional plainspoken English soldier, who enters praising Marfisa's 'gigglers') are the low comic counterparts to the main protagonists, Landgartha and Reyner. If Marfisa (and thus Landgartha) is Old English and Hubba (and therefore Reyner) is New English, the play begins to take an allegorical shape. Landgartha's betrayal by Reyner corresponds to the Old English sense of betrayal by the New English, after which cohabitation might be possible, but full consummation was out of the question.[19] For Burnell, a prominent Catholic royalist, *Landgartha* was a last-ditch attempt to define a possible relationship between two cultures that were spiralling towards war.

In the months after *Landgartha* was staged, the situation in Ireland deteriorated rapidly. A little over a year later, on 12 May 1641, Wentworth was beheaded for a list of treasonous crimes, among which was the attitude to Catholicism that led him to open a theatre with a resident Catholic playwright. Typical of the pamphlets published in the months before his execution is one claiming that his secretary, George Radcliffe, stopped the Warden of St Werburgh's parish from pulling down 'a Masse-house that was newly erected within foure or five houses of the Castle gate'. 'All men that knew him', writes the pamphleteer, 'might quickly discerne his inclination to that Idoltarous, Babilonian whore'.[20] With Wentworth gone, the theatre in Werburgh Street was closed by the Lords Justice, Sir William Parsons and Sir John Borlase, becoming first a military stable and then 'spolyed and a cow house made of the stage', before falling 'into utter rueine by the Calamities of those times'.[21] On 17 November Ogilby narrowly escaped being blown up along with the rest of Rathfarnham Castle (where he had taken refuge with his Werburgh Street neighbour, Sir Adam Loftus), later was shipwrecked on the voyage home, and arrived in London more dead than alive. At around the same time, the Old English were joining the Irish who had taken over Ulster.

In the exodus from Dublin, Burnell headed south to Kilkenny, where in October 1642 a Confederate Assembly of Old English and Irish formed a government in internal exile, which lasted until 1649. Burnell became an Assembly member, and he was joined by many of the Catholic Old English merchants and noblemen who had been in the audience in Werburgh Street. The city in which they found themselves had a theatrical tradition extending back to at least 1366, when Archbishop Thomas Minot forbade 'theatrical games and spectacles' on church property. On 20 August 1553, two plays were staged at the Market Cross in Kilkenny: *Gods Promises, a Tragedy or Enterlude*, and *A brefe Comedy or Enterlude of Johan the Baptyses preachynge in the Wyldernesse*, by John Bale, Bishop of Ossory. Bale presented his plays in a zealous, but short-lived attempt to counter the city's vigorous Catholic mystery cycle tradition, which continued until at least 1639, when a Mathew Hickey was paid 13*s*.4*d*. by Kilkenny Corporation 'for acting a Conqueror's parte at Corpus Christi and at Midsomer time last'. In 1642, a Jesuit college was established in Kilkenny, and in 1644 the 'Schollars of the Society of Jesus, at Kilkenny' performed an original Latin play, *Titus: or the Palme of Christian Courage*, for which a detailed playbill still exists.[22]

Although much attenuated, Irish theatre culture thus shifted its centre to Kilkenny in the 1640s, where at least one new play was published: *A Tragedy of Cola's Furie, OR, Lirenda's Miserie*, by Henry Burkhead (1646). With the battle lines now more or less clearly drawn, *Cola's Furie* is able to dispense with the ambiguous identifications and torturous parallels of its predecessors, *St Patrick for Ireland* and *Landgartha*. Indeed, in his dedication, Burkhead states bluntly that although 'drawn from the historicall records of Forren countryes', 'this small worke' is nonetheless 'fitly applyable to the distempers of this Kingdom'.[23] Should the point be missed, the play refers directly to 'puritans', 'Papists', 'Roundheads' and other contemporary matters. Hence, it would have taken little guessing for the audience to figure out that 'Lirenda' is an anagram for 'Ireland', and the invading 'Angoleans' are the New English of Cromwell's army.

Once this basic framework is in place, it becomes apparent that each of the major male characters represents a real individual: the villainous 'Angolean Governors of Lirenda' Pitho and Berosus are, appropriately enough, Sir William Parsons and Sir John Borlase, the men who ordered the closing of the Werburgh Street Theatre; the furious Cola is Sir Charles Coote (the elder), a New English colonist who had come to Ireland with Mountjoy, and the heroic Osirus is the Earl of Ormond, who also happened to be the great-nephew of Lord Mountgarrett, President of the Confederate Council.[24] Working with these characters based on real (and in most cases living) individuals, the play follows a loose, five-act structure in which events on the stage follow those of the Irish rebellion from 1641 up to the truce of September 1643.

Although there is no record of *Cola's Furie* having been performed, it is entirely possible that it was staged, at least privately. Kilkenny in 1646 had the necessary theatre personnel, and some of the play's most powerfully theatrical moments suggest that it was at least intended for the stage. These include two disturbing torture scenes, strategically placed at the ends of acts II and III (in the first, a sixty-year-old man is racked, in the second a woman is 'drawne aloft, with burning matches between each finger'); there is also a masque, a ghost scene, an antimasque performed by drunken soldiers. Most tellingly, there is a speech indicating that the whole production was at least intended for performance on New Year's Day. The main character, Cola, is a 'mounster tyrant', a type which can be traced to Marlowe's *Tamburlaine* and ultimately to Seneca. 'A Turke could not [be] more brutish villaine than he', says one character. Cola indulges his motiveless lust 'to hang, to racke, to kill, to burne, to spoile'[25] until his death at the end of act IV, whereupon a lesser tyrant, Tygranes (Lord Moore of Mellifont), takes up his cause, before being blown to bits by a cannonball (offstage, it should be noted).

As well as the glimpse it affords of the frightening, haunted world of Ireland during the early 1640s, *Cola's Furie* shows an emerging politicisation of theatrical spectacle. Shirley's awareness of New English Protestants in his audience in 1639 may well have led him to write those scenes in *St Patrick for Ireland* in which theatrical illusion and idolatry merge and are exposed. Writing for an almost exclusively Catholic, royalist audience in Kilkenny, Burkhead has no such concerns. Just before his death, Cola is confronted by 'Revenge with a sword in one hand, and a flaming torch in the other followed by three spirits in sheets', including the spectres of two Irish-speaking farmers he had hung earlier in the play. Cola refuses to credit these supernatural visitations, dismissing them as 'a plot of some conjuring Papist / to vex me with these filthy strange affrightments', and he is subsequently shot dead by a half-seen, possibly supernatural, figure. In pointed contrast to this, Abner (an Irish general who has been identified as Sir Thomas Preston, the Confederate commander-in-chief) sees a masque-vision in which Mars and Mercury tell him that the gods 'are now resolv'd' to let the 'sorrows' of the 'discontent *Lirendeans* . . . be dissolved'.[26] Unlike Cola, he accepts the vision, and is able to force a ceasefire. Accepting visions, Burnell tells his audience, is part of their Catholic, royalist identity, not shared by their iconoclastic, Protestant counterparts.

'We hope in time', wrote one of the Catholic Confederation's leaders, Lord Castlehaven, 'the storm being passed, to return to our old Government under the King'.[27] While this was to happen in Castlehaven's case, in the years of Cromwellian rule between 1650 and 1660 most of the land that had been in the hands of Gaelic and Old English landlords was confiscated, and promised to supporters of the Puritan cause, some already established in Ireland, others recent arrivals from England and Scotland. Of those who did manage to keep their land, some (including Castlehaven) had spent time with the future king in France, where they had enjoyed the vibrant theatre culture of the French court. Hence, when Charles was restored to the throne in 1660, there was no mistaking the link between the theatre and sound monarchist views, and the stage beckoned as an avenue of political rehabilitation. As a prologue directed towards an Irish viceroy a few decades later put it: 'Players, tho' not in favour with the Law, / Have ever suffered with the Royal Cause.'[28]

Among those who were ready to reap the rewards of loyalty was John Ogilby. When Charles made his ceremonial progress through London on 23 April 1661, it was Ogilby who was commissioned to design the triumphal arches and write the masques staged on the streets through which the king passed. In these performances, allegorical figures such as Rebellion are banished by Loyalty and Monarchy, to the accompaniment of songs, such as one sung by an allegorical figure representing Concord promising: 'No Discord in th' Hibernian Harp! / Nought but our Duty, flat, or sharp.'[29] Realising that his star was once more in the ascendant, Ogilby petitioned the king for a renewal of his title as Master of the Revels in Ireland, which Charles had granted to Sir William Davenant in 1660. The king rescinded Davenant's claim, and, on 8 May 1661, issued a patent stating that the monarch 'thought fitt that our subjects of our said Kingdome of Ireland should enjoy the like priviledges in that kind as our subjects here in our Kingdome of England', and granting Ogilby, 'his heires, and assigns' the exclusive right to build theatres and stage 'all Comedies tragedies Operas and other enterludes of what kind soever decent and becoming and not prophane and obnoxious'.[30]

Patent in hand, Ogilby began work on a new Dublin theatre in Smock Alley, a few hundred yards to the north of Werburgh Street, near the rapidly developing quays along the River Liffey. While Davenant and Thomas Killigrew were making the first London theatres out of converted tennis courts, when Ogilby's new theatre opened in October 1662 it was the first Restoration theatre to have been built and designed as a performance space from the ground up, starting with an empty cobbled yard. Measuring 39 feet wide and 66 feet long internally (12 metres by 20 metres), the Smock Alley theatre had a proscenium arch that more or less equally divided a stage reputedly just under 30 feet (9 metres) deep into an apron acting area and a rear stage, which could accommodate pictorial flats and side-wings for scenic illusions. Building a proscenium arch was, in its own right, a statement of political allegiance, for up until this point, its use had been confined to exclusively royalist theatres, such as Davenant's home, Rutland House, and the Cockpit, to which an arch was added in 1658; it was also a feature of Richelieu's Palais-Royal in Paris, where Charles and followers such as the Earl of Ormond had been in exile.

Although the proscenium arch opened up new scenic possibilities, the Smock Alley theatre was very much an actor's theatre. Most of the acting would have taken place on the square forestage, putting the actors in closer contact with the audience than with the painted castles and forests behind the proscenium. Surviving prompt books make it clear that there were two doors on either side of the apron (uniquely referred to as the 'East' and 'West' sides of the stage) over which were rooms with casement windows, known as 'lattices'. These were used as performance areas or let out to members of the audience, as the play demanded. Finally, above the proscenium, there was a 'music loft' for the musicians[31] at a time when music formed an important component of the pleasure of theatre-going.

In the early months of its operation, few of these features would have been used, for when the theatre opened in October of 1662 Ogilby was offering plays that had been performed in Werburgh Street (such as Fletcher's *Wit Without Money*, staged on 18 October 1662) on a bare stage. 'We have a new Play-house here', one observer wrote to a friend in London, 'which in my Opinion is much finer than D'Avenant's; but the Scenes are not yet made.'[32] And yet, even before the stage was fully operational, the 'fineness' of the original Smock Alley theatre was evident in the decoration of the auditorium. The pit contained rows of cloth-covered benches, where the 'lords and ladies' sat. Above them were 'three stories of galleries', in which 'those of the greatest quality sat lowest. Those next in quality sat the next above; and the common people in the upmost gallery.'[33] Where the Werburgh Street theatre had a single box for the Lord Deputy, Smock Alley had an entire gallery of boxes adjacent to the viceregal box, suggesting that as Dublin's population grew, the audience became more socially diverse, and hence felt greater need for sequestration in the auditorium. Indeed, the increased number of galleries, and the passing of handbills announcing plays at coffee houses, taverns and shops, indicates a desire (or more to the point, a financial need) to reach out beyond the environs of Dublin Castle to the wider population of Dublin – or at least to those portions of the population with the disposable income and leisure to attend a performance which customarily began at three-thirty in the afternoon.

Although it was a public theatre, Smock Alley would rely doubly on the support of the court growing up around the new Lord Lieutenant, the Earl (now Duke) of Ormond: both directly for patronage, and for the social cachet to attract audiences who were not part of the inner circles at Dublin Castle. Initially, however, the theatre operated almost as a private court theatre. The first original play Ogilby staged was *Pompey*, a translation of Corneille's *Le Mort de Pompée* by Katherine Philips, one of the rising stars of the Dublin viceregal court. *Pompey*'s première on 10 February 1663, was followed two weeks later by *The Generall*, written by one of the most powerful men in Ireland, Roger Boyle, first Earl of Orrery. For the many in the Smock Alley audience who turned out to watch these plays, the act of attending the theatre – particularly to watch sumptuously staged neo-classical tragedy on a proscenium stage – was an act of fealty to the king. Indeed, as Ormond said to his son, 'it is of importance to keep up the splendour of the government'.[34] Much of that 'splendour' was to be found on the stage of the new theatre, particularly in the exotic Egyptian setting of *Pompey*, or the Sicilian setting of *The Generall*. At the same time, there was more to the politics of the theatre in Restoration Dublin than simple spectacle.

'When I had the honour and happiness the last time to kiss his majesty's hand', wrote Orrery to Ormond in January of 1661, 'he commanded me to write a play for him . . . Some months after, I presumed to lay at his majesty's feet a tragi-comedy, all in ten feet verse and rhyme . . . because I found his majesty relished the French fashion of plays, than English.'

Orrery (when he had been plain Lord Broghill) had been closely associated with Charles I in the 1640s; then, in October of 1649 – the same month in which Cromwell massacred more than two thousand inhabitants of Wexford – he joined the Parliamentary forces, and by 1657 was one of Cromwell's closest advisors. Three years later, he had switched sides again, and was a confidant of Charles II, writing that he loved the king 'a thousand times more than myself'.[35] So, when Charles hinted at a taste for French neo-classical drama, with its conflicts of loyalty and honour, Orrery recognised that here was a forum in which he could make a case for the tragic nobility of regicide. Taking advantage of a fit of gout in 1660, he wrote *The Generall.*

The Generall is a piece of court theatre of a very specialised kind, a piece of public negotiation directed as much at Ormond, the Lord Lieutenant, as at a general audience. Set during a rebellion in which a legitimate king and a usurper struggle for power, the play is clearly about Ireland in the 1640s and 1650s, just as the general who sides with the usurper is clearly Orrery himself. 'Disgrace I feare lesse than to be unjust', he says at one point. ''Tis such to take and then betray a trust.' Elsewhere, another character observes:

> Sometimes hee [the King] thinkes, the Rebells being nigh,
> That wee and they are in Confederacy,
> Then straight hee thinkes, from honour or from spight,
> Wee scorne our selves, butt by our selves to right.[36]

Torn between 'disgrace' and injustice, 'honour' and 'spight', 'scorne' and 'right' (the rhyming couplets here working to point up the parallelism), Orrery's play puts on public display the irreconcilable tensions that had placed him (like so many others) in impossible positions during the middle decades of the seventeenth century. What is more, his vocabulary here – words like 'Confederacy' and 'Rebells' – leave little doubt as to what is being discussed. Eight months before *The Generall* was staged, Orrery had given Ormond the pragmatic reasons why those who had fought against the king must be rehabilitated. 'The act of oblivion, free pardon, and indemnity', he told Ormond, 'if it is not very cautiously drawn and worded, may destroy the great bill of settlement.'[37] *The Generall* continued this argument in the public arena of the theatre by outlining the conditions in which pardon, rather than punishment, is both just and prudent.

Meanwhile, another Dublin was taking shape at the margins of the world of high politics. The city's population would double in the decade between 1660 and 1670, and many of the city's new inhabitants were living in expectation of land either promised or confiscated during the 1640s and 1650s. 'There must bee new discoverys made of a new Ireland', commented an exasperated Duke of Ormond, surveying a country in which 'gentleman's seats were built, or building everywhere'. For others, however, who 'Nature thought it fit / To give some nought but... Wit', as the writer Richard Head was to put it, Dublin in the 1660s was a place in which the most extravagant fantasies of social mobility were worth dreaming. 'Swimming for their Lives, these misrules think, / 'Tis better catch at any thing, then sink.'[38] Head himself was one such self-confessed 'rogue', and in his play *Hic et Ubique: or, the Humors of Dublin*, published in 1663 (and possibly staged in Dublin privately sometime over the previous three years) we see the first traces of a radically fluid Irish stage character who, unlike the protagonist of heroic tragedy, lives only in the present moment. Over the next three centuries, in wildly varying social contexts and theatrical forms, such characters would establish themselves as one of the points of continuity on the Irish stage.

Head's Dublin in *Hic et Ubique* is a place where anything is possible, populated by characters whose success depends on their ability to abandon the entanglements and loyalties of the past. The play opens with Hope-well, Bankrupt, Contriver and Trust-all arriving in Dublin from England with Phantastic, the eponymous Hic, and Peregrine, congregating at the London Tavern (a real Dublin hostelry just across from the old Werburgh Street theatre site). Some, like Bankrupt, are content simply to be in a city where English debts do not need paying; others, like Contriver, have elaborate plans for using the Irish mountains to dam up the Irish bogs, for which 'the King will confer on me little lesse than the Title of Duke of *Mountain*, Earl of *Monah*, or Lord *Drein-bog*'. Among the Dubliners encountered by the English is Colonel Kil-tory, a Cromwellian ex-soldier awkwardly in quest of a wife, who confesses that 'whilst I was scouring the Mountains and skipping the Bogs, I had none of these qualms. I cu'd have then driven a score or two of these white cloven Devils without pity or regard.' While he is capable of raping Irish peasants – as his Irish servant Patrick tells it, of 'putting the great fuck upon my weef' – Kil-tory is at a loss when it comes to courtship 'since Mrs *Peace* came acquainted with us', and he is eventually cheated out of his land by Hope-well's wife.[39] The present, in *Hic et Ubique*, clearly belongs not to the military conquerors, no matter how ruthless, but to schemers with the wit and commercial sense to read a rapidly changing situation.

The scars of the past were not so easily healed, however, and by 1669 the decade which had opened as a new era in the theatre in Dublin was to close on a note that would presage the difficulties that lay ahead. Ogilby, who had kept up his map-making and publishing interests, returned to England early that year, just before John, Baron Roberts, took over the post of Lord Lieutenant from Ormond. Roberts was a Presbyterian, and, as one of his co-religionists, Patrick Adair, put it: 'The public players he stopped . . . as well as other vicious persons.' They remained 'stopped' until Roberts was replaced the following year.

Smock Alley had barely re-opened, when, in December 1670, it came to an even more spectacular halt during a production of Ben Jonson's *Bartholomew Fair*. Near the end of act IV, a character named Zeal-of-the-Land Busy is placed in the stocks on stage. In Jonson's script, Busy is a Puritan; however, in the 1670 Smock Alley production, he would seem to have been dressed as a Presbyterian clergyman – 'to teach great persons to deal with like severity toward them', Adair believed. 'I am one', Busy declaims, 'that rejoiceth in his affliction, and sitteth here to prophesy the destruction of fairs and May-games, wakes and Whitsun-ales, and doth sigh and groan for the reformation of these abuses.'[40] As Busy groaned and sighed, so too did the upper gallery, before splintering and falling 'on the middle one, where gentlemen and others sat, and that gallery broke too, and much of it fell down on the lords and ladies', killing 'a poor girlie'. 'Such providences', noted Adair, 'have a language if men would hear.'[41]

There were structural flaws in more than the galleries of Smock Alley. In the early 1660s, the Dublin theatre had been often in advance of its London counterpart: Smock Alley was the first purpose-built Restoration theatre; both *Pompey* and *The Generall* have claims as the second English neo-classical tragedy; and Philips was the first woman to have a play publicly staged. A decade later, however, the Dublin theatre was still locked into a dependence on the court at Dublin Castle, which meant that its fortunes were tied to the vagaries of political appointments in a way that was becoming less and less true on the other side of the Irish Sea. Hence, during the early 1670s – the years in which Aphra Behn began writing for the stage and the second Drury Lane theatre was built in London – Smock Alley, under the management of William Morgan, was closed almost as often as it was open.

Under a sympathetic administration, the theatre was to all appearances healthy. In 1676, Joseph Ashbury took over the management from Morgan, just as the Duke of Ormond was preparing to return for a third term as Lord Lieutenant. In 1677, the company used Ormond's position as Lord Chancellor of Oxford to perform in the university, becoming the first Irish actors to tour outside the island. Four years later, in 1681, the Smock Alley players (by then about thirty in number) went to Edinburgh, where they staged Nathaniel Lee's *Mithridates* for the royal family at Holyrood House. They were also building up their stock of scenery. Surviving Smock Alley prompt books show that by the mid-1670s, the theatre had standard sets for 'Court', 'Towne', 'Grove' and 'Castle', to which could be added a rear shutter of 'ye shipps'. These basic scenic properties, along with others for interior scenes, allowed the company to stage *Hamlet*, *Julius Caesar*, *King Lear*, *Macbeth*, *Othello*, *Troilus and Cressida*, *Henry VIII*, *Henry IV: Parts 1 and 2*, *The Merry Wives of Windsor*, *A Midsummer Night's Dream*, *Twelfth Night*, *Measure for Measure*, *The Tempest*, and possibly *The Comedy of Errors* – more or less the staples of the Irish stage for the next century or more.

However, the taste for pre-Restoration works exposed a deeper malaise. 'You are of late such Antiquaries grown', chastised one prologue of the period, 'that no regard's to modern writers shown.'[42] The problem was not simply audience taste. Already, one of the economic facts of the Irish theatre world was beginning to make itself felt; a playwright could make more money in London than in Dublin, simply because there were more theatres and a larger population. Consequently, in the decade after 1669, only three original plays were premièred in Smock Alley: *Agrippa, King of Alba* (1669) and a translation of Corneille's *Nicomede* (1670), both by John Dancer, and *Belphegor* (1677) by John Wilson. Dancer was an officer in the Horseguards with 'a great esteem of French Playes', while Wilson was Recorder of Londonderry. Writing in the neo-classical style that had already become *passé* in London, there was a sense in which Smock Alley had become locked into a dependence on court approval (with its corresponding theatrical style) that cut it off from the reinvention of the theatre world taking place in London, to which Irish writers and actors of real ability were increasingly drawn.

A case in point is the Irish-born Thomas Southerne. His play *The Disappointment* first opened in London, before being picked up by Smock Alley in late January 1685. *The Disappointment* has an intricate double plot, in which a character named Aphonso tests his wife's constancy while a rake, Alberto, is tricked into marrying the mistress he has jilted. Like many plays of the period, it makes sex into a metaphor for just about everything, at one point comparing old prostitutes who become bawds to 'lawyers past the exercise of the Bar' who are 'consider'd for their Experience [in] Civil government'.[43] In short, Southerne was capable of writing precisely the sort of play that could have helped Smock Alley consolidate the educated, prosperous audience who patronised the pit and boxes; but, as would so often be the case, he did not live in Dublin.

In the same week that Smock Alley first staged *The Disappointment*, the theatre found itself facing far more pressing problems than the lack of a resident playwright. Charles II died on 6 February 1685, and was succeeded by his Catholic brother, James. When James appointed the Catholic Earl of Tyrconnell as Lord Lieutenant in 1687, the largely Protestant court dispersed, taking with it Smock Alley's *raison d'être*. 'When Doubts & Fears distract the Troubled Age', lamented a prologue read in the theatre on 14 October 1687, 'What suffers most is the forsaken stage / . . . Our poor Broken Troop neglected Lye, Heartless, benumm'd & cold as Winter Flyes.' Ashbury struggled on with a shrinking company until 1689, finally closing the theatre around the time of the Siege of Derry. It remained closed over the next two troubled years, and it was not until after the Treaty of Limerick was signed in October 1691, that he decided it was time to resume business.

Just before Christmas 1691, Ashbury offered a free performance of *Othello*, in which he played Iago and Robert Wilks played the title role. Most of the other male roles were taken up by officers of Ashbury's old regiment, the King's Guard, who had been closely associated with the theatre since the Restoration, and are addressed in one prologue as 'Defenders of the Pit'.[44] The performance was repeated when the theatre re-opened to the public on 31 March 1692 as part of the official celebrations to mark William of Orange's victory, and it looked as if the old ties with the castle had survived yet again. However, things were not to be so simple.

The theatre in Ireland had made the transition from private entertainments – such as Mountjoy's 1601 production of *Gorboduc* – to the public performances in Werburgh Street theatre under the patronage of the court at Dublin Castle. The transition had taken place at a time when court life had been governed by a set of tastes that valued spectacle and illusion, so it is no coincidence that the first three major writers for the Irish stage – Shirley, Burnell and Burkhead – all had Catholic ties. This ethos continued to develop when the centre of theatrical activity shifted to Kilkenny, and was formalised after the restoration of Charles II, when the theatre was defined as a right granted by the monarch. The explicit links to Catholicism may have been broken in the decades after 1662, but the ties to Dublin Castle – where many Irish actors held army commissions – were so strong that Smock Alley became a sort of court theatre attended by the public. When William of Orange became king, the ethos of the court at Dublin Castle would undergo a radical change, as would the understanding of the king's power to grant rights, including the right to stage plays. Consequently, the entire meaning of theatrical performance would change in Ireland after 1692.

A night at the theatre 1

Pompey by Katherine Philips
Smock Alley
Tuesday, 10 February 1663

There might never be a king in Dublin Castle, but when the carriage and retinue of the Duke of Ormond, Lord Lieutenant of Ireland, swept out of the castle gates shortly after three o'clock on the afternoon of Tuesday, 10 February 1663, he was, as usual, greeted by a fanfare and salute suitable for royalty. And, as usual, making his progress the short distance to Smock Alley Theatre, he found the streets half-blocked by horses, carts and country people selling rabbits, cheese, tallow or ducks. Meanwhile, from the opposite direction an equally imposing procession was bringing Roger Boyle, Earl of Orrery, from his Dublin residence of Thomas Court past Christchurch and down Fishamble Street. Around the same time, a group of students were making their way up Dame Street from Trinity College, while from the tavern on Cork Hill, in a slightly more dishevelled procession, lawyers, booksellers and demobbed soldiers were walking the few hundred yards to the theatre, some getting no further than the prostitutes who worked the area.

The occasion on that February afternoon was the first production of a verse tragedy, *Pompey*, translated from the French of Pierre Corneille by Katherine Philips. The air of anticipation in the city's streets was due in part to the novelty of theatre-going, for the first performance at Smock Alley had taken place only four months earlier, and it would be some time before a regular repertoire would be established. It was also the case, however, that Dublin in 1663 had the frenzied uncertainty of a gold rush town, a place where there were fortunes to be made and lost in a game for which rules were still being written. Many of these hopes were pinned on Ormond, who had arrived in Dublin only eight months earlier as the first Lord Lieutenant appointed by Charles II, bringing with him the expectation that he would settle the almost six thousand land claims that were the legacy of two decades of warfare and dispossession.

So, as the candles were being lit inside Smock Alley, the streets around Dublin Castle swarmed with courtiers attached to the new viceregal establishment, jostling with claimants, counter-claimants, their advisors, dependants, the dispossessed, the speculators and the parasites. Some were Catholic Old English or Irish landed families, loyal to the monarchy during the conflict, who now wanted restitution of their confiscated lands; others were Protestant New English settlers, former Cromwellian soldiers, or adventurers, who claimed equal title to those same lands on the basis of promises made during the interregnum. There were clearly more claims than land, and consequently the situation grew more tense as the winter progressed. Only a few weeks prior to the first production of *Pompey* (the timing of which may not have been coincidental), the Court of Claims first convened under Sir Edward Dering to ascertain the innocence (or otherwise) of the dispossessed. Three days after the play was performed, Ormond was confronted with a petition from an angry group of adventurers and soldiers, incensed that so many Catholic families were being found innocent. A month later, another group of disgruntled army officers was discovered plotting to seize Dublin Castle.

The production of *Pompey* at Smock Alley on 10 February 1663, was at the heart of this scramble, and its author Katherine Philips embodied the contradictory mixture of loyalty and guilt, opportunism and idealism, which made Dublin so volatile in the winter of 1663. Like many people in Dublin at the time, Philips was not Irish at all: she was an English royalist, who had written Cavalier poetry throughout the 1650s. However, her husband, James Philips, was a Cromwellian adventurer awaiting the outcome of a land claim in Ireland. Leaving her politically embarrassing husband behind in Wales (while still hoping they might find themselves in possession of an estate confiscated from an Irish royalist) Philips moved to Dublin shortly after the Restoration, and quickly worked her way to the epicentre of power. Famed for her wit, and admired for her poetry, she had exactly the qualities required by Ormond in creating a cultured viceregal court to manifest the splendour of the monarchy. Philips (calling herself 'the matchless Orinda') gave her individual stamp to the coterie at the heart of court life by forming a Society of Friendship whose members addressed each other by mock classical names, and whose inner sanctum included the Chairman of the Land Settlement Commission, Sir Edward Dering ('the noble Silvander'), Ormond's daughter, Lady Mary Cavendish ('the bright Policrite') and Lady Anne Boyle ('the adored Valeria') daughter of Roger Boyle, the Earl of Orrery.

Orrery had already written his own verse tragedy, initially called *Altemera*, which would be staged as *The Generall* two weeks after the production of *Pompey*. In some respects, Orrery and Philips could not have been more different; Orrery had been born into one of the most powerful families in Ireland, and although he had been passed over for the post of Lord Lieutenant, he remained an important power broker. Philips, by contrast, was scrambling to make her way in court. And yet, in the uncertain years of the early 1660s, both found themselves playing a similar game, using the theatre as a means of political rehabilitation. Indeed, Philips had barely begun translating Corneille, when (as she coyly put it in a letter written in August 1662) 'my good Fortune has favour'd me with the Acquaintance of my Lord Orrery . . . By some Accident or another my Scene of *Pompey* fell into his Hands, and he was pleas'd to like it so well, that he sent me the *French* Original'.[1]

Of course, neither the hands into which it fell, nor the choice of *Le Mort de Pompée*, was accidental. 'But when you wonder at my bold design', wrote Philips on the flyleaf of the copy of *Pompey* she sent to the Countess of Roscommon, 'Remember who did the high task enjoin; / Th' illustrious Orrery.' Similarly, Corneille's *Pompée* was an ideal choice not only because it was French, but because the story was well known in the circles in which Philips moved, if only through North's translation of Plutarch's *Life of Pompey*. Indeed, Philips had already compared Charles II to Pompey in several poems written prior to the Restoration, including one entitled 'On the Numerous Access of the English to Wait Upon the King in Flanders': 'As Pompey's Camp, where e're it mov'd, was Rome, / They that asserted thy Just Cause go hence / To testifie their joy and reverence.'[2]

There was, however, a certain irony in using Pompey as an image of the English king, for the historical Pompey had supported the Republican Senate against Caesar's attempts to rule alone, making him in some respects closer to Cromwell. On the other hand, after his defeat by Caesar at the battle of Pharsalus, Pompey (like Charles after his defeat by Cromwell at the battle of Worcester) became a ruler in exile; to make matters even more complicated, when Pompey sought refuge in Egypt, the Pharaoh, Ptolemy XIII, had him beheaded, thus neatly conflating the motif of exile with that of regicide. The historical parallel was thus more suggestive than precise, for if Pompey becomes a sort of portmanteau image of both Charles II and his decapitated father, who then corresponds to Caesar, the victorious ruler; and who is Ptolemy, the foreign king behind the murder?

When the first performer stepped in front of the Smock Alley curtain at three-thirty on 10 February 1663, and the babble of voices in the auditorium ebbed slightly, questions like these would have been in the audience's minds. In the upper gallery sat shopkeepers and rural gentry, while in the cloth-covered benches of the pit, soldiers, students, lawyers and other denizens of the coffee houses and taverns were carrying on debates begun earlier in the day. In the open second gallery were men and women from the fringes of court life, many of them awaiting the results of their land claims. The boxes of the first gallery were, however, the real centre of attention, for they held some of the most powerful people in Ireland, their rank indicated by their proximity to the Duke of Ormond. Orrery was almost certainly close at hand, as would have been Sir Edward Dering. Katherine Philips was possibly seated nearby, although one tradition has it that she acted in the performance, and this is not beyond the bounds of possibility.

In any case, the boxes of the first gallery were more or less level with the stage, lit with equal brightness and every bit as colourfully costumed, so there was a very real sense in which the performance space extended 360 degrees around the inside of the auditorium. The first words spoken from the stage that afternoon would have reinforced this feeling, for they were addressed from the stage to Ormond in the viceregal box, and had been written by Wentworth Dillon, Earl of Roscommon, who would have been seated nearby:

> The mighty Rivals, whose destructive Rage
> Did the whole World in Civil Armes engage
> Are now agreed, and make it both their Choice,
> To have their Fates determin'd by your Voice.

A surge of uncertain attentiveness must have swelled through the theatre as the prologue began, leaving in its wake a little less chatter from the pit, and a little less noise from the upper gallery. Which 'mighty Rivals'? Ireland had just come out of two decades of 'destructive Rage', and rivalry of the land claimants was still fierce. By failing to mention the play's fictional situation (Egypt in 48 BC) at the beginning of his prologue, Roscommon leaves open the possibility that he is commenting directly on the current situation in Ireland. The speech is, after all, directed to Ormond, who had been a Royalist commander in Ireland in 1648, while his 'mighty Rival', Orrery – possibly sitting next to him in the theatre in 1663 – had been in charge of Parliamentary forces from 1649 onwards.

Like most prologue-writers of the period, Roscommon is telling the audience how to interpret the performance. The play, he suggests, will provide a forum in which 'mighty Rivals' can acknowledge both victory and defeat, and in which the audience can applaud both equally. 'Success, 'tis true, waited on Caesar's side', he continues, 'But Pompey thinks he conquer'd when he dy'd.'[3] The conventions of tragedy turn death and defeat into a form of victory, without necessarily turning the agent of that defeat into a villain. 'Pompey thanks false Egypt for its Treachery', wrote one of Philips' admirers in a later poem, 'Since that his Ruine was so sung by thee.'[4] If it is possible to applaud the defeated, the victorious, the guilty and even the dead, so too may it be possible to find some similar form of acceptance for the 'mighty Rivals' seated in the extended stage of the theatre auditorium. Indeed, the very ambiguity of Pompey's allegorical relationship to the events of the 1640s and 1650s helps here, for Pompey was both the exiled, beheaded ruler, and the defender of the Republican Senate – both Charles and Cromwell, as it were. 'Of what Doubt can Pompey's Cause admit', asks Roscommon, 'Since here so many Catos judging sit?'[5], thus referring to one of Pompey's most principled followers. All of you, Roscommon told his fellow audience members, are followers of Pompey.

Katherine Philips (whether on the stage or seated in the boxes) was very much the centre of this spectacle of reconciliation and new possibilities, if only because the initial production of *Pompey* marked the first occasion that a play written by a woman had been given a public performance in English. 'A Woman translate Pompey!' exclaims a later poem praising Philips:

> Yes, that bold work a Woman dares Translate,
> Not to provoke, nor yet to fear men's hate.
> Nature does find that she hath err'd too long,
> And now resolves to recompence that wrong:
> Phoebus to Cynthia must his beams resigne,
> The rule of Day and Wit's now Feminine.

The presence of women on the stage in Smock Alley during that first 1662/3 season was one of the most visible signs that the theatre was entering into a new era, for the women who began acting in Smock Alley in October 1662 would have been among the first English-speaking actresses to appear on a public stage. Within a few years, the association of actresses and playwrights with prostitutes would make the theatre a dangerous place for women to make a living, and in the later decades of the seventeenth century there would be scarcely any plays by women performed in Smock Alley. However in 1663, not only was the soil of theatrical tradition thin in Dublin, the notion of a court and its decorum was still being invented. For those few brief years, just as an ex-soldier could find himself lord of a vast estate, so too could a woman writer have her work performed and applauded by a Lord Lieutenant, finding success in that most masculine of forms, neo-classical verse tragedy.

'Something of grandeur in your Verse men see', wrote one of Philips' friends, 'That they rise up to it as Majesty.'[6] As well as working out how 'mighty Rivals' – both political and sexual – might co-exist in the post-war world, the performance of *Pompey* provided its audience with the kind of spectacle that was part of the business of maintaining the power of the monarchy. Since his arrival in Ireland in July of 1662, Ormond made a point of having his movements marked by fanfares in an attempt to invest Dublin Castle with some of the majesty lacking in a viceregal court from which the king would always be absent. For his part, Orrery recognised the power of the theatre to provide awe-inspiring pageantry, and 'advanc'd a hundred Pounds towards the expence of buying *Roman* and *Egyptian* Habits' for Philips' play[7] – a considerable sum of money, considering that the chapel and stables Orrery built in his home in Charleville cost £1,500. Unfortunately, no descriptions of the costumes survive, but given their cost, and keeping in mind Philips' comments on a production of *Othello* in Smock Alley (in which 'the Doge of Venice and all his Senators came upon the Stage with Feathers in their Hats, which was like to have chang'd the Tragedy into a Comedy'), it is possible to imagine plenty of cloaks, elaborate armour and Egyptian headdresses (but no feathers – although they would become obligatory for tragic heroes within a few years).

Philips is very clear that the money was for costumes only, which would suggest that the production used Smock Alley's standard tragic palace set, which would have been relatively new at the time. It is possible that John Ogilby would have had a hand in designing these, and if so we might expect to find the type of neo-classical ornament (pillars festooned with complex allegorical figures) that he used for Charles' cornonation arches. Stage directions calling for characters to be 'discovered' suggest that *Pompey* used the flats and side-wings (yet another innovation in 'the French fashion') just coming into use in London. As with Corneille's original, all the action in Philips' *Pompey* is confined to a single location (Ptolemy's palace in Alexandria) and the central event (Pompey's murder) takes place offstage. Hence, while there is enough movement from room to room in the palace to allow some use of the new stage machinery, it would seem to be the case that the real spectacle was produced by the changing parade of costumes.

For all its visual splendour, at *Pompey*'s core are its long speeches, written in even meter and rhyming couplets to be declaimed from downstage on the stage apron, with little movement but plenty of gesture. So, as the curtains parted after the prologue, we can imagine Ptolemy, probably played by Joseph Ashbury, splendidly robed, stepping forward from the pillared side-wings to pick up the prologue's meditation on 'great Rivals Destiny':

> That distress'd Leader of the Juster side,
> Whose wearied Fortune hath all Help deny'd
> A terrible Example will create,
> To future times, of the Extreams of Fate.[8]

Ptolemy's 'future times', were, of course, the audience's present, thus renewing the prologue's invitation to read the play allegorically. Ptolemy's dilemma would have been familiar to many people in the audience who had lived through the wars of the 1640s and 1650s. To offer Pompey sanctuary might be just, but it would bring down the wrath of Caesar on Egypt; to kill him would be unjust, but would save the country. As Ptolemy attempts to unravel the ethics of this impossible situation, more than a few eyes in the audience must have glanced in the direction of Orrery, who had been faced with a similar choice when he had abandoned Charles I to join forces with Cromwell in 1649:

> That is unsafe, and this ignoble is;
> I dread injustice, or unhappiness;
> And angry fortune each way offer me
> Either much danger, or much infamy.

Between the 'unsafe' and the 'ignoble', between 'injustice' and 'unhappiness', 'danger' and 'infamy', the play argues that civil war places statesmen in impossible positions – whether in the Mediterranean or in Ireland. 'Let's no more debate what's Just and fit', concludes Ptolemy at the end of the opening scene, 'But to the World's vicissitude submit.'

Equally, however, more than one member of the audience would have listened carefully to Cleopatra's justification for Ptolemy's actions, reminding her brother of their debt to Caesar, who took their side: 'When none that bold Rebellion could withstand, / Which rob'd our Father, of his Crown and Land.' Indeed, the vocabulary here – 'Rebellion', 'Crown' and 'Land' – was precisely that being used only a few hundred yards away in Dublin Castle at the Land Settlement hearings. However, the most powerful moments must have been those in which Achoreus describes the beheading of Pompey with words that echo accounts of the beheading of Charles I:

> His great Soul fled, his Body did expose
> To th' greedy Eyes, of his inhumane Foes:
> His Head, which tumbled on the blushing Deck,
> (By vile Septimus sever'd from his neck.)
> Upon Achillas lance we fixed see,
> As after Battles Trophyes use to be:
> And to conclude a Destiny so sad,
> The Sea was all the Sepulcher he had.
> To fortune now, his slaughter'd Corps resign'd,
> Floats at the Pleasure of the Wave and Winde.[9]

Almost everyone in the Smock Alley audience had felt the impact of the execution of Charles I. Some, like Orrery, had been close to the event; others had felt its repercussions only indirectly; some had suffered, and others had risen under the new regime; some had believed regicide to be a sin, others had supported it as just and necessary. No one could have listened to these words in 1663 and felt nothing.

At this point, the performance of *Pompey* risks reawakening the trauma of regicide that it is trying to contain. It may have been an awareness of this that led Philips to break with the neo-classical unities of plot and time (which her French source material follows so rigorously) by introducing a series of dances, songs and a masque. For instance, act I ends with 'an Antick dance of Gypsies', while act III concludes with a 'Military Dance' (probably performed by officers of the garrison), and there is a 'Grand Masque Danc'd before Caesar and Cleopatra' to end the evening – all 'made (as well as the other Dances and Tunes to them) by Mr John Ogilby', returning to his original profession as a dancing master. The musicians accompanying the dancers would have been in the music loft, located directly above the proscenium arch, and seem to have included some of the best musical talent Dublin could muster. At least one chorister from Christchurch Cathedral, a Mr Lee, was later reprimanded for 'having sung among the stage-players in the Play-house, to the dishonour and disgrace to the members and ministers of this church'.

These musical interludes provide a harmonious counterpoint to the harsh choices offered by tragedy, and the same is true of the songs which Philips introduces, 'set by several Hands; the first and fifth admirably well by Philaster [John Jeffries], the third by Doctor Pett; one Le Grand, a Frenchman, belonging to the Duchess of Ormond, has by her Order, set the fourth, and a Frenchman of my Lord Orrery's the second'.[10] So, if Ptolemy is caught between 'danger' and 'infamy', the song which follows his deliberations suggests a third way:

> Since affairs of the State, are already decreed,
> Make room for Affairs of the Court,
> Employment, and Pleasure each other succeed,
> Because they each other support.

The infernal machine of Corneillean tragedy thus propels its victims towards an inevitable fate, and the play ends with Ptolemy dead, Caesar in control of Egypt, and Cleopatra on its throne. At the same time, running parallel to the harsh exigencies of tragedy are the harmonies of song, culminating in the afternoon's most purely theatrical moment, a masque, beginning with a song by 'two Egyptian priests':

> Then after all the Blood that's shed,
> Let's right the living and the dead:
> Temples to Pompey raise;
>
> Set Cleopatra on the Throne;
> Let Caesar keep the World h'has won;
> And sing Cornelia's praise.

Even as the final curtain closed on this vision of harmony, Philips had a further card to play. *Pompey* has an epilogue, which invites the audience to 'censure as you think fit, / The Action, Plot, the language or the wit', but defies anyone to find 'one line severest Virtue need to flye'.[11] In one sense, there is nothing remarkable in this epilogue, other than its choice of author: Sir Edward Dering, who was then chairing the Court of Claims. Instituted to put the Act of Settlement into practice, the court was trying to find an equitable distribution of the land after more than half a century of dispossession. Old and New English, surviving Gaelic aristocrats and Cromwellian adventurers – including Philips' own husband – all wanted to find a place for themselves on the island. By August of 1663, the court would collapse under the pressures of so many conflicting demands, leaving almost five thousand claims unconsidered. While it was in operation, however, it searched in vain for a way to draw a line under the traumas of the first half of the seventeenth century. Indeed, there is a sense in which its terms of reference had been defined on the Smock Alley stage when Philips' *Pompey* sang of the need to 'right the living and the dead'.

CHAPTER 2

Stage rights, 1691–1782

On 4 November 1712, 'being the anniversary for the birth, landing and marriage of William III', Joseph Ashbury applied for permission to have a celebratory prologue read before a special production of Nicolas Rowe's *Tamerlane* at Smock Alley. The Tory administration of the time had never really accepted William or his successor, Queen Anne, and consequently forbade such a use of the theatre. Among the many Whig supporters of William and Anne in the pit that evening was Dudley Moore, and just before the curtain rose he scrambled up out of the pit to declaim William's virtues from the stage:

> His generous Soul for *Freedom* was Design'd,
> To pull down Tyrants, and unslave mankind;
> He broke the Chains of Europe; and when we
> Were doom'd *for Slaves*, he came and *set us free.*

The effect was, quite literally, to bring the house down. Ladies wearing orange ribbons cheered and ladies wearing red roses hissed; seats were torn up, and the performance was postponed amidst servants brawling in the upper gallery, brandished swords in the pit and an indecorous exodus of silk and taffeta from the boxes. Moore was brought to trial for 'Riotous and Seditious Practices', but was later triumphantly turned free by a Grand Jury of Whigs. Within days, he would be alternately celebrated and reviled by what would become the obligatory post-riot fusillade of pamphlets and satirical poems. 'We think it were fit', one Tory journal jeered at its Whig opponents:

> You should stay in the Pit,
> Unless each has a mind to turn Play'r.
> Think not to invade,
> Our privilege and trade,
> As you would the Prerogative Royal.[1]

The long tradition of using the theatre as a public arena for hammering out the subtleties of Irish political life was beginning to move in a new direction.

In more ways than one, the spectre of William of Orange haunts the Irish theatre of the eighteenth century, just as he haunts the politics of the period. Indeed, many of the post-1691 generation of playwrights and actors bore the scars of the war that consolidated William's claim to the throne. Thomas Southerne, for instance, had used the success of *The Disappointment* in 1685 to gain a captaincy in King James' army; when James was defeated in 1690, Southerne returned to the theatre, writing his two most successful plays, *The Fatal Marriage* (1694) and *Oroonoko* (1695). On the Williamite side, George Farquhar had been born in Derry, where he lived for a time in the early 1680s under the governorship of George Philips, whose son, William Philips, also became a playwright. Farquhar's father, an Anglican clergyman, was burnt out of his home during the Siege of Derry, while Philips, a Tory with Jacobite leanings, found himself out of political favour after 1691. Both men attended Trinity, where they had been preceded a few years earlier by the Leeds-born William Congreve, whose father was garrison commander in Youghal, County Cork during the war. Like Southerne before them, Philips, Farquhar and the Dublin-born Richard Steele later supplemented their writing careers by taking up military commissions, as did key members of the Smock Alley company, including the actor Robert Wilks.

There was, then, a compact triangle of influence, with Smock Alley, Dublin Castle and Trinity College at its corners. This was a world in flux, where land was being confiscated and redistributed on a massive scale, making possible spectacular slides both up and down the social ladder. Catholic supporters of James were finding that noble bloodlines were no protection against dispossession, while sons and daughters of tradesmen or soldiers holding the right political cards were moving into a freshly minted aristocracy, joining the New English who had arrived in the previous century; together, along with a few adaptive survivors from the older aristocratic order, and aspiring lawyers, clergymen, merchants and soldiers, they would form what would become known as the Ascendancy. In short, it was a time when new identities could be improvised against backdrops where the paint was still wet.

And yet, there was a crack in the foundations underlying this shining new edifice. In the immediate environs of Smock Alley, it was possible for long periods to overlook or ignore it; outside of Dublin, however, where

Catholics or Dissenters were usually in the majority – and from 1695 onwards, excluded from many of the basic rights accorded to Anglicans – there was no forgetting that this was a society founded on dispossession and exclusion. In the plays performed at Smock Alley, this was seldom mentioned directly; however, outside the capital, two plays suggest traces of a lost popular theatre culture in which the brutal reality of what happened in the early 1690s never faded: *Ireland Preserv'd; or, The Siege of London-Derry* (1705) by John Michelburne, and *The Battle of Aughrim; Or, the Fall of Monsieur St Ruth* (1728), by Robert Ashton. Michelburne was a Williamite commander at the Siege of Derry, while Ashton was a journeyman shoemaker from Dublin with strong Williamite sympathies. In spite of their differing backgrounds, both fashioned William's victory into stage images that quickly became assimilated into Irish folk culture.

Michelburne (rather immodestly) makes himself the hero of *Ireland Preserv'd*, a loyal and wily soldier who defeats the treachery of the Jacobite Governor of Derry, Landvill, while holding out against the besieging Jacobite army. The play has a loose, episodic structure, alternating back and forth between the armies inside and outside of Derry's walls. It ends abruptly in the final desperate hours of the siege, with the news that King William's fleet has arrived – news that reaches Michelburne as he heartily devours a dog. By 1787, *Ireland Preserv'd* was published in at least six Irish editions (three in Belfast, one each in Strabane and Newry), and William Carleton has described entire communities in rural Ulster acting the play in barns and kilns in the early years of the nineteenth century.

The same was true of Ashton's *Battle of Aughrim*. According to Carleton, when the Protestant farmers of Fermanagh got together to stage these plays, local Catholics were often recruited to play the Catholic roles, 'the consequence was, that when they came to the conflict with which the play is made to close, armed as they were on both sides with real swords, political and religious resentment could not be restrained, and they would have hacked each other's souls out had not the audience interfered and prevented them'.[2] It is possible to imagine a Catholic farmhand or linen-maker, sword in hand, playing the French general St Ruth in a torchlit Ulster barn, prophesying the return of King James: 'James shall return, and with great pomp restore, / Our Romish worship to the land once more, / And drown these Heretics in crimson gore.'[3] In a moment like this, we glimpse the crack in the foundations, which more theatrically sophisticated plays of the period plaster over.

Similarly, in Mitchelburne's *Ireland Preserv'd*, there is a moment in which a defender of Derry refuses an invitation to surrender. 'We have taken commission from king William and queen Mary', he declares, 'and we resolve to maintain their right, and this city, for their interest; and will stand up for the honour of our country, against any *rebels* that are enemies to it.' The scene then immediately changes to 'the Irish camp', where the Jacobite general rages: 'No proposals will do with these *rebels*, there will be nothing done against this damned town! but a formal siege. Did you observe how they fired their cannon, which fell in the midst of our men, without respect of persons, although the king was there?'[4] Something very curious is going on here with the words 'rebel' and 'king': for 'the Irish', led by English and French generals, the 'king' is James, upon whom the 'rebels' inside the city walls have so traitorously fired; for the defenders of Derry (who are also Irish, including several characters who are Gaelic speakers), William is 'the king' who will defeat the 'Irish rebels'.

This little incident in *Ireland Preserv'd* encapsulates the central political problem which defined the cultural life of eighteenth-century Ireland, whether for farmers staging Michelburne's play in a Fermanagh barn, or for policy-makers in Dublin Castle attending Smock Alley. If William III and his successors were to be other than rebels and usurpers, the Glorious Revolution of 1688-9 had to be legitimated; however, almost any argument that could be used in relation to 1689 had the potential to be used again (and again, and again . . .), opening up a vista of endless revolution. For the most part, this difficulty was overcome with arguments taken from John Locke's *Second Treatise of Government* of 1689, which redefined the monarchy's power as a contract or 'Trust, which is put into their [the rulers'] hands by their Brethren'.[5] If the ruler impinges upon the rights and liberties of his subjects (as James II was said to have done), the contract was void; on the other hand, as long as those rights remained intact, any rebellion was a crime against what Locke would call the 'Laws of Nature'. In England, while acceptance of this new constitutional arrangement was by no means universal, the Lockean argument was gradually absorbed into the political culture as a whole, and by the 1720s 'the rights of Englishmen' could be spoken of as a comforting platitude.

In Ireland, by contrast, the issue remained raw and unresolved; any decision made by the Irish parliament was subject to the veto of the English Privy Council, a disability further compounded by the Declaratory Act of 1720, passed 'for the better Securing of the Dependency of Ireland upon the Crown of Great Britain'. For the vast majority of the Irish population who were members of the Catholic or Dissenting churches, the monarch's claim to be a defender of liberty was even more tenuous. A series of penal laws passed by the new regime, beginning in 1695, restricted basic rights to education, religious worship, and, most importantly, property, which was the key to the Lockean social contract. In short, Ireland constantly brought to the surface the contradictions lurking in the new consensus. 'I could never imagine', wrote the Irish Whig MP and philosopher William Molyneaux in *The Case of Ireland's Being Bound by Acts of Parliament in England, Stated* (1698), 'that those Great *Assertors* of their *Own Liberties* and *Rights* [the English Parliament], could ever think of making the least Breach in the *Rights* and *Liberties* of their *Neighbours*, unless they thought that they had *Right* to do so.'[6] Molyneaux's argument, blended with deep residual loyalties to the Catholic King James, would eventually evolve into a distinctively bifocal Irish political vision, fixed simultaneously on the pre-1689 Jacobite past and on some unnamed future utopia in which the rights and liberties so tantalisingly promised – but never delivered – by the new constitutional arrangement would suddenly appear.

The theatre was not only a place in which rights and liberties could be debated; it was a manifestation of those rights and liberties. When he created the office of Master of the Revels in Ireland in 1662, Charles II announced that he was establishing a legal basis for the Irish theatre because he 'thought fitt that our subjects of our said Kingdome of Ireland should enjoy the like priviledges in that kind as our subjects here in our Kingdome of England'.[7] After 1691, the concept of a monarch granting 'priviledges' changed, but the link between the freedom of the theatre and the monarch's role as the guarantor of that freedom survived. Hence, the simple act of speaking from a stage was a political act, and was understood as such, with the consequence that when the discrepancies between the rights of the king's English and Irish subjects were felt most painfully, the Irish theatre became a place where (from one side of the political fence) it was possible to demonstrate that the monarch was fulfilling his end of the social contract and (from the opposite point of view) it was possible to glimpse a set of liberties absent elsewhere in society.

This new understanding of the theatre was to change both the repertoire and the culture of Irish theatre-going, accelerating changes that were already underway in the 1670s and 1680s. The theatre for which Katherine Philips had written had been largely an appendage of the Dublin court, and it behaved accordingly. At the same time, the Viceregent did not directly fund the theatre, so it was necessary to reach an audience wider than the confines of Dublin Castle. By the time John Dunton visited Smock Alley in 1699, he would note: 'The Play-house is free for all Comers, and gives Entertainment as well to the Broom man, as the greatest Peer.'[8]

There were not many places in early eighteenth-century Ireland in which the 'Broom man' and 'the greatest Peer' could hiss and cheer in the same room. In theory, everyone in the theatre was united around the figure of the Lord Lieutenant, represented even in his absence by the viceregal box, just as the state was supposed to be bound together by the monarch. This meant that the 'government nights' on which the Viceroy was bodily present continued to be of great importance to the theatre's licensed place in Irish culture. Indeed, only a few years after Dudley Moore had been tried for marking William of Orange's birthday from the stage, a production of *Tamerlane* before the Lord Lieutenant on 4 November became a fixture in the theatrical calendar. In the 1730s, the Duke of Dorset commanded thirty performances, while his successor the Duke of Devonshire, commanded fifty-four. On such occasions, the viceregal court attracted the rest of fashionable Dublin (with ladies being granted free admission to the boxes) who in turn attracted the tradesmen who sat in the middle gallery, while servants (who arrived as early as four o'clock to secure their masters' seats for the six o'clock performance) would move to the gods to watch the play with the rest of 'the Mob'.

Emulating the viceregal privilege, 'ladies and gentlemen of quality' could request a particular play, often as a charity benefit. The theatre historian John C. Greene records nearly 180 such requests in the period between 1720 and 1745, along with eighty charity benefits, for everyone from a 'distressed foreign Gentleman' to 'distressed Freemasons'.[9] On such evenings, as on the government nights, the lady or gentlemen concerned made it a point of honour to ensure that the theatre was filled. Indeed, throughout the century the fully illuminated, horseshoe shaped auditorium placed the audience on display as much as the actors. Notices appeared in Dublin newspapers in 1761, for instance, requesting gentlemen not to pirouette on the benches in the pit during the performance, while from the same period there is an account of a splendidly bedecked young dandy displaying his finery by reclining at full length on the rail of his box, with his back to the stage – the effect of which was somewhat spoiled when he lost his balance and fell into the pit, amid general laughter. In short, aristocratic patronage (inextricably tied to the viceregal court) worked two ways: the theatre provided an arena for displaying what was often newfound social status, while those making the display kept the theatre financially afloat. A masque written in 1748 by Nicolo Pasquali for a 4 November government night neatly captures this relationship, as a hymn sung by Hibernia praising William's victory ushers in the allegorical figures of Commerce and Plenty.

Commerce and Plenty, however, were gods with their own imperious demands, and there was a growing awareness among the post-1691 generation of the theatre as a kind of model marketplace. From the beginning, this is evident in the work of George Farquhar whose first play, *Love and a Bottle* (1698), introduces a character named Lyrick – a poet who spends most of his time trying to market his verses with lines echoing Farquhar's own views in his *Discourse Upon Comedy* (1701). The wit of a play, Lyrick says at one point, lies not in the poet's mind, but in the audience's response: 'Nothing's ill said, but what's ill taken; so nothing's well said, but what's well taken.' This is something more than the customary compliment to the audience; it is consistent with Farquhar's belief that a good play is not one which follows a prescribed set of rules, but one of which the audience approves. 'The rules of English comedy', he later writes, 'don't lie in the compass of Aristotle, or his followers, but in the pit, box, and galleries'. What emerges, quickly and clearly, in Farquhar's work is the idea that commerical success demonstrates that the play contributes to the common good. 'No, no, Sir', he insists, '*ipse dixit* is remov'd long ago, and all the rubbish of old philosophy . . . and their infallibility is lost with all persons of a free and unprejudic'd reason.'[10]

This is a vitally theatrical idea. That which is right – whether politically or theatrically – is not laid down according to some ancient set of authorities; it is tested, moment by moment, in the presence of the community who make up a theatre audience. And so, Farquhar creates characters who are constantly testing, in an almost improvisational way, what the audience will accept, initially in Roebuck, the hero of *Love and a Bottle*, and later in Farquhar's most popular stage creation, Sir Harry Wildair, the hero of *The Constant Couple* (1699) and *Sir Harry Wildair* (1701). Both characters – Roebuck and Wildair – share a refusal to be bound by rules of behaviour which are not in their own interest; in particular, they are utterly contemptuous of the abstract precepts of honour, which guided tragic heroes like Katherine Philips' Pompey. 'I find that Honour looks as ridiculous as Roman Buskins upon your Lordship', Sir Harry declares, 'or my full Peruke upon *Scipio Africanus*.' Similarly, when the affronted Colonel Standard in *The Constant Couple* challenges Wildair to a duel, Sir Harry tells him: 'I am a baronet, and have eight thousands pounds a year. I can dance, sing, ride, fence, understand the languages. Now, I can't conceive how running you through the body should contribute one jot more to my gentility.'[11]

Such Falstaffian pragmatism may make Sir Harry Wildair or George Roebuck seem like a strange incarnation of the Williamite hero; but there is a sense in which they are precisely that. Moreover, there is a sense in which both characters are Irish: 'An *Irish-man*, Madam, at your Service', announces Roebuck at the beginning of *Love and a Bottle*, while for almost three decades, the role of Wildair was all but owned by the Irish actor and former Williamite soldier, Robert Wilks. It was later taken over by another Irish performer, Peg Woffington, who played it as a breeches part from 1740 onwards.[12] At the same time, we need to remember that elaborate statements of allegiance to the new dispensation frame the adventures of these shape-changing characters. *Sir Harry Wildair*, for instance, is dedicated to William as the king who 'first asserted our Liberties at home against Popery and Thraldom'. Moreover, Farquhar's plays have streaks of vicious anti-Catholicism running through them, from the lecherous Irish priest, MacShane, disguised as a Frenchman in *The Beaux Stratagem* (1707), to Sir Harry Wildair's boast of raping six nuns in five nights as his way of being revenged upon a French Catholic priest who had refused to bury his wife. By the time we reach the end of *Sir Harry Wildair*, Farquhar has defined a new type of theatrical character, less the conventional libertine of the old Restoration comedy than libertarian of the new Whig order, bound to his country and his monarch not by an extended aristocratic lineage, but by a contract of reciprocal rights in a marketplace whose freedoms depend upon the exclusion of those who have a differing view of things – Frenchmen, Catholics, and anyone associated with the old regime.

In many ways, therefore, Farquhar's return to Dublin in 1704 to play Wildair in a command performance of *The Constant Couple* before the Lord Lieutenant is a defining moment in the Irish theatre of the period. By the middle of the century, only Shakespeare and Colley Cibber would be produced more frequently than Farquhar on Irish stages. And yet, while his plays form a part of the emerging Anglo-Irish identity, they are set in England, written for the London stage, and their Irishness can only be produced through an act of translation. The problem here – and it would persist for many years to come – was economic rather than purely cultural. With the payment of royalties more than a century away, playwrights earned their livings through the proceeds of benefit nights. In the London theatre, this was traditionally the third, sixth, and ninth night of a run (and so on in multiples of three), and this practice would seem to have been followed in Dublin. The difficulty in Dublin, however, was that there was not a large enough theatre-going population to sustain a play for more than a few nights, so there is no evidence of any playwright ever receiving a nine-night benefit. On more than one occasion, a playwright opened, closed and had his benefit all on the same night.[13] Hence, Irish stages in the early decades of the eighteenth century echoed with the ghosts of its missing writers: Farquhar, Southerne, Steele (patent-holder for Drury Lane for a time), and Susanna Centlivre, to which can be added those with Irish associations, such as Congreve and even Joseph Addison, who was twice chief secretary in Dublin Castle. In many cases, their plays were being performed in London by actors who had begun their careers in Smock Alley, with Wilks being joined later by James Quin, Charles Macklin and Spranger Barry.

At a time when the English theatre was filled with Irishmen, and the Irish administration was filled with Englishmen, an understandable sense of grievance simmered through Anglo-Irish culture in the 1720s, fuelled by more fundamental issues such as the status of the Irish Parliament, and trade inequalities. And yet, these were also the years in which a distinctive Anglo-Irish identity, which would last for almost two centuries, began to take shape. It was most visible in the great Palladian country houses of the period, of which Castletown in Celbridge (built in 1722) is a luminous example. Less obvious, but equally lasting, many of the Anglo-Irish would develop an abiding interest in antiquarianism, seeking new ways of renegotiating the relationship between past and present. While the real flowering of this antiquarianism would not come until later in the century, it was present in Irish dramaturgy in the 1720s in two plays: Charles Shadwell's *Rotherick O'Connor, King of Connaught, or the Distress'd Princess* (1720) and William Philips' *Hibernia Freed* (1722).

Both plays are protests against what Shadwell denounces in his prologue as the 'Forreign Stories [that] do our Stage Adorn'. The first thing to have struck any audience seeing these plays in the 1720s would have been the setting: unlike most tragedies of the time, which were set in Greece, Rome or some even more exotic location, these plays were set in Ireland and featured Irish characters, who nonetheless managed to be every bit as exotic as their classical counterparts. In *Rotherick O'Connor*, Shadwell turns to material that would be used in Daniel Maclise's influential nineteenth-century painting, *The Marriage of Strongbow and Eva*, and later in plays by Yeats and Lady Gregory: the twefth-century invasion by the Norman Strongbow at the invitation of the dethroned

King of Leinster, Dermot MacMurrough, to defeat his father, Rotherick O'Connor, King of Connaught. Philips goes back even further, to a ninth-century invasion of Ireland by a Viking king, Turgesius, in which O'Brien, King of Ireland, lies besieged on the 'Hill of Tarah', waiting to be saved by O'Neil, the King of Ulster.

Given that the social order of Ireland in the early eighteenth century had been shaped by invasion, it is no coincidence that both of these plays turn to moments of invasion, although in very different ways. Shadwell was a Whig, and a strong supporter of the Williamite settlement, and so he sets out to demonstrate the benightedness of Ireland before 1691, 'When each King Govern'd by his Inclinations, / When Church and Clergy, were the Monarch's Tools.' 'Learn then from those unhappy Days of Yore', he admonishes his listeners, 'To scorn and hate an Arbitrary Power, / To Praise and Love those Laws that make you Free.' His Rotherick is a conventional stage tyrant, 'a Rebell with a Tyrant's Power' who has 'usurp'd' the 'lawfull Right' of Dermot's father, aided by a 'fawning, pious, cringing Priest', who 'Can first confess and then absolve' the tyrant's crimes; by contrast, the Norman Strongbow, who invades Ireland and defeats Rotherick may be bloodthirsty, but he is no tyrant.[14] Philips, on the other hand, was a Tory with Jacobite leanings, who dedicates *Hibernia Freed* to a Gaelic aristocrat, Henry O'Brien, Earl of Thomonde. 'What is so noble,' he asks, 'as to free one's Country from Tyranny and Invasion?'[15] Hence, his play reverses the equation, so that the virgin-raping Turgesius is the invader, while the noble Irishmen, O'Brien and O'Neil attempt to repulse him.

Although Shadwell and Philips were from opposite sides of one political fence, they were on the same side from the point of view of the majority Irish-speaking population, and this makes pre-conquest Irish history a minefield for them. For Shadwell, invasion is a form of deliverance; for Philips, it is a potential catastrophe. However, neither writer can fully commit himself to his position, for to do so would be to unravel the contradictions of a political culture based on the Lockean social contract holding a colony by force. Hence, Strongbow may save Ireland from tyranny in *Rotherick O'Connor*, but he is an ambivalent saviour, as any invader who conquers by force of arms must be. 'Let Skreiks [*sic*] and Groans, the Musick of the Field', he declaims,

> In one continued Clamour, fill the Skies,
> And cover o'er the Ground so high with Blood,
> That Shoals of gasping, dying Enemies,
> May float, and swim about, upon the Surface.[16]

This is not the sort of thing kings were supposed to say after 1691, and so Shadwell cannot bring himself to allow his Irish heroine, Eva, to marry her supposed deliverer, thereby defusing the play's potential triumphalism.

For the Jacobite Philips, the situation is even more difficult, as his Viking invader, Turgesius, opens up some uncomfortable vistas in Irish history. 'Another Nation shall revenge my Death', Turgesius announces in his obligatory dying speech.

> And with successful Arms invade this Realm
> . . . [My Soul] shall rejoyce to see the Land subdu'd,
> And Peasants Hands with Royal Blood embru'd.

Suddenly, every invader of Ireland since the ninth century begins to look like the progeny of Turgesius – whether Williamite, Cromwellian, Elizabethan or even Norman. While this might have seemed like a fair interpretation to a dispossessed Gaelic family, it was not going to endear the play to the audiences in Smock Alley, most of whose ancestors (and, in many cases, very immediate ancestors) were, in one form or another, invaders. At that point, an Irish bard, Eugenius, jumps in to salvage the situation, prophesying:

> Another Nation shall indeed succeed,
> But different far in Manners from the *Dane*.
> . . . They shall succeed, invited to our Aid,
> And mix their Blood with ours; one People grow,
> Polish our Manners, and improve our Minds.[17]

At that point, however, the damage was done, and there is no record of a production of the play at Smock Alley.

Comedy provided a more secure footing for creating a distinctive Anglo-Irish identity, but only slightly so, since there was always the danger that comic Anglo-Irish characters would be confused with the comic Irish servants – the Teagues and the Macahones – who had been conventional since the early Restoration, and whose lineage goes back to the Elizabethan play, *Sir John Oldcastle* (1600).[18] For instance, when Farquhar's Roebuck first arrives in London at the beginning of *Love and a Bottle*, and introduces himself to Lucinda as 'an Irish-man', she recoils in horror. 'A mere Wolf-dog, I protest', she cries, and teasingly begs him for 'some News of your Country' of which she has heard 'the strangest Stories'. Roebuck assures her that Dublin is just like London: 'We have ladies and whores; colleges and play-houses; churches, and taverns; fine houses and bawdy-houses: in short, every thing that you can boast of, but fops, poets, toads and adders.'[19]

Similarly, in the first post-1691 play to be set in fashionable Dublin, William Philips' *St Stephen's Green* (1700), there is a 'pert conceited [Irish] fop', Vainly, who declares that 'Breeding and Conversation' are not to be had in Ireland. A group of Irish gentlemen then proceed to question him about the quality of Irish wine, food, society and ladies – all, according to Vainly, are excellent. 'Why thou worthless Contemptible Wretch!' expostulates one of the Irish characters, Sir Francis Feignyouth. 'Do you entertain Strangers with your aversion for your Country, without being able to give one Reason for it?'[20] Unfortunately, claiming that Dublin is more or less like London does not help to establish a distinctive Anglo-Irish sense of identity. As if responding to this awareness, the perilous position of a relatively new aristocracy lacking a fixed sense of identity surfaces continually in the Irish comedies of this period. In Shadwell's *The Sham Prince, or News from Passau* (1718), for instance, Sir William Cheatley arrives in Dublin, borrowing huge amounts of money and courting an heiress simply by claiming to be the Prince of Passau. Similarly, in *St Stephen's Green*, servants are mistaken for gentlemen, just as earlier, in Farquhar's darkest play, *The Twin Rivals* (1703), an evil twin can pass himself off as his virtuous brother.

One response to this situation is a developing pride in anything that might mark out the Anglo-Irish from their English contemporaries. Even mild vices could be of use. Hence, we find the forerunner of the 'hard-riding country gentlemen' (who were to gallop over so many pages of nineteenth-century Irish fiction) in Sir Jowler Kennel, a hunting-obsessed Irish landowner affectionately mocked in Charles Shadwell's *Irish Hospitality; or Vertue Rewarded* (1717). 'I hope you are not apt to be jealous, for I must own I love my Hunt's-man mainly', Sir Jowler says in what is supposed to be a marriage proposal. 'Now if you can't sleep with a good many Dogs upon the Bed, why, none but *Beauty*, *Ranger*, *Cæsar* and *Sweetlips*, shall lye of my Side; and if you have an aversion to Smoaking, as I know some Ladies have, why I'll Chaw, 'tis all one to me' – to which the lady replies demurely: 'Pray Sir *Jowler*, are these your good Qualities, or your bad ones?'[21] In a sense, it did not matter; any qualities would do, as long as they could be claimed as distinctively Anglo-Irish – although sleeping with hunting dogs must not have seemed like the most secure basis for a cultural identity.

These early efforts to establish a distinctive Irish theatre repertoire were not helped by the state of the theatre infrastructure at the time,

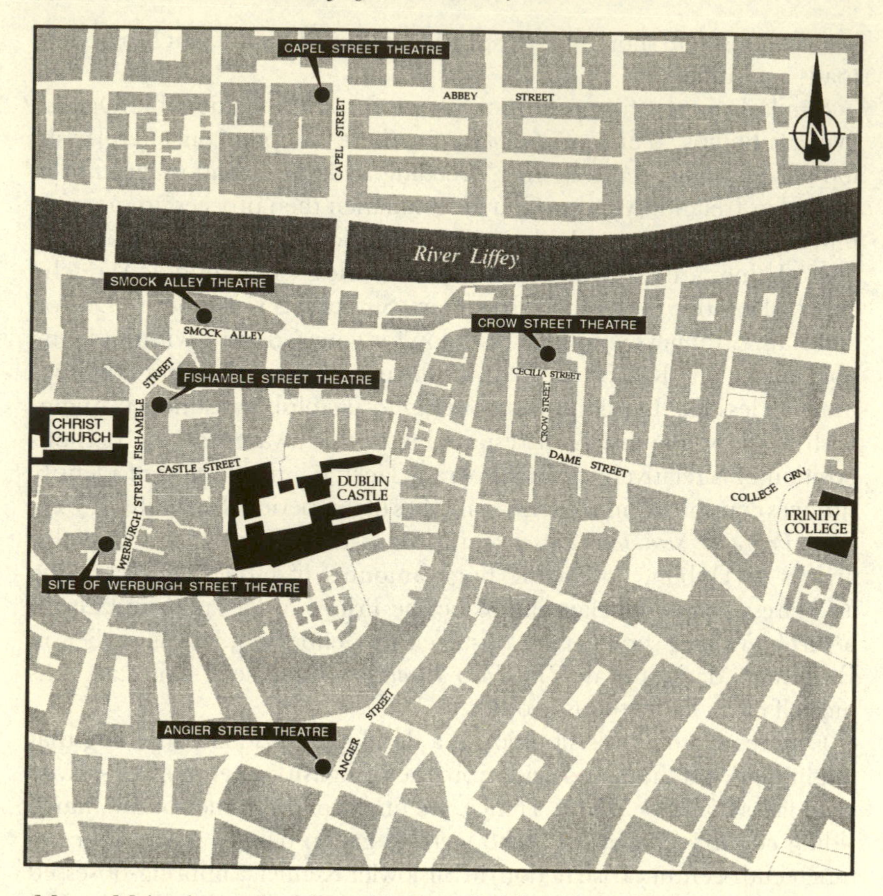

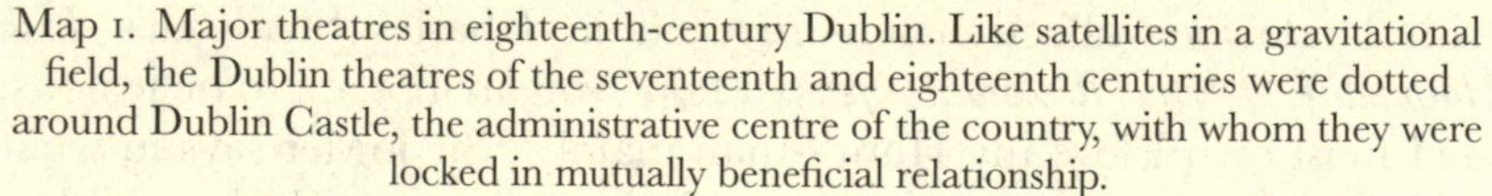
Map 1. Major theatres in eighteenth-century Dublin. Like satellites in a gravitational field, the Dublin theatres of the seventeenth and eighteenth centuries were dotted around Dublin Castle, the administrative centre of the country, with whom they were locked in mutually beneficial relationship.

which was growing increasingly outdated. In 1720, Joseph Ashbury, who had inherited the title of Master of the Revels in Ireland from its original holder John Ogilby, died in Dublin at the age of eighty. After his death, Thomas Elrington took over the running of an increasingly decrepit theatre; Elrington collapsed and died in 1732, and in 1734 the building followed him, when 'Part of the House' fell down. By this time, however, its new proprietors, a group of Dublin gentlemen, were already planning a new building, which opened two years later, on 9 March 1734, in Aungier Street (near St Stephen's Green) with the old Smock Alley company in residence. Meanwhile, a group of actors who had initially set

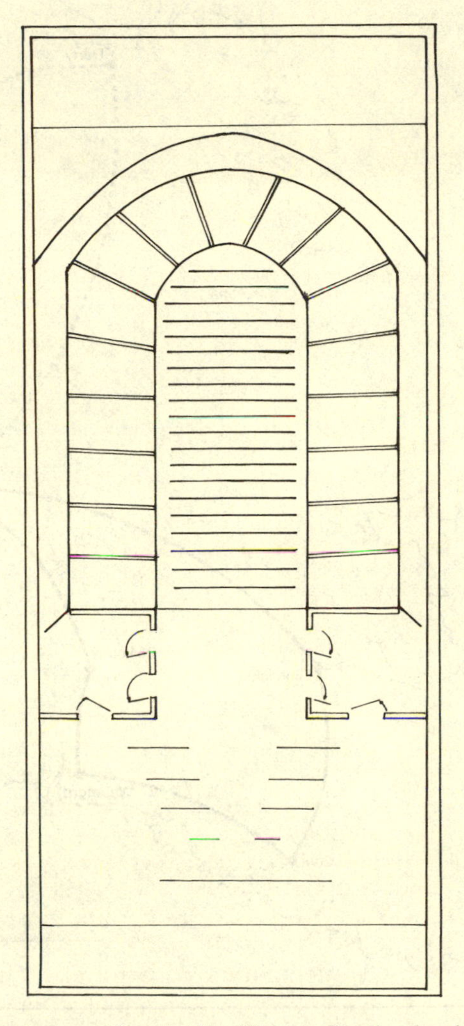

Plan 1. A conjectural plan of Smock Alley Theatre, Dublin, showing the stage, boxes and pit as they may have appeared after the theatre was rebuilt in 1735. Work carried out by archaeologist Linzi Simpson for Temple Bar Properties in the mid-1990s has determined the length and width of the building, and the location of the proscenium arch, while the two sets of doors in the forestage are a well-documented feature of the Smock Alley stage. Other dimensions are conjectural. The building was used as a church from 1811 until 1990, and is now a Viking adventure centre.

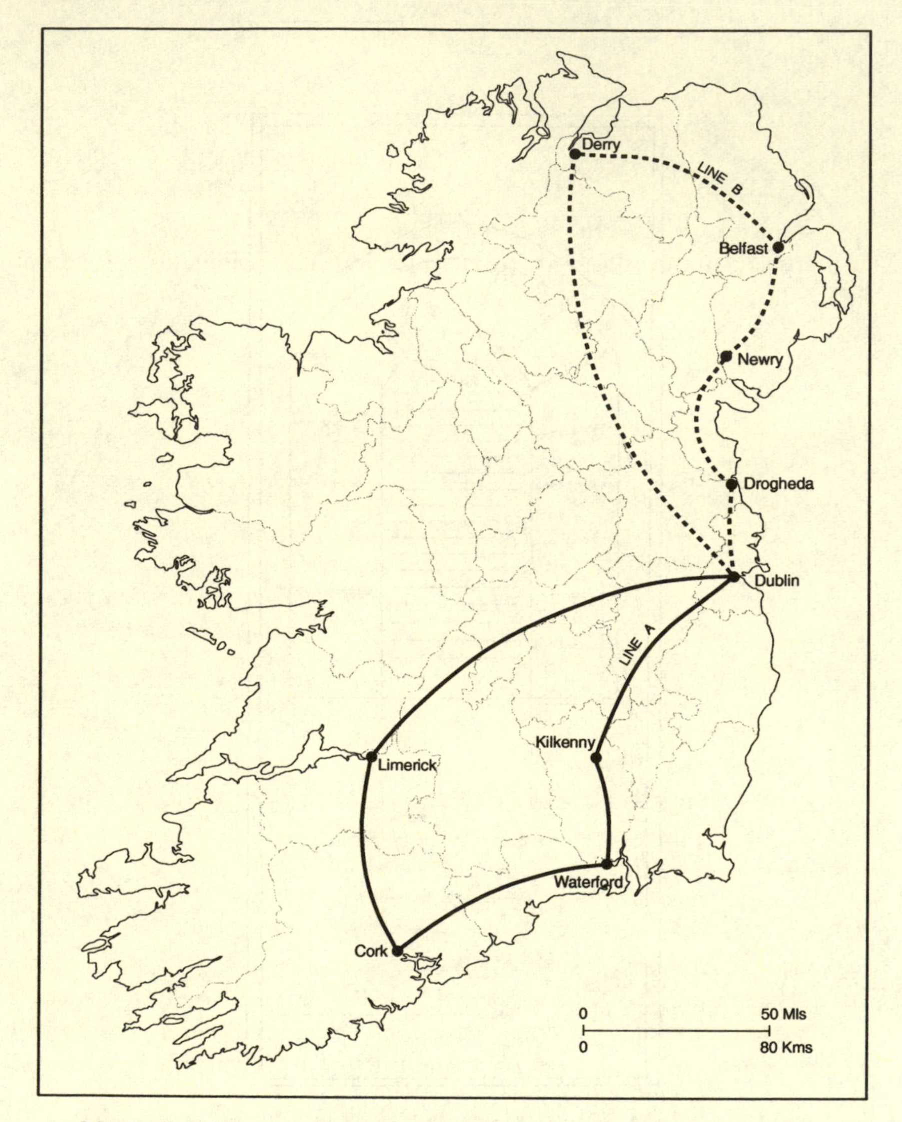

Map 2. Ireland: routes of tours carried out by Smock Alley and Angier Street companies *c*. 1740. The geography of Irish theatre began to take form in the decade after 1735, when rival Dublin companies travelled south and north respectively during the summer season, establishing theatre cultures along an axis that ran from Belfast to Cork, with Dublin at its centre.

up in a 'booth', or temporary wooden theatre in Dame Street, and later in a more permanent structure on a site now occupied by the Guinness Brewery, on Rainsford Street, took over the old Smock Alley site. Using the shell of the existing structure, they began building a new theatre, which opened on 11 December 1735.

By the mid-1730s, the Irish theatre was fundamentally different to what it had been when Ashbury first took the stage in *Pompey* in 1663. Very quickly in the mid-1730s, two new theatres had come into existence in Dublin, where before there had been only one. For the first time there was a competitive marketplace, and in the scramble for new audiences, the Dublin theatre introduced some long-overdue reforms in staging. The sight of stagehands wheeling side-wings and flats on and off the stage was replaced in 1741 with what would appear to have been a drum-and-shaft system, in which a large barrel located beneath the stage controlled a number of counterweighted lines, creating an effect in which borders, cloudings, and drops all moved at once, allowing magical transformations of the stage. Over the next few years, although the new Smock Alley still had a large forestage from which actors usually entered and exited via doors on either side of the proscenium, Irish theatre was taking the first steps towards a performance style whose pleasures would be increasingly visual.

The new competitive world of the late 1730s and early 1740s also brought with it the beginnings of what would become one of the most important phenomena in Irish theatre: professional touring. There had, of course, been earlier ventures outside of Dublin. In the 1690s, Ashbury had gone to Kilkenny with the Smock Alley players, including Wilks, and in 1713, they had travelled to Cork for the summer, establishing a makeshift theatre in a converted malthouse. By the middle of the 1730s these irregular peregrinations had become regular summer circuits encompassing Limerick, Waterford and Kilkenny, as well as Cork. Hence, when the old Smock Alley company moved to Aungier Street, they kept their summer circuit; in 1736 they built the first Irish purpose-built theatre outside of Dublin, the Theatre Royal on Dunscomb's Marsh, Cork, which remained in use until 1760. This left the new proprietors of Smock Alley without a source of summer income, so in 1736 they ventured north to Belfast, and by 1741 were playing a regular northern circuit which also took in Derry and Newry. In each of these cities, smaller, more erratic, theatre cultures would emerge. Hence, by 1741, a basic map of the geography of the Irish theatre had been traced; it would last until the 1930s.

While it benefited the rest of the country in the long term, in the short term this first taste of competition was almost catastrophic. The two companies played to half-empty houses in Dublin for seven years, until, at the beginning of the 1743–4 season, they joined forces, eventually hiring as their manager a twenty-six-year-old actor who would have a profound influence on the Irish theatre: Thomas Sheridan. We get an early glimpse of Sheridan in a short afterpiece *The Brave Irishman; or, Captain O'Blunder*, written while he was still a student at Trinity, and first performed in 1743. The title role, the 'first *counter*-Stage Irishman'.[22] has all the standard features of the stage Irish servant: he carries a shillelagh, is loyal to the point of naìveté, never far from a fight or a song, and, most importantly, twists language into unexpected shapes with his 'bulls', or illogical logic. In spite of this, he is a gentleman, and consequently he is speaking as much to a potentially confused theatre audience as to the stage mob who mock him after his first entrance when he indignantly declares: 'You Shons of Whores, don't you see by my Dress and Behaviour, that I'm a Shentleman-Stranger.' Although he speaks like a stage Irish servant, he shows through his actions – like Roebuck before him – that he is more of a gentleman than the English and French grandees who mock him, singing at the curtain: 'The English they are drones as plainly you can see, / But we're all brisk and airy, and lively as a bee.'[23]

For Sheridan, however, this was far more than a piece of light entertainment. 'We are told', Sheridan would later write in his *Course of Lectures on Elocution* (1762), 'that amongst the savages of North America, the spokesmen who come down with what is called a Talk to our governors, deliver themselves with great energy untutored by any schoolmistress but nature. But were these savages to be taught our written language by our masters, we should soon find them delivering themselves as ill as we do.' O'Blunder provides Sheridan with an early exploration of this idea. While it is true that O'Blunder's lack of 'any school-mistress but nature' is exaggerated for comic effect (and, indeed, Sheridan would later devote considerable time and energy into achieving 'uniformity of pronunciation') there is no mistaking the idea that his natural eloquence flows from an intuitive nobility.[24] If the eloquence of the spoken word is the basis of civilisation, then those institutions founded on eloquence become the exemplary civilising bodies: parliament, universities, the courts, the church, and, of course, the theatre. In *Captain O'Blunder*, Sheridan incidentally helps to provide a culture that was beginning to pride itself on its oratorical skills with a caste mark more powerful than an affinity for foxhounds.

The seriousness with which Sheridan understood the role of the theatre in Irish society helps to account both for his influence, and for the trouble he would provoke. His first taste of the latter came on 14 July 1743, when he refused to appear in the most orthodox of Whig plays, Addison's *Cato*, on the grounds that both the musicians and his costume were missing – a refusal that was misinterpreted as a political gesture in the heated political climate in the months leading up to the Jacobite rebellion of 1745. Having settled that row, Sheridan again courted controversy when he mounted a production of Henry Brooke's attack on political corruption, *The Patriot* on 4 December 1744. Under its original title, *Gustavus Vasa: The Deliverer of His Country*, the play had been banned in England under the Licensing Act of 1737. The Act stipulated that all new plays had to be approved by the Lord Chamberlain's Office prior to production. The Act had never come before the Irish Parliament, however, so its jurisdiction in Ireland was a legal grey area. Hence, deciding to stage *The Patriot* was an assertion of the right of the Irish Parliament (an image of which appeared on the Smock Alley curtains) to legislate for Ireland. In the end, the play ran for three nights, no action was taken, and that seemed to be the end of the matter – although *Gustavus Vasa* would be claimed by a much more assertive patriotism in the 1780s, and flaunting the Licensing Act would continue to be a way of asserting Irish liberty as late as 1909.

When real trouble came, it came unexpectedly. On 19 January 1747, a revival of Vanburgh's *Aesop* was going reasonably well – that is to say, the musicians had been pelted with oranges from the upper gallery before the curtain went up, the pit was noisy, with the occasional beau pirouetting on his bench to display his new wig, and the stage exits were more or less blocked by the chairs of gentlemen flirting across the auditorium with the masked ladies in the boxes. Suddenly, a drunken Trinity student from Galway, Edward Kelly, stumbled up out of the pit, across the stage, and into the green room, where he accosted an actress, a Mrs Dyer. Kelly told her that he would, as she put it, 'do what her husband Mr Dyer, had done to her, using the obscene expression'. Another young Trinity student of the time, Edmund Burke, saw Kelly put his hands 'under the actress's petticoats'.[25] Sheridan intervened, and Kelly was turned out of the dressing rooms, only to reappear in the pit, where he continued to hurl invectives and the occasional orange at Sheridan, who in annoyance stepped out of character and declared (in lines echoing Captain O'Blunder): 'I am as good a Gentleman as you are.'[26] When the performance was finally finished, Sheridan found Kelly in his dressing room demanding an apology; exasperated, the actor, still in costume, used Aesop's walking stick to give Kelly 'the Usage he deserved', a beating which one witness says was received 'with Christian patience' – suggesting perhaps that Kelly was too drunk to put up much of a fight.

Over the next week, the theatre teetered on the verge of open rioting, and was closed for a time; there were brawls on the streets of Dublin, fuelled by the inevitable pamphlets and satires, ultimately leading to a court case, the division of Trinity students into pro and anti-Sheridan factions and finally ending with Kelly's public humiliation in the Front Square of the College and his imprisonment. In retrospect, given that Irish theatres were rowdy at the best of times, it might seem remarkable that what started as a drunken brawl should have escalated into a civil disturbance; however, what set events spiralling out of control was Sheridan's claim to be 'as good a gentleman' as Kelly. Kelly's refusal to accept Sheridan's status re-opened an uncomfortable question asked by Farquhar's Roebuck, Shadwell's *Irish Hospitality*, and Sheridan's own *Captain O'Blunder*: what *is* an Irish gentleman? In a culture in which hereditary title offered uncertain footing, the question revolved – like so much in Ireland in the eighteenth century – around the question of rights and privileges. Was it possible to be an obnoxious drunk, attempt to rape an actress, and still be a gentleman? For Kelly and his supporters, this was precisely the point, although they were reluctant to say it in so many words. 'Shall we tamely View our Honours torn', Kelly is made to ask in a satirical poem published by Sheridan's supporters,

> 'And on Plebian Backs our Badges worn?
> And unreveng'd behold those hated Sights,
> Nor crush th' Invaders of our antient Rights?'[27]

The problem was, of course, that 'ancient rights' in mid-eighteenth-century Ireland were often neither ancient nor rights.

The Kelly riots were only partly about Sheridan asserting his own status as a gentleman-actor; they were equally about the role of the theatre in Irish society. When Smock Alley would erupt in rioting a decade later during a production of Voltaire's *Mahomet*, Sheridan would wearily quote Colley Cibber to the effect that 'I so often had occasion to compare the State of the Stage to the State of a Nation, that I yet feel a Reluctancy to drop the Comparison, or speak of the one, without some Application to the other.'[28] The stage, for Sheridan, was not simply a part of society; it was a model of society. Writing in the aftermath of the Kelly riots, he denounced anyone who attempted to disrupt the audience's consensual choice to enjoy a play as 'open Enemies of their Country. They destroy the very Fundamentals of our Constitution, they trample Liberty under Foot, and introduce Anarchy and Confusion to the Subversion of all Order and Right.'

There is thus a political edge to the practical reforms Sheridan was able to bring about after 1747, ensuring that actors were paid, and doing away with 'two great Nuisances universally complain'd of . . . the Upper-Gallery which us'd to be constantly so noisy . . . and the Crowds that us'd to assemble on the Stage itself'.[29] He raised admission to a hefty half crown in the Upper Gallery, where servants traditionally sat (and from where they launched their traditional missile, the orange), making it, in his words, 'one of the quietest parts of the house'. In the summer of 1747, he also built a separate, covered entrance to the galleries on the west side of the building, adding extra entrances to the pit on the eastern side, as well as providing access to the lattices from the box room at the front of the building.

As well as decreasing congestion in the theatre, these changes also increased the social segregation of the theatre, so that not only did different social classes sit in different parts of the theatre, they also entered and exited through different doors. Indeed, the existence of elaborate doors on the northern end of Smock Alley suggests that some privileged members of the audience may have entered the building from the stage end, perhaps crossing the stage to reach their seats. At the same time, however, Sheridan took what was considered the outrageous step of forbidding beaux from sitting on the stage itself, or hobnobbing with the actors and actresses in the green room during the performance. The net result of these changes was a sharper definition of the class structure as it was mirrored by the theatre auditorium, removing some forms of aristocratic privilege, while entrenching a more middle-class sense of decorum throughout the theatre as a whole.

Looking back on his career in the year in which he gave up the management of Smock Alley, 1758, Sheridan would maintain that all that he had done in the theatre – making the house more orderly, compelling respect for actors, regularising theatre business – was in the service of 'a Stage of Liberty', whose model was 'a State wherein the Lives and Properties of all Subjects are equally under the Protection of the Laws; wherein no Man shall be restrained from saying or doing any thing that is consistent with Reason and Truth'.[30] With the Theatre Royal's monopoly on the Irish stage effectively broken, however, Sheridan's 'Stage of Liberty' had to confront the possibility that a fickle audience, deciding perhaps that they liked to sit on the stage, would patronise another theatre. One of the actors in Smock Alley, George Stayley, satirised this situation in a short comic play, *The Rival Theatres* (1759), in which a lady of fashion remarks that the best theatre is not the best regulated, but the newest. When reminded that a new theatre will not always be new, she responds: 'Then I hope Mr Somebody will come over, and build another House.'[31]

In 1759, the latest 'Mr Somebody' was the popular Dublin actor, Spranger Barry, who the previous year had made public his plans for a new theatre on Crow Street. Sheridan, in turn, responded with a proposal (which proved deeply unpopular) that Dublin should have only one theatre, run by the actors as a 'Commonwealth', so that their 'Advancement is the reward of Merit, not Caprice', with all surplus profits going to charity, and government acting as the main shareholder – in short, a state theatre. 'The Dublin Stage', declared Sheridan in a manifesto of 1758, 'will never remain long in a flourishing Condition whilst it is the Property of a private Person.'[32] The theatre may have been the expression of its audience's will for Sheridan, but equally it was too important to be left to the whims of the marketplace.

In the years immediately after Sheridan left Smock Alley in 1758, there were many who would come to believe in retrospect that he had been right. Shortly after Barry opened in Crow Street in 1760, and obtained the title of Master of the Revels, Henry Mossop returned from an acting career in London to take charge of Smock Alley, setting off yet another theatre war. As had been the case in the 1730s, the existing audience was not large enough to support two theatres, so both companies increased their touring and raised production standards to widen their audience bases. Barry, for instance, built a large new theatre on George's Street in Cork, and instituted a regular season in Limerick, where a permanent theatre was constructed in 1770. This in turn led to a consolidation of the theatre cultures in Cork, Limerick and Belfast.

Meanwhile back in Dublin, Barry worked at building up the stock of scenery, and an inventory of the Crow Street Theatre records four different bells located under the stage for sound effects ('thunder bell, alarm bell, large bell and curtain bell'), as well as a large number of flats and wings, some generic, but a few representing Irish scenes, including a 'waterfall in the Dargle'.[33] For their part, members of the Smock Alley company were also increasing their stock of scenery, and in February and March of 1772 they made use of an Indian elephant on display in Dame Street for a production of Shakespeare's *Henry VIII*.

However, in the same week that King Henry made his entrance 'clad in burnished gold and riding an elephant', Thomas Sheridan was once again in Dublin, chairing a meeting in a hotel just off College Green, at which the Irish parliament was urged to establish 'one good theatre in this city'.[34] Competition in the theatre, as in the Irish economy as a whole, was destructive, because the market was never really free, being constantly twisted by the magnetic pull of London. Leading English actors could always be lured to Ireland for a lucrative run in a favourite role. David Garrick, for instance, was a frequent visitor, and first acted *Hamlet* on a Dublin stage. Similarly, Peg Woffington was for a time in the Smock Alley company, and both careers are typical of their time in this respect. Hence, the careful development of an Irish company could be upstaged by a rival bringing in a star name from London for a season, while, in a tradition going back to James Quin and Robert Wilks, successful Irish actors almost invariably found themselves drawn to the more lucrative stages of London.

In London, theatres were getting bigger and runs getting longer, thereby widening the gap between what a playwright could earn in London and in Dublin. Consequently, the two Dublin theatres were continually tripping over each other in an attempt to stage the latest London play. For instance, when Sheridan's wife, Frances, wrote *The Discovery* in 1762, it was premièred at Drury Lane with Sheridan and Garrick in the lead roles; it was not until later that year that the two rival Dublin theatres, Smock Alley and Crow Street, both mounted productions at the same time, each playing to half-full houses. This was a pattern that would be repeated again and again in a period during which much of the new work on the London stage – particularly in Drury Lane – would come from Irish pens. In the 1760s, London audiences flocked to see musical comedies by Isaac Bickerstaff, such as *Love in a Village* (1762) and *The Maid of the Mill* (1765); comedies by Arthur Murphy, including *The Way to Keep Him* (1760), *All in the Wrong* (1761), and *The School for Guardians* (1767); more comedies by Hugh Kelly, such as *False Delicacy* (1768) and *A School for Wives* (1773); and Richard Cumberland's *The West Indian* (1771). In the same period, Oliver Goldsmith's two plays – *The Good-Natur'd Man* (1768) and *She Stoops to Conquer; or, The Mistakes of a Night* (1773) – were both staged in Covent Garden. All of these writers were born in Ireland; none of them wrote plays set in Ireland or had careers in Ireland, although their plays would be performed in the Dublin theatres. Leaving Cork Harbour in 1747, Murphy wrote: 'there is nothing stirring in this place at present but barrels of beef and firkins of butter, under which denomination I would also comprehend the people',[35] and this sense that an Irish career was not worth the effort continually undercut any attempt to create an Irish theatre like that imagined by Sheridan.

Against this background, the career of Charles Macklin appears as a sort of spectral image of what the Irish theatre of the period might have been. By the time Macklin arrived to act in Crow Street in 1757, he was already an ambivalent icon of Irishness; rumours circulated that he had been born on the battlefield at the Boyne in 1690, that 'at the celebrated siege of Derry in King William's time, he had three uncles within the walls, and three without'.[36] He almost certainly killed a fellow actor early in his career; at the same time he was a living embodiment of Sheridan's theories of the superiority of natural eloquence over artificial oratory, and was widely acknowledged to have been responsible, along with Garrick, for introducing a more interpretative style of acting. Unlike the generation of actors who preceded him, he made speeches sound like speech, with an effect that consigned him to the theatrical wilderness early in his career, and, as public taste shifted, brought him acclaim for his 1741 performance as Shylock in *The Merchant of Venice.* Throughout his career, he shuttled back and forth between Dublin and London, even establishing his own theatre in Capel Street in 1770. However, it is in his work as a playwright that he shows what might have been if the theatre in Ireland had been able to support playwrights who were willing to write for Irish audiences.

Macklin's plays for the London theatre, such as *The New Play Criticiz'd, or the Plague of Envy* (1747) and *Love à la Mode* (1759), contain characters 'of Irish distraction' (as one of them puts it) not unlike Sheridan's Captain O'Blunder – that is to say, they are forcefully Irish, and yet acceptable to English audiences. Even King George II approved, although he objected to Macklin's definition of 'an Irish-Englishman' as a type of 'outlandish Englishman'. However, Macklin's first play to be set in Ireland, *The True-Born Irishman,* was written for the Crow Street theatre, and its reception would demonstrate the growing gulf between Dublin and London audiences. When it opened on 14 May 1760, the house was full, and it quickly became a fixture in the Irish repertoire; however, when it was retitled *The Irish Fine Lady* for Covent Garden in 1767, it failed dismally. 'The audience are right', Macklin acknowledged. 'There's a geography in humor as well as in morals, which I had not previously considered.'[37]

The True-Born Irishman dusts off a conventional plot – here, the mysogynistic *Taming of the Shrew* story – in which the hero (in this case, a Dubliner, O'Dogherty) must 'cure' his wife of an obsession. 'The Irish Fine Lady's delirium', O'Dogherty calls his wife's particular fixation, 'or the London vertigo; if you were to hear her when the fit is upon her – oh, she is as mad – the devil a thing in this poor country but what gives her the spleen, and the vapours – and such a phrenzy of admiration for every thing in England.'[38] By the end of the play, O'Dogherty catches his wife in an intrigue with the English fop, Mushroom, and compels her to give up her English pretensions, chief of which is the claim that her name is not O'Dogherty, but Diggerty. 'Why they have not such a name in all England as O'Dogherty – nor as any of our fine sounding Milesian names', proclaims Macklin's hero when his wife has vowed not to 'vix' him again with the name Diggerty.

O'Dogherty is not the first Macklin hero to identify himself as a 'Milesian', or Gael; Sir Callaghan O'Brallaghan in *Love à la Mode* is equally proud of being one of 'the true old Milesians' who are 'the tick blood of the nation'.[39] Macklin's library (which at his death in 1797 amounted to over a thousand items, most collected since the loss of his earlier library in a shipwreck in the Irish Sea in 1772) contained all of the standard works of the newly emerging Irish antiquarian movement: Charles Vallancey's *Collecteana de Rebus Hibernicis* (1770), Wynne's *History of Ireland*, and other similar works.[40] Macklin's Milesian heroes are thus early indicators of a trend that was to become one of the dominant strands in Irish cultural life over the next two decades; a growing sense of kinship between the Gaelic culture the Penal Laws had so thoroughly repressed, and a Protestant Anglo-Irish patriotism, meeting on the common ground of antiquarian studies – a meeting which Joep Leerssen argues 'stands at the beginning of Irish nationalism proper'.[41] 'And though the Milesians have been dispossessed by upstarts and foreigners, buddoughs and sassanoughs', declares O'Dogherty in *The True-Born Irishman*, 'yet I hope they will flourish in the Island of Saints, while grass grows or water runs.'[42] Spoken by the hero at the end of a fairly conventional comedy, these lines could sound innocent enough. And yet, just two months after they were first spoken, the first meeting of the Catholic Committee met in Dublin to argue for a relaxation of the Penal Laws.

From 1691 onwards, the rhetoric of rights and liberties never left the Irish stage, but by the time Macklin returned to Dublin, it had begun to mutate. In 1758, in one of his pamphlets arguing for the creation of an Irish national theatre, Thomas Sheridan recalled for his readers the inspiring effect of the first production of Joseph Addison's *Cato* in 1713. 'Let us call to mind', he urges his readers, 'the noble spirit of Patriotism, which that Play then infus'd into the Breasts of a free People, that crowded to it. There *Cato* breath'd again in Life; and tho' he perish'd in the Cause of Liberty, his Virtue was victorious, and left the Triumph of it in the Heart of every melting Spectator.'[43] In 1775, Sheridan was still playing Cato (and was 'astonishingly well received', much to his son's amazement). And yet, in the decades between 1713 and 1775, the idea of dying for 'liberty' and 'patriotism' which a play like *Cato* or *Tamerlane* inspired in 'the Heart of every melting Spectator' was taking on a sharper, more radical edge.

The same factor that made it so difficult to keep a theatre financially afloat in Dublin – the proximity to London – helped to give the Irish theatre its political edge. Plays about liberty in London could be absorbed as platitudinous in any but the most disturbed periods; in Dublin, they continually opened up uncomfortable questions about the position of the vast majority of the population whose liberty was so severely curtailed. William Philips and Charles Shadwell had discovered this in the 1720s, when their plays *Hibernia Freed* and *Rotherick O'Connor* unintentionally questioned the rights conferred by conquest. Gorges Edmond Howard encountered the same problem in 1773 when he returned to the material that Philips had used in *Hibernia Freed* with a play entitled *The Siege of Tamor.* Once again, a valiant, besieged Irish king struggles with the tyrannical Danish invader, Turgesius, reopening awkward questions about invasion, tyranny, liberty and armed resistance. In his epilogue, Howard tells his audience that he hopes they may learn, from this account of Irish courage and love of liberty, 'how they are favour'd, / Who dare for freedom and their Country bleed'.

We get a sense of the volatility of the period when we remember that Howard was no revolutionary. He was closely associated with the court party in the Dublin Castle administration. Equally, however, he had acted as a solicitor for the Catholic Committee seeking amendment of the penal laws. 'These laws are, as they now stand, a reproach to a civilized nation, and an affront to Christianity', he declared. 'They are against common right, and several of them totally opposite to the principles of a free constitution.'[44] A character 'could not have fallen into a greater dilemma', Macklin wrote to Howard after reading *The Siege of Tamor*, 'than that of being obliged to surrender his religion, his country, and its liberties, to the cruelty of a Tyrant.'[45] Macklin, a convert from

Catholicism whose family had lost their land in Derry in 1691, presumably knew what he was talking about.

When someone close to the political establishment like Howard was writing plays about heroes 'Who dare for freedom and their Country bleed', it was a sign that the situation was moving closer to violence. By the mid-1770s, the American colonies had began to assert their rights to independence. Within a few years, as the Volunteer movement began to spread throughout Ireland, Irish Presbyterians and some Catholics would take up arms (*albeit*, in defence of their king) under the leadership of Anglo-Irish landowners. Meanwhile in Irish public debate, the language being used over issues such as restrictions on Irish trade was becoming more and more intemperate. As the ground became more unstable, the widening gap between perceptions of English liberty and Irish liberty began to alter the dynamic of the relationship between the theatre worlds of Dublin and London; and it was precisely at this moment that Thomas Sheridan's son Richard Brinsley Sheridan shot to prominence in the London theatre world, premièring three plays in 1775 (*The Rivals*, *St Patrick's Day* and *The Duenna*) and taking over the management of Drury Lane the following year.

Although his near contemporaries in the London theatre world – Kelly, Murphy and Cumberland – used Irish characters in their plays (Goldsmith restricted his Irish speculations to his prose and verse), Sheridan alone used the stage to stoke the new sense of threat in English / Irish relations. When *The Rivals* first opened on 17 January 1775, there was thus a swift, and unexpected, backlash against the play's Irish character, Sir Lucius O'Trigger who, as his name suggests, is an avid duellist. Writing in the London *Morning Post*, on 21 January, a contributor calling himself as 'A Briton' was furious. 'It is the first time I ever remember to have seen so villainous a portrait of an Irish Gentleman, permitted so openly to insult the country upon the boards of an English theatre.' As Joep Leerssen has argued, the objection to O'Trigger was not mounted by any Irish interests in London, but by English theatregoers who had become used to a type of stage Irishman who was blundering, perhaps, and inordinately proud of his country, but honest, loyal to his English masters and determined to be of service. Sir Lucius O'Trigger, violent and bloodthirsty, was an affront to this new convention, so much so that Sheridan was forced to withdraw the play after only one performance, recasting and rewriting the character so that his duels had some justification. According to a mollified *Morning Post*, the new O'Trigger 'wipes off the former stigma undeservedly thrown on the sister kingdom'. 'If the condemnation of this Comedy (however misconceived the provocation) could have added one spark to the decaying flame of national attachment to the country supposed to be reflected on', Sheridan wrote later, 'I should have been happy in its fate.'[46]

Of all the Irish theatre exiles of the 1770s, Sheridan's absence was the most strongly felt. The memory was still fresh of his father, Thomas Sheridan, and his battles to establish the dignity of the Irish stage; indeed, Thomas Sheridan was still acting on Irish stages, appearing in Cork and Limerick in July of 1776, later filling the Crow Street Theatre (now under the management of Thomas Ryder) for twenty-two performances between November and March. Although Richard Brinsley Sheridan had not lived in Ireland since he was a child (nor was he to return), his public statements on Ireland (particularly after he became a Member of the Westminster Parliament in 1780), and the Irish productions of the plays he wrote in a brief, dazzling burst in the late 1770s (following up *The Rivals* and *The Duenna* with *The School for Scandal* in 1777, and *The Critic* in 1779) increasingly took on a patriotic fervour.

This was particularly true of his farce, *St Patrick's Day*, which opened in Covent Garden on 2 May 1775. Although dismissed as a trifle by many of his English contemporaries and never staged in Drury Lane during Sheridan's management, it quickly became a fixture on Irish stages and was published in two Dublin editions by 1789. Like much of Sheridan's work, its plot is entirely conventional: a wily recruiting officer, Lieutenant O'Connor, tries to win permission to marry the daughter of the crotchety Justice Credulous. Within this flimsy framework, the play helps define the complex mixture of pride in being Irish and pride in living under the British Constitution that was becoming an increasingly explosive mixture. 'You are the two things on earth I hate most', Credulous tells O'Connor: 'an Irishman and a soldier . . . Renounce your country and sell your commission, and I'll forgive you.' 'If you were not the father of my Lauretta', O'Connor retorts, 'I would pull your nose for asking the first, and break your bones for desiring the second' – upon which Credulous immediately relents.[47]

In performance, the play contained a hidden charge, not immediately obvious in the script. By writing a play that calls for marching and drumming, set on St Patrick's Day, Sheridan provided a legitimate excuse to play the piece of music known as 'St Patrick's Day', which was rapidly becoming the unofficial Irish national anthem. By the late 1770s, an Irish theatre orchestra who either played or omitted to play 'St Patrick's Day' (depending on the political mood of the audience) could find themselves being pelted with oranges; Sheridan's play provided them with a way around the dilemma, by incorporating the music into the performance.

As voices calling out for 'St Patrick's Day' became more imperious, it was clear that the mood in Irish culture was changing. The 'flame of national attachment' was being fanned by a wind blowing from across the Atlantic, and while Sheridan was taking over the management of Drury Lane, back in Dublin one of his cousins, also named Richard, was raising his glass, along with Napper Tandy and other members of the Free Citizens of Dublin, to toast 'Our fellow subjects in America now suffering persecution for attempting to assert their rights and liberties.'

On 4 November 1779, the annual government performance to commemorate King William's birthday was planned to go ahead as it had since the beginning of the century; however, in the hours before the curtain rose, several thousand armed Volunteers assembled around the statue of William of Orange in College Green, draping one side of the statue with a banner proclaiming 'The Glorious Revolution'; on the other side, more ominously, were the words: 'Free Trade – or Else!!' In the sixty-seven years since Dudley Moore had clambered up on to the Smock Alley stage to praise William as the defender of Irish rights, the Irish theatre had grown rapidly, becoming a commercial enterprise and spreading from one struggling Dublin theatre to include Cork, Belfast, Limerick, Derry and Waterford. And yet, many people still thought of the Irish stage as a sort of alternative parliament, both an embodiment of Irish rights and the place in which rights denied could be debated – or, if necessary, demanded. This high sense of purpose had energised the theatre of the eighteenth century, sometimes to the point of violence; and it was with this legacy that it entered into a new epoch, when an independent Irish legislature finally did come into existence in 1782.

A night at the theatre 2

Mahomet by Voltaire
Smock Alley
Saturday, 2 March 1754

Even before the curtain went up on the evening of 2 March 1754, it was clear that there was going to be trouble.

Although (as he was fond of reminding Dubliners) Thomas Sheridan had done much to make the theatre a place of 'Order and Decency' during the years of his management of Smock Alley, play-going in eighteenth-century Ireland was, at the best of times, a noisy, boisterous, contact sport, a public bearpit in which servants, parliamentarians, butchers, Trinity students, haberdashers and 'ladies of quality' debated art, sex, politics, and fashion. However, the sound that rumbled out from the auditorium to the green room on that Saturday evening in March of 1754 was different from the usual playhouse tumult – less leavened with hilarity, perhaps. When the three chimes of the prompter's bell finally signalled the start of the performance, the actor West Digges, who had the opening speech, knew he was in for a rough night, particularly when he saw that the most volatile parts of the house, the pit and galleries, were filled to capacity, while the more sedate boxes were ominously empty.

The play to be performed was Voltaire's *Mahomet* – 'in Point of Story Characters, Incidents, and Moral, one of the most unexceptionable Plays that could be perform'd', as Thomas Sheridan was to write later.[1] In theory, Sheridan was right, for Voltaire's verse tragedy resembles nothing so much as Addison's *Cato*, the definitive Whig play of the era. Alcanor (the character played by Digges) is the governor of Mecca, ordered by the besieging tyrant Mahomet (acted by John Sowdon) to surrender the city. Mahomet holds Alcanor's son and daughter, Zaphna (Sheridan) and Palmira (played by Peg Woffington), as hostages. After many intrigues, Alcanor, like Cato, dies defending the city, having made the painful decision to sacrifice his children rather than surrender, declaring: 'My country's now my family.'

If nothing else, the events of 2 March 1754 should remind us that the ways in which audiences make sense of plays cannot always be controlled, particularly at moments of political instability. The anger brewing in the Smock Alley pit on that evening had its roots in a confrontation that had taken place in the Irish Parliament on 17 December 1753, when a faction within the Irish House of Commons, led by its Speaker, Henry Boyle, put on a show of strength by voting down what became known as 'the Money Bill'. The Bill would have allocated an Irish treasury surplus to the payment of the national debt of Great Britain. Although the Protestant landowners and merchants of what was known as the 'Country Party' were all vociferous in their loyalty to the king, they objected to subsidising their English counterparts. And so, in what would become an increasingly common paradox, they found themselves in conflict with the king's representative, the Duke of Dorset, who was Lord Lieutenant.

The Money Bill debate brought to a head a simmering sense of animosity that had existed since at least the time of the Declaratory Act in 1720, which had defined the English Parliament's right to pass legislation that was binding on Ireland. Around the country throughout the winter of 1753/4, members of the Country Party defining themselves as 'Patriots' began to define more sharply their contradictory sense of grievance and loyalty. So, on New Year's Day in Cork, for instance, a group of Patriot 'Independent Freeholders from the Province of Munster' drank a series of toasts that began with drams to honour 'The King and the Royal Family', and ended (with those not comatose forty-eight drinks later) pledging that 'all Favourites imported, from the elder Sister, to vote against the Younger, be despised by Majesty, and the Sons of Liberty'.[2]

Thomas Sheridan was drawn into this political maelstrom by, as Benjamin Victor put it, 'Wit and good Company, which have destroyed the ablest and wisest Men from the Beginning of the World.' Like all managers of the Theatre Royal before him, Sheridan was dependent upon the patronage of the Lord Lieutenant, in whose wake the fashionable world followed, trailing their financial dependants behind them. Sheridan was thus delighted when the first Duke of Dorset returned for a second term as Lord Lieutenant in 1750, for the duke was a keen theatregoer. Capitalising on his good fortune, Sheridan founded (and funded) an elite private dining society, the Beefsteak Club, among whose thirty members were Dorset, his son Lord George Sackville, and senior parliamentarians from the Court Party who looked after Dublin Castle's interests in Parliament.

When the Beefsteak Club gathered for their weekly meal in a house adjacent to Smock Alley Theatre, its only female member, the actress Peg Woffington, took her place at the head of the table as its honorary president. Woffington's involvement with the club is in many ways indicative of the ambiguous place of the theatre – and more specifically of actresses – in the culture of mid-eighteenth-century Ireland. Sheridan's daughter, Alicia LeFanu, would later write that Woffingon's company 'was sought after by men of the first rank and distinction. Notwithstanding . . . her moral character was such as to exclude her from the society of her own sex. Mr Sheridan found it impossible, therefore, to introduce her to his wife.'[3] An actress might dine every week with the most powerful men in the country, but she would not have been allowed to sit in a box with the 'ladies of quality' in her own theatre. In a similar way, the theatre may have been close to the centre of power in Irish society, but it could never be fully shielded by that power.

As the Beefsteak Club met for its weekly meals during January of 1754, the battle over the Money Bill continued to rage only a few blocks away in the chambers of the Irish Parliament on College Green. Although it was clear that the country was heading into a major political crisis, Dorset, his wife, and members of his court attended the theatre on 2 February, to watch the first performance of *Mahomet*. Sitting in his viceregal box, the duke noted with disapproval that there was a large, noisy clique from the Country Party, sitting in the pit, who showed their disapproval of Sheridan and Woffington by greeting their entrances with stony silence, while greeting the words of West Digges (playing Alcanor, the hero who stands up to tyranny) with wild applause. Three days later, on 5 February, Dorset decided that enough was enough, and he prorogued the Irish Parliament.

Near the end of the first act of Voltaire's play, the character of Alcanor declares: 'Power is a Curse when in a Tyrant's Hands.'[4] For a Lord Lieutenant to shut down an elected Parliament was considered an act of tyranny; to do so three days after he had applauded a play condemning tyranny seemed like the rankest hypocrisy, and this point was not lost on anyone. 'Every line carries with it its point', reported the *Dublin Spy* newspaper of the play. 'If it had been calculated purely for the Meridian of Ireland, the acumens which run through some of the Spirited Speech could not carry a keener edge.' The *Spy*'s comments and plot summary were hastily reprinted in mid-February as a pamphlet,

A Grand Debate Between the Court and Country at the Theatre-Royal, in Smock-Alley. 'Mr Digges who played the Part of *Alcanor* had a great Advantage', the *Spy* claimed, 'for he was the Chief Engine that play'd against the Court or *Mahomet's* Party: Bravos of Applause thundered from the Pit where the Friends of Liberty clapped every Spirited Speech which came from the Patriot Mouth of *Alcanor*.'[5] Outside of Dublin, the Patriotic 'Independent Electors of the Antient, Loyal and ever Memorable Town of Inniskillen' (after their obligatory first loyal toast to the king) drank to the proposition: 'May Peg Woffington clap all the Court Party' ('clap' here carrying the double meaning of 'to infect with gonorrhoea'). Similarly, Patriot clubs around the country lifted their glasses to the toasts: 'May *Mahomet* never be able to Impose on the People of Ireland' and 'The Spirit of *Alcanor* Possess every Friend at Liberty', while giving 'groans' 'for the Female President of the Beefsteak Club' and 'for the Mis-Manager of *Smock-Alley*'.[6]

Sheridan had every reason to expect trouble, therefore, when he announced a second performance of *Mahomet* for 2 March. At the same time, he had little choice in the matter. He had long insisted that his theatre was at the service of the public, and to prove this point he had instituted a system whereby the box-keeper took requests for performances of particular plays. The Patriots of Dublin, spurred on by pamphlets such as *A Grand Debate*, flocked to the box office throughout February of 1754, filling pages with requests for *Mahomet*, and interrupting performances of other plays with calls for it. To have refused to perform *Mahomet* would have been to expose as a sham Sheridan's claims that he acted in all he did solely upon 'that divine Principle impressed upon our Natures – LIBERTY' (making his theatre very much like the Irish Parliament, as many would be quick to point out, which could do whatever it pleased, as long as it pleased the Lord Lieutenant). In the end, Sheridan was forced to agree to a second performance, even though it meant walking into a trap of his own making.

Sheridan thought he was better equipped to face down a protest than proved to be the case. On the eve of the performance, Friday, 1 March, he gathered the actors together in the green room to instruct his cast on their duties. 'Every Man born under our happy Constitution, has a Right to think as he pleases, and speak his Sentiments', Sheridan told them, 'provided, they are not repugnant to the Laws of the Land, and the Rules of Civil Society'. However, he went on to 'lay it down as a Maxim that the Business of an Actor is to divest himself as much as possible of his private Sentiments, and to enter, with all the Spirit he is Master of, into the Character he represents.' The actor who neglects this, he continued, 'ought to be looked upon by the Publick, as an Incendiary . . . for, supposing Persons of a different Way of thinking should take it into their Head to resent, and oppose this Behaviour, the Theatre in that Case, instead of being a Place of Pleasure and Entertainment, would become a Scene of Riot and Disorder'. When the actor West Digges, who was playing Alcanor, then asked what he was to do if requested to repeat a passage, Sheridan told him with libertarian *hauteur*: 'I do not give you any Order upon this Occasion, you are left entirely *free to act as you please.*'

When the curtain rose at six-thirty on the evening of Saturday, 2 March, it was clear that most of the audience had decided in advance to make West Digges' Alcanor their hero, and in this they did not have long to wait. The opening scene of Voltaire's play is a short, expository dialogue between Alcanor and his confidante, Pharon (acted by Tottenham Heaphy), in which Alcanor works himself up to a state of righteous anger, exclaiming:

> If, ye Powers Divine!
> Ye mark'd the Movements of this nether World,
> And bring them to account, crush, crush those Vipers,
> Who, singled out by a Community
> To guard their Rights, shall for a Grasp of Ore,
> Or paltry Office, sell 'em to the Foe![7]

There were several editions of this translation of the play in print when Digges spoke these lines, so it seems certain that many of the audience knew the play. In any case, the audience knew this speech, for it was greeted by a wild, premeditated, cheer from the pit. The cheering continued for some minutes, becoming mixed with cries of 'Encore, Encore'. 'The Actor seemed startled', noted a backstage observer, 'and stood some Time motionless; at last, at the continued Fierceness of the Encores, he made a Motion to be heard; and when Silence was obtained, he said, "It would give him the Highest Pleasure imaginable to comply with the Request of the Audience; but he had his *private Reasons* for begging that they would be so good to excuse him, as his *Compliance would be greatly injurious to him.*" '

The audience then began to call for Sheridan. The Smock Alley treasurer, Benjamin Victor (who was later to write a *History of the Theatres of London and Dublin*), was standing next to Sheridan in the wings at the time; he recalls that, like so much else at the time, the issue for Sheridan was one of rights. 'They have no Right to call upon me', Sheridan fumed. 'I'll not Obey their call.' He forthwith ordered his sedan chair, removed his costume, and returned across the Liffey to his home on Dorset Street.

Meanwhile, back in the theatre, the curtain was lowered, and first the prompter, then Peg Woffington, and finally Digges himself, made futile efforts to pacify the audience, initially requesting the 'Liberty' to continue the production. When this was of no avail, they offered to refund the audience's tickets. A friend of Sheridan, a Mr Adderley, went into the pit, and attempted to reason with 'some Gentlemen whom he saw in a Knot', asking them 'what they meant to do? They said, they would call for the Manager. He asked upon what Pretence? They said, because he had forbid Mr Digges to repeat any Speech upon an Encore. He told them he took upon him to affirm that the Fact was not so, for that he had conversed with Mr Sheridan upon that Subject the Day before.'

Still the call went up for 'the Manager'. When the audience were informed, again by the hapless prompter, that Sheridan was no longer in the building, the gentlemen in the pit decided that they would wait one hour for him to return. The stage was now being bombarded from the galleries, not only with the customary oranges, but, as depositions taken afterwards were to attest, with bottles, stones and brickbats (the presence of which, Sheridan would later claim, proved the whole incident to have been premeditated). Very quickly, the boxes emptied of the few ladies and their escorts present, the middle galleries were abandoned, and a crowd began to form outside the theatre as news of the disturbance buzzed through the taverns and coffee houses in the streets and alleyways surrounding Smock Alley.

Finally, at around eight o'clock, two 'Persons of Gravity and Condition' rose from the pit, and hoisted themselves up into the boxes. 'God bless his Majesty, King George, with three Huzzas!' a voice cried above the confusion, and with three 'huzzas', those nearest the walls began tearing down the wainscotting, while others, in the centre of the pit, began smashing the benches. The group nearest the front of the pit scrambled up on to the stage, drawing their swords to slash the curtain with its twin pictures of Trinity College and the Irish Parliament buildings. Others wrenched out the candles, which illuminated the stage, to set a number of small fires, and then scrambled through the rents in the curtain, to begin hacking at the scenery meant to represent the streets and walls of Mecca.

As the vanguard in the pit were flooding on to the stage, the throng outside the theatre had pushed their way past the box-keepers, and the rioters in the galleries began shoving their way down the stairwells to get closer to the action. The two groups met up in the boxroom, which they pulled apart, hauling a grate full of hot coals into the centre of the room, and piling it high with broken benches and wainscotting to make a bonfire. Seeing that they were about to be burned alive 'rouz'd six of the Servants belonging to the Theatre to a desperate Courage' and they rushed the group in the boxroom, dousing the coals and preventing the fire from consuming not only the theatre but 'probably the whole Quarter of the Town, as the Buildings stand so close there'.

Backstage, most of the actors had long since slipped out of the building, although a group of stage carpenters and an armed 'centinal' had decided to make a last stand by barricading themselves in the wardrobe room to defend one of the theatre's most valuable assets, the costumes. Later, some of this same group worked their way around to the windows overlooking the front of the building, from which they proceeded to fire on the crowd gathered outside, although there are no reports of anyone being hit.

Benjamin Victor, aware that Sheridan had no intention of returning, had waited until the first 'huzza' before making his own speedy exit. Victor went across Dame Street to Dublin Castle, where the Lord Lieutenant sent him in quest of the Lord Mayor who 'excused himself, as being ill of the Gout; then the Town-Mayor and I went in Pursuit of the High-Sheriffs to their Houses, and from thence to the Taverns, where we heard they were; but we could find no Magistrate, till one o'clock in the Morning, above a Deputy Constable'. When he finally returned to Smock Alley with an unwilling posse of constabulary, the few candles still in place had guttered and the main body of rioters had dispersed, although it was to take another hour to clear the darkened building of the most determined core of protesters.

By the time the theatre was finally emptied at two o'clock, Victor found himself all but alone in the dark, amid the heaps of scorched and splintered wood, shattered glass, torn draperies, the air damp and heavy with gunpowder and singed velvet. The total damages, according to Sheridan's later (and by no means unbiased) estimate, amounted to the considerable sum of £9,000 (to put this in context, three days later £6,000 was enough to save a leading Dublin bank from collapse). In spite of the damage, the structure of Smock Alley was intact, the costumes safe, and the company were able to resume performances later that season, although without their usual stock of scenery – and without Thomas Sheridan.

A notice in the *Dublin Journal* of 2–5 March informed the public that 'Mr Sheridan, lately Manager of the Theatre Royal . . . has entirely quitted the Stage, and will no more be concerned in the Direction of it.' This was, of course, only temporarily the case; he was back in Dublin in 1758 lobbying unsuccessfully to secure a monopoly on the Dublin stage, and he was not to retire completely from theatre management until 1780. However, when he awoke on the morning of Sunday, 3 March 1754, Sheridan seems to have been resolved to quit the theatre forever, and to dedicate his life to his great project of reforming the educational system and the English language. 'The Play-House was looked upon as a Common, and the Actors as *feræ Naturâ*', he wrote bitterly a few years later. 'To such an absurd height had Popular Prejudice risen, that the Owners were considered as having no Property there, but what might be destroyed at the Will and Pleasure of the People; that the Actors had not the common Privileges of British Subjects.'

Sheridan's daughter, Alicia, later hinted that Digges deliberately misinterpreted his vague instruction to 'act as you please' to settle a long-standing petty dispute with Sheridan. Victor also believed that Sheridan's enemies from the time of the Kelly riots seven years earlier were making use of the tense political climate, and suggests that it was not entirely coincidental that it took him more than five hours to find a magistrate on the night of the riot. What is more, while the Duke of Dorset was quick to step in afterwards with an offer of full compensation and a pension for Sheridan (both were refused on the grounds that acceptance would prove the Patriots had been correct in labelling him a Castle lackey), the Lord Lieutenant's lack of response on the night demonstrates that he realised a military response (the barracks in Dublin Castle were only minutes away from the theatre) would have tipped the scales between a popular protest and civil war. He might have been willing to have dinner with Peg Woffington, but he was not going to send out the army to save her. In short, as Victor put it, 'the Manager had, in this dispute, quite lost the Favour and Protection of the Public. Nay, even the Courtiers all agreed he should have stroaked the growling Lion, and not have gored him.'

In the weeks before the riot, Sheridan had written in the *Dublin Journal* that because he believed the theatre 'was a Place calculated for amusement, I was in hopes that Party itself would be glad to be refreshed from its Labours'. This declaration of the theatre's independence from party politics brought a swift response from a pamphleteer writing as 'Libertus'. 'The Theatre', responded Libertus, 'has ever been the very Place where the People have distinguished their Patriot Spirit; and when their Remonstrances have been, by ministerial Influence, obstructed by the *Powers* that be, this has been always the *Succedaneum* they have made Use of, to shew their Sense of whatever Grievance or Oppression they have laboured under.'[8] More clearly than any other event of the period, the *Mahomet* riot showed that the Irish theatre had the potential to expose the gulf between the rhetoric and the reality of Irish liberty; more importantly, it showed that when that gulf became too great, Irish people would see the theatre as a forum for pursuing their rights, even to the point of violence.

CHAPTER 3

'Our national theatre', 1782–1871

According to Lady Morgan, Ireland's 'National Theatre' first came into being on 20 December 1784 with a performance that 'was to be altogether national, that is, Irish, and *very* Irish it was':

> The play chosen was *The Carmelite* by Captain Jephson, with an interlude from Macklin's farce of *The Brave Irishman*, and a farce of O'Keeffe's, *The Poor Soldier*. The overture consisted of Irish airs ending with the Volunteer's March, which was chorused by the gallery to an accompaniment of drums and fifes . . . My father wrote and spoke the prologue in his own character of an 'Irish Volunteer'. The audience was as national as the performance; and the pit was filled with red coats of the corps to which my father belonged.

There is a telling mixture of fantasy and truth here. When Morgan's father, the actor, singer, and theatre manager Robert Owenson opened his theatre in Dublin's Fishamble Street, it was known not as the 'National Theatre Music Hall' (the name by which Lady Morgan remembers it) but alternately as 'The Music Hall' and as the 'City Theatre'; moreover, its first production was neither *The Carmelite* nor *The Brave Irishman* (the former, in any case, written by Richard Cumberland, not Robert Jephson, and the latter by Thomas Sheridan, not Macklin); its first offering was *The School for Wives* by Molière.

Having said this, by the end of their first week of operation, it was clear that Owenson and his company were trying to do something which would justify his daughter's subsequent memory of her father 'giving his theatre the name of "National" . . . at a time when the glorious body of Irish Volunteers became the Prætorian bands of the land, not to impose, but to break her chains'.[1] On 27 December 1784, Owenson's company offered a bill made up of *The Wonder: A Woman Keeps a Secret*, Sheridan's *The Brave Irishman* as an afterpiece, and a 'prelude' by Owenson called *The Manager and the Irish Actor* featuring 'a medley, adapted to the most favourite Irish lilts, called "The Humours of St. Patrick's Day; or,

Thady Mullowny's Journey to Dublin" ', which included 'a description of the City, the Tavern, &c. and of the Volunteers marching from the royal Exchange, to be reviewed in the Phoenix park'.[2]

Owenson's courting of the Volunteers is part of the beginning of a shift in the theatre's place in Irish political culture. The Volunteer movement was a loosely associated group of Irish militias, first mustered in Ulster in response to the American Revolution of 1776. While pledging their loyalty to the Crown, the Volunteers quickly began to develop their own agenda, and without ever firing a musket in anger, the existence of between 30,000 and 40,000 armed men resolving to achieve 'the more equal representation of the people', and pledging to 'root corruption and court influence from the legislative body',[3] gave real political muscle to many of the same issues which had motivated the Patriots who had demolished the Theatre Royal during the *Mahomet* riots of 1754. The Volunteers' show of strength in College Green on 4 November 1779 had played a key role in the establishment of an independent Irish parliament; by the mid-1790s, the more radical Volunteers would form the vanguard of the United Irishmen.

In this same period, the Irish theatre world was also expanding. Playbills and records of performances from the 1780s and 1790s exist not only for larger towns – Cork, Belfast, Derry, Limerick, Waterford and Kilkenny (where Owenson was to build a theatre in 1785) – but also for Antrim, Lisburn, Newry, Ennis, Wexford, Sligo, Athlone, Castlebar, Clonmel, Tralee, Youghal, Bray, and New Ross. Sensing the climate of opportunity, Owenson arrived in Galway in the summer of 1783, where he found an enthusiastic supporter of the theatre in the local Volunteer colonel, Richard Martin, one of the largest landowners in Connemara. Martin built a small theatre in Kirwan's Lane between Cross and Quay streets, to the rear of his Galway townhouse. Contemporary accounts suggest that the building seated 'about one hundred persons' in a raked auditorium with no boxes or gallery. Although small, the theatre was ornately decorated, with a rose and ribbon pattern framing the proscenium, culminating in the figures of Tragedy and Comedy and the motto 'Vive la Bagatelle'.[4]

On Friday, 8 August 1783, Owenson used the Kirwan's Lane theatre to present the verse tragedy, *Douglas*, a play which had so impressed Thomas Sheridan earlier in the century that he had a medal struck in honour of its Scottish author, John Home. Lieutenants in the local Volunteer corps played most of the male roles in Owenson's production, with Martin taking the part of the villain, Glenalvon, while his wife

At the THEATRE, KIRWAN's-LANE.

ON Friday Evening, the 8th of Auguſt, 1783, will be preſented the celebrated Tragedy of

DOUGLAS.

Douglas,	Captain NUGENT.
Old Norval,	Major TRENCH.
Lord Randolph,	Mr. TONE.
Officer,	Lieutenant MOOR.
And, Glenalvon,	Colonel MARTIN.
Anna,	Mrs. SOPHIA CHEVERS.
AND, LADY RANDOLPH,	Mrs. R. MARTIN.

To which will be added a Farce call'd

ALL THE WORLD's A STAGE.

Sir Gilbert Pumpkin,	Colonel MARTIN.
Captain Stanly,	Captain NUGENT.
Harry Stukely,	Lieutenant MOOR.
Simon,	Lieutenant COSTELLO.
Watt,	Lieutenant DALY.
And, Diggory,	Mr. TONE.
Miſs Kitty Sprightly,	Mrs. SOPHIA CHEVERS.
And, Miſs Bridget Pumkin,	Mrs. R. MARTIN.

By particular Deſire of the Ladies and Gentlemen,

STAGE 1l. 2s. 9d. PIT 4s. 4d.

Tickets to be had of Mrs. R. MARTIN; and of Mr. Owenſon at the Theatre.

The Ladies and Gentlemen requeſt that no Hoops may be worn at the Theatre on the above Occaſion.

To begin preciſely at Seven o'clock.

GALWAY: Printed by B. CONWAY, at the Volunteer Print-

Photograph 1. This playbill for a Galway production of John Home's heroic tragedy *Douglas* in 1783 advertises a number of local Volunteer officers in leading roles; the 'Mr Tone' who played Lord Randolph was Theobald Wolfe Tone.

(who had previous acting experience) was the heroine, Lady Randolph. The Martin family tutor, Theobald Wolfe Tone, played Lord Randolph, a nobleman torn between two loyalties, who finds relief only in battle. 'Free is his heart who for his country fights', Randolph tells his wife. With the benefit of hindsight, there is something both prophetic and ironic in the image of Wolfe Tone standing on stage in full battledress, declaiming in the doomed character of Randolph:

> Peace in this world I can never enjoy . . .
> I am resolved. I'll go straight to the battle, where the man that makes
> Me turn aside, must threaten worse than death.[5]

Douglas is one of a group of heroic tragedies (including Rowe's *Tamerlane*, Addison's *Cato* and Voltaire's *Mahomet*) that were very much a part of the rhetoric of rebellion in the years leading up to 1798. *Douglas*, for instance, was published in at least five Irish editions before 1814: three in Dublin, and, significantly, one each in Belfast (1766) and Newry (1786), the heartland of the Volunteer movement. It rose to particular prominence after a viceregal command performance for the Duke of Rutland in Smock Alley on 20 June 1784, where there was a disturbance after some gentlemen in the pit called out for the orchestra to play the 'Volunteer March'. Similarly, Robert Owenson's Volunteer-supported production of *Douglas* in Galway had been anticipated in Limerick three years earlier, when the local Volunteer colonel, Thomas Smyth, organised a performance of the play at Limerick's New Theatre Royal. These productions of *Douglas*, in turn, are part of a wider Volunteer involvement with the theatre, extending from command performances in Belfast to interludes written specifically for Volunteer audiences, such as *The Female Volunteer: Or, The Humours of Loughrea* (no longer extant) performed in Cork in 1780, or Mary O'Brien's *The Fallen Patriot*, in which the allusively named Freeport (there was a trade dispute on at the time) declares that 'when the gilded fool shall sneer at virtue, I'll thunder in his ears Liberty and my Country'.[6]

Owenson believed this patriotic fervour would support a 'national' theatre; however, an attack in the *Freeman's Journal* (at that point in its long history a government organ virulently opposed to Volunteer politics) suggests that the real enthusiasm for a patriotic theatre came not from the gentlemen in the pit, but from the occupants of the upper of the two galleries in his theatre. 'Were it not', jeered the *Freeman*, 'that the Manager's singular and forcible merit in droning out planxties and acting spalpeen characters, secured him a round of heel-applause from his good friends in the gallery, we should be apt to stile the *Prelude*, performed last night, a jumble of the greatest balderdash that ever insulted the stage.'[7] Although there is a particular vitriol in this report, it is by no means unique. From the early 1780s onwards, there is evidence of a vociferously patriotic upper gallery, populated by a growing audience of servants, small tradesmen and labourers who could be moved by the badges of nationality.

Unfortunately for Owenson, cheers from an upper gallery (where seats cost only 1*s*. 7½*d*., compared to 5*s*. 5*d*. for the boxes) were not enough to run his little 128-seat theatre. In 1786 he sold his share of the theatre, turning to an enterprise in which he could be confident of strong support from Irish gentlemen of all political stripes: he became a wine merchant. The failure of this 'national' theatre was due to more than Owenson's hopeless managerial skills (although they helped); staging patriotic or 'national' Irish plays in the 1780s was a delicate business. Although Irish politics were becoming increasingly divisive and acrimonious, what had been true in the 1730s was still true in the 1780s. 'Dublin can afford no more than one audience', wrote an anonymous pamphleteer, contributing to the debate over the 1786 'Act for Regulating the Stage in the City and County of Dublin' (26 Geo. III, Chap. 57). While the Act confirmed that performances would be restricted to the patent theatres, it left open the possibility that new patents might be issued, and this worried the existing theatre managers. 'It therefore must consequently follow, that when two Theatres contend for existence, one of them must fall.'[8] An enforced monopoly may have been good for business, but it also meant that all shades of political opinion had to be accommodated in the same auditorium, with opponents from across the floor of the Irish parliament seated side by side with those who resisted the very existence of that parliament, while in the gods even the most seditious sentiments could be assured of at least a partial raucous cheer. In the smaller Irish cities, this enforced intimacy of antagonists was even worse.

Choosing an Irish play for such an audience was sometimes like choosing the bomb that might do the least damage; the trick, as playwright John O'Keeffe discovered, was to mould sentimental comedies into parables of reconciliation, heavily laced with Irish music and displays of Irish landscape, making them distinctively Irish, but less dangerous than tragedies drawn from Irish history. O'Keeffe's career followed what would become an increasingly common trajectory, writing his first plays for Irish theatres outside of Dublin, before moving to Dublin, and ultimately to London.

In the spring and summer of 1770, the Smock Alley manager, Thomas Ryder, hired O'Keeffe to adapt his 1767 play, *Harlequin in Waterford* to a northern setting for Ryder's new Mill Gate Theatre in Belfast. The play became *Harlequin in Derry*, complete with scenery showing the north of Ireland, some of which was no doubt reused in O'Keeffe's next work, *The Giant's Causeway; or, A Trip to the Dargle* which was staged in Belfast on 25 May 1770 and featured a giant capable of flying from the Antrim coast to the Wicklow mountains, thus providing occasion for 'an elegant View of the Giant's Causeway, the Dargle, and the Waterfall of Powerscourt'.

Three years later, O'Keeffe continued in the newly popular mode of virtual tourism with a piece for the Cork Theatre Royal entitled *Tony Lumpkin's Ramble Thro' Cork*, which borrowed a character from Goldsmith to offer audiences views of 'the Mall, Red-House Walk, Sunday's Well, Coffee-Houses, Taverns, &c'.[9] The Cork play, along with one he had written for the Theatre Royal in Limerick (both southern theatres were under the management of Tottenham Heaphy) was later performed in Dublin, 'with great applause', as O'Keeffe recalls. On 15 April 1777, he followed up his Dublin success with *The Shamrock*, staged at Crow Street, a lost play which entertained audiences with 'Irish characters and customs, pipers, and fairies, foot-ball players, gay hurlers' and Irish melodies, some taken from the harpist Toirdhealbhach Ó Cearbhalláin (Turlough Carolan). 'I chose the airs (Irish) myself', O'Keeffe later recalled, 'and it was a pleasing performance.' The following year he adapted his Tony Lumpkin play for a London audience, where it was staged at the Haymarket, and by 1779 he had had his first major London success, *The Son-in-Law* (also at the Haymarket). By 1800, there had been 1,200 performances of his plays in London.

The Ireland of O'Keeffe's plays is a pastoral world out of time. In his *Recollections* he describes the Ireland of his youth as a place where 'there were no gypsies – no poor rates – no pawn-brokers; the word village was not known; but every group of cabins had a piper and a schoolmaster; and before every cabin door, in fine weather, there was the Norah, or Kathlene, at her spinning wheel . . . The milkmaid always sung her melodious Irish tunes while milking'.[10] As a memory, this is an astounding fabrication for someone born and raised in the centre of Dublin. Nonetheless, of the more than seventy plays he wrote (comedies, light operas, and farces) many use characters who are from this Irish fantasy world, and three of his extant works are set entirely within it: *The Poor Soldier* (1782), *The Prisoner at Large* (1788) and *The Wicklow Mountains* (1795).

The dates of O'Keeffe's two most popular Irish plays – *The Poor Soldier* and *The Wicklow Mountains* – tell a story in themselves. Although *The Poor Soldier* was a reworking of *The Shamrock*, its rewriting in 1782 coincides with the creation of an Irish parliament, and so the new play can be seen as heralding a new set of possibilities for class and sectarian mobility. Like most of O'Keeffe's work, *The Poor Soldier* stays close to convention: a landlord, Lord Fitzroy, is in love with one of his tenants, Norah, who in turn is loved by Pat, the 'poor soldier', who wins her in the end. The play's religious politics, however, stretch conventions, for Fitzroy is a Protestant landlord, and Norah is the niece of the local Catholic priest, Father Luke, acting *in loco parentis*.

To put *The Poor Soldier* in context, Irish Catholics had their rights to lease and inherit land restored only four years before the play's 1782 début; in the same year that the play was running in London and Dublin, two further bills granted Catholics rights to limited land ownership and education. Hence, when Fitzroy first mentions the possibility of marriage to Norah in a conversation with Father Luke, the priest raises two objections: 'Her religion and her country'. 'My dear Sir', Fitzroy tells him with a magnanimous sweep, 'be assured I am incapable of an illiberal prejudice against any one, for not having first breath'd the same air with me, or for worshipping the same Deity in another manner.'[11] Today this sounds like impeccably bland liberalism, but in the Ireland of 1782 dismissing the importance of 'worshipping the same Deity in another manner' was dangerously subversive of the basic structures of Irish society going back to the Williamite settlement.

When Lady Morgan mistakenly recalled that *The Poor Soldier* was the first production of the Irish 'National Theatre' in 1784, therefore, her grasp of detail may have been shaky, but her understanding of the play was acute. Like Lady Morgan herself, O'Keeffe had an ability to make challenging ideas palatable to a wide audience by encasing them in unobjectionably conventional forms. That *The Poor Soldier* was to the taste of its audience can be gauged by the fact that it went through eighteen editions in Dublin alone before 1800 and was almost continuously in the repertoire of Dublin's Crow Street theatre after 1782; moreover, it was performed regularly in Cork from 1784 onwards, and later in Limerick and Belfast (1785), Wexford (1788), Kilkenny (1789), Waterford (1792) and Ennis (1797). When it was first produced in New Ross on 17 May 1789, the bill included a recitation of 'Thady O'Shaughnessy's Description of the Volunteer Review', and the first Derry production in 1793 included an 'occasional address' by an actor in the uniform of a Derry Volunteer (1793).[12]

By the time O'Keeffe wrote *The Wicklow Mountains* in 1795, a change had taken place in Irish society. First performed in the same year in which the United Irishmen became a secret society, and the Orange Order was founded, it was originally an opera entitled *The Wicklow Goldmine* before O'Keeffe turned it into a play which uses a range of stock Irish characters: the benevolent landlord, the shy but feisty Irish *colleen*, the devil-may-care stage Irishman, the stern-jawed romantic stage Irishman. However, he introduces a new figure: a violent member of a secret society who is on the side of good. Bearing the name of a legendary seventeenth-century rapparee, Redmond O'Hanlon wears the distinguishing oak bough of the Oakboys; and yet, he is variously identified as a Defender, a Whiteboy, a Heart of Steel, and a 'capital Peep O' Day boy' – an unlikely combination, given that the Oakboys, Hearts of Steel, and Peep O' Day boys were Protestant secret societies, while the Defenders and vast majority of Whiteboys were their Catholic antagonists. Even more improbably, he is the local constable.[13]

O'Keeffe's Redmond O'Hanlon points the way to an Irish theatre that will increasingly try to define and resolve the contradictions of Irish society. Both Catholic and Protestant, outlaw and lawman, O'Hanlon acts like a stage villain, but saves the heroine; moreover, he is the spokesman for the play's populist politics. 'See you not what heavy grievances we lay under', asks O'Hanlon, 'our great landlords spending their money abroad, their stewards patch by patch enclosing our commons, and their parsons with their rich livings leaving us in the claws of their cursed griping tithe proctors.' O'Keeffe imagines a world from which these grievances could vanish, as a gold mine is discovered, and its wealth distributed evenly among the people, 'as grass is given to feed the native flocks that bound over the surface of the earth'. In this new dispensation, 'instead of the unhappy necessity of punishing crimes', says the wise and kindly landlord, 'we might prevent their commission, by awakening them [the poor] from the idleness of despondency'.[14] This dream of a new order free from sectarian differences, in which the poor are redeemed from violence and the landlords learn their duties (and keep their land), would be dreamed many times in the next century. O'Keeffe may not have been the first to formulate it, but he certainly was one of the most influential, with initial productions of *The Wicklow Mountains* in Covent Garden and Crow Street (1796), Derry (1798), Kilkenny (1799) and Limerick (1805) and frequent revivals well into the 1840s.

John O'Keeffe's plays are part of a new Irish cultural formation, evident in other ways in the final years of the eighteenth century. Smock Alley – which had been in operation more or less continuously since

1662 – closed its doors for the final time on 2 January 1788; in July of 1788 the theatre was advertised for sale, and in August its most influential manager, Thomas Sheridan, died. In that same year, what are arguably the first works of Irish theatre history were published: Robert Hitchcock's *Historical View of the Irish Stage* and Joseph Cooper Walker's 'Historical Essay on the Irish Stage', published in the *Transactions of the Royal Irish Academy*. There had been earlier attempts at placing the Irish theatre in an historical context, notably W. R. Chetwood's *General History of the Stage* (1749), Thomas Wilkes' *General View of the Stage* (1759) and Benjamin Victor's *History of the Theatres of London and Dublin* (1761) although most of these works are primarily memoirs. Hitchcock and Walker were the first to treat Irish theatre history as a discipline in its own right; moreover, by writing for the Royal Irish Academy, Walker (a respected antiquarian whose *Historical Memoirs of the Irish Bards* had appeared two years earlier) was sending out a clear signal that the theatre in Ireland was an integral part of the Irish cultural landscape, not simply an exiled annex of London.

In retrospect, we can see the Irish theatre world of the nineteenth century taking shape in the 1780s and 1790s; at the time, however, it seemed more chaotic than ever. Smock Alley's final manager, Richard Daly, was also manager of the Crow Street Theatre, and he had closed the older theatre in order to end the competition that had existed between the two theatres since 1758. Unlike his predecessors, however, Daly was not an actor, and so lacked the vital direct link with his audiences to which Sheridan, Mossop, or Macklin had been able to turn in times of crisis. He was also compulsively quarrelsome, and shortly after the closure of Smock Alley became embroiled in a long, complex series of law suits against John Magee, editor of the patriotic *Evening Post*. Magee's supporters fought back by staging regular riots in Crow Street from 1790 onwards. So, when Frederick Jones, who had been managing the Fishamble Street theatre, began lobbying to wrest the patent away from Daly in 1796, Daly had little choice but to relinquish it. Jones promptly closed Crow Street for redecoration, reopening it on 29 January 1798, only to have it closed again for eight weeks when martial law was declared on 30 March after the arrest of United Irish leaders. The theatre was closed again by martial law in the summer of 1803 after the aborted rising led by Robert Emmet.

In the short term, the failed rebellions of 1798 and 1803 – whatever else might be said about them – were bad for theatre business. On both occasions Jones attempted, unsuccessfully, to claim compensation from the government. In the long term, the United Irishmen and Robert

Emmet would have long, lingering afterlives on the Irish stage, and by the end of the century the 1798 play would be a well-established genre. In the immediate aftermath of Emmet's rising, the kind of cultural nationalism that would make these plays so popular by the end of the century was still percolating, disrupting rather than stimulating theatre-going. At the same time, however, the demand for Irish material on Irish stages was growing, and in 1804 it erupted in a vigorous pamphlet war.

A pamphlet attributed to John Wilson Croker (later a prominent Tory MP) entitled *Familiar Epistles to Frederick Jones, Esq. on the Present State of the Irish Stage*, went through three editions in 1804 and 1805, and occasioned a series of responses, including one from Lady Morgan. After pointing out that Jones had a 'despotic monopoly' on the theatres of Dublin, Cork and Limerick, Croker attacked him for neglecting Irish plays, and for casting English actors in Irish roles. 'Can we not ourselves produce / These novelties for Irish use?' asks the 'First Epistle'. Jones responded: 'This Isle more wit produces, / Than is sufficient for her uses.'[15] The *Epistles* had little effect on the amount of Irish material Jones presented, although they did lead Lady Morgan to write an opera, *The First Attempt*, staged on 28 February 1807, in an attempt to prove that Irish plays could succeed.

If nothing else, the *Familiar Epistles* debate should tell us something about the liveliness of Irish theatrical life in the opening years of the nineteenth century. It is common to assume that when the Irish Parliament ceased to meet after the Act of Union came into effect on 1 January 1801, social life in Dublin withered. This image of a sad and decaying post-Union Dublin, its great Georgian squares empty, does not, however, sit easily with the busy social life recorded in a surviving diary from the period. Attending the first viceregal theatre visit after the Act of Union, the anonymous diarist noted 'splendour & good acting of all kinds going forward – a crammed house – great displays of fashion . . . The Viceregal boxes fitted up in all the grandeur of silk & velvet, gold and silver, carvings & gildings, fanciful, elegant.'[16] By 1805, the city was home to *The Theatric Magazine*, a substantial weekly journal devoted to the stage. Similarly, a mock heroic epic published in 1806, *The Amazoniad*, recounts the events of a viceregal command performance in Crow Street, in which a lady, discovering that her place in the box next to the Lord Lieutenant has been taken, attempts to evict the usurper by pouring a pot of tea down her décolletage. 'The tea meand'ring down her bosom flew', records her chronicler, 'On the smooth orbs the milky currents glide / Thus thaws bedew the snow-crown'd hillocks' side.' Not to be bested, the tea-besplattered invader responds by cramming a half-chewed orange into her rival's mouth, 'And stopt at once her triumph and her breath.'[17]

In spite of such ructions, Frederick Jones built up theatre audiences in the opening decades of the nineteenth century, generating particular enthusiasm for opera. So, when in 1819 the patent passed to Henry Harris, he was able to demolish the old Crow Street Theatre, and commence work on a much larger replacement, the Theatre Royal in Hawkins Street, just outside the walls of Trinity College. Even though Ireland was still recovering from the economic crisis and famine of 1817, Harris raised more than £50,000 to execute a design for the theatre by Samuel Beazley, a theatre architect who had made alterations to Drury Lane in London.

The Hawkins Street Theatre used an existing building previously owned by the Dublin Society, which provided two dressing rooms, a property room, a large, glass-roofed painting room, a band room, green room, several offices and a spacious public saloon. The auditorium, on the other hand, was completely new, in 'the shape of a Horse-Shoe', as one contemporary describes it. 'There are two tiers of enclosed Boxes, supported by fluted columns, with open lattices above them upon each side, even with the first gallery; the ornaments upon the panels are chaste and tasteful, and the drapery of crimson and light blue with which the boxes over the stage doors are hung gives to the whole a very elegant appearance.'[18] The basic layout of the auditorium was an evolved version of those preceding it, with a large pit, 45 feet (13.5 metres) across, two rows of boxes, lattices (small screened boxes on either side of the proscenium) and two galleries. Each part of the auditorium had its own entrances and lobbies, and the lavishly decorated viceregal box had its own special state entrance.

The Hawkins Street Theatre was thus the first major nineteenth-century Irish theatre, and unlike its predecessors it was designed for producing stage spectacles. It was originally lit by candles, but in October of 1823 gas was introduced, thus allowing controlled dimming of house and stage lights. Acoustically, the house was very good, and, in the boxes at least, comparatively intimate, with a distance of only 52 feet 6 inches (15.75 metres) from the centre box to the lip of a stage, which, at 60 feet (18 metres) deep and 75 feet (22.5 metres) wide, was larger than the pit. The proscenium opening was just over half this width, which meant that Dublin actors still had a long, shallow forestage, while behind them a full fly system and seven sets of sliding wings made possible new forms of stage

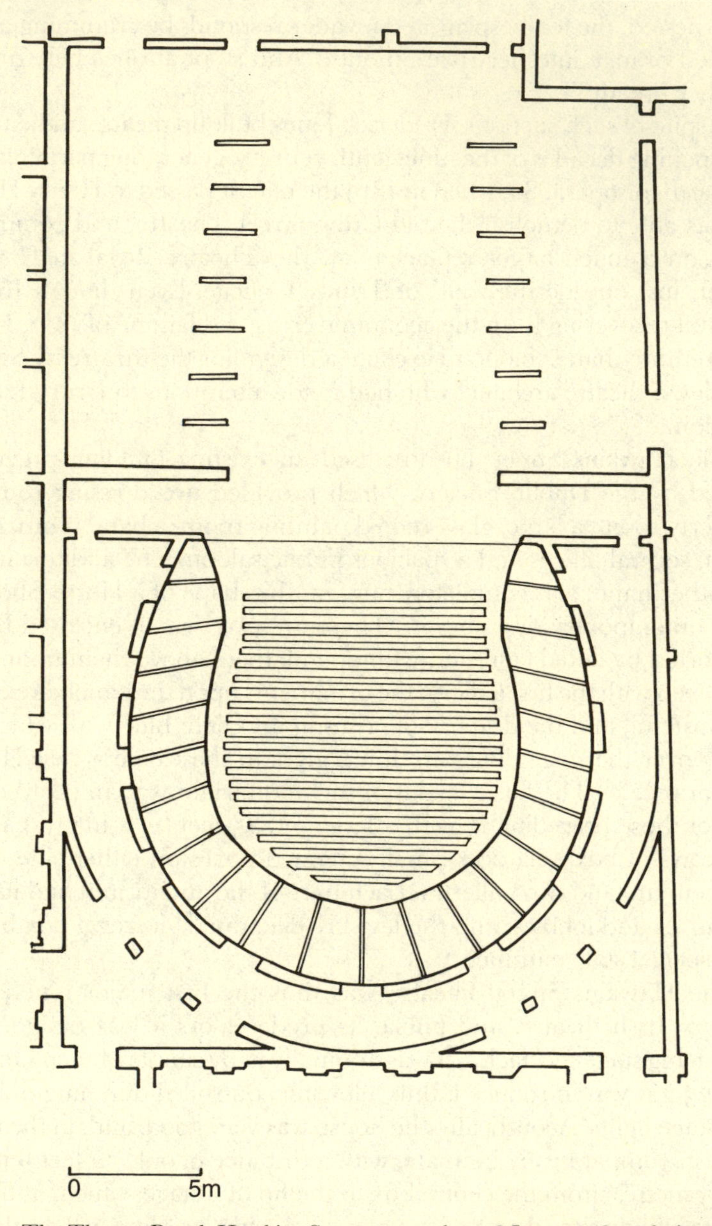

Plan 2. The Theatre Royal, Hawkins Street, opened on 18 January 1821, designed by Samuel Beazley. 'The Theatre, before the Curtain, presents to the eye the shape of a Horse-Shoe, and is admirably constructed for the accommodation of the spectators', wrote one observer. Until its destruction by fire on 9 February 1880, it was the main Irish theatre of the nineteenth century.

spectacle, with a specially fitted vamp trap allowing magical appearances and disappearances. And yet, in spite of the stage size, the view from the upper gallery was very poor. This was the cause of disturbances in the theatre on more than one occasion, most notably in October 1821, when spikes were installed on the gallery rails to prevent intrepid theatregoers from climbing down from the galleries into vacant upper boxes.

The opening of the Hawkins Street Theatre on 18 January 1821, was heralded by the launch of a new theatre magazine, *The Theatrical Observer*, the first of at least nine similar journals, including *The Drama*, *Dramatic Argus*, *Dramatic Review*, *The Stage* and *The Theatre*, which flowered briefly in Dublin during the early 1820s. While only four to eight pages long, these remarkable little papers were published daily, six days a week; 'written, for the most part, about the solemn hour of twelve', as *The Stage* noted in its first issue; 'printed in the witching time of night, and published before the play-loving folk forsake their pillows in the morning'. They seldom lasted longer than eighteen months, collapsing as much from exhaustion on the part of their writer/proprietors, as from their dependence upon the variable fortunes of the theatre. While they lasted, however, this miniature theatre press provided a breathless day-by-day account of a city in which social life revolved around the rowdy, boisterous experience of going to the theatre. *The Theatrical Observer* of 8 February 1821, for instance, wished that 'the Gods [would] be less uproarious, and that they would not throw orange-peels on the stage, which they do to the peril of the actors' limbs'. Similarly, *The Drama* for 30 November recounts a fistfight between its reviewer (a Trinity student) and an actor who had been the object of a particularly scathing critique in that morning's edition.[19]

While orange throwing and the occasional brawl had been part of theatre-going for over a century, *The Theatrical Observer* also charts the beginning of a major change in the theatre's role in Irish life, as it took a further step away from the patronage of Dublin Castle. This might not have been obvious on 22 August 1821, when George IV made the only visit to a Dublin theatre by a reigning monarch, watching a production of *The Duenna* and *St Patrick's Day* by Richard Brinsley Sheridan, who remained something of an Irish hero. Just over a year later, however, Orangemen attacked the Lord Lieutenant during a state visit to the theatre. While Lords Lieutenant would continue to visit the theatre until the early twentieth century, by the mid-1820s it was clear that the old reciprocal relationship between the castle and the theatre was unravelling as the campaign for repeal of the Act of Union gathered force.

On 23 May 1825, for instance, competing calls for cheers for 'the Duke of York' and 'O'Connell and the Catholic Association' degenerated into an exchange of bottles and wooden blocks. In January 1831, a viceregal visit to the theatre ended with fistfights and an audience member addressing a political harangue to the house from the middle gallery. Two years later, a bottle-throwing episode on 26 April 1833 led to an audience member from the upper gallery being sentenced to six months hard labour; not long after, a box-keeper died when he was thrown down four flights of stairs. In May 1835, the Lord Mayor of Dublin tried unsuccessfully to sue the *Freeman's Journal* (whose politics had swung to support for Daniel O'Connell and the Repeal movement) when it was claimed that he was orchestrating the Orange riots, which were an almost nightly event throughout that spring.

Looking at the repertoire of the Irish theatre for the first half of the nineteenth century, there is little to suggest that performances were so politically volatile. In May and June of 1821, for instance, the Theatre Royal offered its audiences *The Vampire*, a spectacular gothic melodrama; two plays based on Sir Walter Scott novels, *The Heart of Mid-Lothian* and *Rob Roy Mac Gregor*; O'Keeffe's operetta, *The Castle of Andalusia*; and Shakespeare's *Richard III*. Among the accompanying farces (programmes at this period never included less than two pieces), only O'Keeffe's *Poor Soldier* was by an Irish writer, and the most popular was *Aladdin*, a pantomime with elaborate scenic effects (including a genie who disappears into a quart bottle). In part, the theatre's manager, Henry Harris, was simply trying to bring in as big an audience as possible by not offending anyone – an increasingly difficult thing in a period when the battle lines were being drawn with increasing sharpness between opponents and supporters of Catholic Emancipation and the Act of Union.

The increased size of the theatre (Jones' Crow Street theatre had seated approximately a thousand spectators; Hawkins Street could accommodate 3,800) meant that theatre audiences were even more diverse than they had been in the eighteenth century. Admission prices in 1821 remained much as they had been for almost a century: Boxes, 5*s*.5*d*.; Pit, 3*s*.3*d*.; Middle Gallery 2*s*.2*d*.; Upper Gallery 1*s*.1*d*. Where a manager such as Sheridan had only to fill a comparatively small number of boxes with an almost exclusively aristocratic Protestant audience to be sure that the rest of the theatre would fill in their wake, in the forty years between 1780 and 1820 the increasing enfranchisement of Irish Catholics meant that things were no longer so simple. Hence, a nineteenth-century manager had to fill two rows of boxes, a lower (or 'middle') gallery, upper galleries, and, later, the stalls which gradually took over what had been the pit, with an audience whose fluid class divisions were confusing even to contemporaries, and whose contending political and sectarian allegiances could easily erupt into violence.

This placed the Dublin theatre manager in a difficult situation. In London, a rapidly expanding theatre world had divided along class and political lines, so that increasingly theatres catered to more or less like-minded audiences. In Dublin, the Theatre Royal had to accommodate gentlemen and ladies along with an increasingly prosperous merchant class in the boxes, while the working classes – some of whom were Orangemen, and some of whom supported Repeal – still sat in the galleries. The situation remained this way for some time, partly because of the restrictions imposed by the patent system, and partly because of the continued belief that Dublin could support only one theatre. Indeed, when a new theatre, the Adelphi, opened on a site behind Trinity College on 26 December 1829, it lasted a little over a year before the manager of the Theatre Royal, J. W. Calcraft, hired it for a fixed rate of £225 per year in order to close it down in the belief that competition would kill both theatres.

The virtual monopoly of the Theatre Royal only came to an end in 1844 when the new owner of the Adelphi, John Charles Joseph, purchased a dormant theatrical patent, demolished the old theatre, and began work on what would later become one of the most important theatres of the period: the Queen's Royal Theatre, which opened in October, 1844. According to testimony given by Joseph in 1857, the Queen's Royal Theatre could hold 'about 1950 persons, giving 750 to the pit, 200 to the boxes, 400 to the lower gallery, and 600 to the upper'.[20] Even if we accept his claim that the theatre was usually only half filled (the larger Theatre Royal would make a similar claim) this means that by the early 1850s, there were almost three thousand Dubliners in the theatre on any given night.

The Irish theatre outside of Dublin was also expanding. While the practice of touring companies playing smaller towns continued throughout the century, new theatres were being built in the larger centres, including the Theatre Royal in Wexford, which was built in 1830 and is still in use as the home of the Wexford Opera Festival. In Limerick a new Theatre Royal was built by Joseph Fogarty in 1841 in Lower Mallow Street, and in Waterford, the theatre established in the City Hall in 1784 was extensively remodelled in the 1850s. In 1866, Cork theatre emerged from a low period in the early nineteenth century with the building of the Athenaeum Theatre (later known as the Opera House) on Lavitt's Quay. Not all of the theatres built outside Dublin in this period were successful; however, the fact that entrepreneurs were willing to invest in larger and larger theatres attests to the basic vitality of the theatre. If there was a problem with the Irish theatre in the middle decades of the nineteenth century, it was not the problem of finding an audience; it was the problem of finding an Irish repertoire.

As early as the *Familiar Epistles* pamphlet war of 1804–5, there were demands for Irish material on Irish stages. The daily theatre press of the early 1820s, for instance, launched a series of campaigns for more Irish plays, and reprinted large sections of Hitchcock's *Historical View of the Irish Stage* to give ballast to the argument that a distinctive Irish theatrical tradition existed and needed to be maintained. In its 7 March 1821 edition, *The Theatrical Observer* commented that it had no objection to an Englishman – Harris – managing 'our national Theatre'; however, it did object to a steady theatrical diet of the plays from the London stage as a consequence. 'If a native of India of the Hindoo Cast, were to succeed Mr Morrison as the keeper of his Tavern', the *Observer* continues, 'he might as well insist on his Guests eating no dishes but such as Hoschenee, Hurrabubbub, Rice, and Cayenne Pepper Soup, because the inhabitants of India prefer those viands to Beef Steaks and Potatoes.'[21]

Some theatre managers resorted to the expedient of introducing Irish songs into existing plays, giving the stage a delightfully absurd 1826 production of *Faust* in which the characters sang popular Irish ballads. More successful were the pantomimes, which had become an established feature of the repertoire (usually, although by no means exclusively staged at Christmas) by the early 1820s. While making use of a standard set of characters – Aladdin, Harlequin and, later in the century, the Widow Twankey – these plays invariably introduced local jokes and allusions, and increasingly made use of Irish mythological material (often of dubious authenticity) as in the Theatre Royal's 1840–1 pantomime, *O'Donoghue of the Lakes, or Harlequin and the Leprechaun*, or its 1844–5 offering, *Harlequin Shaun na Launthera, or Fin Macoul and the Fairies of Lough Neagh.*

What was really needed, as *The Drama* claimed on 2 January 1822, was work by Irish playwrights. This should not prove difficult to provide, the writer claimed, because Ireland 'outnumbers England and Scotland together, in fine and approved stage-writers – Maturin the first – and Sheil, the most successful of our tragic poets, are Irishmen. . . . Banim, and Knowles, young dramatists of eminent success, and considerable poetical powers, are also our countrymen'. *The Drama* goes on to plead with Harris to make 'our fine Theatre a school of native genius, to the benefit of the country and the Patentee, and the mutual glory of both'.[22] None of the dramatists mentioned here – James Sheridan Knowles, Charles Robert Maturin, John Banim and Richard Lalor Sheil – was able to earn a living exclusively from the theatre. Knowles was the most successful of the group, becoming one of the most eminent playwrights of the 1820s and 1830s, although he turned to lecturing and novel-writing in the 1840s; Sheil, Maturin and Banim abandoned the theatre even earlier: Sheil through the pressures of his political career, while Banim and Maturin became novelists, with Maturin also retaining his stipend as an Episcopalian clergyman.

The difficulty in making a living experienced by Irish playwrights of the period was a more acute form of the problem faced by their English counterparts. Playwrights were usually paid a flat fee for their work, ranging anywhere from £50 to the £600 that Knowles received from Covent Garden for his play *Love* in 1839. Irish managers could only offer fees on the lower end of the scale because a smaller audience base meant that a run of four or five nights was considered good in Dublin, whereas a successful play could run for twenty (and in some cases many more) performances in London. Even with a career in London, playwrights could have difficulty making a living. For instance, Knowles' total earnings from his entire thirty-year theatrical career amounted to £4,600, whereas in 1840 Chapman and Hall paid Dickens £3,000 for a six-month copyright to *Barnaby Rudge*.[23] Dramatists thus found themselves with two options if they wanted a reasonable (and reasonably steady) income: either to become exceptionally prolific (which usually meant learning to churn out genre pieces and adapt novels and French plays) or to use the fame that came from being a respected dramatist to kickstart a more dependable career in politics or fiction.

Richard Lalor Sheil is a case in point. He had recently graduated from Trinity College and was reading law at Lincoln's Inn when he wrote his first play, *Adelaide: Or, The Emigrants* for Jones' Crow Street theatre in 1814. 'While Irish genius soars through every clime', announces the play's preface, 'And gains new laurels from the hand of time, / Why should her sons to foreign nations roam, / Nor trust the native patronage of home?'[24] However, when the play later transferred to London, he found that no matter how much he might be 'fired with patriot ardour' and 'daring to claim, / From his own land the just award of fame', even a moderately successful London production paid better than 'native patronage'. Hence, his later works, including *The Apostate* (1817) *Bellamira*

(1818) and *Evadne, or the Statue* (1819) were all first produced in London – although *The Apostate*, with its meditations on religious and political loyalty makes an interestingly oblique commentary on his later political involvement with the campaign for Catholic Emancipation.

Plays like *The Apostate* provided a tantalising glimpse of what the Irish theatre might accomplish if Irish writers wrote for Irish stages. Similarly, John Banim's *Damon and Pythias*, written with help from Sheil, uses a form that goes back at least as far as Addison's *Cato*, as its hero, Damon, resists the rule of a tyrant, Dionysus, given power by a corrupt senate. 'I blush to look around and call you men!' Damon tells the senators. 'What! with your own free willing hand yield up / The ancient fabric of your constitution, / To be a garrison, a common barracks.'[25] Staged only twenty years after the passing of the Act of Union by an Irish Parliament whose support was garnered largely by offers of what were euphemistically called 'salaries without office', a Dublin audience needed no prompting to recognise the denunciation of legislators who had exchanged a senate for a barracks. The play became the most successful of Harris' opening season at the new Theatre Royal in 1821, and would later be performed throughout Ireland.

Sheil and Banim are part of the first wave of newly confident Catholic elite that emerged in the years leading up to Catholic Emancipation in 1829. Increasingly detached from the Gaelic culture of eighteenth-century Ireland, they began moving steadily into areas which had been the almost exclusive preserve of Protestant gentlemen: politics, law, journalism, and, of course, the theatre. Sheil and Banim would be followed by others, including Gerald Griffin, whose *Tragedy of Aguire* was rejected by Macready in 1823, but whose *Gisippus* was staged posthumously in 1842, and would be played in Dublin as late as 1905. As was the case with Banim's plays, Griffin's verse tragedies are almost unrecognisable as the work of the author known for his novels of Irish peasant life. Meanwhile, as Sheil was making political speeches about the 'ardent eyes and beaming countenances of the humblest tillers of the earth' in pursuit of 'the attainment of their political rights',[26] a new note was beginning to enter Irish Protestant writing, in both fiction and drama; it is a note of estrangement and alienation. It is present in Charles Robert Maturin's gothic play *Bertram* (1816) which opens with the profoundly displaced hero pulled from a shipwreck and asked to name his homeland. 'The wretched have no country', he tells his rescuers. 'That dear name / Comprizes home, kind kindred, fostering friends, / Protecting laws, all that binds man to man – But none of these are mine; – I have no country.'[27]

It is not entirely fair, of course, to make an anguished writer like Maturin symptomatic of an entire culture; at the same time, it is true that the Protestant Ascendancy, who had been the backbone of the Irish theatre, were an increasingly embattled class. In this regard, the career of James Sheridan Knowles is emblematic. A nephew of Thomas Sheridan, and cousin to Richard Brinsley Sheridan and the playwright Alicia LeFanu, Knowles began his career with plays for the theatres in Waterford (*Leo; Or, the Gypsy*, 1810) and Belfast (*Brian Boroimhe*, 1811, and *Caius Gracchus*, 1815) before his best-known work, *Virginius*, opened in Glasgow in 1820. Five years later he made his London début with *The Fatal Dowry*. By 1834, two of the leading actors of the age, William Charles Macready and Edwin Forrest, were touring in competing productions of *Virginius* – 'unvaryingly powerful in its effects upon my audience', as Macready later recalled. *Virginius* would earn Knowles acclaim as the 'poet of liberty' in the United States, resulting in an invitation to meet Andrew Jackson at the White House. 'I never shook hands with a European with so much pleasure', Jackson is reported to have said afterwards. Meanwhile, Knowles' early play, *Brian Boroimhe*, had taken on a life of its own.

Brian Boroimhe was based on a now lost play, *Brian Boroimhe (The Victorious)* by Daniel Mara which had played Crow Street on 24 January 1810. Mara's play, in turn, had a theatrical genealogy going back to Gorges Edmond Howard's *The Siege of Tamor* (1774) and ultimately to William Philips' *Hibernia Freed* (1722) all of which belong to a sub-genre of Irish plays (later developed in John Banim's 1821 play, *Turgesius*) in which a besieged Irish army resists an invasion by lustful, barbaric Danes. In Knowles' *Brian Boroimhe*, the Danish tyrant, Tormagnus, arrives on stage after the spectacular entry of the Danish ships sailing into Dublin Bay, and urges the Irish to 'renounce your faith, your monarch, and your cause, and you are free'. Brian Boroimhe's lieutenant, O'Donoghue of the Lakes, chooses death over 'all the honours apostacy could purchase from corruption', and by the play's end stands bravely on the scaffold, from which he declaims: 'Think ye the gaze of thousands on the public execution can appall the patriot soul?'[28] These were strong words for a play first staged only eight years after the execution of Robert Emmet.

When *Brian Boroimhe* appeared in Dublin at the Theatre Royal on 27 April 1821, it was 'much applauded by the galleries', according to *The Theatrical Observer*, and to the 'disgust' of the rival *Stage*: 'These *clap-traps* only suit the vulgar taste of the galleries, and we were glad to find, that when they were introduced in this Play, the galleries were the only applauding quarters of the house.'[29] As well as reaching a popular nationalist audience in the upper gallery of the Hawkins Street theatre in 1821, the play was revived during the 1831/2 season and toured throughout the south of Ireland, playing in Clonmel and Kilkenny during the summer of 1834. More importantly, it reached the United States, opening in New York at the Chatham Gardens Theatre on 22 January 1827, and it was playing in New York in the winter of 1834/5 as Knowles was visiting the White House. 'My plays', wrote Knowles to a friend while on that tour, 'are too liberal for the aristocratic illiberals of Ireland.'[30] It was still being performed in New York at the time of the Young Ireland Rising in 1848, by which point Knowles had become too illiberal for his younger self; he had stopped writing for the theatre to take clerical orders, vociferously denouncing the errors of Popery. 'All that the Book of Revelations alleges with Babylon', he declared in 1849, 'has been fulfilled in the church of Rome.'[31]

Meanwhile, *Brian Boroimhe* continued marching on, featuring as the St Patrick's Day production at New York's Lafayette Theatre as late as 1870. A surviving playbill for that production is emblazoned with the words 'St Patrick, Liberty, or Death'[32] and promises processions with banners bearing shamrocks and harps, and Irish songs between the acts. What is more, although *Brian Boroimhe* was never published in Ireland, and was omitted from the 1856 London edition of Knowles' collected works, there was an inexpensive American edition as early as 1828, and by 1853 Samuel French in the United States had added the play to its list of standard acting editions, along with his *Virginius*, Banim's *Damon and Pythias*, and Griffin's *Gisippus*.

Of course, playwrights can never fully control the ways in which their plays will be interpreted by a particular audience; however, with the opening of the United States (and New York in particular) as a theatrical market in the years before the establishment of enforceable copyright legislation, plays intended for Irish and English audiences were being presented in the vastly different circumstances of North America. This in turn changed the dynamics of the Irish theatre in fundamental ways, reorienting the Dublin–London axis that had dominated Irish theatre since the 1630s. As the American tour became an established practice, and as the number and size of American theatres burgeoned in the 1830s, a London production was no longer the only, or even the most important, prize for an aspiring Irish actor or dramatist. There was now a new world to conquer – a world increasingly populated by an

Irish diaspora capable of applauding sentiments too nationalistic (or too Catholic) for the London stage.

The theatrical world was thus remapped in the middle decades of the nineteenth century in ways that were to be more than just economic, and the Irish actor and dramatist who would be most spectacularly successful in reading this new map was Dion Boucicault. He was by no means the first Irish dramatist to set his sights on America; indeed, as early as 1797 John Daly Burk, a Trinity graduate, had established himself as one of the pioneering playwrights of the newly independent United States with plays such as *Bunker Hill; Or, The Death of General Warren* (1797). However, when Boucicault stepped off the boat in New York on 18 September 1853, after more than a decade writing plays for the London theatre (including major successes with *London Assurance* in 1841 and *The Corsican Brothers* in 1852) it set in motion events that would transform the theatrical world. Boucicault and his wife Agnes Robertson acted together in his New York plays, and in 1859 they had a massive success with his anti-slavery drama, *The Octoroon*, which earned them $1,363 in its first week at New York's Winter Garden Theatre. When they demanded more, they found themselves out of a job, while the play continued without them for another two months.

Boucicault resolved not to make the same mistake again, and when he wrote *The Colleen Bawn* the following year, he took control of all aspects of the production from the very outset. After an initial run at the Laura Keene Theatre which earned them enough money to buy two houses in New York, Boucicault and Robertson went to London, where they negotiated, for the first time ever outside a patent house, an arrangement with a London theatre manager in which the playwright was paid a substantial royalty for every performance. Boucicault also began restricting the number of performance licences granted to provincial English theatres, forcing them to book his entire production as a touring show. *The Colleen Bawn* ran for ten months at the Adelphi, longer than any previous play in London theatre history. Queen Victoria went to see it three times – 'one could appreciate it even more the 2nd time', she commented in her diary. By the end of their first year in London, between royalties, touring company franchises and acting, Boucicault and Robertson had earned £23,000.

Consequently, when he arrived in Dublin in April 1861 for a twenty-four night run at the Hawkins Street Theatre, Boucicault was the Irish theatre's first international superstar. The *Catholic Telegraph* announced that he had 'commenced a new era in Irish character'. 'We are indeed

Photograph 2. Dion Boucicault as Myles-na-Coppaleen in *The Colleen Bawn*. 'Mr Dion Boucicault's personification of the reckless, hearty, honest Myles is one of the most genuine, humorous, and unexaggerated representations of low Irish character we have ever seen on the stage', claimed the *Dublin Evening Mail* in 1861.

delighted to see that there is now a fair chance of having the Irishman placed before the public as he really is', it commented, 'and that instead of a blundering blockhead, with jigs, howls, and shillelaghs, we have the true son of the sod represented, bold and courageous even to recklessness, with all his virtues and virtuous errors, ready to sacrifice his life to save that of a fellow-creature.'[33]

What makes this Irish praise for the authenticity of *The Colleen Bawn* all the more remarkable are the conditions of its writing. Boucicault would later claim that walking down Broadway one rainy night in March of 1860, he picked up a copy of Gerald Griffin's novel, *The Collegians*, when sheltering in Bretano's Bookshop. The next day he wrote to the theatre manager Laura Keene, 'I have it! I send you seven steel engravings of Killarney. Get your scene painter to work on them at once. I also send a book of Irish melodies, with those marked I desire Baker to score for the orchestra. I shall read act one of my new Irish play on Friday: we rehearse that while I am writing the second, which will be ready on Monday.'[34]

Of course, Boucicault had more to hand than a novel, a set of engravings, and some Irish melodies when he sat down to assemble *The Colleen Bawn*; he also had at his disposal the palate of recognisable characters, situations, and scenic devices that had come together since the eighteenth century to form what had become known as 'the Irish play'. The scenic set pieces with which *The Colleen Bawn* opens, for instance, providing views of the Lakes of Killarney and the Gap of Dunloe, were part of a genre of virtual tourism which went back to O'Keeffe's pantomimes of the 1760s. These had remained popular in Hawkins Street productions such as *St Patrick and the Golden Shamrock* of January 1835, whose attractions included a 'View of Killarney Lake and Distant Mountains'. Moreover, a surviving prompt book for *The Colleen Bawn* shows that Boucicault saw light as part of the language of the theatre, so that in performance, the first important piece of narrative information is contained not in the dialogue, but in a lighting cue (preserved in an early prompt book) in which the heroine signals to her forbidden lover: 'Green lights on. Lights down to begin. Signal light ready. Light in window.'[35]

When morally weak Hardress Cregan did make his entrance in *The Colleen Bawn*, he carried with him a genealogy that can be traced back as far as Charles Shadwell's *Irish Hospitality* (1717), but is more immediately related to the Irish hero of John Baldwin Buckstone's *Green Bushes; Or, A Hundred Years Ago*, which was staged at London's Adelphi Theatre in 1845, and was still popular with Dublin audiences in the 1920s. Indeed, the comparison between *The Colleen Bawn* and *Green Bushes* is worth pursuing, for while Buckstone claims to have travelled through 'some of the Irish localities' in his play, *Green Bushes* was simply one genre piece among the more than two hundred he wrote. *Green Bushes* also features a villainous Irish servant (like Danny Mann in *The Colleen Bawn*) a helpless Irish colleen for him to plot against (like Eily O'Connor in Boucicault's play) and a faithful Irish servant who is responsible for resolving the plot (corresponding to Myles-na-Coppaleen in *The Colleen Bawn*). This is not to say that Boucicault is unduly indebted to Buckstone (although the two men knew one another, and in the 1840s Boucicault had written plays for Buckstone's Haymarket Theatre in London). It is simply the case that, writing under pressure, both dramatists used generic characters and situations they knew would produce a particular response from their audiences. 'Playmaking', as Boucicault once put it, 'is a trade like carpentering. Originality, speaking by the card, is a quality that never existed. An author cannot exist without progenitors any more than a child can. We are born of each other.'[36]

Boucicault's understanding of his craft in these terms helps to explain why he was so prolific, telling a Parliamentary Commission in 1866 that he had written between 180 and 200 plays. It also helps to explain how the Irish play could emerge from its roots in sentimental comedies such as O'Keeffe's *Poor Soldier* in the late eighteenth century to become one of the most popular theatrical forms of the second half of the nineteenth century. By the 1840s, it was not necessary to be Irish to write an Irish drama, nor was it necessary to be a great artist in the Romantic mode, gifted with a heightened sensibility. In theory, anyone with a good knowledge of the theatre could write an Irish play, and many did, including Edmund Falconer, who played Danny Mann in Boucicault's original London and Dublin productions of *The Colleen Bawn*.

While he was still acting with Boucicault, Falconer wrote his own star vehicle, *Peep O' Day: or Savoureen Deelish* (1861) based on a short story by John Banim. Using a plot that resembles both Buckstone's *Green Bushes* and O'Keeffe's *Wicklow Mountains*, Falconer's play is set during the 1798 rebellion, and involves Harry Kavanagh, an Irish peasant (*albeit*, a peasant who is about to publish a novel) falsely accused by his landlord of being a member of the United Irishmen. The basic materials of the play are thus purely conventional, including one of the favourite Irish set pieces of the period: the brawl at Dublin's Donnybrook Fair. The *Oxford English Dictionary* lists 1900 as the earliest use of the word 'donnybrook' to mean 'a scene of uproar, disorder, and free fighting'; however, there were Donnybrook scenes as early as the pantomime *Friar Bacon and the Brazen Head*, performed at Hawkins Street in 1821. So, when Falconer's play was staged at New York's Broadway Theatre in 1868, the stage manager had little doubt as to what was required. 'Irish Fair scene', he wrote in his prompt book: 'Large and small tents some to be pulled down. A great quantity of padded stones, fish, vegetables, dead cats and other things to pelt with . . . a good many stuffed sticks.'[37]

Writing an Irish play by putting together stock components may sound easy enough, but in practice it involved a delicate political balancing act. For instance, the barrage of dead cats in the Donnybrook scene is interrupted by the hero, who tells the combatants that 'these fights only waken [*sic*; 'weaken'] our power', and then proceeds to remind them of what is at stake by singing the nationalist song, 'The Shan Van Vocht':

> Yes, Ireland shall be free,
> From the centre to the sea,
> And hurrah for liberty,
> Says the Shan Van Vocht.

In the same scene, however, there is a British army officer sympathetic to the rebel on the run (who, of course, is not really a rebel) and the play differentiates between the 'gintlemen and real soldiers' of the army and 'the make believes and dirty bluffs of [Irish] yeomanry'.[38] Hence, played before an audience who roared approval for 'The Shan Van Vocht', *Peep O' Day* could be an incendiary piece of political theatre; played before an audience who applauded the good-hearted British soldiers, it was something else entirely.

Holding together the ambivalent politics of these Irish plays of the 1850s and 1860s are two key conventions, both inherited from earlier theatrical forms: the conciliatory ending and the rebel hero. *Peep O' Day*, for instance, ends with pardons for rebels who turn out not to have been rebels after all, as does Boucicault's own 1798 play, *Arrah-na-Pogue* (1864). Similarly, a character like Myles-na-Coppaleen in *The Colleen Bawn* might be an illicit poitín distiller, and hence an outlaw; but he is also the wittiest character on the stage, and the one who makes a spectacular dive into the lake to save the heroine in the play's most famous moment. Other similar plays end with the marriage of an Irish colleen and a British officer, or the last-minute intervention of a kindly landlord – all conventions that work towards the resolution of political antagonisms.

By bringing together adversaries (or by combining contrary qualities in the same character), the Irish play becomes a parable of reconciliation, equally capable of playing as a command performance before the Lord Lieutenant in Dublin (as happened with *Arrah-na-Pogue* on 25 November 1864) or filling theatres in New York or Boston, where many in the audiences would have had strong Fenian sympathies (as was the case with *Peep O' Day*, which played in at least two separate Boston productions and a New York production in the twelve months between January 1867 and January 1868). Indeed, *Arrah-na-Pogue* is particularly interesting in this regard, for it originally contained a rebel ballad, 'The Wearing of the Green', to which Dublin Castle objected when the play arrived in Ireland in 1864. A surviving prompt book shows that Boucicault obligingly replaced it with a long speech in which an Irish landlord leaps to the defence of the wrongly accused peasant hero, Shaun the Post.[39] Capable of such accommodations, the Irish play had little difficulty in exporting its highly palatable brand of Irishness all over the globe, so that there would be a Paris production of *Arrah-na-Pogue* by the end of the 1860s, followed by productions in Toronto, Sydney, and elsewhere.

After circling the globe for several decades, the Irish play finally touched down in Ireland in its fully fledged form on the evening of 1 April 1861, when *The Colleen Bawn* opened at the Theatre Royal in Hawkins Street, clearing the way for the Irish plays which would follow it later in the decade. The Theatre Royal in 1861 was, in many ways, a different place from the theatre that had opened in 1821. The basic structure of the building had remained more or less unaltered, although the boxes had been converted into the dress circle and second circle, where a growing middle class paid 5 shillings and 3*s*.6*d*. to watch *The Colleen Bawn*. This audience who sat 'entranced, save where the feelings of the entire house were roused by some soul-inspiring lines connected with Ireland', were thus not the artisans and servants who had stomped their feet in approval from the upper gallery when Robert Owenson had sung his patriotic songs in the 1780s. Like the leaders of the Fenians themselves, most of the new audience in the Theatre Royal were middle class and many of them were Catholic, a generation consolidating their place in Irish life in the decades after the Famine of the 1840s.

When Boucicault stepped out on the stage of the Theatre Royal in his oversized coat and battered hat as Myles-na-Coppaleen, it was more than just the actor who was coming home. While there had been Irish plays performed in Ireland prior to 1861, none had been as successful as *The Colleen Bawn*. For much of the 1840s and 1850s the stage of the Theatre Royal had been taken up with opera, and the single most profitable evening in Irish theatre history before 1861 had been the 1848 appearance of the Swedish soprano, Jenny Lind, for whom prices were raised to what contemporaries considered a 'preposterous pitch' of £1 10*s*. for the dress circle, bringing in a reputed £1,600. That a Swedish soprano singing in Italian should have been the theatrical highlight of a year in which tens of thousands of Irish people died of hunger suggests how far the Irish theatre had drifted from the rest of Irish culture in the 1840s. Meanwhile, in London and New York, the pieces of the Irish play were being welded together and tested by a hitherto unimaginable diversity of audiences, just as railway and steamship lines were opening up to bring them home. By the time a new Irish theatre – the Gaiety in Dublin – opened in November 1871, the Irish theatre was about to become both more national and more international than at any previous point in its history.

A night at the theatre 3

She Stoops to Conquer by Oliver Goldsmith and *Tom Thumb*
Theatre Royal, Hawkins Street
Saturday, 14 December 1822

The conspiracy was hatched in the Shakespeare Tavern, on the edge of a grimy alleyway known as Leinster-market, directly across from the canopied state entrance to the Theatre Royal on Hawkins Street. From the tavern windows, the six men huddled around a table on the evening of Wednesday, 11 December 1822 – John and George Atkinson, James Forbes, William Graham and two more brothers, Henry and Mathew Handwich – could see the elaborately decorated door by which the Lord Lieutenant of Ireland, Richard, Marquis Wellesley, would enter the Theatre on Saturday evening. As they drank toasts to the 'Glorious, Immortal and Pious Memory' of William of Orange, the men talked of their hatred for Wellesley, and a plan began to take form.[1]

All six men were members of the Orange Order, an exclusively Protestant organisation that had come into being in 1795 'for the defence of our persons and properties, and to maintain the peace of the country'. By 1822, the Order had spread from its origins in rural Ulster to include Irish Protestants of every social strata, from large landowners and baronets to solicitors, small tenant farmers, soldiers and artisans – like those drinking in the Shakespeare Tavern on that December evening. William Graham, for instance, was a journeyman shoemaker, and Mathew Handwich a journeyman carpenter; the Atkinsons, slightly higher up the social ladder, were clerks in the Customs House.

The men were not all members of the same Lodge. James Forbes and William Graham were Deputy Master and Secretary, respectively, of Lodge 1660, while the Handwiches belonged to Lodge 780, of which Henry was Deputy Master. The Atkinsons were members of a smaller, less prestigious Lodge 1612, which met in a tenement house owned by a Mrs Daly in Werburgh Street. They knew one another, however, from the public demonstrations on 12 July (the anniversary of the Battle of the Boyne) and 4 November (William of Orange's birthday), when Orange Lodges from all over the city congregated at the equestrian statue of William III on College Green (just around the corner from the Theatre Royal) painting it orange and bedecking it with Orange regalia. Almost without exception, these displays of loyalty degenerated into street brawls, turning the city centre into a battleground where Orangemen and Dublin's Catholics fought each other with fists, bludgeons and bottles.

Early in 1822, it was becoming clear that the biannual riots were going to be worse than usual that year. Shortly after his appointment as Lord Lieutenant in 1821, Wellesley initiated a policy of conciliation towards middle-class Catholics, meeting with Catholic leaders and inviting Catholic Bishops to viceregal levées. In those same months, apocalyptic prophecies circulated among the Catholic poor, foretelling 'in the year 22 the locusts will weep' and triggering the massacre of several Protestant families by Catholic secret societies in Limerick and Tipperary. Wellesley responded by reintroducing an insurrection act and suspending *habeas corpus* in the 'disturbed' areas of the southwest, but this did little to calm Protestant fears. Hence, by the summer of 1822, Orange fears were at a fever pitch, and Wellesley instructed the Lord Mayor, John Smith Fleming, to prohibit Orange processions to the College Green statue, thereby putting himself into direct conflict with the Order.

The July prohibition was ignored, leading to more violent street riots than ever before, and the situation went from bad to worse when a group of Orangemen in Cavan desecrated a Catholic church by leaving the severed head of a calf on the altar. When Orangemen arrived at the College Green statue on 4 November they found it surrounded by soldiers, and in the ensuing mêlée fought with soldiers of the same king to whom they had sworn an oath 'to the utmost of our power, to support and defend'. Not for the last time, the Orange Order found itself in a hopelessly contradictory situation, and it responded by personalising the political situation, attacking 'that honest, but deluded man, Lord Wellesley'. 'We have now an exclusively Popish Conspiracy', wrote the Orange leader, Sir Harcourt Lees, 'the object being to separate the Government, and to murder every Protestant in Ireland.'

All of these events were on the minds of James Forbes and his Orange brethren as they drank in the Shakespeare Tavern on 11 December, having just heard that Wellesley would be attending the Theatre Royal the following Saturday for a production of Goldsmith's *She Stoops to Conquer*. Two days later, on Friday, 13 December, there was a meeting of Lodge 1612 on Werburgh Street, at which money was raised for Forbes and William Graham to each buy six pit tickets for the following evening.

Throughout the afternoon of 14 December, members of the Lodge prepared for the evening ahead, gathering whistles, bludgeons, and printing handbills. By late afternoon about thirty of them were drinking, first in their Lodge (ignoring the injunction to temperance in their oath) and later in a small tavern run by James Flanagan in Dame Court. As they left Flanagan's to go to the theatre, Henry Handwich told them: 'Boys, be wicked.'

Meanwhile, throughout the city there was excitement over what was to be Wellesley's first state visit to the theatre, and by five thirty in the afternoon a large crowd had gathered in the mud of Hawkins Street, still torn up from the building of the theatre a year earlier. It took until seven o'clock, just before the Lord Lieutenant's entourage cantered into view, before the street was fully cleared of the carriages, which at one point had been stopped back as far as College Green in one direction, and the Liffey quays in the other.

A few minutes later, Wellesley began to make his way up the private staircase of the state entrance, while inside the theatre James Forbes, positioned in the lattices, let loose a shower of handbills with the slogan 'No Popery!' Most of these drifted towards the stage and pit, although a few fell into Wellesley's box, and were quickly scooped up by his aide-de-camp, Henry Webster. In the pit directly beneath the viceregal box, William Graham was busily distributing more handbills, while throughout the auditorium the cheers for Wellesley mixed with cries of 'No Popish Lord Lieutenant' and 'Baldy-pated Wellesley go home out of that.'

Shortly afterwards, Lord Mayor John Smith Fleming appeared in his box, and a pack of playing cards was hurled at him – a reference to his nickname in the pro-Orange press, 'The Knave of Clubs'. Fleming instinctively caught the deck, and stood in embarrassment for a moment before being cheered by the Lord Lieutenant and his party, who seemed determined to make light of the protests. In the upper gallery, however, the situation was deteriorating rapidly. Mathew Handwich had already thrown a few punches, and John Eastham, a labourer who was sitting on the left side of the gallery, became so alarmed that he tried to climb down over the parapet into the middle gallery.

In spite of the ructions at the top of the theatre, however, the curtain rose on Oliver Goldsmith's *She Stoops to Conquer*, with John Liston, the most respected comic actor of his time, as Tony Lumpkin, and the actor-manager Percival Farren playing Marlowe. The first noticeable disruption came in the middle of act II, as the characters of Marlowe and Hardcastle sit down to a glass of ale, when there was a call from the pit for them to drink the Orange toast, 'The Glorious and Immortal Memory'. The audience laughed. By the end of the fifth act, however, the noise in the theatre was becoming intolerable, and the calls of 'No Propery', and 'A cheer for the Calf's Head' mingled with the sounds of whistles blown and rattles shaken. 'Tonight the gallery is ours, boys', one Orangeman was heard to say to another and by the end of the play, bludgeons – about a metre long, painted white with square corners – were on open display.

When the curtain finally dropped on Goldsmith's play, the orchestra made an attempt to salvage the situation by launching into a quick version of 'God Save the King', which Wellesley conspicuously joined the audience in singing. Having played their trump card, the orchestra next tried 'Patrick's Day' (the closest thing Ireland had to a national anthem at that point). Then the real problems started. There were strenuous calls from the upper gallery for the Orange song, 'The Boyne Water', and Henry Handwich, sitting three rows from the edge of the gallery just above the Lord Lieutenant, took a final swig from the bottle in his hand before giving it a side-arm toss over the edge of the parapet. Philip Ryan, an exciseman from Galway, and Bernard McNamara, a physician, sitting in the middle gallery directly below Handwich, both looked up just in time to see it fly over their heads, hit the curtain, drop to the stage, and roll towards the orchestra. Mr Barton, the director of the orchestra, stopped the music, and held up the bottle. There were cries of 'shame, shame' from some parts of the house, and Major George Harris of the 7th Hussars, sitting in the lower gallery across from Handwich, got up from his seat and began to push towards the top of the house, as did a magistrate, John Crosby Graves, who was sitting in the box next to Wellesley.

The roars from the upper gallery were becoming louder. James Forbes in the lattices was blowing his whistle for all he was worth. Another young Orangeman, George Graham (no relation to William Graham) was sitting in the front row just left of centre in the upper gallery, banging a watchman's rattle against the railing. When the rattle splintered in half, he hurled the pieces downward. One piece about eight inches long hit the cushion of the box beside the Lord Lieutenant. Fortunately, it was occupied by Lady Rossmore, who was deaf and almost blind. 'I was not in the least alarmed', she later testified. James Tiernan, a chandler sitting a couple of rows away from Graham in the gallery, was considerably more upset, and called out 'shame, shame'. He was promptly bludgeoned on the head from behind. Others in the upper gallery, including a jeweller, Michael Farrell, began to edge warily towards Handwich and Graham, just as the first plainclothes policemen arrived in the upper gallery. From the Lord Lieutenant's box, his private secretary (rumoured to be his illegitimate son), Captain Edward Johnson, was elbowing his way to the middle gallery, where he appeared at the parapet and addressed 'you one shilling and two shilling men' in the upper gallery (jeers). 'Some wretch has insulted his Excellency, and thrown a rattle at the Lord Lieutenant's head ("shame, shame"). It is monstrous that his Excellency should be thus treated (cheers and hisses).' Meanwhile, directly above him, the police were pulling people from the upper gallery. 'Why are you blowing that whistle', the magistrate Graves demanded of Forbes, whose place in the lattices was separated from the upper gallery only by a row of spikes. 'For fun', Forbes told him, whereupon he was arrested, along with the Handwich brothers and George Graham.

After the arrests had been made, the house quieted enough for the afterpiece, *Tom Thumb*, to be played in relative peace, with Liston again taking the lead role. Afterwards, the Lord Lieutenant left with his dignity more or less intact. The arrested Orangemen were dragged to the College Street police station, only a few buildings away from the theatre, where Graves decided that they could be released on bail. Once back on the street, they returned to Flanagan's tavern, where they resumed drinking, and were joined by the Atkinsons, William Brownlow, who had been in the pit, and William M'Culloch, who had thrown some handbills from the upper gallery. Forbes was particularly incensed about his arrest, and two attorneys drinking in the tavern at the time heard him pound his fist on his table and declare: 'Let them transport me, it's the worst they can do; I don't care a damn, provided Papists and Popish Governments are put down.' He then drank the toast: 'Here's confusion to John Smith Fleming, the Popish Lord Mayor, the bloody Marquis Wellesley, and all Popish Governors', to which the others lifted their glasses. The riot was effectively over; however, its aftershocks were only beginning.

The 'Protestant interest' (which included, but was by no means confined to, the Orange Order) was well organised, with considerable influence in both publishing and politics. In the immediate aftermath of the riot, Sir Harcourt Lees wrote *An Address to the Orangemen of Ireland Relative to the Late Riot at the Theatre Royal, Hawkins Street*, which laid down the basic – if contradictory – outlines of the Order's official position on the riot. In part of the pamphlet, Lees condemned any hint of an Orange attack on the king's representative, claiming (incorrectly) that it was physically impossible to throw a bottle from the upper gallery to the stage. Instead, Lees proposed an implausible 'Papists' plot' in which 'a hired

Ribbonman, sitting near the Orchestra, under hand, flung a bottle over the lights, against the curtain . . . determined under the villainous cry of Orange Assassination, to break up that powerful and loyal Institution, as well as freemasonry altogether'.

At the same time, Lees by no means wanted to discount the validity of the protest. 'The Orangemen contemplated nothing farther than a few harmless hisses', he announced, 'and long and loud my gallant Boys, may you continue them, against every Protestant Advocate for the extension of political power to Jesuits, to carry their murderous plans against our lives and properties into full effect'.[2] As for George Graham – there was little doubt that he had thrown the rattle – he had every reason to attack Wellesley, for Graham was 'son to a man, who was taken out of his house by the rebels in 1798, and actually cut in pieces at his own door', although other reports stated that he was only sixteen years old at the time of the riot, and therefore had not been born in 1798. Another version of the story claimed that he had thrown away the rattle in youthful panic when the police began to move into the gallery. Summing up his case, Lees argued that Graham and Handwich had good reason to do what they did not do.

There was palpable delight in Catholic circles at the spectacle of the Orange Order in open battle with Dublin Castle. 'You may imagine what a curious revolution it is in Dublin', wrote Daniel O'Connell in the days after the riot, 'when the Catholics are admitted to be the only genuine loyalists. For the first time this truth has reached Dublin Castle.' He later offered Wellesley a thousand men to track down the perpetrators, writing to his wife: 'I confess it would amuse me to have one good day's running after the rascals.'[3] Meanwhile, the government parties began putting around their version of events, with *Wilson's Dublin Directory* for 1823 concluding its 'Annals of the City of Dublin' with an inflated report of 'a quart bottle and a heavy log of timber' flung at the Lord Lieutenant 'by assassins in the upper gallery, providentially without effect'.[4]

It was becoming clear that Dublin Castle were taking the incident seriously as the arrests continued. William Graham and William Brownlow were arrested on 23 December, later joined by six others, including a baker, an officer's servant from the 5th Dragoon Guards, and the Atkinson brothers. The real shock came, however, when the Attorney General, William Conyngham Plunket, announced that the rioters were to be charged with conspiracy to murder the Lord Lieutenant. Plunket had been the author of the Catholic Emancipation Bill in 1821, and had been sitting beside Wellesley in the Theatre Royal on the night of the riot. He thus had solid political reasons for wanting to use the occasion to face down the Orange Order; however, in treating the protest as an assassination attempt he badly overplayed his hand.

Immediately, playbills for an imaginary theatre under the Lord Lieutenant's patronage appeared around Dublin, announcing fictional productions of *Much Ado About Nothing* and *Killing No Murder*. A satire was circulated, in which Richard Wellesley appeared as Shakespeare's Richard III, declaiming: 'Assassins vile have maimed my noble person!!' In the taverns, ironic addresses were read out: one from the fictitious society of 'Scene Painters, Sign Painters, and other Dawbers', congratulating the theatre's drop curtain on 'its late miraculous escape from the malignant efforts of an assassinating association', while another to the now- famous bottle from its fellow 'Quart, Pint and Magnum Bottles' expressed their 'abhorrence of a wretch who could endanger the existence of a vessel so dear to all Irish hearts'. All considered, Wellesley and Plunket found themselves facing a public relations disaster:

> Have you heard, or who has not,
> Of this dreadful Orange plot,
> Which lately reared its horrid head,
> To strike our Lord Lieutenant dead; . . .
> That they might not be detected,
> With hellish prudence they selected
> . . . implements so unfit,
> A broken rattle and a bit
> Of wood – that some men even still
> Notwithstanding P [lunket]t's skill
> And legal knowledge (silly elves!)
> Have not yet convinced themselves,
> That these wretches did intend
> His Ex [cellenc]y's life to end.[5]

And yet, mockery was the least of Plunket's problems. The Grand Jury before whom the Orangemen were to be arraigned would be selected from a panel chosen by the Dublin Sheriff, Charles Thorpe, who had Orange associations. Three days after the riot, on 17 December, Thorpe was playing cards with one of the rioters, William Graham, in a private house off St Stephen's Green. 'I have an Orange panel in my pocket', he told Graham. 'Be damned to the Marquis Wellesley. We shall do no good in this country until he is out of it.' And, sure enough, when the trial for conspiracy went ahead in January 1823, the Grand Jury returned the bill marked '*ignoramus*', indicating that they considered there to be insufficient evidence for the trial to proceed to a petty jury. It was later found that jurors had been curt to the point of rudeness with witnesses who tried to provide evidence of a conspiracy.

Infuriated, Plunket convinced two of the accused, John and George Atkinson, to turn state's evidence, and, ignoring the Grand Jury's verdict, proceeded with a highly unusual *ex-officio* prosecution against Henry and Mathew Handwich, George Graham, William Graham, William Brownlow and James Forbes. While this was legal, it came so close to infringing on the civil liberties of which Irish Protestants boasted, that it provoked widespread anger. 'An Old Juror', complained in *The Warder* newspaper, for instance, that Plunket's actions were 'arbitrary and oppressive'.[6] One did not have to be an Orangeman to be uneasy about this procedure. Nonetheless, the second trial began on 3 February 1823, with the risible charges of conspiracy to murder and attempted murder replaced by charges of conspiracy to riot and rioting. The petty jury of twelve men (chosen once again from a panel selected by Sheriff Thorpe) heard evidence and legal argument until mid-afternoon on 7 February, when they retired. Twenty-four hours later, they had still not agreed on a verdict, and informed the court that they were not likely to agree, except in the case of William Brownlow, whom they acquitted. The court had no choice but to turn all of the accused free. 'Haven't I managed things well', Sheriff Thorpe said proudly when the news reached his office.

The most immediate response to the collapse of the trial was the establishment of a Parliamentary Committee, who passed over testimony concerning working-class Orange activists to focus on Orange influence in the legal system, concentrating on Sheriff Thorpe's role in rigging the juries. One senior Orangeman, Sir Abraham Bradley King, spent an afternoon eloquently avoiding questioning, before finally admitting that even if ordered otherwise by a court of law, he would uphold the Orange oath to 'always conceal and never will reveal' the secrets of the Order. The Committee's report made clearer than ever before the extent to which the Orange Lodges were not only outside of government control, they were capable of undermining government policy. Indeed, the administration became so worried about the Lodges in the aftermath of the riot that they were for a time suppressed under the Unlawful Societies Act of 1825.

The riot's impact on the Irish theatre was equally significant. When Plunket made his opening address to the jury in the second trial, he needed to find a legal precedent for proceeding from *ex-officio* information. In a situation not without its ironies, the precedent he found was over a century old, and also arose from an attempt to prosecute the instigator of a theatre riot. After Dudley Moore had invaded the Smock Alley stage on 4 November 1712 to proclaim the virtues of William of Orange, he too had been tried by a jury who shared his political convictions, and, like the defendants in the Bottle Riot case, he had been set free, forcing the state to try to by-pass the usual procedures. While this may have been a solid legal precedent, the recourse to *ex-officio* prosecutions on two occasions was eloquent testimony to the difficulties in prosecuting theatre disturbances. If anything, Plunket's choice of precedent suggested that theatre riots tended to push the legal system to its self-defeating outer limits.

This point was further sharpened by Chief Justice Charles Kendal Bushe's summation to the jury, which produced an important legal definition of the rights of Irish theatre audiences. 'An audience may cry down a play, or hiss, or hoot an actor', he told the jurors; 'an audience may be noisy, but not riotous; besides, this must be the feeling of the moment; if not, it becomes criminal.' Later, in 1907, Bushe's ruling was to form the basis of the ruling in the trials of the protestors against John Millington Synge's *Playboy of the Western World*. Hence, for almost a century, the events of 14 December 1822 confirmed the legal status of the theatre as a place of public protest, provided that protest was not premeditated; and premeditation, like conspiracy, was notoriously difficult to prove in court.

The riot had a further effect. Since its establishment in the seventeenth century, the theatre in Dublin (and, more indirectly, elsewhere in Ireland) had relied upon a mutually beneficial relationship with the Lord Lieutenant. Government nights had given the theatres both immediate profit and the long-term warrant of respectability; the theatres, in turn, had given the Lords Lieutenant an opportunity to be on public display before a cross-section of the community, asserting an unspoken claim to rule by popular acclaim, not mere force of arms. When Henry Handwich threw a bottle in the presence of the Viceroy, the fragility of this exchange was exposed in a way that had never happened before. Consequently, while Wellesley and his successors by no means stopped going to the theatre completely after 1822, they grew warier. It may have been the opposite of what the conspirators who met in the Shakespeare Tavern originally intended, but their actions on the night of 14 December 1822, helped to make the Irish theatre a place of resistance to direct British rule.

CHAPTER 4

'That capricious spirit', 1871–1904

At first, the actor Richard Younge could not understand what was happening. As the head of the English touring company performing T. W. Robertson's *M.P.*, Younge was used to acclaim. Since *Caste* (1867), Robertson's plays had been heralded as part of a new, serious theatre, eschewing extravagant sentiment and stock characters for what were seen as realistic representations of middle-class life. However, as Younge looked out from the stage of Dublin's Theatre Royal on 28 August 1871, he saw none of the usual heads nodding approval; instead, all he could see were faces contorted with anger. An orange hit the stage nearby, and as the roaring and hissing in the auditorium became louder, he realised that the people in the pit and galleries were objecting to the character of Mulhowther, an unreconstructed stage Irish villain who had somehow gone unnoticed by English audiences. Stepping out of character, Younge pleaded with the audience to 'allow the piece to proceed without interruption', telling them 'it was the author's right to portray any character he pleased'. In the end, however, the audience won, and a few days later notices in the Dublin newspapers informed patrons that 'the Irish character of "Mulhowther" . . . has been entirely changed'.[1]

By 1871, what would prove the central tension in the Irish theatre culture for the next fifty years was already clearly defined. On the one hand, a popular nationalism had become deeply entrenched in Irish public life. There was no mistaking it: it was there in newspapers, magazines, speeches and in the crowd of 60,000 people who lined Dublin's streets for the funerals of three Fenians executed for killing an English police sergeant. It was also present, *albeit* in a more constitutional form, after the foundation of the Home Rule movement in 1870. And yet, in the same years that Irish culture was becoming more self-consciously national, the new rail and steamship routes and the growth of English and American touring companies were making Ireland a part of a theatre world that was increasingly multi-national. Richard Younge may not have realised it at the time, but when he stepped on to the Hawkins Street stage, he was stepping into what was already a cultural battlefield.

Indeed, while the audience of *M.P.* were howling down Mulhowther, workers not far away on South King Street had begun construction of the Gaiety Theatre, designed by one of the most important theatre architects of the period, C. J. Phipps. Opened on 27 November 1871 by two Irish brothers, Michael and John Gunn, the new theatre marked 'a distinct parting of the ways' with previous theatrical practice, in that it did away completely with the 'old-fashioned system of "the stock Company" '. Although touring shows had been appearing since the 1820s, traditionally the main Dublin theatres had been primarily repertory theatres, maintaining a resident company and mounting their own productions for most of the year. By the early 1870s, however, there were enough good touring companies that it became possible to run a dedicated touring house all year around, without the expense of maintaining a full staff of performers and technicians. So, the Gunns decided to 'give to the public of Dublin, on the stage of this new Theatre, the best in variety and excellence that the world can afford',[2] home-producing only their own annual Christmas pantomime.

As the numbers of good touring companies increased, they not only stimulated the theatre world in Dublin, they also sent out ripples around the country, helping to decentralise the Irish theatrical world. Touring was about reaching as many audiences as possible, so companies usually made the most of their Irish visit by playing Belfast, Cork and sometimes Limerick or Waterford. In the case of Belfast, this new situation coincided with a period of industrial prosperity whose most visible indicator was the opening of the Harland and Wolff shipyard in 1862, and was to lead in 1895 to the construction of what remains the most magnificent theatre on the island, the Grand Opera House, designed by Frank Matcham. In this new theatre, two and half thousand theatre patrons sat in an auditorium encircled by sinuous balconies, decorated with Orientalist plasterwork in a cream and gold colour scheme. From these plush surroundings, the audience faced a deep stage, 33 feet 6 inches (10 metres) wide by 52 feet (15.6 metres) high, with a full fly system and electric lighting (also introduced in the Gaiety in the late 1880s).

The construction of the Belfast Opera House consolidated the northern end of the Irish theatrical axis, which already ran roughly north–south from Belfast to the Gaiety and Theatre Royal in Dublin to the Athenaeum Theatre (later the Opera House), which opened in Cork in 1866. For English travelling companies, this created an attractive circuit.

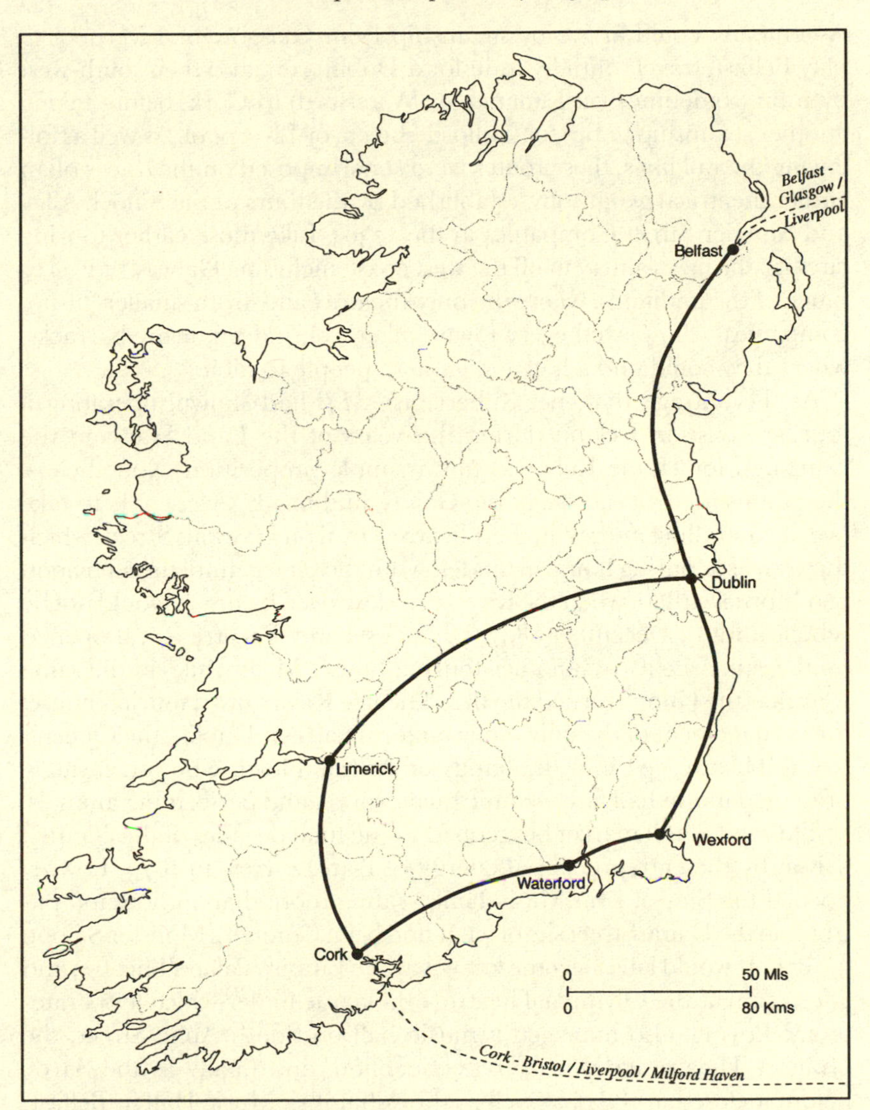

Map 3. Ireland: routes of English touring companies, *c.* 1890. By the 1890s, the geography of the Irish theatre had settled into a Belfast – Dublin – Cork axis first established in the 1730s. Typically, a company arriving in Belfast would travel to Dublin and take the train south to Cork, before sailing back to England.

A company could arrive by steamship from Glasgow or Liverpool to play Belfast, travel south by train for a Dublin run, and then south-west by train (sometimes via Limerick or Waterford) to Cork, before taking another steamship to Bristol, Milford Haven, or Liverpool. As well as following the rail lines, these routes were superimposed on the traces of an earlier theatrical geography, established by the tours of the Smock Alley and Aungier Street Companies in the 1730s. Like those earlier touring circuits, the new routes cut off the west coast, including Galway, as well as much of the midlands, where the only theatre came from smaller 'fit-up' companies, who played every town, village, or, indeed, army barracks, where they could find a hall and enough people to fill it.

As the outrage that met Robertson's *M.P.* had shown, operating a touring house in Ireland during the years of the Land War and the campaign for Home Rule was not a simple proposition. Nonetheless, the Gunns made a success of the Gaiety, and in 1874 were able to take over a controlling interest in the Theatre Royal on Hawkins Street, which they ran as a touring house in tandem with the Gaiety until the afternoon of 9 February 1880, when the Royal was destroyed by fire. It would not be rebuilt until 13 December 1897, when a second Theatre Royal opened on the same site as yet another touring house. Meanwhile, in the same year that the Gunns turned the first Theatre Royal into a touring house, the management of the only other major theatre in Dublin, the Queen's Royal Theatre, fell into the hands of Arthur Lloyd, who increasingly presented music-hall fare – comic turns, songs, and performing animals.

This end of the market burgeoned in the final decades of the century, driven by the entrepreneurial energy of Dan Lowrey. In 1879, Lowrey opened the Star of Erin Music Hall, seating more than a thousand patrons on the Dame Street site of what had been Connell's Monster Saloon in 1855. It would later become known as the Empire Palace Theatre, and later again as the Olympia Theatre – the name under which it operates today. Lowrey also managed a music hall on South Anne Street, the Grafton Theatre (known later as the Bijou, and finally as the Savoy before it closed in 1884), as well as the Alhambra Music Hall in Belfast.

This is not to say, however, that Irish theatres of the period presented an unbroken procession of what W. B. Yeats would witheringly call 'Musical Comedy'. When the Gaiety opened in November of 1871, its first production was Oliver Goldsmith's *She Stoops to Conquer*, and over the following decades the Gunns brought to Dublin much of the best mainstream theatre of the period, of which melodrama and musical comedy constituted only a part. Goldsmith and R. B. Sheridan were played regularly, although Shakespeare, as always, continued to dominate the non-musical repertoire. In the final decades of the nineteenth century, there were almost annual productions of *Hamlet*, and at a time when all of the major Shakespearean actors toured, Beerbohm Tree, the Kendals, F. R. Benson and Henry Irving were all regular visitors to Ireland. Indeed, it was while in Dublin that Irving met his future business manager, Bram Stoker, during a 1876 appearance.

Contemporary plays from the London theatres also toured, and the time lag narrowed steadily between London and Dublin openings. The D'Oyly Carte Opera Company brought Gilbert and Sullivan to Irish audiences, and plays by T. W. Robertson (the 1871 reception of *M.P.* notwithstanding) appeared frequently, as did those of Arthur Wing Pinero, whose *The Second Mrs Tanqueray*, with Mrs Patrick Campbell in the title role, played Dublin several times shortly after its London première in 1893. It was as touring shows, as well, that the works of Oscar Wilde began to trickle on to Irish stages, as *Lady Windermere's Fan* and *The Importance of Being Earnest* made brief appearances in Dublin. Wilde himself lectured on 'Beauty, Taste, and Ugliness in Dress' and 'Art in Modern Life' from the Gaiety stage as part of a speaking tour in January 1885. This, however, was the last time he was to visit Dublin. After his trial in 1895, touring productions of his plays faded away, and it was to be thirty years before his plays became a part of the Irish repertoire.

While it is true that much of what appeared on the Gaiety stage originated in England, this was not exclusively the case. The American actor Edwin Booth appeared at the Gaiety, as did a number of Wild West plays, whose pleasures included trick rifle-shooting and lariat twirling. American touring shows also began to include Ireland on their European itinerary, so that Irish audiences saw melodramas like *Rip Van Winkle* and *Uncle Tom's Cabin*, with a 1902 production of the latter featuring 'real Negroes' – a luxury the Irish fit-up companies who regularly toured the play around the country had to do without. But then, performers in blackface make-up were by no means unfamiliar to Irish audiences. The minstrel show was popular with Irish audiences as early as 1837, when the Theatre Royal had a hit with Thomas Dartmouth Rice and his 'Jim Crow' act, performed in blackface. Rice's success encouraged a string of 'minstrel' performers throughout the century, including Eugene Stratton, who played the Theatre Royal in the 1890s.

If the minstrel show constituted one end of the spectrum at the main Irish theatres, opera – which appeared much more frequently – was the other end. Italian opera, which for much of the 1840s had almost completely overwhelmed the sound of the spoken word on Irish stages, continued to be popular, although the Gunns also had a taste for Wagner, so that by the late 1880s at least one week a year the Carl Rosa Company presented *Tannhäuser* or *Tristan und Isolde*. In addition to opera, Irish audiences were fond of non-English language theatre and performers. In June of 1881, Sarah Bernhardt filled the theatre to capacity with *La Dame aux Camélias* and *Frou Frou*, in which she was ecstatically received by the audience in the gallery. In the following decade, the Gaiety hosted the Comédie-Française actor, Constant-Benoît Coquelin, the Italian actress Adelaide Ristori and her countryman, the Shakespearean actor Tommaso Salvini. In the early years of the twentieth century, the Gaiety and Theatre Royal would bring in sporadic, but influential, touring productions of Maeterlinck, Sudermann, and Ibsen.

By any standards, this is a rich and varied diet – the theatrical equivalent of everything from American fast food to French *haute cuisine* – and it would be a mistake to condemn it as bad simply because it was not Irish. 'Practically any sort of entertainment was available in the bigger theatres', actress Maire Ni Shiubhlaigh later recalled. 'The playgoer had the choice of anything from the Hamlet or Othello of Martin Harvey, right down the line to the broadest farce or melodrama.'[3] And yet, there was an irony here: amid this cornucopia of choice, there was often little room for Irish plays on Irish stages. The demise of the Irish repertory companies, combined with the tight control that Boucicault held over his copyright while his plays were at their most popular, gave rise to an anomalous situation: plays about Ireland, often written in response to political events in Ireland, were being premièred in New York or London with American or English casts, only arriving in Ireland a year or so later as touring shows.

One of the best examples of this phenomenon is Boucicault's *The Shaughraun*, which opened at Wallack's Theatre in New York on 14 November 1874, nine months after the first Home Rule MPs were elected to Westminster. Throughout the late 1860s and early 1870s, the Fenian movement had created a culture of nationalist resistance that could be highly theatrical in its own right, where a shadowy world of informers, hairsbreadth rescue attempts and underdog rebels existed parallel to the more mundane world of land reform politics and parliamentary elections. Earlier Irish plays set in the 1790s, like Edmund Falconer's *Peep O' Day* and Boucicault's *Arrah-na-Pogue*, shared this ethos; however, *The Shaughraun* goes a step further, making its hero, Robert Ffolliott, a Fenian. Leaving no doubt as to the play's links with the world of its audience, the villains hint that they are relying on 'the late [Fenian] attack on the police-van at Manchester, and the explosion at Clerkenwell Prison in London' to 'warrant extreme measures' in the capture of Conn the Shaughraun, the starring role Boucicault created for himself.[4]

Like its predecessors, *The Shaughraun* performs a delicate balancing act. It opens up conflicts – between unjust legality and just illegality, English and Irish, landowners and peasants – and then resolves them with a mélange of conventional devices. In this case, a lost letter appears at a crucial moment revealing that Robert Ffolliott has been pardoned, thereby allowing the English soldier pursuing him, Captian Molineux, to marry Ffolliott's sister, Claire. By supporting authority and resistance to authority at the same time, an Irish play like *The Shaughraun* could be all things to all audiences. This, of course, is why it would be so successful as part of the new global entertainment culture.

At the same time, the audience's part in the play's reception was something Boucicault took very seriously. 'The jury is composed here, as it was composed in Greece, of the people', he later wrote, 'and the drama is, therefore, made by collaboration of the people and the poet.'[5] In other words, Boucicault was not simply slipping a surreptitious Fenian hero to a world audience; audiences were already willing to accept the legitimacy of such a hero, Boucicault believed, and his job was simply to make their willingness manifest using the standard tools of his trade. Hence, in what was both a publicity stunt and a working out of this idea, Boucicault published an open letter in 1874 to the British Prime Minister, Benjamin Disraeli, pleading for the release of the remaining Fenian prisoners in British gaols, claiming that the more than 20,000 people who had applauded *The Shaughraun* supported his claims. Disraeli may have ignored the letter, but the audiences continued to applaud, as Boucicault revived the play again and again, in Ireland, England, the United States, Canada, and later in Australia and New Zealand.

As plays like *The Shaughraun* spread around the world, it was only a matter of time before someone decided to produce Irish plays in Ireland. So, in 1884 – the same year in which the Gaelic Athletic Association was founded – the Queen's Royal Theatre became self- proclaimed 'Home of Irish Drama', although – ironically – this was only after its management passed to an English entrepreneur, J. W. Whitbread. Whitbread shared the Gunns' belief that the days of the resident company were gone. Economically, it made more sense to put together a touring production, which could easily play a series of one or two week runs at different theatres, amounting to several hundred nights, rather than to attempt the starkly impossible task of filling a two thousand seat theatre in the same city for a year. At the same time, Whitbread wanted to maximise the Irish audience for Irish plays.

His solution, as he explained to an interviewer in 1893, was to create a resident touring company, which would open a play at the Queen's, where the audience knew the actors and almost guaranteed them a welcome. Buoyed by reports of genuine Irish applause, the show would then set off around the touring circuit, travelling to Belfast, Cork, Glasgow, and then on to Bristol, Manchester, London and after that possibly New York or even Sydney, so that by the end of a tour some of Whitbread's productions would boast of more than two thousand performances. If this figure is accurate, given theatre sizes at the time and houses which were roughly 60 per cent full, many of his plays would have been seen by a total audience of more than three million people worldwide. Meanwhile, when Whitbread's own shows were out conquering the world, the Queen's acted as host to other touring companies, whenever possible bringing in Irish plays, so that for approximately a third of the year, or about fifteen weeks annually, the Queen's presented Irish material.[6]

In creating an Irish identity for his theatre, Whitbread brought into being something that did not exist at any of the other major Irish theatres of the time: an audience with a collective identity carried over from play to play. 'It was like the palmy days of the drama to see the way the floor of the pit was covered with orange-peel before the end of the play & the exclamations of "isn't she a lovely character" or "isn't he a grand character" were ever in the air', wrote the inveterate theatregoer Joseph Holloway, watching an Irish play in full flight at the Queen's:

> At times, when the 'bad character' held the stage one could scarcely hear with the din made by the small boy element on the top. And as for cheering & hissing they seldom ceased for a moment. Now the hero said something that met with the entire approval of those in front, & even the informer had their say & the audience were up in arms against them – hissing, howling & wishing for their death with all their might & main of lung power. A genuine Queen's audience (like today's) to one not used to it must be a curious sight & a new experience indeed![7]

While other Irish theatres of the period brought together a Wagnerite audience, or a minstrel show audience, or a musical comedy audience for a single night, the Queen's was able to forge something like a community, where the theatre became a noisy, active place in which the audience worked with the performer in the creation of a play.

Photograph 3(a) A view of the audience, Queen's Royal Theatre, Dublin. Audiences in the Queen's Royal Theatre, could be 'as noisy and excitable as I ever saw inside a theatre', wrote Joseph Holloway. This photo of a comparatively sedate crowd was taken when the theatre re-opened after renovations in 1909.

Photograph 3(b) Exterior of Queen's Royal Theatre, Dublin, shortly before its demolition in 1969.

Among the performers most popular with the 'genuine Queen's audience' was Hubert O'Grady, who had won the affections of Dubliners by playing Conn in *The Shaughraun* during a 1877 revival at the Gaiety. 'His style of acting is quiet as a whole', noted Holloway, 'and in his frequent "colloquising" [*sic*] with himself he invariably takes the house into his confidence.' By 1885 O'Grady had founded the Irish National Company, producing his own political melodramas, including *Eviction* (1879), *Emigration* (1880), *The Famine* (1886) and *The Fenian* (1888). Attending what was to be O'Grady's final appearance with his company at the Queen's in October 1899 (although no one knew it at the time), Holloway writes that 'There was murder getting in – the crowd at the pit and gallery doors extended nearly to the tram tracks [which ran down the centre of the street], – but good humour prevailed . . . & the people when they got out of the squash & swelled to their natural sizes again became talkative & ready to enjoy anything.'[8]

In the Irish plays written by O'Grady, and later by Whitbread himself, the genre took on a sharper, more directly political edge. O'Grady in particular was adept at using the tableau – a moment in which the actors freeze in an iconic posture at the end of a scene – to create powerfully resonant moments. For instance, *The Famine*, which first played the Queen's on 26 April 1886, has a scene containing only three lines of dialogue which builds to a stage tableau of a Fenian attack on a police van in Manchester.[9] The attack was, of course, a real-life event, and many in O'Grady's audience would have attended the public funerals of the three men who had been executed for the attack.

As well as being more explicitly political than their predecessors, O'Grady and his peers were becoming increasingly unequivocal in their treatment of one of the key characters in the Irish play: the informer. Indeed, by the end of the century, a substantial part of the pleasure for the audience at the Queen's Theatre came from hissing the informer. 'They hiss him out of love for him!' Holloway exclaimed of Frank Breen, who often played informers at the Queen's.[10] In a sense, Irish melodrama increasingly bound its audience together in what can only be described as pleasurable hatred, where the communal condemnation of a character who betrays his country builds up so that it can be satisfied in the spectacle of his punishment.

This was the model of the Irish play to which Whitbread turned when he began writing plays for his Kennedy-Miller company shortly after he took over the running of the Queen's. His first work was the play *Shoulder to Shoulder* produced in 1886, followed by *The Nationalist* in 1891.

Towards the end of the century he wrote more quickly, producing a group of plays dealing with the 1798 rising: *Lord Edward, Or '98* (1894), *Theobald Wolfe Tone* (1898 – sometimes simply called *Wolfe Tone*), and *The Insurgent Chief* and *The Ulster Hero* (both 1902), the former dealing with Michael Dwyer's involvement in the rebellion in Wicklow, the latter with Henry Joy McCracken in Belfast. In total, Whitbread wrote fifteen plays in the twenty years before 1906, of which four dealt with 1798, putting the theatre at the heart of a movement which saw new centenary commemoration societies and committees being formed almost weekly by the time Arthur Griffith founded the *United Irishman* newspaper in March 1899.

When Whitbread's *Wolfe Tone* opened at the Queen's on 26 December 1898, it thus caught the mood of the moment perfectly. Like much popular theatre, its power lay in the untroubled mixing of wildly heterogeneous ideas and sources. Tone himself is a typical melodramatic romantic lead, distant, chivalrous, only taking an active role in proceedings in the final scenes when he negotiates with Napoleon and Josephine (whose presence in Whitbread's play is explained by the popularity of Willie Wills' play about the couple, *A Royal Divorce*, which had packed the Gaiety the week before *Wolfe Tone* opened, and would continue to be an audience favourite until the 1920s). In fact, *Wolfe Tone*'s real focus is not Tone at all (although the audience's sympathy with him is assumed); it is his servant, Shane McMahon (played by one of the Kennedy-Miller Company's biggest attractions, Tyrone Power) and Shane's struggles to outwit the informer, Rafferty.

When the curtain opened on *Wolfe Tone* for the first time on that December evening, a damp blast of winter air swept through the auditorium, as members of the audience found themselves looking through the stage, whose back doors had been opened on Trinity's New Square, located behind the theatre. Merging the stage world with the real world, Shane is beaten on his first entrance by a group of Trinity students, before being rescued by a United Irishman, Thomas Russell. Hence, the opening few minutes of the play reinforce real class tensions between Trinity students and the predominantly working-class audience who patronised the Queen's, thereby bonding the audience (through their surrogate, Shane) to the republican United Irishmen. The audience is further linked to the United Irishmen through the mutual hatred of the informer Rafferty, played by Frank Breen, who dies in a spectacularly sadistic curtain scene where, attempting to run while chained, blindfolded and screaming for mercy, he is shot by an entire company of French soldiers.

'So perish all traitors!' Tone solemnly reminds the audience, lest the point is missed.[11]

By its second night, the crowds pushing their way into the Queen's to see *Wolfe Tone* were so big that they threatened to block the fire station across the street, and the police insisted that the doors be opened early. Whitbread, wrote the *Dublin Evening Herald*, 'is thoroughly in sympathy with Ireland'. 'This is the sort of play', noted Holloway in his diary, 'that will ultimately put a new spirit into Ireland'[12] – an opinion shared, if with some reservations, by many of those who were already infused with the new militant spirit. 'Though we are not prepared to accept *Lord Edward* or *Wolfe Tone* as ideal Irish plays', commented the *United Irishman* in March 1899, 'they are certainly steps in the right direction . . . These plays will do good, and the Irish Stage, if we may call our theatres such, would be the better of many more of their class.'[13] Whitbread, for his part, was more than willing to court advanced nationalist opinion, holding a special benefit matinée of *Wolfe Tone* for the Wolfe Tone Memorial Fund on 16 September 1899.

As the mainstream became less compromising, theatre audiences became increasingly active. St John Ervine later recalled that as a boy growing up in Belfast, his aunt would bring him to see Shakespeare or anything with the word 'London' in the title, but not Boucicault, much less Whitbread or O'Grady. 'She was fearful', he wrote, 'that there might be a row in the gallery between the Papist and Orange corner-boys who congregated there on "Irish" nights to make a demonstration of their religious beliefs: one side cheering the British authorities, while the other side pelted them with orange-peel and objurgations. Some of these lads, she said, might have a rivet or two in their pockets, purloined from the shipyards.'[14] One of these Orange corner- boys, who grew up to be the playwright Thomas Carnduff, would later recollect coming out second best in a fracas during a production of *Arrah-na-Pogue*, in which he rapidly exited the theatre after 'a terrific kick in the pants sent me hurtling down the stone steps, seven at a time'.[15]

Some of these mêlées were the spontaneous continuation of a venerable tradition of brawling in the galleries (although rivet throwing was an innovation peculiar to industrial Belfast). At the same time, organised protests, which had more or less disappeared from Irish theatres after the Orange riots of the 1830s, began to re-emerge around the turn of the century. In April 1902, for instance, the Cork branch of Cumann na nGaedeal broke up a performance at the Cork Opera House of *The Dandy Fifth*, a jingoistic comedy set in a British army regiment. When the show arrived in Dublin on 14 April, the manager of the Theatre Royal requested the presence in the theatre of a company of real soldiers to reinforce those on the stage (and also, of course, to back up the police officers who supervised all performances in the patent theatres as a matter of course). The Dublin production was hissed and part of the audience began singing 'God Save Ireland', leading to the arrest of eleven protesters – described as 'law students, medical students, clerks and artisans' – one of whom was jailed for a month.

While rivets were flying and language activists were singing 'God Save Ireland' in the big patent theatres, in the drawing room of Duras House, County Galway, on a rainy afternoon in September 1897, W. B. Yeats, Lady Gregory and Edward Martyn decided to start a theatre of their own. 'Though I had never been at all interested in theatres, our talk turned on plays', Lady Gregory later wrote. 'We went on talking, and things seemed to grow possible as we talked, and before the end of the afternoon we had made our plan.'[16] The most remarkable thing about this group – with the exception of George Moore, who would join them later – was their almost complete lack of interest in Irish theatre before they decided to found one. Indeed, they took pride in the fact, with Yeats writing of an unsuccessful attempt to stage an early play with Florence Farr in 1894 as having been 'the first contest between the old commercial school of theatrical folk & the new artistic school'. 'It is a wild mystical thing', he announced, 'carefully arranged to be an insult to the regular theatre goer who is hated by both of us.'[17]

In the beginning, not knowing what was expected made it possible to accomplish the unexpected. Knowing only that they did not want a 'commercial' theatre, the founders of what was initially named the Irish Literary Theatre set about creating a type of theatre that had survived the eighteenth century only in amateur productions staged in the country houses of the landed Ascendancy – a theatre founded on patronage. Indeed, the list of subscribers published in the first issue of *Beltaine* contains enough knights and barons to keep a decent seventeenth-century theatre afloat, with no fewer than seventeen titled patrons on the list, along with three Members of Parliament, the Provost of Trinity College, balanced on the other end of the political spectrum by the stentorian nationalist leader John O'Leary and members of the Irish Parliamentary Party.

In the end, few of these patrons were particularly helpful as sources of income; however, they did provide a way of dealing with the licensing laws, which still confined professional performances in Dublin to the three big patent houses: the Theatre Royal, the Gaiety, and the Queen's.

Although the laws had not been amended since 1786, in the final years of the nineteenth-century Irish managers of the patent theatres were insisting on their monopoly as firmly as ever, issuing a public warning on 17 January 1898 threatening to prosecute anyone who staged for 'hire, gain, or any kind of rewards . . . any Interlude, Tragedy, Comedy, Prelude, Opera, Burletta, Play, Farce, Pantomime'. In the kind of manoeuvring at which he was to become so adept, Yeats cleared this first hurdle. He formed a strategic alliance with the Amateur Dramatic Defence Association, headed by a Dublin solicitor, Francis R. Wolfe, lobbied the liberal unionist MP W. E. H. Lecky (who was one of the Theatre's patrons) and finally convinced a nationalist MP, Timothy Harrington, to slip the necessary amendment into the concluding sections of the Local Government Act of 1898 (61 and 62 Vict.).

Carried through in the slipstream of far-reaching legislation which defined the powers of local authorities, an innocuous-looking clause empowered the Lord Lieutenant to 'grant an occasional licence for the performance of any stage play or other dramatic entertainment in any theatre, room, or building where the profits arising therefrom are to be applied for some charitable purpose or in aid of the funds of any society instituted for the purpose of science, literature, or the fine arts exclusively'. It also carried the proviso that 'The licence may contain such conditions and regulations as appear fit to the Lord Lieutenant, and may be revoked by him.'[18] Legally, at least, the Irish Literary Theatre thus began its life under the patronage of Dublin Castle. Each of its performances prior to 1904 had to be personally approved by the Viceroy, who could (at least in theory) shut them down on a whim.

Having thus altered the legal status of the theatre, Yeats, Gregory and Martyn set about transforming the theatre itself. Precisely how they were to do this, however, was caught in a tangle of contradictions from the very outset. Shortly after that famous afternoon in Duras House, the founders of the Irish Literary Theatre produced their statement of purpose:

> We propose to have performed in Dublin in the spring of every year certain Celtic and Irish plays, which whatever be their degree of excellence will be written with high ambition, and so to build up a Celtic and Irish school of dramatic literature. We hope to find in Ireland an uncorrupted and imaginative audience trained to listen by its passion for oratory . . . We will show that Ireland is not the home of buffoonery or of easy sentiment, as it has been represented, but the home of an ancient idealism. We are confident of the support of all Irish people, who are weary of misrepresentation, in carrying out a work that is outside all the political questions that divide us.[19]

Leaving aside for a moment the disingenuous claim to be 'outside' of politics, there are two underlying assumptions here: both would prove liberating, even if they were wrong.

In the first place, the suggestion that there was a need to create, *ad ovum*, 'a Celtic and Irish school of dramatic literature' effectively erases a dramatic tradition going back at least to the seventeenth century – a tradition which, through plays like those of Charles Macklin, had helped create the notion that there was such a thing as 'the Celtic' in the first place. Because it chose to ignore the existing Irish theatre history, the Irish Literary Theatre was able – indeed, it was compelled – to imagine afresh its relationship to Irish history. What is more, if there was no prior Irish theatre worth mentioning, it followed that there could be no Irish theatre audiences, and hence the fantasy of 'an uncorrupted and imaginative audience trained to listen by its passion for oratory'. This, of course, completely ignores the existence of discerning and sophisticated theatre audiences, who were familiar with an increasingly wide range of theatrical forms. As the more clear-sighted John Millington Synge (who was later to join Yeats and Gregory) wrote to a friend in 1904, 'The Dublin audiences who see Mme Rejane in Ibsen, Mrs P. Campbell in Sudermann, Olga Netherstole in *Sapho* etc. are hardly blessedly unripe.'[20] Vocal in their likes and dislikes, Irish audiences were capable of shouting down plays that offended them, and equally capable of blocking the street in front of the Queen's in their enthusiasm to see plays by Boucicault, Whitbread or O'Grady, which they by no means considered 'misrepresentations'.

In a sense, the Irish Literary Theatre came into being by imagining an empty space where in fact there was a crowded room. From this basic – *albeit* enabling – contradiction, others arose. The Irish Literary Theatre was supposed to win 'the support of *all* Irish people', a notion reinforced by the group's increasing use of the word 'national'; at the same time, Yeats was railing in private against the 'regular theatre-goer', admitting in the Theatre's new journal, *Beltaine*, that he was writing for 'that limited public which gives understanding', and that he would 'not mind greatly if others are bored'.[21]

Muddying the waters even further, *Beltaine*'s successor, *Samhain*, held up Ibsen and the theatre of Norway as an example for Ireland. 'If Irish dramatists had studied the romantic plays of Ibsen, the one great master the modern stage has produced', Yeats announced in 1901, 'they would not have sent the Irish Literary Theatre imitations of Boucicault, who had no relation to literature.'[22] Given that there had only been two Ibsen plays seen on Irish stages at that point – *A Doll's House*, performed by the amateur Players' Club on 14 December 1897, and an earlier touring production of *An Enemy of the People* – the importance of Yeats' qualifying word 'romantic' (indicating presumably a preference for the Ibsen of *Peer Gynt* or *Brand*) would have escaped anyone who equated Ibsen with risqué social realism. Consequently, when it became obvious that Yeats hated realism as much as he hated the 'commercial' theatre, there was not a little confusion among those working with him who thought they had been helping to create an Irish Ibsenite theatre for 'all the Irish people'.

If contradiction was a way of life – indeed, a philosophy of life – for Yeats, it was also the fuel that made the Irish Literary Theatre so dynamic and embroiled it in an almost perpetual state of civil war, both backstage and with its audiences. When the Irish Literary Theatre's first play opened on 8 May 1899, with Yeats' *The Countess Cathleen*, it became obvious that, apart from anything else, the new company had a genius for managing publicity. Before the play even opened, a debate in the letter columns of the English newspapers brought over two leading reviewers, Arthur Symons and Max Beerbohm, while Yeats himself made sure that *Beltaine* helped to shape the expectations of the audience. However, more effective than any friendly puffing was the attack launched on the play by Frank Hugh O'Donnell, who had read the script in advance (earlier published versions went back as far as 1889 and 1895). Writing to the *Freeman's Journal* in late April, and later publishing his comments as a pamphlet, *Souls for Gold*, he denounced the play as offensive. *The Countess Cathleen*, declared O'Donnell, is full of 'wild incoherencies . . . revolting blasphemies and idiotic impulses which sicken and astonish'. 'Mysticism?' he asked. 'Nonsense. This is not Mysticism. The great mystics are intellectual and moral glories of Christian civilisation. This is only silly stuff, and sillier, unutterable profanity.'[23]

In one sense, he was right. Although not clearly set in any precise historical period, *The Countess Cathleen* takes place during a time of famine and this in itself was enough to provoke controversy. By the end of the nineteenth century, the Famine of the 1840s had taken its place in the popular Irish nationalist version of history, most forcefully argued by John Mitchel, as an instrument of conquest to 'scourge our people from their own land'. 'If you will only look back to the years gone by', declares a character in the curtain line of Hubert O'Grady's *The Famine* (which would return to the Queen's five months after *The Countess Cathleen* for yet another packed run) 'you cannot but be convinced that all our trials and troubles can be traced to the great distress during The Famine.'[24] In

Yeats' *Countess Cathleen*, by contrast, the Famine provides a landlord – an equally hated figure in the traditional versions of events, and the villain of O'Grady's play – with the opportunity to become the saviour of her people by offering her soul in exchange for those of all of her tenants. The guardian landlord's sacrifice is then blessed by an Angel in a final *deus ex machina*:

> The Light of Lights
> Looks always on the motive, not the deed,
> The Shadow of Shadows on the deed alone.[25]

From the point of view of the sharply defined pieties of nationalist Irish history, this was blasphemy.

Arthur Griffith, editor of the *United Irishman*, would later claim that he had hired a few dozen coalmen to sit at the back of the theatre and cheer anything that might offend the Catholic Church on *The Countess Cathleen*'s opening night. However, while there was jeering, foot stomping and cheering, most of the audience were simply bewildered. For Joseph Holloway, it was not until a year later that he grasped what had been going on, when he saw Maeterlinck's *Peleas and Melisande* at the Theatre Royal. 'Be the Lord Harry', exclaimed a friend sitting next to him, 'it is Yates [*sic*] all over again.' 'He had seen the latter's *Countess Kathleen* [*sic*] performed at the Irish Literary Theatre', explained Holloway, 'and the style – full of weird mystic suggestiveness leading to nothing really dramatic seemed to him (& indeed to me also) to coincide strongly with our own poet's mannerisms of thought & strange mystic fancies.'[26] Like many others baffled by the deliberate obscurity of this first wave of Irish modernist theatre, Holloway thought Yeats could be sorted out by a good lesson in how to write a play. In a lecture to the National Literary Society in 1900, Holloway took to task 'the non-playgoing high-and-mighty literary critics who pretend to know all about what stage work ought to be, and despise all real playgoers, like myself'. If the Irish Literary Society really wanted to know what theatre was all about, he told them, they should see 'a revival of *Lord Edward, or '98* at the Queen's Theatre'.[27]

The 'weird mystic suggestiveness', which puzzled Holloway and infuriated O'Donnell, was to be the hallmark of the plays produced by the Irish Literary Theatre in its early years. Although no one would have admitted it, the stage world of the conventional Irish play was solidly secular, in that all of the machinery necessary for the resolution of the plot was displayed (often spectacularly) before the audience's eyes. By contrast, the real focus in *The Countess Cathleen* is a world of demons, angels and abstractions, only fleetingly illuminated when the Angel descends in the play's closing moments; for the rest of the performance, the onstage world is only a cipher for a spiritual world elsewhere. Similarly, those audience members who returned to the Antient Concert rooms the following night for Edward Martyn's *The Heather Field* would see a play about a landowner obsessed with a field that is both real (in this case, real enough to bankrupt an estate) and symbolic of a 'disposition too eerie, too ethereal, too untameable for good steady, domestic cultivation'.[28]

When the Irish Literary Theatre announced its second season for 19 February 1900, apart from the inclusion of George Moore's political comedy, *The Bending of the Bough*, both Alice Milligan's *The Last Feast of the Fianna* and Edward Martyn's *Maeve* confirmed the first season's impressions. If Martyn's *The Heather Field* had resembled Ibsen's *The Master Builder*, then *Maeve* (described by its author as 'A Psychological Drama') begins by resembling *Hedda Gabler*, in that it deals with a woman who refuses to bind herself to anything but an ideal beauty. However, in its closing scenes it suddenly changes direction, moving into a lengthy dream sequence in which Queen Maeve and a chorus of boy pages tempt the central character to join them in 'Tir-nan-ogue'. With its anguished linking of present and past, *Maeve* is an unusually subtle attempt to find in Irish mythology an alternative to mundane reality. However, in turning to Irish mythology it was part of a wider trend, which went back to the antiquarian studies of the late eighteenth century, evolving through the work of poets such as Samuel Ferguson and Aubrey De Vere in the middle of the nineteenth century, and culminating in the publication of Standish James O'Grady's *History of Ireland: The Heroic Period* in 1878. At a time when poems and prose narratives based on the exploits of Maeve and Cuchulain were appearing regularly, these plays helped to establish the basic parameters of what was seen at the time as the future of Irish drama.

'If the aim of the Irish Literary Theatre is to create a national drama', commented the *Daily Express*, 'it is obvious that the development of Miss Milligan's method is the proper road to reach ultimate success.'[29] In fact, with a handful of notable exceptions (most of which are supplied by Yeats), the Irish mythological play was something of a *cul de sac*. Partly this was due to an historical myopia, which failed to recognise that plays like Milligan's *Last Feast of the Fianna*, James Cousins' *The Sleep of the King* (1902) or Bulmer Hobson's *Brian of Banba* (1902), in which heroes wearing horned helmets spouted interminable purple prose, resembled nothing so much as Shadwell's *Rotherick O'Connor* (1720) come back from the dead. The mythological play only appeared new because it was so archaic.

The weaknesses of the form were apparent as early as 1901, when the Irish Literary Society staged *Diarmuid and Grania*, written by Yeats and George Moore. In spite of an attempt to raise production standards by hiring a respected English actor, Frank Benson, to play the lead (sporting a fetching pair of tartan trews) and a score by Edward Elgar, the play was a flop. Its authors' greatest triumph, wrote Frank Fay, was to have 'written in English a play in which English actors are intolerable. Even amateur Irish actors could give a meaning which escapes experienced English professionals'.[30] As a case in point, Fay directed his readers (with a forgivable touch of nepotism) to the one-act play directed by his brother, William Fay, which had accompanied *Diarmuid and Grania*: *Casadh an tSúgáin* by Douglas Hyde.

Casadh an tSúgáin was prophetic of the future direction of the Irish theatre in a number of respects. It was one of the first plays ever mounted in the Irish language, following closely behind an anonymous work entitled *Imtheach Conaill* produced in Letterkenny on 18 November 1898, and P. T. MacGinley's *Eilís agus an Bhean Déirce*, staged by Inginidhe na hÉireann at the Antient Concert rooms on 27 August 1901. *Casadh an tSúgáin* was also the Irish Literary Theatre's first peasant play. Although peasant cottages had been on Irish stages since at least the time of John O'Keeffe, this would be the first time that audiences would watch a play set entirely in a cottage interior. By 1911, the company would have used more or less the same set sixteen times, and by the middle of the twentieth century it would be embarrassingly ubiquitous. The plot, too, was to be reworked again and again on the Irish stage, as a woman is forced to choose between an unimaginative farmer and a volatile wandering poet. In a sense, this was a domesticated version of the plot of Edward Martyn's *Maeve*, and it would be used again in Padraic Colum's *The Land* (1905), in Synge's *In the Shadow of the Glen* (1903) and later in *The Playboy of the Western World* (1907). *Casadh an tSúgáin* is thus an encapsulated version of much that was to take place on the Irish stage in the first half of the twentieth century.

The contrast between the Benson Company's performance of *Diarmuid and Grania*, and the Gaelic League's performance of *Casadh an tSúgáin* also defined the question of performance style. As early as the 1900 production of Moore's naturalistic comedy, *The Bending of the Bough*, Joseph Holloway had complained in a review entitled 'The Art of Gazing into Space' of the Irish Literary Theatre's 'irritating fault of speaking to the house'. 'What could be more inartistic or unnatural', he asked 'than the way the four members of the Corporation got into line about a yard and a half behind the footlights, and about two paces apart, and, staring out at the audience all the time, commenced to converse to each other for all the world like mechanical figures with their "buttons" pressed.'[31] Although it seemed strange to Holloway, this new style of acting was an important innovation, largely the work of Frank Fay. Fay, writing regular theatre reviews in the *United Irishman*, was chaffing against the emotive, gestural style of acting current on the stage of the time, championing instead actors such as Coquelin, who had played the Gaeity in 1899. Reviewing *Casadh an tSúgáin*, he noted that 'the acting reminded me of French acting, on a small scale, of course'. 'The other day', Yeats wrote the following year, 'I saw Sara Bernhardt and De Max in *Phedre* and understood where Mr. Fay had gone for his model.'[32]

It makes sense, therefore, that Frank Fay and his brother Willie should have come together with Yeats and Lady Gregory, who had consolidated their positions as the leaders of the Irish Literary Theatre, gradually pushing aside Moore, who returned to writing fiction, and Martyn, who had become heavily involved in the language movement and would later found the Theatre of Ireland in 1906. Willie Fay had a long history of involvement with the theatre, some of it professional, learning his trade in melodramas by authors like J. B. Buckstone and Boucicault, while his brother Frank had gained a reputation as an acting coach who insisted that his students attend the theatre with him on every possible occasion. 'From the front row of the sixpenny gallery', Maire Nic Shiubhlaigh would later recall, 'we watched the work of every great figure of the time, while he painstakingly examined each performance.'[33] Bringing with them key players from the Ormonde Dramatic Society and the dramatic class of Inginidhe na hEireann, including Maud Gonne, Nic Shiubhlaigh, Padraic Colum, James Cousins and Frederick Ryan, they reformed as W. G. Fay's Irish National Dramatic Company. By April 1902, they were ready to stage *Cathleen ni Houlihan.*

Cathleen ni Houlihan must go down in Irish theatre history as the play no one could spell, including its supposed author. 'Is it Houlan or Hoolan', Yeats asked Lady Gregory in May of 1902 when preparing the text for publication; 'Is it Ni or Ny?'[34] Programmes, playbills and reviews alternately spell 'Cathleen' with a 'C' and a 'K', 'Houlihan' was spelled with every imaginable combination of vowels, and one review in a Cork newspaper anticipated by forty years its translation into Irish, referring to it as *Caitilin Ni Uallachain.* This elusiveness may have been a symptom of its hybrid authorship. The play was originally attributed to Yeats, was copyrighted under his name, and still appears in his *Collected Plays*.[35] He would later claim that he had dreamed the plot and Lady Gregory had written it down, although evidence in Lady Gregory's diaries and a comparison with her later plays suggest she did rather more than this, and it is now included in an edition of her plays as well. In a sense, the play's resistance to print media and lack of a clearly ascertainable author is entirely appropriate: this play about a young man who is transformed by a half-remembered piece of folk memory quickly wove itself into its audience's own sense of communal memory. What is more, it did so by working with, rather than against, the existing theatre culture.

The initial production in St Teresa's Hall on 2 April 1902, could not have been seen by more than five hundred people over three nights, most of whom could barely see as the venue extended over two connected rooms, and the sounds of billiard balls and music-hall ballads from the adjoining building were audible throughout the performance. The stage, according to Nic Shiubhlaigh 'did not give much room for movement or extravagant gesture', was almost completely filled by the set, which wobbled as the actors squeezed by it backstage. Playing the title role, Maud Gonne arrived ten minutes before the curtain went up, unprofessionally (but impressively) sweeping through the audience in full spectral costume as the Poor Old Woman. Production photos from that first night show that, in spite of her limited experience on the stage, she had mastered 'the art of staring into space', with dark eye make-up accentuating the whites of her eyes. Holloway thought that she played the title role 'with creepy realism . . . [she] chanted her lines with rare musical effect, and crooned fascinatingly, if somewhat indistinctly, some lyrics'.[36]

In spite of some uncertain initial production values, *Cathleen ni Houlihan* had a power which, not long after, made Yeats uneasy. In terms of its basic plot, *Cathleen ni Houlihan* did not differ greatly from earlier plays presented by the Irish Literary Theatre. Edward Martyn's *Maeve*, Alice Milligan's *Last Feast* and Hyde's *Casadh an tSúgáin* all involved comfortable domestic worlds thrown into disarray by the entrance of a character from another, possibly supernatural or mythological, order of things, who offers the possibility of instantaneous, magical transformation. These earlier plays, however, could only imagine this transformation in terms of vague intimations of 'Tir-nan-ogue'. By setting *Cathleen ni Houlihan* in 1798, the ideology of the transformation play became manifest, as the yearning for a redeemed world was rooted in the same imaginative politics being staged nightly at the Queen's. This time, no one was baffled.

Cathleen ni Houlihan firmly re-established Yeats' nationalist credentials, initially winning over any of the Fay brothers' followers who doubted his commitment to the national cause and suggesting that it was possible to create a new theatre for 'all Irish people'. The company now began to stage plays more frequently, beginning with performances of five new plays in October 1902, including a revival of *Cathleen ni Houlihan* on 26 October as part of a programme sponsored by Cumann na nGaedeal. Five months later, rechristened the Irish National Theatre Society, the group returned to the Molesworth Hall and the balance of power shifted away from the Fays back to Yeats and Gregory, with a bill on 14 March 1903 made up of Gregory's *Twenty Five*, and Yeats' *The Hour Glass*. In October, they revived *Cathleen ni Houlihan*, premièred another new play by Yeats, *The King's Threshold*, and introduced the first work by the writer who was, briefly, to become with Yeats and Gregory the third member of the Society's uneasy ruling triumvirate: John Millington Synge.

Synge's *In the Shadow of the Glen* pushed beyond the breaking point – not for the last time – the contradictions that had been present in the Irish National Theatre Society since the manifesto of 1897. The play's basic plot resembled the 'stranger in the house' trope explored earlier by Yeats, Colum and Martyn: a woman named Nora, living in a Wicklow glen, decides to leave her husband for a wandering tramp. 'I'm thinking it's myself will be wheezing . . . lying down under the heavens when the night is cold; but you've a fine bit of talk, stranger, and it's with yourself I'll go.'[37] The first production of *In the Shadow of the Glen* did away with a standard feature of theatrical performance at the time: the footlights, instead lighting the stage with three large limelights, one from either side of the stage, and one from the back of the hall. By substituting a form of light which attempted to mimic a harsh natural light for one that was recognisably theatrical, and by doing so on a stage on which real objects were used instead of theatrical props, the visual aspect of the performance proclaimed that this was realistic theatre. However, as Ibsen had found when he had written a play about a woman named Nora who walks out of her loveless marriage, when the version of 'reality' presented on stage does not conform with what many in the audience think of as being real, removing the sheen of theatricality could be a dangerous strategy. As a review in *The Leader* put it, the play looked like 'an evil compound of Ibsen and Boucicault'. 'This subject', sniffed Holloway, 'no matter how literary-clad, could never pass with an Irish audience as a "bit of real Irish life".'[38]

In one of those debates which rage all the more fiercely because neither side could disprove the other, this 'scandalous slur' on 'Irish womanhood' – 'which we all of us know are the most virtuous in the world' – became a national issue. Yeats, who had by now learned the value of controversy, goaded the combatants in a letter published in the *United Irishman* the week before the play opened, asking: 'What is a National Theatre?' 'Only that theatre', he declared, 'where the capricious spirit that bloweth where it listeth, has for a moment found a dwelling place, has good right to call itself a National Theatre' – to which James Connolly replied sharply: 'If Ireland were self-governed, self-centred in speech and thought . . . *then* our dramatists might choose their field of action from China to Peru, and our national dramatic literature would be none the poorer.' And so the basic unresolved tensions present from the beginning were intensified: was this theatre to serve the national cause by reflecting Irish life as it was (a tendentious enough proposition in its own right); or was it to be an oblique witness to Irish freedom by providing a vehicle for the 'capricious spirit' of 'the half-dozen minds who are likely to be the dramatic imagination of Ireland for this generation'?[39]

Unfazed by the row, Yeats left the theatre shortly before midnight after the first performance of *In the Shadow of the Glen* on 17 October 1903, to send a telegram to Lady Gregory in London: 'Enthusiastic audience no trouble whatever.'[40] He had good reason to be cheerful. A long-time acquaintance, Annie Horniman, had just told him that she was prepared to subsidise the theatre. Meanwhile, Yeats himself was about to embark upon a lecture tour of the United States, where he would be the first Irish playwright since James Sheridan Knowles to be invited to lunch at the White House. In his absence, the seemingly inexorable expansion of the Theatre's repertoire continued with Pádraic Colum's *Broken Soil* in December 1903, hailed by Oliver St John Gogarty as 'national drama in the fuller sense, perhaps, than any yet presented'.[41]

'I have got the prospect of receiving a sum of money quite unexpectedly', Horniman wrote to the National Theatre Society Secretary, George Roberts, on New Year's Day, 1904. 'So let us hope that your days in the Molesworth hall will be numbered.'[42] That same month, the company premièred Yeats' *The Shadowy Waters*, Seamus MacManus' *The Townland of Tamney*, followed by Synge's *Riders to the Sea* on 25 February 1904, at which point it became clear that the company had a major writing talent in Synge. The following month, *Riders to the Sea* featured prominently in their English tour, helping to repeat the success of their first tour the previous year. 'All the players are as happy as babies', Yeats wrote to a friend, 'and I anticipate no difficulty in keeping the company together for another year at least.'[43]

A month later, in April 1904, Horniman wrote a long-expected letter to Yeats. 'I am taking the hall of the Mechanics Institute in Abbey Street', she wrote, 'and an adjoining building in Marlborough Street.' As the Mechanics Institute, and from 1901 as the National Theatre of Varieties, the 'hall' was a small theatre, which had presented variety, some early films, and the occasional Irish play, performed in contravention of the patent laws. The 'adjoining building' (much to the delight of Dublin's wits) was the city morgue. Joseph Holloway, who was an architect when he was not attending the theatre (which was seldom), was retained to oversee the renovation, and the design he produced finally forced the National Theatre Society to confront, in the unappeasable medium of bricks and mortar, the two big questions which had been there from the start: who was to be the audience for this 'national' theatre, and what was its appropriate theatrical form?

Horniman wanted the new theatre to be a pure modern space of the kind pioneered by Wagner's *Festspielhaus* in Bayreuth in 1876, with no boxes or gallery, and a single, raked fan-shaped auditorium, funnelling all of the audience's attention towards the stage. 'I am having a plan of the Bayreuth Theatre sent to Mr Holloway', she wrote to Roberts in May 1904, 'so that he can see how the seats are arranged so as to make them all good.'[44] Horniman then set off to see Bayreuth for herself, leaving Holloway to ignore Wagner's great innovation. Instead, he drew up plans for a fairly traditional auditorium that sat 562 patrons in a pit, stalls, and single curved balcony running around three sides of the house. At a time when the capacity of the Gaiety was 1,400 and the Queen's 1,950 (with 600 in the upper gallery alone) this was relatively small, although still considerably larger than the ninety-six-seat Molesworth Hall the company had been using. In the end, the most Wagnerian feature of the theatre was the electric chandelier Horniman sent over from Nuremberg.

The Abbey was smaller than its competitors partly because it lacked the upper tiers of galleries that allowed a working-class theatregoer with sixpence and a head for heights to choose between *Wolfe Tone* at the Queen's or *Hamlet* at the Gaiety. Seat prices had always been high by the standards of the time in the Molesworth Hall (where tickets were one, two or three shillings, depending on location), and the directors continued this practice in their new home, where tickets were fixed at three shillings for the stalls, two shillings for reserved seats in the balcony, and a shilling in the pit. This effectively excluded the sixpenny audience from a theatre

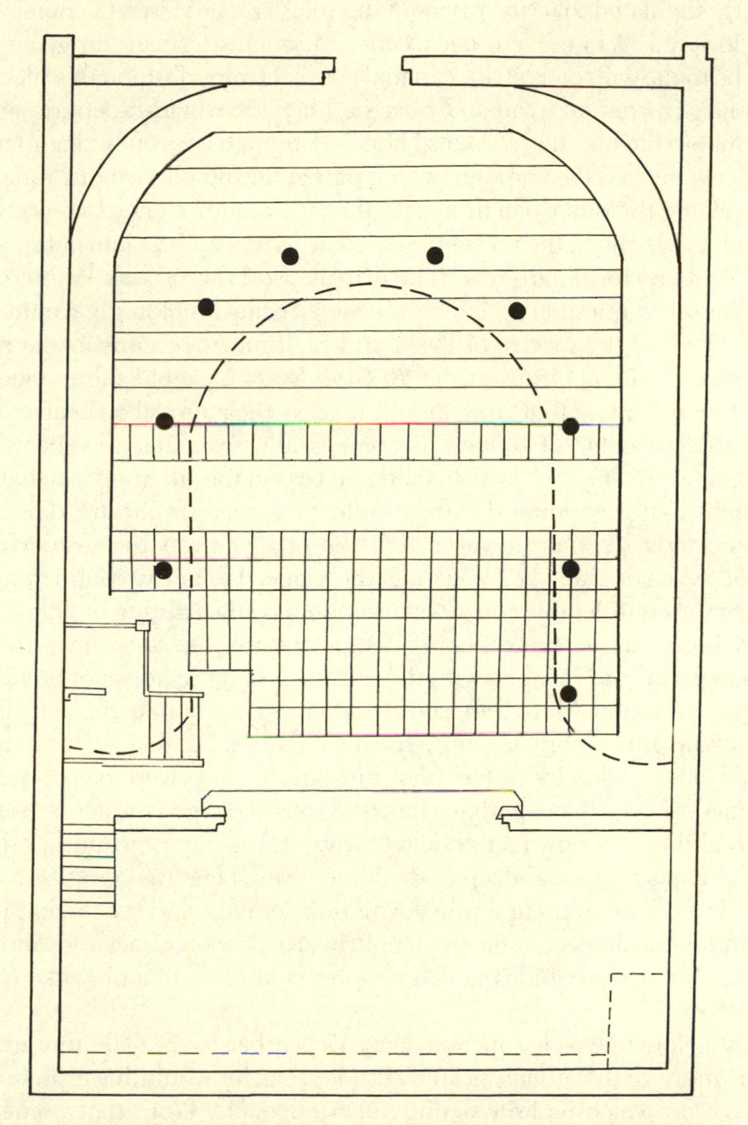

Plan 3 When the Abbey Theatre designed by Joseph Holloway opened on 27 December 1904, it was not the modern performance space for which Yeats and Annie Horniman had hoped. Instead, it was a scaled-down nineteenth-century theatre, which confined the actors to a small square behind the proscenium arch.

which, when it had been the Mechanics Institute, had prices as low as twopence and fourpence. Indeed, the lease drawn up by Horniman clearly stipulated that 'the prices of the seats can be raised of course, but not lowered . . . to prevent cheap entertainments from being given'. 'It will be to the gain of us all if I can make this the most fashionable place in Dublin', Horniman wrote to Roberts. 'Then the would-be smart people will follow and take the 3/- seats I hope.' Although its proposed upmarket audience helped the company win a patent (granted in August 1904) by convincing the other patent houses that it would not encroach on their popular audiences, the message was clear to at least one journalist, who wrote: 'The Horniman-Yeats Theatricals: No Low Persons Wanted'.[45]

The other question to which the new theatre building gave an answer involved the spectre of Ibsen and realism. As recently as the public debate over *In the Shadow of the Glen*, Yeats had told the readers of the *United Irishman* that they should take as their model a theatre 'that will reflect the life of Ireland as the Scandinavian theatre reflects the Scandinavian life'[46] – which made it reasonable to suppose that he thought that a national theatre should be a realistic theatre. His own plays clearly showed, however, that the opposite was the case. Meanwhile, when it came to designing the stage, Holloway found himself facing the considerable constraints imposed by the existing building. Initially, there was no scene dock, workshop, paint-room or even wardrobe, although this was rectified with the purchase of more adjacent buildings in 1905 and 1906. More importantly, he cut 10 feet (2.9 metres) off either side of the proscenium, leaving a frame of modest but reasonable dimensions: 21 feet wide by 14 feet high but only 15 feet deep (6.3 by 4.2 by 4.5 metres), which meant that a backstage cross obliged the actor to leave the building, trot down a public laneway, and re-enter by another door. About half as high and deep as the Gaiety, the stage was completely unsuited to the monumental transformations of light and space Yeats was beginning to discover in the work of Edward Gordon Craig and Adophe Appia, but was ideal for the claustrophobic box-set of a play like *Riders to the Sea*.

Just before the Abbey opened on 27 December 1904, Yeats announced (with more than a touch of ingratitude) that he would have preferred a stage on which realistic acting was impossible. From that point on, however, his struggle for a non-representational theatre would become a rearguard action, and by the end of 1910 forty-nine shows (out of a total of sixty-three) would use box-set interiors, putting the Abbey firmly on the road to a realistic production style which would dominate until the early

1960s. Opening its doors for the first time with Yeats' *On Baile's Strand*, *Cathleen ni Houlihan* and Lady Gregory's *Spreading the News*, its founders could reflect on the fact that they had created something which had been talked about for centuries: a theatre with a completely Irish repertoire, producing twenty-four new plays by thirteen new writers in five years, in the process beginning to shift the balance of power in the theatre from managers to playwrights. And yet, on that same December night, as Maire Ni Shiubhlaigh was playing Cathleen ni Houlihan with 'weird beauty and intense pathos' at the Abbey, across the Liffey almost two thousand people were howling for the informer's blood in Whitbread's *Sarsfield* at the Queen's.

A night at the theatre 4

The Playboy of the Western World and *Riders to the Sea*
by John Millington Synge
Abbey Theatre
Tuesday, 29 January 1907

'I feel we are beginning the fight for our lives', Lady Gregory wrote to John Millington Synge while his *Playboy of the Western World* was in rehearsal on 14 January 1907; 'and we must make no mistakes.'[1] The Abbey management had been worried about the new play from the start, closing the rehearsals to even their most devoted hangers-on, such as Joseph Holloway, who, of course, knew that something was afoot. 'Mr. [W.A.] Henderson, [the Abbey business manager] was looking gloomy at the Council Meeting of the National Literary Society', he noted in his diary, 'and I knew something was wrong at the Abbey.' 'There were too many violent oaths', Lady Gregory later wrote of the script, 'and the play itself was marred by this. I did not think it was fit to be put on the stage without cutting.'[2] Accordingly, she made sure that the problems would not rebound on Yeats, whose short farce, *The Pot of Broth* (which she had largely written) was scheduled to be performed on the same bill. 'It would be an injustice to Yeats to put a slight thin peasant farce with your elaborate peasant work', she wrote cajolingly to Synge, urging *Riders to the Sea* as an alternate curtain-raiser; to Yeats she wrote tersely: 'I was determined that Synge should not set fire to your house to roast his own pig.'[3]

The Pot of Broth was out, and *Riders to the Sea* was in, but Synge's pig was still going to roast. The auditorium on the opening night of *The Playboy of the Western World* was completely full, with box office receipts of £32 14*s*.10*d*. showing that every possible seat had been sold (in addition to which there were always friends and relations of the directors to be given complimentary seats). *Riders to the Sea* was listened to with the reverential silence it demanded. Indeed, two months earlier, in November 1906, Yeats had inserted a tetchy notice in the Abbey's journal, *The Arrow*, claiming 'Several complaints have reached us, that, at a recent performance of Mr Synge's *Riders to the Sea*, the effect of the play was all but destroyed, by the opening and shutting of the door to the Stalls.' 'At

Bayreuth, nobody is allowed to enter the auditorium till the Act is over', he told his readers, appealing to them 'to endeavour to be seated before the rise of the curtain at 8.15'.[4] In the light of what was about to happen, it is also worth keeping in mind that the previous issue of *The Arrow* had announced, for the first time ever, 'Sixpenny Seats in a part of the Pit', where seats had originally cost a shilling.

Yeats' injunctions against rattling the stall-doors were part of a programme of modifying audience behaviour that included the abolition of half-price tickets after nine fifteen (a practice still followed at the Queen's), and the darkening of the auditorium during the performance. Such changes made possible a play like *Riders to the Sea*, which demands an audience's full attention, beginning with the barely audible tap, tap, tap of the spinning wheel, and developing a steady, relentless build, through static, low-key performances. At the same time, these reforms were bringing to an end the centuries' old pleasures of theatre-going, which involved talking to other people, smoking, commenting on the play, applauding or hissing the characters, eating oranges, calling out witty responses to the action on the stage, and getting up for a drink when the action hit a dull spot. In the place of the traditional active audience, the Abbey was doing its best to create an audience who sat silently in the dark, staring intently at the stage, offering up the requisite round of applause only when the play was over – all restrictions a Queen's audience would have considered the equivalent of a custodial sentence.

When *Riders to the Sea* came to an end on 26 January with the line 'no man at all can be living for ever, and we must be satisfied,' it was followed by a short break, during which the orchestra played. Then *The Playboy of the Western World* began. At first the audience were receptive, laughing at most of the right moments, but increasingly uncertain how they were supposed to respond to this strange tale of a young man, Christy Mahon, played by Willie Fay, who wanders into a remote Mayo community claiming to have killed his father. It was by the same author as *Riders to the Sea*, which also dealt with a death in a small community in the West of Ireland, but this time everyone on the stage seemed to be uncommonly pleased with the killing, welcoming the self-proclaimed murderer into the pub which was the play's one set, and setting him up with the publican's daughter, Pegeen Mike. 'I'm thinking this night', says Christy, 'wasn't I a foolish fellow not to kill my father in the years gone by', upon which the curtain came down for the end of the first act. The audience duly applauded, and backstage Lady Gregory dashed off a telegram to Yeats, who was in Aberdeen giving a lecture: 'Play great success.'

So it continued through the beginning of act II. However, the audience was becoming increasingly uneasy, as adulation is heaped on the murderer. The audience became even more uncomfortable when Christy's dead father (who is not, of course, dead) reappears. Then, about fifteen minutes from the end of the play, the mood suddenly changes, the humour darkens, and Christy chases his father outside to kill him again, presumably with greater finality. It was at this point that the audience, like the villagers on the stage, turned nasty. In quick succession, Christy attacks his father with a shovel offstage, and returns to announce that he will marry only Pegeen Mike, even if offered 'a drift of Mayo girls standing in their shifts itself', whereupon one of the characters pulls off her petticoat to provide him with a disguise. It was supposed to be 'a drift of chosen females', but Willie Fay fluffed probably the most famous line of his career, making the insult even worse by making it more specific. By now, there was a bedlam of hisses and yells in the auditorium, but fortunately only about ten minutes of performance time left. So it was with considerable relief that the actors playing Christy and Old Mahon finally marched off leaving Pegeen Mike to lament her loss of 'the only Playboy of the Western World', before joining them in an anxious backstage retreat to the green room. When the house finally cleared, Lady Gregory sent off a second, more famous, telegram to Yeats: 'Audience broke up in disorder at the word shift.'

The next day was Sunday, so the theatre was dark. When Joseph Holloway went out for his afternoon walk on Pembroke Road, he met Frank Fay, Willie Fay and Willie's wife, Brigit O'Dempsey, who was playing Sara Tansey in *The Playboy*. 'We chatted about last night's fiasco.' 'The players had expected the piece's downfall sooner', Willie told him. Holloway praised the acting and told them 'It was a fine audience to play to. It frankly did not like the play and frankly expressed itself on the matter, having patiently listened to it until the fatal phrase came and proved the last straw'.[5]

Yeats arrived back in Dublin the following day, Monday, just in time to see a tiny audience take their seats, with fewer than eighty people sitting in a theatre capable of holding more than five hundred. If Saturday evening had been a case of an audience honestly protesting against a play it did not like, Monday was a completely different affair. After listening politely and patiently to *Riders to the Sea*, about forty members of the audience sitting in the pit (identified by Yeats as supporters of Arthur Griffith), began stomping their feet, booing and hissing as soon as the curtain rose on *The Playboy of the Western World.* The actors trudged through the sea of abuse for a while, until Willie Fay stopped the performance, announcing that he was a Mayo man himself, and threatening to call the police. As a patent theatre, the Abbey was entitled to police protection, but this threat only incensed the audience further, as did the arrival of half a dozen police officers, who stood around stolidly but ineffectually until Lady Gregory and Synge asked them to leave. From the stalls, Lord Walter Fitzgerald made a short speech pleading for the actors' right to be heard, but he too was hooted down. And so the performance continued, for the most part inaudibly, and even when the players had made their final, merciful exit the rumpus continued until both the house and stage lights were put out, finally silencing the remaining protestors with darkness.

'With the coming of Yeats', the newspaper editor W. P. Ryan commented to W.A. Henderson, 'I knew that the trouble would be aggravated.'[6] He was, of course, absolutely right. 'The position of attack is far stronger than the position of defence', Yeats had told Frank Fay a couple of years earlier,[7] and true to his own advice, he went on the attack. He began the day on Tuesday by accompanying Synge, who was miserable with influenza, to the Metropole Hotel, where he gave an interview to the *Freeman's Journal*, in which he declared the autonomy of art, and the need for exaggeration in great art. Of course, Yeats did not expect those who had protested the previous night to understand this, he said, because he could see 'the people who formed the opposition had no books in their houses' – a sentence the *Freeman's Journal* helpfully set in large type when it printed the interview the next day. He went on to say that such 'commonplace and ignorant people' were incapable of following a great leader because they had wrapped themselves up in 'societies, clubs, and leagues', and 'they have been so long in mental servitude that they cannot understand life if their head is not in some bag'.[8] Synge volunteered that the offensive word 'shift' was used in Douglas Hyde's *Love Songs of Connaught* (*albeit*, in Irish), but Yeats was providing much more interesting copy, and Synge's remarks were ignored in the ensuing battle. Meanwhile, back in the theatre, Lady Gregory was doing her bit by suggesting to a nephew that it would be useful if he could bring along to the theatre that night 'a few fellow athletes' from Trinity College, 'that we might be sure of some able-bodied helpers in case of an attack on the stage',[9] not realising that since the eighteenth century mobs of drunken Trinity students had been used in Dublin to provoke – not prevent – theatre riots.

Shortly after seven o'clock that evening, a crowd began to gather around the pit-door of the Abbey on Marlborough Street. By seven-thirty the forty or so young men waiting for the doors to open noticed a posse of policemen being let in through the stage door. At ten to eight, the house doors opened, and there was a rush for the sixpenny seats in the pit. At about eight o'clock twenty Trinity students entered the building in varying degrees of inebriation, and were given free seats in the more expensive stalls. They were accompanied by a Galwayman in a large overcoat (a later satire refers to him as 'Napoleon'), who decided to get things moving by offering to fight anyone in the pit, before standing up on a chair to make a speech, which came to the resounding conclusion: 'I am a little bit drunk and don't know what I am saying' – words duly reported in the next morning's papers. Most of the audience, including the pit he had offered to fight, enjoyed his performance, and so he obliged their interest by weaving his way up to the side of the stage, and playing an unsteady waltz on the theatre's piano, before being escorted back to his seat by the stewards, protesting 'they won't allow me to speak although I am a Labour member' (general laughter). Yeats and Gregory were by now in the theatre, and at eight-fifteen precisely the curtain went up on *Riders to the Sea* to an auditorium only half full. As had been the case on previous nights, and as would be the case for the rest of the week, it was listened to in respectful silence, and enthusiastically applauded when it was over.

At that point Yeats stood up to pour oil on the hot coals by announcing that there would be a public debate on *The Playboy* and 'the freedom of the theatre' the following Monday, at the same time warning the audience that 'no man has the right to interfere with another man who wants to hear the play'. The play would be performed until it was heard, he told them, 'and our patience will last longer than your patience'. Then, at three minutes past nine, after a few Irish airs from the orchestra, the curtain went up for the third time on *The Playboy of the Western World.* The opening scene was listened to politely, but when Christy made his entrance the audience in the pit started to stomp their feet and make as much noise as possible, while those in the stalls cheered and clapped with equal vigour, forcing the management to turn up the house lights. The Galwayman took this as the cue for some fisticuffs, and Yeats at first tried to restrain him, and then returned to the stage, which the actors had abandoned. Yeats pleaded with the audience to listen to a play by 'a distinguished fellow-countryman of theirs', telling them they would impair the Irish reputation for 'courtesy and intelligence', at which point someone in the audience began to blow on a bugle. Meanwhile, the Galwayman was calling out to him, 'Woa, woa, you chap there. Woa, be a sportsman', while trying to shake free from the friends who were holding him, in the process upending some of the chairs in the stalls. After he was finally evicted by Synge and Ambrose Power, the burly actor playing Old Mahon, Yeats announced that 'we have persuaded one man who was, I regret to say, intoxicated, to leave the meeting. I appeal to all of you who are sober to listen.'

A voice from the pit: 'We are all sober here' (loud applause).

After a short conference, Yeats, Lady Gregory and Synge called in the police, who had been backstage throughout, and, with the help of another of Gregory's nephews, Hugh Lane, began pointing out particularly noisy members of the pit to be evicted. More police arrived, and the orchestra added an extra level of unreality to proceedings by striking up a few jaunty tunes to accompany the arrests. An uneasy calm descended, but as soon as the houselights went down and the play recommenced, the uproar started up again under the cover of darkness, with the stalls and the pit stopping just short of open warfare with one another as cries of 'That's not the West' were repeated again and again. One member of the audience suggested that the police arrest Christy Mahon for the murder of his father, at which the whole house laughed. The police, aided by the managers, continued to pick out members of the audience, some of whom were simply evicted, while others were taken into custody and later charged. In the course of the next hour, things continued more or less like this, with the curtain lowered from time to time when the performance became more than usually inaudible. The Galwayman reappeared, like a belated Old Mahon, in the third act at around ten-twenty, his head reeling from more drink rather than from the blow of a loy, and repeated his offer to fight anyone in the pit. He was forestalled, however, by his friends in the stalls launching into a rousing chorus of 'God Save the King', which was matched by an equally energetic version of 'God Save Ireland' from the pit, by which time it was ten-thirty, and the final curtain fell on the poor shell-shocked actors.

Once they were finally outside the theatre, the groups in the pit and stalls continued taunting each other as they crossed the Liffey on the students' way home to Trinity, picking up supporters in the street. The name-calling finally erupted into a violent brawl in Westmoreland Street, just outside the walls of the college (and a police station), where there were further arrests. By the next evening, Wednesday, the house had picked up, with about 420 in attendance, and, in spite of the publication earlier that day of Yeats' provocative interview with the *Freeman's Journal*, the night was less rowdy, although it was still difficult to hear much of the play, and the police continued to arrest protestors in the audience. Once again, there were fights in the street afterwards. The worst was over, however, and as the week went on, the protests gradually lost some of their energy. Indeed, they were becoming self-parodic, so that when on Thursday night Old Mahon describes Christy as 'a poor fellow would get drunk on the smell of a pint', someone in the pit called out 'That's not Western life', to the general amusement of the whole house. The Saturday matinée, although thinly attended, was relatively quiet, and by the final performance on Saturday evening Abbey decorum had re-established itself. 'If we can hold our audiences now for a few weeks', Synge wrote to Lady Gregory a week later, 'we shall be in a better position than ever.'[10]

Throughout the affair, it is possible to trace a thread of drunken hilarity weaving its way through the more serious strands, and by the time of the great debate on the freedom of the theatre on Monday, 4 February, this had worked its way to the surface. Contributions ranged from a long, and much interrupted, account of the Covent Garden riots by the theatre historian W. J. Lawrence, to a medical disquisition on sexual melancholia at which 'many ladies, whose countenances plainly indicated intense feelings of astonishment and pain, rose and left the place'. John B. Yeats made a sly speech about Irish piety, provoking the audience to call on Yeats to 'kill your father'. 'Where's the loy?' someone called from the back of the hall. Yeats, in full evening dress, stood up to speak several times, and, in the words of one biographer, made a speech more 'deliberately offensive to a Dublin audience' than any he had ever made in his life, perhaps trying to shock them into seriousness. He claimed that he would not be swayed by intimidation, and that 'we' – the Protestant directors of the Abbey – 'have not such pliant bones, and did not learn in the houses that bred us a so suppliant knee ("Oh", groans and hisses).'[11] Much of what was said, however, was inaudible, and although there were some informed speeches from the stage, the real performers were, once again, in the audience which kept up a barrage of heckling throughout the night. 'I was sorry while there that we had ever let such a set inside the theatre', Gregory wrote to Synge the next morning, 'but I am glad today, and think it was spirited and showed we were not repenting or apologising.'[12]

By the time the Monday night debate had concluded, it was clear that the *Playboy* riots had offended against an imaginative geography, which idealised the western seaboard (the part of the country most remote from English influence) as the home both of what Synge had called 'Cuchulainoid' heroics, and of an equally sentimentalised notion of Irish femininity. These were, of course, political issues, manifestations of divergent understandings of nationality separating the lower-middle-class, predominantly Catholic nationalist, audience who sang 'God Save Ireland' in the sixpenny pit, from the upper-middle-class, predominantly unionist, audience who sang 'God Save the King' in the three-shilling stalls. At the same time, the schism between these two groups was also social, and their conflict was in part the product of conflicting understandings of correct theatre etiquette.

When the first protestors were brought to trial, the judge, Justice Mahony, took no account of the fact that the offences had been committed in a theatre, and fined them all the maximum forty shillings, as if they had been disturbing the peace by screaming abuse at passers-by in the street. However, those charged later in the week came up before Justice Wall, who had taken the time to look up precedents for theatre rioting, and had come upon Charles Kendall Bushe's instructions to the jury in the Bottle Riot eighty-four years earlier. 'The rights of an audience in a theatre are very well defined', Justice Wall told the court. 'They might cry down a play which they disliked, or hiss and booh the actors who depended for their positions on the good-will of audiences, but they must not act in such a manner as had a tendency to excite uproar or disturbance.' The only condition limiting this right to 'cry down a play' was that the action must be spontaneous. 'If premeditated by a number of persons combined beforehand to cry down a performance or an actor', Wall said, citing Bushe, 'it becomes criminal.'[13]

Of course, an audience used to paying sixpence for their seats knew this, for codes of behaviour more than two centuries old persisted in the galleries of the large theatres. In the Abbey, with its stern warnings against late-comers rattling the stall doors, there had been a conscious effort on the part of the proprietors to restrict the rights of a theatre audience to something more in line with upper-middle-class notions of decorum. Much of the heckling and hissing Yeats and Gregory found so offensive was in fact the audience asserting its traditional rights. Joseph Holloway, who appreciated the responsiveness of the audience at the Queen's Theatre, recognised as much when he had praised the audience's 'frankness' on the opening night of the *Playboy*. So too did Justice Wall, who imposed the minimum fine of ten shillings on the protestors brought before him, telling the court he thought the matter should never have come to trial. Newspaper comment across the political spectrum drifted towards his position, praising the protestors who were voicing a genuine dislike of the play, condemning protestors who had planned a disturbance, and almost uniformly denouncing the Abbey's decision to involve the courts in a situation governed by clearly understood protocols of audience behaviour. In the end, Synge's *Playboy* may have helped change what would be performed on Irish stages; but equally its first run would change what happened in Irish auditoria. 'The stage became spectators', concluded *The Abbey Row*, a satirical account of the affair, 'And the audience were players. Whether the play was good or bad, / It really didn't matter.'[14]

CHAPTER 5

'Not understanding the clock', 1904–1921

'Each of us dreams of some city or season in the history of the world in which he would especially desire to have lived', observed a commentator in a Dublin magazine, *To-day*, in 1904.

> One looks back in his ecstasies to the Athens of Pericles, and another meditates rapturously on some discoloured Tuscan village in the days of Michael Angelo. For myself, if I had the choice, I would take no year I ever heard of in exchange for the present . . . The score of new movements which have filled recent years in Ireland with strange hopes have affected Dublin in a degree scarcely to be equalled anywhere else.[1]

For many, it was as if a wrinkle in time had occurred, and the year 1904 had folded into 1604 or 1504. These were the years in which Synge would make his famous comparison between 'those of us who know the people' in Edwardian Ireland and 'the Elizabethan dramatist taking down his ink horn and sitting down to his work using many phrases that he had just heard'; or in which Patrick Pearse would claim that 'there is in our playwrightship something of the naïveté of the Moralities and Mysteries'[2] – thinking perhaps of Douglas Hyde's Mystery play, *Dráma Breithe Chríosta* (1902). As usual, it was Yeats who found the best phrase for a time so temptingly out of joint. 'You and I and Synge', he mused in an open letter to Lady Gregory, 'not understanding the clock, set out to bring again the theatre of Shakespeare or rather perhaps of Sophocles.'[3]

If the opening years of the twentieth century were a time of an imagined innocence for the Irish theatre, by 1904 it was an innocence under pressure. In the early days of the Irish Literary Theatre, the actors had been amateurs, and consequently had not undergone the strict, but unofficial, system of apprenticeship by which professional actors of the time learned their craft. Of course, Frank Fay had herded the young actors to the sixpenny gallery of the Gaiety and Theatre Royal, before moving back to a cramped rehearsal space for vocal exercises. However, with the exception of Willie Fay, none of the first Abbey company had experienced the more usual introduction to the actor's art at the time, such as playing the Second Constable in *The Shaughraun* on a six-month tour of the English provincial theatres. Yeats recognised the value of this wise naïveté early, writing that 'the more experience an actor has had of the stage . . . almost of a certainty the worse [he is] for my theatre'.[4] Following his cue, when the National Theatre Society first played London in March 1903, the *Daily Express* approved of their 'simple and homely' performance, which it contrasted favourably with the usual offerings of the London stage, on which there was 'too much complication, too much "business", and too much vulgarity'.[5]

It was not just training that made the new Irish actors different; equally important in the neophyte years was the effect of playing in performance spaces such as St Teresa's Hall or the Molesworth Hall, where the small stages forced the actors from the beginning to use voice rather than movement. 'When they do move', enthused *The Times Literary Supplement* during the 1903 London tour, 'it is without premeditation . . . even with a little natural clumsiness, as of people who are not conscious of being stared at in public. Hence a delightful effect of spontaneity.'[6] To match its painfully tiny stage, the Molesworth Hall had only six rows of seats, so that all ninety-six audience members were close to the low stage, and almost at eye-level with the actors. Since the Restoration, almost all theatres had been designed so that half of the people in the audience (in the pit and stalls) were below the actor's line of sight, and half above (in the case of the upper gallery, considerably so).[7] A good actor in a traditional theatre such as the Queen's or Belfast Opera House had to learn how to use the rake of the stage, working the entire audience, making eye contact with theatregoers in the pit, the stalls, and up to the highest gallery, pulling them all together in a virtuoso performance of inclusivity. The distinctive practice of 'staring into space' – playing in almost perfect stillness, eyes front – which marked early productions of the Irish Literary Theatre and the Irish National Theatre Society, could only have been developed in theatres in which the entire audience, seated at a height to stare back, was already a communal unit before the performance began.

The renovated Mechanics Institute, to which the company moved in 1904, with its single balcony and raked stage, retained something of the intimacy of those early spaces, although the balcony forced actors to play above their line of sight. However, the real transformation of this inanimate, intimate style of acting took place outside of Ireland. Although the 1903 London tour netted only £13 profit, it was a critical

Photograph 4. Playboys of the Wild West. Cultures collide when the Abbey company dress as cowboys while on their 1911 US tour with Shaw's pastiche Wild West play, *The Shewing Up of Blanco Posnet.* This linen cloth was sold during the tour to raise money for Hugh Lane's collection of paintings. Portraits at the bottom are: Yeats, Abbey actors Sara Allgood, Eithne Magee and Sidney Morgan (top row), and J. A. O'Rourke, J. M. Kerrigan, Udolphus Wright and Fred O'Donovan (bottom row).

success, and soon the company began to feel the same pressures that had forced Boucicault and Whitbread to take to the road. While helping to organise the 1904 London tour, Stephen Gwynn told the National Theatre Society's secretary, George Roberts, that the company could make £160 to £170 per night if they rented the Royal Court in Sloane Square – and this was at a time when the Society's account books show net cash assets of £75, most of which had been donated.[8]

So, in 1904 the National Theatre Society began annual visits to London, Oxford and Cambridge, moving on to a tour of England, Scotland and Wales in 1906 and 1907, where they played theatres such as the Albert Hall, Leeds, the Theatre Royal, Cardiff and the Edinburgh Lyceum. In September 1911, the company set out on their first American tour, playing thirty-one cities in five months, returning in February 1912, and then promptly setting out again for a five-week engagement of twice-nightly shows at the London Coliseum, with its revolving stage and more than 2,000 seats in four tiers. Immediately afterwards, they set out on a tour of English variety theatres. Looking up at the sheer precipice of the auditorium from the centre of the Coliseum's cavernous stage (later used for ballet and ice-skating shows) it must have seemed a long way in a short time from St Teresa's Hall on Dublin's Camden Street. At that point, the days of staring into space were at an end.

It is hardly surprising, given this velocity of change, that a series of internecine battles raged in the Abbey from 1904 onwards, as it transformed itself from a group of amateur players who could initially only perform a few weeks a year, to a fully professional company, managing a theatre and meeting touring commitments. 'Under the Old Society', Lady Gregory wrote in 1905, 'those of us who had private means of any kind, were liable for all we possessed, and it was impossible to go on that way when the business of the Society was growing into larger proportions. Every other change followed logically from that first one.'[9] One of the earliest moves towards professional status came on 24 October 1906, when the National Theatre Society registered itself under the corporate name by which it continues to trade, the National Theatre Society Limited, with Yeats, Lady Gregory and Synge as directors, and Frederick Ryan as Secretary – but without many of the actors with whom the Society began, who left in protest at what they saw as a betrayal of their ideals. 'I think we have seen the end of democracy in the theatre', Yeats wrote to a friend, 'for I go to Dublin at the end of the week to preside at a meeting summoned to abolish it.' For the first time, the actors began to receive salaries, although, as Terence Brown points out, even the top rate of 15 shillings a week offered to Frank Fay was only what a cook in service earned at the time.[10] By January 1907, the directors had hired Ben Iden Payne (who had been with the Benson touring company) on a salary of £500 per year to direct everything except peasant plays, which remained the preserve of Willie Fay. Although Payne lasted only a short time, by January 1908 Willie Fay, Frank Fay, and Brigit O'Dempsey all felt they had been pushed far enough from control of the company they had helped to found, and quit. The core group of performers who remained – Sara Allgood, J. M. Kerrigan, Máire O'Neill and Fred O'Donovan – increasingly came to see themselves as professional actors rather than as cultural revolutionaries.

While in its business offices the Abbey was shaping itself into something like a professional theatre, its directors still acknowledged a duty to startle audiences out of complacency, and so it made sense that they should have kept in contact with George Bernard Shaw, who had a genius for it. 'I am not an ordinary playwright in general practice', Shaw once wrote. 'I am a specialist in immoral and heretical plays.'[11] Shaw had originally written *John Bull's Other Island* in 1904 with at least one eye on a possible Abbey production: but the directors had rejected it, Shaw claiming that it was 'uncongenial to the whole spirit of the neo-Gaelic movement',[12] Yeats saying that they did not have the actors to play it (both of which were true). In 1909, just as *The Playboy of the Western World* was ceasing to shock Irish audiences (it was revived after Synge's death on 24 March of that year) the Lord Chamberlain's Office in London provided the perfect opportunity for Shaw to come to the Abbey, when it banned Shaw's 'Sermon in Crude Melodrama', *The Shewing-Up of Blanco Posnet.*

Blanco Posnet was a deliberate snare, designed to trap the English censorship laws in their own absurdities. Using a setting borrowed from a Wild West play and originally written to be played as a children's charity benefit, it is just the sermon that Shaw claimed it to be, as Blanco, a horse-thief about to be lynched, reveals that he gave up the horse he had stolen to save a sick child. Blanco is disgusted with himself for his weakness, feeling that having spent years trying to 'give God the good-bye', God had caught him in the end. 'He's a sly one', Blanco tells his accusers. 'He's a mean one . . . He lets you run loose until you think youre shut of Him; and then, when you least expect it, He's got you.'[13] Of course, the story of a sinner surprised by Christian charity was one that had been heard innumerable times from the pulpit; but the Lord Chamberlain still could not pass a play that called God 'a sly one', and banned it on grounds of blasphemy.

Shaw sent *Blanco Posnet* to Yeats and Lady Gregory, who made it clear that they were spoiling for a fight by announcing that they would stage it on 25 August 1909, during the busiest week of the Irish theatrical calendar (coinciding with the Royal Dublin Society's Horse Show). According to the letter of the law, they were entitled to stage the play, for the Lord Chamberlain's writ did not extend to Ireland. Indeed, as the theatre historian W. J. Lawrence reminded readers of the *Freeman's Journal*, Ireland's exclusion from the Lord Chamberlain's jurisdiction had been tested shortly after the 1737 Licensing Act became law, when Thomas Sheridan staged a version of Henry Brooke's banned play, *Gustavus Vasa* in 1744. At the same time, most plays staged professionally in Ireland (including those of the Abbey, whose account books record fees paid to the Censor's Office) were submitted to the English censor so they could be toured. Moreover, the patent (which the Abbey had held since 1904) had been granted by the Lord Lieutenant, who was entitled to withdraw it if they breached its terms by staging offensive material.

Consequently, both Dublin Castle and the Abbey were holding strong cards when they settled into a game of bluff and brinksmanship, with the authorities threatening to revoke the Abbey's patent, and the theatre responding by making the issue into a national one. 'If our patent is in danger', Yeats and Lady Gregory declared in a public statement on 22 August 1909, 'it is because the decisions of the English Censor are being brought into Ireland.' This forcibly recruited the hard-line nationalists who had opposed Synge's *Playboy*. 'We are bound to stand by the Theatre in its fight against the imposition of British Censorship', wrote an out-manoeuvred Pearse in *An Claidheamh Soluis*.[14] For their part, the Abbey directors made sure that things did not get out of control as they had during the *Playboy* riots by hiking the price of pit tickets eightfold, to four shillings, thereby excluding the sixpenny audience who had objected so forcibly to the *Playboy*. In the end, the Castle blinked, hoping for objections from the churches once the play was staged; none were forthcoming, and *Blanco Posnet* played to large (and well-heeled) audiences, most of whom enjoyed it, but left a bit mystified as to the source of the controversy. In the end, it was an almost perfect public relations victory for the Abbey.

From the Abbey's point of view, the timing of the *Blanco Posnet* row was propitious, for the Dublin theatre world was in transition. Just three weeks after the *Playboy* riots, on 18 March 1907, the Queen's had closed for extensive renovations. It remained closed for two years, re-opening in 1909 with the auditorium rebuilt by the Dublin architect R. J. Stirling as a tight horseshoe, with a balcony and upper gallery extending further than the old galleries, and a much shallower pit. While the sightlines, particularly from the boxes, were poor in the new theatre, the acoustics were superb, and the audience were much closer to the stage than they had been in the original house – a situation which suited the old Queen's audience perfectly, in that it was now easier than ever for them to talk back to the actors on the stage. However, J. W. Whitbread's patent had expired during the renovation work, and for the first few years after re-opening the new management made little effort to re-establish its status as 'the Home of Irish Drama'.

This meant that for a period of about five years after 1907, the Abbey was the only patent theatre in Dublin to offer Irish plays on a regular basis, further accelerating its assimilation into the theatrical mainstream. At the same time, the theatre's patron, Annie Horniman, was becoming increasingly worried about its nationalist agenda, and the situation was not helped by the deterioration of her personal relationship with Yeats. The final straw came when the theatre failed to close to mark the death of Edward VII, and by the end of 1910, Horniman and her annual subsidy were gone to Manchester to set up a repertory company with Iden Payne. No longer dependant on patronage, the reconstituted National Theatre Society Limited was now a fully commercial theatre with fixed capital of £1,000, divided into £1 shares – 376 of which were held by Yeats and Lady Gregory. By 1911, the Abbey was paying its first regular royalties to its playwrights (which may explain why the 1911–12 season was dominated by anonymous Medieval morality plays). In the same year, the new company had its licence renewed for a further twenty-one years, with no objections from the other major patent holders.

By 1910, the original amateur ethos of the Abbey was threadbare. 'Most of them are professional actors', complained William Archer, 'inasmuch as they make acting the business of their lives. Nevertheless, their general style is one of imperfect accomplishment.'[15] At around the same time, Yeats was beginning to realise that the early minimalism of Abbey scenography was getting tired. In the beginning, he had insisted that play designs used no more than two (or at most three) basic colours: one for the backdrop, the other for the costumes. As Abbey staging began to drift toward a more conventional naturalism, however, what had been hailed originally as a refreshing visual restraint increasingly revealed the story hidden in the Abbey account books. Records for the year ending 31 December 1903, for instance, show that in the early years, scenery was the company's biggest expenditure after hall rental. By contrast, in the financial quarter ending May 1911, the Abbey spent nothing on scenery, and only slightly more on props (£6 7*s*.6½*d*.) than was spent on stationery and stamps (£4 16*s*.3½*d*.). Often, the only figure entered for scenery is an actuarial amount to cover depreciation.[16]

Consequently, Yeats was elated in January 1910 when he found what he thought was a cheap but aesthetically exciting solution in Edward Gordon Craig's designs for a series of moving screens, which would allow transformations of light and space without the need for hydraulics or a fly system. 'We shall have a means of staging everything that is not naturalistic', Yeats wrote excitedly to Lady Gregory on 8 January 1910, 'and out of this invention may grow a completely new method even for our naturalistic plays.'[17] By the summer of 1910, Yeats had Joseph Holloway at work on removing the rake from the Abbey's stage (since the screens moved on castors, and would have rolled off a sloping stage) and by January of the following year, they were used in a new production of his play, *The Hour Glass*, and in a new play by Lady Gregory, *The Deliverer*. Over the next five years, Yeats put much effort into rewriting his earlier plays with Craig's innovations in mind. By 1915, however, the screens were gathering dust in the Abbey lumber-room, partly because they had an alarming tendency to fall over, and partly because Craig would not license their use on tour.

By 1911, a playwright could earn as much in royalties from three nights in a large venue as the theatre's manager earned in an entire financial quarter. It was thus a cause for frequent begrudging comment that plays by the Abbey directorate featured so prominently in the tour programmes. At the same time, while touring tied the Abbey more closely than ever before to the world of commercial theatre, it also spread its myth. In New York during the winter tour of 1911–12, *The Playboy of the Western World* met with organised riots far more violent than anything experienced in Dublin, with the actors at the Maxine Elliott Theatre weathering a barrage of rotten vegetables and stinkbombs. However, Theodore Roosevelt joined Lady Gregory in her box for the play's second New York performance, and by the end of the tour Gregory would tell the New York *Sun* that 'the whole intellect of America is with us'. Moreover, after the tour was over, Eugene O'Neill, Susan Glaspell and Robert Edmond Jones would all speak of its influence on their work in the American theatre, with Jones in particular influenced by the 'very simple' set designs, even as audiences at home were beginning to tire of the same bare sets.[18] Similarly, as Dublin audiences increasingly associated the theatre with undemanding rural comedies, the tours helped to forge a link between the Abbey and one of the lessons of modernism: art did not soothe or moralise – it surprised and shocked.

As the Abbey players roamed America, trailing the rich odour of stinkbombs and scandal, they attracted increasing media and scholarly attention around the world. As early as 1904, newspaper readers in Sydney, Australia were being told about the 'Celtic Renaissance', while Yeats would remark in a 1908 programme note that 'in Japan there are some who believe very erroneously that we are a great success, and even making money.'[19] By 1912, there were two studies of Synge in print: Francis Buckley, *John Millington Synge* (London, 1912); P. P. Howe, *J. M Synge: A Critical Study* (London, 1912). Meanwhile, Maurice Bourgeois, at work on yet a third, was hounding the Abbey's long-suffering business manager, W. A. Henderson, for information about the playwright. When Christy in *The Playboy of the Western World* says he is to go 'coaching out through limbo with my father's ghost', Bourgeois wanted to know, 'is Limbo the village where the play takes place, and if so, can it be identified with some actual village in the West?'[20]

If the Abbey's international image originated in phantom villages in the west of Ireland, its personnel increasingly came from the Belfast/Dublin/Cork touring axis that had been the spine of Irish theatrical geography for almost two hundred years. For instance, the Abbey's two most prominent managers between 1910 and 1920 – Lennox Robinson and St John Ervine – were from Cork and Belfast, respectively. Robinson grew up about twenty miles outside Cork city in Ballymoney, but when 'something special' was playing at the Cork Opera House 'a late train would be run to Bandon and Clonakilty, and there was a junction on that line only six miles from home'. 'My sister and I would seize such opportunities', he later recalled, 'parking our bicycles at Gaggin Junction . . . and getting to Ballymoney after midnight.' On the other end of the touring circuit in Belfast, Ervine was watching many of the same shows. 'I date the beginning of my serious interest in the theatre', he later wrote, 'from the visits of Forbes-Robertson and Gertrude Elliott and Henry Irving and Ellen Terry to the Grand Opera House in Belfast about the year 1900.'[21]

Robinson and Ervine were not the only ones watching attentively from the galleries of their local opera houses. Many of the period's most popular playwrights came either from Cork (including T. C. Murray, R. J. Ray and J. Bernard MacCarthy) or from Belfast and its environs (George Shiels and Rutherford Mayne). For almost all of them, an apprenticeship in the theatre began in the gallery or pit of the local opera house, watching Shakespeare, Pinero, Boucicault, Wild West shows, and everything else that came along. The big touring shows, with their displays of virtuoso acting and spectacular stage designs, gave this generation a passion for the theatre they were to keep all their lives. And then, the Abbey touring company arrived in Cork in 1907, and Belfast in 1908, presenting a form of theatre that was equally compelling, but was also simple. The sets could be built by any carpenter, the lighting was usually a basic amber wash, the acting was spartan, the plays were seldom more than one act long, and were often written in something more or less approximating the speech of real Irish people. More than one person in those early audiences looked at these productions, and thought: I can do that. Indeed, extending the touring circuit one step further north, in 1908 Graham Moffat in Glasgow wrote his first play, *Annie Laurie*, and founded the Scottish National Players after seeing the Abbey on tour.[22]

Hence, it makes a kind of symbolic sense that the Ulster Literary Theatre's founding myth is set on the same Dublin–Belfast train that carried the touring companies. In 1902, two members of the Protestant National Association, Bulmer Hobson and Lewis Purcell had set up what they had hoped would be the Ulster branch of the Irish Literary Theatre. For Hobson, in particular, the new theatre was intended to be one of the cultural arms of a non-sectarian revolution. However, when they travelled to Dublin to put the idea to Yeats, Hobson and Purcell found him 'haughty, aloof' and unwilling to expand the franchise. Later that evening, as the train carried them back to Belfast, disappointment turned to defiance. 'We decided to write our own plays', Hobson later recalled. 'And we did.'[23]

By November 1904, the newly named Ulster Literary Theatre had a base at 109 Donegall Street in Belfast, and its own journal, *Uladh*. 'Ulster has its own way of things', announced *Uladh*. 'At present we can only say that our talent is more satiric than poetic. That will probably remain the broad difference between the Ulster and the Leinster schools.'[24] As manifestos go, this was to prove more than usually accurate. Between 1904 and 1930, the Ulster Literary Theatre produced forty-seven original plays, of which only six were mythological plays; the majority were either political satires or rural comedies with a satiric edge, and these would be the company's most successful productions. Indeed, shortly after the Abbey made its first appearance in Belfast on 30 November 1908, George Morrow responded with a Synge pastiche, *The Mist That Does Be on the Bog* (1909), followed in 1912 by a hugely popular mythological parody, *Thompson in Tir-na-nOg* (1912).

As early as 1905, in Lewis Purcell's *The Enthusiast*, the basic features of the Ulster comedy as it would survive into the 1960s were already in place: a distinctive double-edged satirical comedy, directed equally against the divided community and its would-be saviour, made palatable by the comic use of dialect. In *The Enthusiast*, for instance, James McKinstry returns home from university in Belfast to his County Antrim farm, decked out in a 'white, india-rubber tap coat and yella' boots' to preach the gospel of the co-operative movement to farmers split along sectarian lines. Near the end of the play, the McKinstrys' hired man, Rab, gives an account of the mass meeting called up by James to set up a farming co-operative. 'Then Andy Moore got up – no' young Andy, the oul man – an' he said they were goin' till upset the Crown and Constitution, an' at the wind up he axed Jamie if he cud gie scripture for it, an' Jamie as much as said he cudn't. Then somebody shouted "Socialism", and Ned Grahme – he wuz drunk – he shouted it was a Fenian thing, an' he kep' shoutin' that the whole time. An' sez I to myself, "this is goin' to be the warm meetin." '[25] *The Enthusiast* 'really did impress me', recalls one audience member, 'because for the first time I saw the kind of people that I knew and lived among in County Antrim and County Derry there alive and talking as they talked.'[26]

In many respects, however, the most important Ulster play to be staged in the first decades of the twentieth century was neither a comedy, nor was it staged in Belfast. It was St John Ervine's tragedy, *Mixed Marriage*, first performed at the Abbey on 30 March 1911. That it should have been staged at the Abbey had less to do with the sensitivities of Belfast audiences than with what was already evident as the Abbey's greatest strength: its ability to absorb talent from other theatrical centres on the island. Set in the home of a working-class Protestant family in East Belfast at the time of a shipyard strike (possibly the Belfast dock strike of 1907), *Mixed Marriage* crosses class and sectarian loyalties by making the romantic relationship of a Catholic girl, Nora, and a Protestant boy, Hugh, emblematic of the potential for unity in a divided working class. 'Can't ye see, they're doin' the very thing ye want Irelan' to do', says Hugh's mother. 'It's Cathlik an' Prodesan joinin' hans thegither.' However, as the play moves inexorably to its frightening fourth act, in which the family are huddled together in the familiar kitchen set made unfamiliar by the riot which rages outside, Hugh's mother acknowledges that 'It's a quare hard job til stap bigotry wance it's started.' The play ends with Nora rushing off-stage into the riot, to be killed. As an apparently intractable sectarianism came to be seen as one of the defining features of Ulster society, so too would the basic *Romeo and Juliet* plot, first used in *Mixed Marriage*, become a defining feature of Ulster dramaturgy.[27]

While the Ulster Literary Theatre was creating its own identity on the northern end of the Irish theatre axis, the same process was underway on the southern end. When the Abbey brought *Riders to the Sea* to Cork on 15 and 16 September 1907, among those in the small audience of about fifty was Lennox Robinson, who later recalled: 'It came on me as a flash, as a revelation. Play-material could be found outside one's own door, at one's own fireside.'[28] Also in the audience that night was Daniel Corkery, who one week later sketched in his diary the idea for his first play. Corkery had been involved three years earlier with the short-lived Cork National Theatre Society, and in November 1908 established the Cork Dramatic Society, 'to do for Cork what similar societies have done for Dublin and Belfast'. Based in An Dún, an old Gaelic League room over a livery stable on Queen Street, he was soon joined by Terence MacSwiney, who would write four of the eighteen original plays the group would stage.

As was the case in Belfast and Dublin, the Cork Dramatic Society struggled with the gap between what its founders wanted to accomplish, and what it could reasonably stage or expect its audience to enjoy. While Corkery would later become (unfairly) emblematic of a puritanical cultural xenophobia, both he and MacSwiney saw the modernist Europe-wide revolution in theatrical form as akin to their own revolutionary project. 'The natural thing for a city to do is build itself a theatre', he wrote, suggesting that the bare stage of the Chinese theatre would provide a good model.[29] By September 1910, Corkery was defending Synge's scandalous work *The Playboy of the Western World* to the venerable Cork Literary and Scientific Society by brandishing the twin icons of theatrical modernity, Ibsen and Maeterlinck, while MacSwiney was writing in the introduction to his play, *The Revolutionist*, that 'the audience that accepts the elaborate convention will accept the simple one, which leaves the way open for a return to freer methods in our management of the stage'.[30]

While Corkery and MacSwiney struggled, not always successfully, to put their theories into practice, writers associated with the Cork Dramatic Society who worked within more conventional dramatic forms quickly found themselves taken up by the Abbey. Indeed, in 1910 the Abbey mounted three successive productions by Cork alumni: *Harvest* by Lennox Robinson, *The Casting-Out of Martin Whelan* by R. J. Ray, and *Birthright* by T. C. Murray, which opened on 27 October 1910. Set entirely in the ubiquitous farmhouse kitchen box set, the rural Ireland of

Birthright is utterly unlike that of Synge's timeless peasants, who live in a kind of dazed awe at 'all the great states and territories of the world'. The rural Ireland of *Birthright* was a little over a generation old. It was a place of late marriages and large-scale emigration, dominated by the new class of small-landowning farmers, some of whom had gained control of their land as recently as 1903, when the Wyndham Act had been passed. 'When I bought this place thirty years ago with the bit o' money I made in the States', demands Bat Morrissey, a first-generation farmer-proprietor, 'what kind was it? Who drained the western field that was little better than a bog?'[31] Bat's son Hugh, however, is more interested in socialising with the priest and playing hurling than he is in farming, and as the generational conflict escalates to the point at which Hugh is beaten to death, it becomes clear that *Birthright* is suggesting that Irish modernity was archaic even before it was fully formed.

Murray's critique of an outdated modernity is typical of the playwrights known as the 'Cork Realists'. This group initially included Lennox Robinson, whose early plays, such as *The Clancy Name* (1908) and *Patriots* (1912), are equally a departure from the 'ancient idealism' of the Irish Literary Theatre's original manifesto. *Patriots*, in particular, captures the mood of the years in which Yeats wrote 'September 1913', with its well-known refrain 'Romantic Ireland's dead and gone, / It's with O'Leary in the grave.' James Nugent, a nationalist revolutionary, released after eighteen years in prison, returns home to find that his wife has become a shrewd businesswoman, turning their shop into one of the most successful small businesses in the town, while the League he helped to found now spends its time listening to talks such as 'Through the Apennines with a Camera'. Nugent resolves to hold a mass rally, but no one shows up. 'You'll never get me to believe that the spirit that animated the men of '48 and '67 is dead,' Nugent tells one of his erstwhile supporters. 'Not dead, James', he is told, 'but grown wise. Ireland is to be very prosperous, very well-to-do one of these days, but it's never going to fight again.'[32] And yet, a year after *Patriots* had its première, the Cork Dramatic Society, which gave Robinson his start, had collapsed, largely due to the founding of a Cork branch of the Irish Volunteers in December 1913. 'Gradually An Dún became a hall for drilling', Corkery later recalled. 'Even our actors took to drilling. Somehow we dissolved.'[33]

There is a strange sense of simultaneous exhaustion and exhilaration in the cultural life of Ireland in the years immediately preceding the 1916 Rising. 'We want a flash of lightning to clear the air', says a character in MacSwiney's *The Revolutionist*, written over the winter of 1911–12 (but not staged until 1921). On the one hand, plays like Robinson's *Patriots* give the impression of a national struggle which had run its course; on the other, there was a dizzying proliferation of societies whose aims blur the distinctions between cultural development and armed revolution – societies in which people who had never written a play before in their lives were turning to esoteric theatrical models in an attempt to re-invent the stage, and then rushing from rehearsals to the drill hall; or in which experienced actresses like Maire Nic Shuibhlaigh were forsaking straight theatre for variety shows to raise money for guns.

The most important of these groups was the Theatre of Ireland, formed by a group who broke away from the Abbey in 1906, and included among its members Padraic Pearse, Edward Martyn, Padraic Colum, Constance Markievicz, Joseph Mary Plunkett and Thomas MacDonagh. Maintaining close links with both the Abbey and the Ulster Literary Theatre, they staged not only Purcell's *The Enthusiast* in May 1908, but also more forcefully revolutionary plays, such as MacDonagh's *When the Dawn Has Come* (1908), set in an Irish revolutionary council fifty years in the future. Similarly, in April 1910, Casimir Markievicz set up his own Independent Dramatic Company to stage his patriotic melododrama, *The Memory of the Dead: A Romantic Drama of '98*, with his wife, Constance, and Abbey actor Seaghan Connolly in the lead roles. Indeed, it is tempting to see in many of these plays a foreshadowing of what lay ahead, particularly in a play such as Pearse's *An Rí* (1913), a short, intense piece structured like Yeats' *Cathleen ni Houlihan*, which builds quickly to an epiphanic revelation of the glory of self-sacrifice. 'Before Pearse fired a shot', claims W. I. Thompson in an influential argument, 'he rehearsed insurrection by writing a play about it.'[34]

Trying to find an open theatre on Easter Monday, 1916, Joseph Holloway saw on a hoarding what he thought at first was an announcement for the Theatre of Ireland, 'signed by T. C. Clarke, Thomas McDonagh, Joseph Plunkett, P. H. Pearse, James Connolly and two others . . . It had a Gaelic heading, and went on to state that Ireland was now under Republican Government, and they hoped with God's help, etc., to do justly by their own countrypeople. It was a long and floridly worded document full of high hopes.'[35] It was, of course, the Proclamation of an Irish Republic. By the time the Rising was over, most of the Theatre of Ireland's founders were either dead (Pearse, MacDonagh, Plunkett), in prison (Markievicz), or, in the case of Edward Martyn, had moved on to other theatre projects. The Abbey was less profoundly affected by the fighting of Easter week, although Seaghan Connolly died in the fighting, while another actor, Arthur Sinclair, was briefly interned. 'My first emotion', Lady Gregory wrote to Yeats, 'was one of deep depression. I thought now everybody in Ireland will turn against idealist politics and even our theatre and our literature. They will think of nothing but burned houses; and it wasn't until the executions that my mood changed.'[36]

In the years immediately before 1916, it was not only in the smaller theatres that the political temperature was on the rise. In the summer of 1912, Wilson Howard's touring company introduced audiences at the Queen's to a subgenre of Russian plays, including *Siberia* and *Under the Czar,* the former advertised as 'An Intense and Engrossing Play Dealing in a Most Descriptive Manner with the Cruel Persecution of Political Suspects'. The following year, during the week of 23 June 1913 – less than two months before the Irish Transport and General Workers Union declared a general strike – William de Lacy and his 'No. 1 Company of Special Artistes' were presenting twice-nightly *From Mill to Mansion: Or, the Story of a Great Strike*, the playbills for which were emblazoned with the logo: 'All we ask is a fair day's wage for a fair day's work, but the masters grudge us even that.' At the same time, a young Dubliner, P. J. Bourke, was writing and performing Irish plays, including *When Wexford Rose* (1910) and *The Northern Insurgents* (1912) in small venues like the Father Matthew Hall. By the end of 1912, he was ensconced at the Queen's with a company of his own in the old actor-manager tradition, staging his own plays, and reviving those of Boucicault, Whitbread and O'Grady. Before long, he was joined by Ira Allen, who had also formed a touring company based at the Queen's, performing a similar repertoire of material, and later writing his own plays. Meanwhile, a burgeoning number of small, travelling fit-up companies were roaming the countryside, playing everywhere from the Curragh Army Camp to church halls in Sligo.

Bourke and Allen picked up where Whitbread had left off in the plays they wrote for the Queen's, making use of iconic tableaux, frequent changes of picturesque scenery (usually advertised on the playbills) and the obligatory informer. However, just as the plays of Whitbread (and, to an even greater extent, Hubert O'Grady) moved away from the conciliatory endings of Boucicault and his predecessors, Bourke's plays take a further step towards unappeasable militancy. So, at the end of *When Wexford Rose*, as the young hero goes into exile in France, he tells General Holt (a real historical figure) that he can 'never know true happiness . . . until

I take my place once more with the men of Wicklow and Wexford in the struggle for Independence'.[37] Moreover, when the play was staged at the Queen's in 1912, the musical interludes (so important in melodrama) were advertised as being provided by 'the McHale Branch Gaelic League, All Ireland Feis Prize-Winners', establishing an important link between melodrama and the 'authentic' Irish culture of the Gaelic League.

Three years later, on 15 November 1915, Bourke's Number One Company of Irish Players hired the Abbey to stage yet another melodrama dealing with 1798, *For the Land She Loved*, as a benefit for the Defence of Ireland Fund. 'The audiences have been a strange lot who insist on smoking & tell the assistant to go to Hell! when informed that No Smoking is allowed', commented Joseph Holloway, unused to seeing the Queen's audience out of its natural habitat. 'They are a law unto themselves.'[38] The Queen's audience not only upset the Abbey's middle-class decorum; it also upset Dublin Castle, who admonished the manager of the time, St John Ervine, for allowing the theatre to be used for such incendiary material. If the politics of the large (and growing) genre of 1798 melodramas had been either ignored or not recognised prior to the 1916 Rising, this was clearly no longer the case, and the Queen's responded, from September 1916 onwards, by staging as much Irish material as possible, drawing on a repertoire going back more than half a century. In 1919, for instance, the theatre staged only four non-Irish plays (including the perennial favourite, *East Lynne*) compared to nineteen Irish plays, ranging from Ira Allen's 1798 drama, *Father Murphy*, to O'Grady's trilogy *Famine*, *Eviction*, and *The Fenian*, Whitbread's *Rory O'More*, Boucicault's *Colleen Bawn* and Bourke's *In Dark and Evil Days*, the advertising posters for which had been censored when they were first posted in 1915. More than ever before, the Queen's was the 'Home of Irish Drama', and would continue thus until the mid-1920s.

The vibrancy of Irish melodrama in the decade and a half after 1910 was only partly due to the over-heated political climate of the time; it was equally the first fruits of a Faustian pact with the cinema. When Sidney Olcott, a Canadian film director with the Kalem Film Company of Florida, began shooting the first Irish fiction films, it was clear that he was targeting the popular theatre audiences. Early films such as *Rory O'More* (1911) and *The Colleen Bawn* (1911) were not only based on popular Irish plays; in many cases, they assumed that their audiences had already seen the full version on stage. Olcott's *The Colleen Bawn*, for instance, runs for thirty-five minutes, trimmed down from a stage play lasting more than an hour and a half, which in turn is based on a three-volume novel. Olcott's film manages to retain most of the play's major scenes by keeping episodes so brief that, for instance, when Danny Mann gestures frantically off-camera to indicate the source of an incriminating letter that is the key to the plot, only an audience who already knew what was going on would know that he was not simply having a fit. Even the titles, which might have carried some of the burden of the narrative, are often given over to explaining that a nondescript shoreline is a 'View of the Lakes of Killarney' – or, in one bizarre instance, that the bed used in a particular shot 'was owned by Daniel O'Connell and was occupied by him'.

The threads that tied the early cinema to the popular theatre are nowhere more evident than in *Ireland a Nation*, a film shot in 1914 by Walter MacNamara, and featuring P. J. Bourke. Its opening sequences use cinematic versions of three subgenres of the 1798 play: the Wolfe Tone play (with its obligatory scenes involving Napoleon); the Michael Dwyer play, which is composed of a series of hairsbreadth escapes from the Yeomanry; and the Robert Emmet play, with its tragic love thwarted by 'the most infamous of things – The Informer'. When *Ireland a Nation* was shown in Dublin in January 1917, the military authorities temporarily banned it after receiving intelligence reports that a scene showing 'the murder of a British soldier by a rebel was greeted with prolonged and enthusiastic applause'.[39] In a re-edited version in the 1920s, *Ireland a Nation* would become something of a Rosetta Stone for reading the politics of the patriotic Irish play, as newsreel footage of a nationalist political rally and the funeral of Terence MacSwiney were spliced on to the end, ultimately creating an extended narrative of Irish history in which the stage world of Whitbread's *Wolfe Tone* bleeds into the real world of the War of Independence.

When such films were initially shown, they drew audiences to the plays upon which they relied. In the case of P. J. Bourke, the *succès de scandale* of *Ireland a Nation* would make him the pre-eminent figure at the Queen's from 1917 until the early 1920s. At the same time, however, cinema was changing the world of the theatre. When the first Irish film company, the Film Company of Ireland, was established in 1916, its main director was J. M. Kerrigan, an Abbey actor who had played, among other roles, the lead in *When the Dawn Has Come* with the Theatre of Ireland. Kerrigan was joined by John McDonagh, also of the Theatre of Ireland, and both directors used Abbey actors such as Arthur Sinclair and Fred O'Donovan in their films. Initially, these actors were able to combine film and theatre careers; within a month of the première of his film *O'Neil of the Glen* in August 1916, for instance, Kerrigan was starring as Broadbent in the

Abbey's first production of *John Bull's Other Island*. However, Kerrigan and other key Abbey performers, including Sara Allgood, were among the first to establish a pattern of actors who would use a reputation created at the Abbey to launch a career in Hollywood. When the indigenous Irish film industry slowed down after 1922, it became increasingly difficult to keep Irish actors at home.

The cinema forced other changes in patterns of theatre-going. By the time Sidney Olcott came to Ireland in 1910, twenty per cent of the films made in Hollywood were Westerns. This initially helped to create a vogue for plays such as *The Sheriff of the Lonesome Pine*, which played the Queen's in May 1913; within a decade and a half, however the cinema would have almost completely supplanted the Western genre of plays. A similar pattern can be seen with the detective play, as it became clear that the cinema could do certain things better, and more cheaply, than the theatre. Virtual tourism – the recreation on stage of real landscapes – had been one of the attractions of theatre-going since the first Theatre Royal on Hawkins Street opened in 1821; a century later, it was the cinema that provided the best 'views of the Lakes of Killarney', and at a considerably cheaper price. The same was true of star actors, so that before long the touring theatre companies began to feel the effects of competition.

This is not to say that the touring companies shrivelled up and died. Nonetheless, in 1910 – the year in which five cinemas opened in Belfast, and the Volta in Dublin and Electric Cinema in Cork opened within a week of each other – the Theatre Royal in Dublin became primarily a variety house, after its acquisition by the Gaiety management. But it did not go without one last riot. On 11 October 1910, during a production of *Sir Walter Raleigh* by William Devereaux, a character made a disparaging remark about the Inquisition. 'Immediately', reported the *Freeman's Journal*, 'a large number of the audience stood up and sang "Faith of Our Fathers".'[40] In 1910 the Gaiety hosted a touring production of Rutherford Mayne's *The Troth*, performed by the Manchester company to which Annie Horniman had shifted her patronage. In 1912, the Gaiety brought back Horniman's new company who played Shaw's *John Bull's Other Island* for the first time before an Irish audience. However, over the next few decades, the Gaiety devoted increasing amounts of stage time to musical recitals and touring opera companies, and relied more than ever on their Christmas pantomime.

The Abbey was one of the main beneficiaries of this realignment of the Dublin theatre world in the years leading up to 1916. As the Queen's increasingly courted an advanced nationalist audience, and the other large patent houses cut back the amount of theatre they presented, the Abbey found itself in more or less sole possession of the mainstream theatre audience. And so, with its directors sneering and kicking, and still courting a reputation for managed scandal, the theatre took possession of the middle ground. The first moves came as early as 1906, when William Boyle's rural comedies provided the theatre with some of its most profitable plays in *The Building Fund* (1905) (which Yeats described privately as 'impossibly vulgar') and *The Eloquent Dempsey* (1906), which the actor Dudley Digges described as 'a magnet that draws even in a deluge'. Similarly, George Fitzmaurice's rural comedy, *The Country Dressmaker* (1907) would eventually notch up 181 performances by 1949. However, when Boyle tried to move in a more adventurous direction with *The Mineral Workers* (1906), a plea for Irish industrialisation, he found audiences unwilling to follow him. In a similar vein, when Fitzmaurice began to develop his own distinctively bizarre folk plays, including *The Pie-Dish* (1908) and *The Magic Glasses* (1913), he was asked why he could not produce another *Country Dressmaker*. By the time he wrote *The Dandy Dolls* (also 1913), which ends with the Hag of Barna sweeping on to the stage, smacking a priest, and then flying off with the main character suspended by his whiskers, the Abbey directors were no longer willing to take a chance on him, and rejected the play.

Although Yeats and Lady Gregory were loath to admit it, after 1910 the Abbey was to a large extent dependent on rural comedies, and this dependence increased when the First World War made touring in the United States impossible. Hence, when Lennox Robinson's *The Whiteheaded Boy* opened in December 1916, it not only provided a much-needed popular success, it was a harbinger of things to come. On its first night, Holloway noted only 'a few stray people' in the audience, but this quickly changed. Houses grew steadily, leading to the inevitable revival; by 1960, it would have been staged for 284 performances, making it the Abbey's most frequently performed full-length play. Although laced with the kind of sardonic wit that was becoming Robinson's trademark, *The Whiteheaded Boy*'s basic plot (already used in one variation by Purcell in *The Enthusiast*) was the prodigal-son story. Such plays were very much in vogue in the English theatre of the time, most notably St John Hankin's *The Return of the Prodigal*, staged in 1907 at the Royal Court Theatre (where Robinson had served a six-week apprenticeship in 1910).[41] *The Whiteheaded Boy* thus joined plays like *The Country Dressmaker* in providing many of the same pleasures that theatre audiences had come to expect from the touring companies (a tightly constructed plot, sympathetic characters, genuinely funny situations), while at the same time filling a demand for Irish material.

In the same 1916–17 season that *The Whiteheaded Boy* was first produced, J. Augustus Keogh took over as manager of the Abbey from St John Ervine, who had been so unpopular that the players had gone on strike for a time. Keogh decided it was time that Irish audiences became better acquainted with Shaw, partly because he had a long history of involvement with Shaw's work, but also because he believed that 'Abbey acting is not acting at all', and he hoped that the discipline of playing Shaw would teach the company stage technique.[42] Over the winter of 1916–17, therefore, just as Shaw's box-office appeal in England began to slump during the jingoistic climate of the war, Dublin audiences were swamped with his work, beginning with the long-delayed first Dublin production of *John Bull's Other Island*, followed by *Widowers' Houses*, *Arms and the Man*, *Man and Superman*, *The Doctor's Dilemma*, and *The Inca of Perusalem*. Even Keogh, however, gratefully gave in to pressure from Dublin Castle not to stage Shaw's only other Irish play, *O'Flaherty V.C.*, a Shavian parable about an Irish soldier, home on leave, who finds his beloved mother and sweetheart more frightening than shellfire in the trenches. *O'Flaherty V.C.* is so subversive of ideals of family and home – dear to both Irish republicans and supporters of the British war effort – that the Abbey would have found few supporters in the controversy that would have been inevitable with a play ironically subtitled *A Recruiting Pamphlet*. The uneasy weeks after the Easter Rising were not the time for such a battle. All concerned (Shaw excepted) were glad when it sunk away quietly.

In some respects, putting *John Bull's Other Island* on with plays like *The Doctor's Dilemma* suggests that Shaw might have written his Irish play even if he had not been born in Ireland. Shaw had long been working with the dialectical play of opposing stereotypes: there is the pacifist/revolutionary in *The Doctor's Dilemma*, the munitions manufacturer/philanthropist in *Major Barbara*, and so on. *John Bull's Other Island* initially seems to be yet another inversion of two stereotypes, with an Irish character, Larry Doyle, who is a 'steady, humdrum' cynic, and an English character, Broadbent, who is an apparently sentimental romantic; meanwhile, one of the two apparently conventional stage Irish characters in the play, Haffigan, is from Glasgow, and the other, Patsy, has, the stage directions tell us, 'an instinctively acquired air of helplessness and silliness, indicating not his real character, but a cunning developed by his constant dread of hostile dominance'. 'Dont you know', Doyle tells Broadbent, 'that all this top-o-the-morning and broth-of-a-boy and more-power-to-your-elbow business is got up in England to fool you, like the Albert Hall concerts of Irish music?'[43]

Of course, this subversion of stereotypes was not new to Irish audiences, who had sharp eyes for distinguishing between insulting and strategic forms of stage Irishry. Indeed, it would be possible to go back at least as far as Thomas Sheridan's *Captain O'Blunder* to argue that the so-called 'typical' stage Irishman had been subverted so often and for so long that a continuous state of subversion is in fact an intrinsic feature of the character's history (and attractiveness). At the very least, it must be said that Shaw came to the process late in its history, and this in turn allows him to pull his English and Irish characters back and forth between the poles of sentimentality and pragmatism with such dizzying dexterity that he clears a space for his real point: national cultural identities, whether Irish or English, are only so much fodder for the forces of free-market capitalism. And so, the play's most powerful moment is the speech in which the defrocked priest Keegan (addressing both Doyle and Broadbent) predicts that 'this poor desolate countryside' will become 'a busy mint in which we shall all slave to make money for you'. After listening politely to him, the Irishman and the Englishman go off hand in hand to choose a site for their hotel.

When *John Bull's Other Island* had first been published in 1907, its preface alone had occasioned a lively debate in Dublin's Contemporary Club; when it was staged in 1916, five months after the execution of Pádraig Pearse, it was the wrong moment to suggest that nationality was redundant. Irish audiences received the play, ironically enough, more or less as a relatively straight-forward comedy. Hence, while running a Shaw season in 1916 was in one sense an act of repatriation for the playwright, it also made the Abbey look worryingly similar to other repertory companies in England, and less like the theatre that had electrified audiences with *Cathleen ni Houlihan* in 1902. Moreover, by 1916 the Abbey's most mercurial figure, W. B. Yeats, was increasingly detached from its day-to-day operations, and stories of his wandering into the theatre and dropping *non sequiturs* were already part of Abbey lore (such as the afternoon in 1915 when he chanced on a rehearsal being conducted by St John Ervine. Staring myopically at the stage, Yeats asked Ervine. 'What is that old sack doing on the stage?' 'That's not a sack', replied Ervine. 'That's my wife.')

This was not simple boredom on Yeats' part. Even before 1913, when he first encountered the Japanese Noh theatre, Yeats was already on his way to creating for himself what he would define in 1919 as 'an unpopular theatre and an audience like a secret society where admission is by favour and never to many'.[44] As first *The Eloquent Dempsey* and later *The Whiteheaded Boy* drew in crowds, it was clear that the Abbey was not to be that theatre. In the decade between 1910 and 1920, Yeats wrote six new plays, and rewrote a number of the earlier works; however, only two of these – *The Green Helmet* (1910) and *The Player Queen* (1919) – along with revised versions of *The Hour Glass* and *The Countess Cathleen*, found their way to the Abbey stage. Consequently, many of the plays of those years were only staged privately, such as *At the Hawk's Well*, which premièred in Lady Cunard's drawing room in Cavendish Square, London on 2 April 1916. Others, such as *Calvary*, would wait for decades to reach the stage.

Even Yeats' powerful theatrical response to the 1916 Rising, *The Dreaming of the Bones* (1919), would have to wait for a production. At the time, Yeats held it back because, as he wrote to Lady Gregory, he thought it was 'too politically explosive'.[45] On the almost bare, abstract Noh stage, with three musicians narrating, a young rebel, fleeing in the night from the Easter Rising, encounters the spirits of Diarmuid and Dervorgilla, who had invited the Normans to Ireland in the twelfth century, and whose story had first been staged by Charles Shadwell as *Rotherick O'Connor* in 1720. In Yeats' play, their spirits are wandering for eternity, forced to remain apart until forgiven by one of their own race. At first, the young rebel fleeing the fighting of Easter 1916 is moved by their plight, but looking around him sees

> that the enemy has toppled roof and gable,
> And torn panelling from ancient rooms;
> What generations of old men had known,
> Like their own hands, and children wondered at,
> Has boiled a trooper's porridge.

As the morning light dawns, he cries 'O, never, never, / Shall Diarmuid and Dervorgilla be forgiven.'[46] The time for forgiveness was past. If the future had been open and mutable at the time of *Cathleen ni Houlihan* in 1902, by the time Yeats wrote *The Dreaming of the Bones* in May and June of 1917, it was locked into the implacable logic of war.

While Yeats drifted in and out of Ireland, Lady Gregory provided the theatre with its real continuity. Yeats acknowledged as much in his open letter of 1919, when he wrote: 'You have done all that is anxious and laborious in the supervision of the Abbey.'[47] New writers tended to bring their work to the theatre in clusters and then fade away, while the pattern of actors leaving the theatre for greener pastures abroad was already well established by the time Fred O'Donovan left in 1918. In the same period, there had been a succession of managers following Ben Iden Payne: Lennox Robinson, Nugent Monck, St John Ervine, J. Augustus Keogh, and then Robinson again. There were, of course, some constants: the theatre's business manager, W. A. Henderson, often seemed like the only person, apart from Gregory, with any notion of how the theatre might continue from year to year. Others, such as Seaghan Barlow, the stage carpenter, did everything from build sets to play small roles. It was Gregory, however, who negotiated with Dublin Castle during the *Blanco Posnet* episode; she and Robinson bore the weight of the tumultuous 1911 US tour; and most contemporary accounts indicate that without her diplomatic skills in the green room, there would have been more defections. In addition, she wrote more for the theatre than any other dramatist of the period, having thirty-one opening nights (including collaborations and translations) at the Abbey between 1904 and 1921. Among these was what would become for many years the theatre's most frequently performed play: *The Rising of the Moon* (1907).

First staged less than two months after Synge's *Playboy*, this short one-act play is both a nationalist recruiting piece and a moment of autobiography for a writer who went from attacking the second Home Rule Bill in 1893 with a satire, *A Phantom's Pilgrimage, or Home Ruin*, to supporting what she later called 'idealist politics'. Set on a quayside in the moonlight, a sergeant stands watch for an escaped Fenian prisoner; a ballad-singer enters, and offers to keep the sergeant company, singing rebel songs 'to keep [his] heart up'.[48] It becomes apparent that the ballad-singer is the fugitive Fenian, but the policeman helps him to escape after hearing him sing the 1798 ballad that gives the play its title, 'The Rising of the Moon'. When the play was first produced, there were some grumblings from Sinn Féin that the play was too kind to the policeman, but really this was only obligatory sniping in the aftermath of the *Playboy* battle. The Unionist *Irish Times* came closer to the mark when it objected that 'The metamorphosis of this worthy officer from being a man burning with zeal to do his duty to a man whose sense of duty is undermined by the recital of a few songs is quite remarkable.'[49] Like *Cathleen ni Houlihan*, which she wrote with Yeats, *The Rising of the Moon* is a play born of the recognition that revolutionary politics are about sudden, magical transformations; so too, at its best, is the theatre. Although Lady Gregory's career as a playwright began later than most, she discovered almost instantly the secret kinship of good theatre and revolutionary politics.

Almost all of Lady Gregory's plays explore this relationship in some way. This was true of *The Image*, for example, first staged at the Abbey in November 1909, and it is equally true of *Aristotle's Bellows*, first staged twelve years later in March 1921. By that point, with the Anglo-Irish War at its most bitter, the truce of 9 July only four months away, and political change of a very real kind underway, Gregory was growing more wary of instantaneous metamorphoses. Indeed, *Aristotle's Bellows* can be seen as an allegorical invitation to reassess the value of revolution. It is a deceptively simple piece, with two characters: Mother, and her stepson, Conal. Conal is searching for the eponymous bellows, which will magically transform the world, righting all wrongs. Mother warns Conal against such dreams, telling him 'It's best make changes little by little the same as you'd put clothes upon a growing child.'[50] Where *The Rising of the Moon* had staged a moment of miraculous transformation, *Aristotle's Bellows* is more circumspect, suggesting that the desire for revolution may be of more value than the brave new world the revolution will bring.

Lady Gregory wrote the sketch for *Aristotle's Bellows* in July 1919. The first Dáil had just met, and at that point it would not have been easy to predict the duration or outcome of the war. As she worked on the play, she noted in her journal: 'For myself I have long tried to do my work apart from politics, my formula has long been "not working for Home Rule but preparing for it".'[51] Like so many others of vastly differing political convictions – from Pearse to Yeats to P. J. Bourke – Gregory had seen the theatre as a means to an independent Ireland. By the time *Aristotle's Bellows* was produced on 17 March 1921, that Ireland (at least in part of the island) was less than a year away. 'A beautiful, sun-shiny day', Joseph Holloway noted of that St Patrick's Day. 'The first thing I saw when I got up was a string of lorries, armoured cars, caged lorries filled with Black and Tans, and military all with guns and revolvers on the ready. They were going towards town.'[52] Within a year, the Black and Tans would be gone; but so too would the Irish theatre's most compelling *raison d'être*.

A night at the theatre 5

The Plough and the Stars by Sean O'Casey
Abbey Theatre
Thursday, 11 February 1926

Irish politics in the 1920s was a continuation by other means of the Civil War. The Irish Republican Army, who opposed the Treaty, called a ceasefire and dumped their arms in May 1923, but they neither surrendered nor conceded the point on which the war had been fought. Consequently, the war did not really end in 1923; rather, it took a new shape, a suspended, vestigial version of what had gone before, in which a midnight knock at the door of a Republican could still mean a search for guns, and in which groups opposed to the Treaty, like Sinn Féin or Cumann na mBan, continued to meet and discuss strategy. Outwardly, however, there was the appearance of calm, as the new Free State government of W. T. Cosgrave set about putting in place the institutions of a new state.

Although the matter was not voted on in the Dáil, by August 1925 the institutions of the new state included a national theatre, the Abbey. 'Dear O'Casey', Yeats wrote to the playwright on 1 August 'On behalf of the Theatre I have invited Mr Ernest Blythe, Minister of Finance and Mrs Blythe to supper on the stage after the performance on Saturday evening, August 8th, and I very much hope that you will be able to come.'[1] That evening, Yeats, flanked by Blythe, announced that the government would be giving the Abbey an annual subsidy of £850. 'We have become the first State-endowed theatre in any English-speaking country', Yeats declared from the stage. Joining him on the stage, Blythe told the audience that the Abbey had done work of national importance. 'The Government recognizes the value of that work, and would continue to recognize it.'[2] The following week, Sean O'Casey submitted the typescript of *The Plough and the Stars* to the Abbey's board of directors, which now included a government appointee, George O'Brien.

O'Brien was quick to foresee that there could be problems ahead for a state-subsidised theatre staging a play which dealt in such a provocative way with the state's founding moment. The play opens in a Dublin tenement in the months leading up to the 1916 Rising, introducing a group of characters who are alternately enamoured and cynical of the uniforms and rhetoric of rebellion. The second act – which O'Brien thought completely unnecessary – moves to a pub, where a prostitute, a barman and the characters from the opening act set up an ironic counterpoint to a patriotic speech being delivered just outside the pub window by a character using the words of Patrick Pearse. Then, in act III, the action moves to Easter Week, as stricken Volunteers and looters drift back to the tenement with reports of the attack on the General Post Office, just off stage. By act IV, all that is left is a numb horror, as the remaining characters huddle in an attic room, their dreams of freedom now as constricted as the stage space, while outside the window Dublin burns and British troops scour the tenements for snipers.

As O'Casey would later point out, this was not the first play to deal with 1916 in a critical way. However, it was the first to do so with such blatant irreverence. After reading over the play, O'Brien wrote to Yeats, suggesting specific cuts in the script. Phrases like 'put your leg against mine', and 'little rogue of th' white breast' in the love scene between Clitheroe and Nora in act I, were to go, as were the words 'Jasus', 'Christ', 'bitch', 'lowsers' and 'lice'. 'The vituperative vocabulary of some characters occasionally runs away with itself', he noted. Similarly, he thought the 'professional side' of Rosie Redmond, the prostitute in act II, was 'unduly emphasized', insisting that her song at the end of the act was especially offensive:[3]

I once had a lover, a tailor, but he could do nothin' for me,
An' then I fell in with a sailor as strong an' as wild as th' sea.
We cuddled an' kissed with devotion, till th' night from th' morning had fled!
An' there, to our joy, a bright bouncin' boy
Was dancin' a jig in th' bed![4]

Yeats, of course, jumped to O'Casey's defence. 'To eliminate any part of it on grounds that have nothing to do with dramatic literature would be to deny all our traditions', he told O'Brien curtly. O'Brien, however, was no fool. Replying to Yeats on 13 September 1925, he insisted that his only concern was that *The Plough and the Stars* 'might offend any section of the public so seriously as to provoke an attack on the theatre of a kind that would endanger the continuance of the subsidy. Rightly or wrongly, I look upon myself as the watchdog of that subsidy.'[5] Walking home from the Abbey with Joseph Holloway on 12 October, O'Brien had confided that he 'wouldn't like the Catholic Truth Society to march with banners up and down outside the theatre, or rows like *The Playboy* ones to occur inside'.[6] Holloway assured him that nothing of the sort was possible.

Perhaps more than any of the other board members, O'Brien recognised that in accepting a subsidy from the Free State government, the Abbey had taken sides in a dangerously stalemated game, in which neither side knew how far the other was prepared to go. In particular, the theatre had aligned itself with Ernest Blythe, who (for the second time in five months) ate a supper on the Abbey stage on 27 December 1925, at a gala celebration marking the theatre's twenty-first anniversary. At that point, Blythe was one of the most despised members of the government among anti-Treaty Republicans.

In the month leading up to the Abbey's twenty-first anniversary dinner, Blythe was to the fore in the damage limitation exercise that followed the leaking of the findings of the Boundary Commission, which more or less confirmed Partition. On 15 January 1926, the Republican newspaper, *An Phoblacht*, published in full a speech Blythe had made back in 1914, when he had stated: 'Under no circumstances must we acquiesce in the cutting up of our country and the division of our people.'[7] Meanwhile, on the streets of Dublin, Republican activists were handing out leaflets juxtaposing his earlier anti-partitionist stance with his more recent claims that 'the work of the Boundary Commission will be eminently satisfactory'. So, when many Irish republicans thought of the betrayal of their ideals in the winter of 1925/6, they thought of Ernest Blythe.

As *The Plough and the Stars* went into rehearsal in January 1926, it became obvious that in making the Abbey his special project, Blythe had made himself vulnerable. O'Casey was already deeply unpopular with most of the Abbey company, after publicly attacking Michael Dolan's 'painfully imperfect' production of *Man and Superman* the previous summer. At the very least, Dolan had become 'O'Casey's greatest enemy', as Gabriel Fallon put it. It was thus with a touch of mischievousness that Lennox Robinson, who was directing *The Plough and the Stars*, cast Dolan in the role of The Covey, the character O'Casey would later admit came closest to his own view. Meanwhile, the actress Eileen Crowe decided shortly after rehearsals started that she would 'not be called "snotty" ' in the part of Mrs Gogan. There is nothing objectionable in 'such words as Snotty, Bum, Bastard, or Lowsey', O'Casey retorted.[8] O'Casey had already agreed to changes in the script, including the cutting of Rosie Redmond's song in act II, after a heated board of directors' meeting on 24 September 1925, and was justifiably annoyed when the actors began calling for more cuts. Nonetheless, he wrote a new part for Crowe – The Woman from

Rathmines, who appears briefly in act III – and rehearsals simmered on as before, with Robinson sitting near the stage, his head bowed and long legs crossed, while O'Casey slouched further back in the stalls in his trenchcoat and hat.

News of the internecine strife at the Abbey spread around Dublin, as it always did, blending with talk of upcoming by-elections, and the deeper rumblings that a major change was underway in the Sinn Féin leadership. Since the end of the Civil War, Sinn Féin, under the leadership of Eamon de Valera, had refused to recognise the legitimacy of the Dáil, and while the party had contested elections, successful candidates had not taken their seats. By early February 1926, however, de Valera felt he had spent enough time in the political wilderness. In the same week that *The Plough and the Stars* was to open, he published a motion to be voted on at the party's Ard Fheis (or annual convention) that would open the way for their involvement in government. In the interim, however, his supporters were in an awkward position. With the Ard Fheis coming up in March, they had to avoid any actions that might land them in prison; at the same time, they needed to show their supporters that they were still the keepers of the militant republican flame.

The first night of *The Plough and the Stars*, on Monday, 8 February, gave little indication of what lay ahead. In spite of rain and thick winter fog, the queue for tickets had begun at four o'clock in the afternoon, and by early evening extended well past Abbey Street. In part, this was because so many seats had been reserved, with members of the government, including Blythe and Kevin O'Higgins, forming a special party who were escorted backstage by Yeats after the performance. There was, as Joseph Holloway put it, 'electricity in the air' on that first night, and O'Casey was called up to the stage to take a bow after the final curtain. 'It was a very excited first night audience', Robinson wrote to Lady Gregory, 'a bad audience to judge a play by'.[9]

The first signs of trouble came during act II on Tuesday night, when Sighle Humphreys began hissing from the back of the pit. Humphreys was at that point Vice President of Cumann na mBan, a Republican women's organisation with close links to Sinn Féin and the IRA. In December 1925, Cumann na mBan had threatened to protest at a showing of a British war film, *Ypres*, announced for the La Scala Theatre in Dublin, successfully forcing its withdrawal. However, Cumann na mBan minutebooks for February 1926 give no indication that there were any official plans to disrupt O'Casey's play. Indeed, in the early weeks of 1926 the organisation was arranging to hire the Abbey for a Republican benefit show, scheduled for 5 March.[10] At the same time, this did not prevent its members from acting unofficially.

On Thursday, 11 February, the Abbey once again was packed, with people standing along the side of the pit and at the back of the balcony. Anyone looking around the auditorium before the play began would have missed neither the large Cumann na mBan presence, nor the prominent members of Sinn Féin, including a legendary gunman (and Sinn Féin TD), Dan Breen – although Breen was to take no part in the demonstrations. The Republican women in the theatre that night were experienced agitators and organisers, some with experience of combat and prison. Moreover, they were a carefully selected group, carrying with them resonances of men who had died in the 1916 Rising: Humphreys was the niece of one of the leaders, while Kathleen Clarke and Maud Gonne were widows of men who had been executed; so too was Hanna Sheehy-Skeffington, although she was not a member of Cumann na mBan, and her husband, Francis Sheehy-Skeffington, had been a pacifist, shot after trying to prevent looting. Fiona Plunkett was the sister of Joseph Plunkett, one of the executed signatories of the Proclamation, while Margaret Pearse was the mother of Patrick and Willie Pearse, and a national icon in her own right, thanks to Patrick Pearse's poem, 'The Mother'. Moreover, both Gonne and another prominent protestor, Dorothy McArdle (whose play about 1798, *Ann Kavanagh*, had been performed at the Abbey in May of 1922) had a history of association with the Abbey itself.

When the Abbey's black and gold curtains parted on 11 February to show Barry Fitzgerald, as Fluther Good, fixing a lock to the door of Nora and Jack Clitheroe's tenement flat, there was a sense of expectancy in the theatre, different from that of earlier in the week, if only because as veterans of the 1916 Rising, the women of Cumann na mBan were part of the world of the play. As O'Casey put it, there were 'two plays': 'one on the stage, the other in the auditorium'.[11] Just how those two performances were to interact with each other did not become clear until act II, when the protestors saw what they had been waiting for: Ria Mooney, playing Rosie Redmond, the prostitute lounging in a pub, waiting for clients, while outside Patrick Pearse tells an unseen group of listeners that 'Bloodshed is a cleansing and a sanctifying thing, and the nation that regards it as the final horror has lost its manhood.'[12] 'Put that woman off the stage', someone yelled, as pennies and lumps of coal began to rain down on the actors. One group in the pit started chanting 'send out O'Casey', while other members of the audience began protesting against the protestors, calling 'put them out'. In the pit, several women stood up to make speeches from their seats, but between being cheered and hooted they were inaudible. Ria Mooney and the rest of the cast continued amid the ruckus, while the houselights were switched on, and Yeats hastily summoned by telephone from Merrion Square.

During the interval, some of the audience left the pit, allowing the protestors to consolidate their positions by occupying the vacant seats. By the time Shelah Richards as Nora Clitheroe entered to tell the other characters of the 'fear glowin' in the eyes' of the rebels, the protestors had begun to rush the stage, where they were repulsed by a group of actors. One republican, named George Lalor, found himself in range of the actor Barry Fitzgerald, who had been playing the part of Fluther, and who, as O'Casey recalled the incident, 'fought as Fluther himself would fight, sending an enemy, who had climbed on to the stage, flying into the stalls with a flutherian punch on the jaw'.[13] When two protestors caught hold of the curtains, and tried to swing on them, Seaghan Barlow pitched in, sending one of the rioters tumbling on to the piano. Meanwhile, another group of actors, led by F. J. McCormick, attempted to distance themselves from the proceedings, pleading with the audience to distinguish between the actors and the play. 'You have no right to earn your bread by insulting Ireland', yelled a voice from the pit.

Upon arriving at the theatre, Yeats called the police, before dispatching to the *Irish Times* a copy of the speech he was about to make before the hastily dropped curtain. Gabriel Fallon, playing the role of Captain Brennan, remembers seeing Yeats pacing backstage, 'as coolly as if he were pacing his eighteenth-century drawing-room in Merrion Square still smiling to himself, apparently oblivious to the pandemonium that raged beyond the curtain . . . [He] then placed himself close to the curtain opening, and after a moment's pause gave the signal.' When he stepped forward, looking (according to Abbey actress Ria Mooney) 'like an ancient Roman Senator', his voice was almost drowned out; but it did not matter, for the press already had his speech:

> I thought you had tired of this, which commenced fifteen years ago. But you have disgraced yourselves again. Is this going to be a recurring celebration of Irish genius? Synge first and then O'Casey. The news of the happenings of the last few minutes here will flash from country to country. Dublin has again rocked the cradle of reputation . . . the fame of O'Casey is born here tonight. This is his apotheosis.[14]

Someone threw a shoe at him.

Yeats was not the only person to make a speech that night. Hanna Sheehy-Skeffington had placed herself in the balcony (strategically the best spot from which to conduct a theatre riot) along with a group of supporters, who struck up a chorus of 'The Soldier's Song', accompanied by a rhythm beaten out with a walking stick on the balcony rail. Throughout the second act, she had tried to make a speech, but nothing was audible anywhere in the auditorium at that point. Indeed, little that anyone said was audible until ten-fifteen, when detectives and uniformed Gardai, 'mystified', as O'Casey put it, 'at anyone kicking up a row over a mere play', had succeeded in evicting most of the protestors from the pit. Then she spoke:

> We are now leaving the hall under police protection (boos and cheers). I am one of the widows of Easter Week. It is no wonder that you do not remember the men of Easter Week, because none of you fought on either side. The play is going to London soon to be advertised there because it belies Ireland. We have no quarrel with the players – we realise that they, at least, have to earn their bread; but I say that if they were men they would refuse to play the parts. All you need to do now is sing 'God Save the King'.[15]

She then marched out of the theatre amid much hissing and whistling, countered with exaggerated applause. The play continued until its conclusion, in which a group of British soldiers sing 'Keep the Home Fires Burning', while Dublin burns in the background.

One of Hanna's friends, Cumann na mBan member Rosamund Jacobs, read of the disturbance in the next day's papers, and hurried over to the Sheehy-Skeffington house on Belgrave Road, to find Hanna dressing to go to the Gaiety, where *Lightin'* by Winchell Smith and Frank Bacon was playing. 'She seems to have quite enjoyed the riot', Jacobs noted in her diary: 'said Yeats was inaudible & that without the rioting her more defensible attack from the balcony would have had little effect & the thing would have fallen flat'. Hanna's teenage son Owen then mentioned that there had been a big 'blow-out' in Trinity the previous night, warning her there might be a few drunken students in the Gaiety. 'Oh, I hope not', Hanna replied primly. 'If there is one thing I dislike, it is rowdyism at the theatre' – upon which she and Owen roared with laughter.[16]

Elsewhere around Dublin, the debate over the play continued in the newspapers, and was later given an extra push at a debate organised by Frank Ryan at the Mills Hall on 1 March, at which O'Casey and Hanna Sheehy-Skeffington emerged as the main combatants. 'In no country save Ireland', she had written earlier in the *Irish Independent*, 'could a

State-subsidised theatre presume on popular patience to the extent of making a mockery and a byword of a revolutionary movement on which the present structure claims to stand.' 'I am one of those', she continued, 'who have gone for over twenty years to performances in the Abbey, and I admire the earlier ideals of the place that produced *Cathleen ni Houlihan* . . . Now, in its subsidised, sleek old age, [it] jeers at its former enthusiasms.' O'Casey responded by asking if 'the Ireland that is pouring to the picture-houses, to the dance-halls, to the football matches, [was] remembering with tear-dimmed eyes all that Easter Week stands for'.[17]

There was, however, by no means universal condemnation of *The Plough and the Stars* among Republicans. Rosamund Jacobs, for instance, records heated arguments over the play in the Radical Club, where on 20 February Kathleen Lynn read a paper 'all against the play, & was fiercely abused by those who were supposed to be proposing and seconding votes of thanks. The proposer apologised to the club for such tripe being inflicted on them.'[18] At the same time, there was widespread agreement that the protest had been an effective means of embarrassing the Cosgrave government (and Ernest Blythe in particular), in that it cast them as the subsidisers of a scandalous attack on the sacred traditions of republicanism. 'The Abbey Theatre's adventurous youth is over', claimed F. R. Higgins in the Sinn Féin weekly, *An Phoblacht*. 'The twenty-first birthday complete, an endowment due to the biddable child is being paid over by a satisfied Minister of Finance.'[19]

However, like any performance, the riot itself began to produce multiple interpretations. Hanna Sheehy-Skeffington was personally opposed to censorship, 'disowning any objection to the play on grounds of "decency", or "morals" ', and insisting that the protest should not be compared to the *Playboy* riots, as it was conducted 'on national grounds only'.[20] Nonetheless, much of the steam in the ensuing debate arose from the perception that the play was immoral. In February 1926, the campaign was well under way that would result later that year in the establishment of a government Committee on Evil Literature, and journals such as *The Catholic Bulletin* not only attacked 'this subsidised system of pouring scorn on the ideals of Easter Week, 1916'; they went further in calling for the censorship of newspapers supporting O'Casey, reserving particular venom for the *Irish Times* – 'the organ of the Ascendancy, New and Old' – and used the occasion to launch a particularly vicious attack on Yeats.[21]

Other old enemies of O'Casey soon joined the pummelling. When *The Plough and the Stars* had been in rehearsal, O'Casey had insisted that it should not be advertised in *The Voice of Labour*, with whom he had a long-running feud going back to his trade union days. Initially, the newpaper gave the play a supportive review, written before the protest; on 20 February, however, it published a second assessment, declaring that 'As a literary effort, the thing is a joke, but as a commercial proposition I expect it will be a huge success in London, where audiences will be found to enjoy anything that libels Ireland.'[22]

Returning home from the debate with Hanna Sheehy-Skeffington on 1 March, his old eye-complaint nearly blinding him, O'Casey found a telegram inviting him to go to London, where *Juno and the Paycock* had just been a major success. Not surprisingly, he went. For their parts, Sheehy-Skeffington and her fellow protestors soon had more important things on their minds. Ten days after the debate, they were delegates at the historic Sinn Féin Ard Fheis at which de Valera would break away to form Fianna Fáil, the party that would hold power in Ireland for much of the rest of the century. Meanwhile, *The Plough and the Stars* soon settled into the Abbey repertoire, eventually becoming the most successful play in the theatre's history. It may not have been obvious during that tempestuous winter of 1926, but both O'Casey's play and de Valera's decision to enter the Dáil were part of the same process of learning to live with the revolutionary energies of preceding decades.

CHAPTER 6

Aftermath, 1922–1951

Three days after the new Irish parliament approved the Anglo-Irish Treaty on 7 January 1922, the Abbey staged its first play in an independent Ireland: T. C. Murray's *Aftermath.* 'You will see', Murray wrote in a prologue (later cut by Lennox Robinson in rehearsals), 'a proud old woman's passionate yearning for the lost land which her people once possessed. You will see how, blinded by ambition, she wrecks her son's life and the lives of others . . . in a word, all the bitter fruit of a harsh old woman's folly.'[1] Although Murray could not have known that his play would open in the same week as the Treaty, he could have been writing a prescription for the culture of Free State Ireland, which was to be dominated by a harsh tone of disappointment, shot through with a resentment that the young should be sacrificed for the ideals and cravings of a previous generation. Murray was not writing an allegory; still it was difficult not to see the 'proud old woman' as Cathleen ní Houlihan.

'A free Ireland would not, and could not, have hunger in her fertile vales and squalor in her cities', Patrick Pearse had claimed. 'A free Ireland would, in short, govern herself as no external power – nay, not even a government of angels and archangels could govern her.'[2] When it became apparent, after the Civil War of 1922–3, the dock-workers' strike of 1923, and the hard winters and wet summers of 1923 and 1924, that there would be hunger in the fertile vales and squalor in the cities of a free Ireland, there was, understandably, a stinging sense of betrayal. This bitterness was to last through the worldwide depression of the 1930s, the economic constraints of the early 1940s, when Ireland's economy, alone in Europe, lacked the adrenalin boost of war, and well into the 1950s. The culture of the period thus rankles with an awareness of limitations, constraints and lost opportunities.

This was particularly true of the theatre, and Abbey-bashing quickly became one of the national pastimes in the new state. In part, this was because those resounding, exquisitely worded manifestos hung around the theatre like so many faded wreaths, reminders of a now-suspect idealism. 'Nothing but a victory on the battlefield', Yeats had declared after the first production of *Cathleen ni Houlihan* in St Teresa's Hall, 'could so uplift and enlarge the imagination of Ireland, could so strengthen the National spirit.'[3] Equally, theatre *per se* lacked an appropriately ancient Gaelic pedigree, and thus could expect little support from purists for whom the only true Irish culture was Gaelic. To make matters worse, the Abbey was the creation of an Anglo-Irish ascendancy which was now decisively on the losing side of history, its directors (Yeats, Lady Gregory, and later Lennox Robinson) all members of a minority Episcopalian faith whose population base was now in the six counties of Northern Ireland which had remained part of Great Britain. In short, the aura of betrayed ideals clung to the Abbey. There could be no worse – or no more appropriate – heritage for an Irish national theatre in 1922.

'Heard a terrific explosion at about 12:30', Joseph Holloway recorded in his diary for Friday, 30 June 1922, later discovering that he had been listening to the Free State army shelling Dublin's Four Courts, which were being held by Irish Irregular forces opposing the Treaty. 'Ireland in my time never witnessed such days of degradation as the past three.'[4] At the same time, in another part of Dublin, Sean O'Casey was working on a play provisionally titled 'On the Run', later renamed *The Shadow of a Gunman*. Set in a Dublin tenement in May 1920, at the height of the War of Independence, the main character in *The Shadow of a Gunman*, Donal Davoren, is not only the shadow of a gunman, he is the shadow of a poet, a writer of inflated, romantic verse who pretends to be a gunman to impress the residents of the tenement in which he lives. As such, he brings together the twin strands of poetic rhetoric and violent revolution which had been winding together ever more tightly in the years leading up to the War of Independence.

At one point, when Davoren's imagined identity is challenged by his room-mate, Seumus Shields, himself a former Volunteer, Davoren tells him, 'I remember a time when you yourself believed in nothing but the gun.' 'Ay', Shields replies, 'when there wasn't a gun in the country; I've a different opinion now when there's nothing but guns in the country.'[5] 'Here was the first play of a new post-war mentality', the playwright Denis Johnston later recalled, 'the first break away from a false set of values that had been slowly poisoning us – the first time we heard expressed on stage emotions that we were as yet hardly conscious of feeling ourselves.'[6]

On 10 April 1923, Liam Lynch, the leader of the anti-Treaty IRA, was shot dead by Free State forces; two days later, *The Shadow of a Gunman* opened for a three-day run. After a slow start, it built to a full house by the final night; 'the largest audience, I think', Lady Gregory wrote in her journal, 'since the first night of *Blanco Posnet*' fourteen years earlier. Passing through the thronged vestibule on that third night, she noticed an armed Free State soldier standing guard, placed there after a threat from Anti-Treaty forces to attack the theatre. In the green room she found a second soldier, 'giving finishing touches to the costume of Tony Quinn, who is a Black and Tan in the play, and showing him how to hold his revolver'.[7] Dealing with events that had taken place only a few years earlier, and set in the Dublin tenements almost within sight of the Abbey, O'Casey's play disconcertingly merged with the world outside the theatre, pointing up the uncomfortable similarities between what had been seen as the glorious struggle of the War of Independence, and the sordid viciousness of the Civil War.

While this produced a powerfully cathartic theatrical experience, it also contributed to the mistaken impression that O'Casey was a tragic realist writer in the mould of St John Ervine or T. C. Murray. The realist label would interfere most immediately with the reception of O'Casey's next play, *Kathleen Listens In*, a one-act satire, greeted at its première on 9 October 1923, by an uncomprehending silence. Gesturing towards O'Casey's dramatic roots, the play is a series of politicised music-hall turns, played out by characters such as 'The Free Stater', 'The Republican', and, most memorably, 'The Man in the Kilts', who pops in from time to time to insist that everyone speak Irish. 'I wish to God!' calls out one character in exasperation, 'they didn't love Kathleen as much as they do!'[8] As *Kathleen Listens In* was in production, however, O'Casey had already started work on a second full-length play for the Abbey, suggested by an incident in the Civil War he was to recall in his *Autobiographies*, the discovery of the body of 'Young Captain Wogan: away in a lone counthry lane, beyond Finglas, half hidden in hemlock. Taken out an' murdhered! Near unrecognisable; his belly kicked in, ears frayed, an eye gouged out, and the nose broken, with a bullet through his brain as an amen. The bastards only left a batthered memory of him! . . . There's Irish freedom for you!' [9]

The 'batthered memory' of Commandant Tancred, a character we never see, dominates *Juno and the Paycock*, which opened on 3 March 1924. 'On a little by-road out beyant Finglas, he was found', the audience are told in the play's opening line, as Mary Boyle reads of her neighbour's death. He is not mentioned again until the middle of the second act, when nearly twenty minutes of song and comic by-play are abruptly interrupted by the mother of the dead Tancred, draped in black and followed by a procession of mourners. As a theatrical image, it conjures up the final moments of Synge's *Riders to the Sea*, when Maurya laments over her dead sons. In *Riders to the Sea*, however, the audience are co-celebrants in the ritual of mourning; in *Juno and the Paycock* they are guilty revellers who have just cheered the Boyles' garrulous neighbour, Maisie Madigan, for her version of 'If I were a blackbird I'd whistle and sing.' The immediate effect of this intrusion of the tragic is a stab of guilt that both makes the audience feel the pain of Mrs Tancred's loss all the more sharply, and, at the same time, makes them resent her for breaking up a great party. Veering wildly between tragedy's solemn satisfactions and the giddy carnivalesque of music hall, *Juno and the Paycock* carves out its distinctive stage world.

This is most evident in the play's final moments. With the stage darkened, and almost empty, Juno repeats the evocative prayer, introduced by the grieving Mrs Tancred in act II, the repetition giving it the resonance of ritual: 'Sacred Heart of the Crucified Jesus, take away our hearts o' stone and give us hearts o' flesh!' Chastened, the audience sit in silence, expecting the final curtain, when Captain Boyle and his sidekick, Joxer, roll on to the stage, looking as if they might have wandered across the Liffey from the Queen's. 'D'jever rade Willie . . . Reilly . . . an' his own . . . Colleen . . . Bawn?' asks Joxer. 'It's a darlin' story, a daarlin' story!'[10] Of course, the play's first audience did know *The Colleen Bawn*, if only because yet another 'darlin' film version of Boucicault's play had its Irish première on 17 March 1924, a fortnight after *Juno and the Paycock* opened.

It took a special kind of acting for the actor Barry Fitzgerald to make an audience applaud Captain Boyle, a drunken blowhard who abandons his disintegrating family. Similarly, even though O'Casey's next play, *The Plough and the Stars*, met with a hostile reception from many anti-Treaty republicans when it was first performed in 1926, it too quickly developed a large audience base, due in a large part to performances like that of F. J. McCormick, who played Jack Clitheroe. When Clitheroe, resplendently foolish in full green dress uniform, calls out 'Death for th' Independence of Ireland' at the end of act II of *The Plough and the Stars*, it required a form of acting very different from the quiet understatement of the first generation of Abbey actors.[11] Indeed, Gabriel Fallon (who played Bentham) was unusual among the company who first performed O'Casey in that on joining the Abbey in 1920 he arranged to take private acting lessons in the traditional Abbey style from Frank Fay in his Upper Mount Street flat. More typical was McCormick, whose acting career began at the Queen's in June 1912 with Ira Allen's Company of Irish Players in a 1798 melodrama, *Father Murphy*. By 1917, Fitzgerald had his own Celtic Comedy-Drama Company, presenting yet another 1798 play, *Pike O'Callaghan* at the Queen's, a theatre in which at least two other members of the mid-1920s Abbey company – P. J. Carolan and May Craig – regularly acted.

Even as O'Casey's Dublin plays were drawing life from the patriotic melodramas, these staples of Irish theatrical life for more than half a century were dying. The Queen's suffered badly during the years of fighting, and was closed for much of 1920 and 1921. By the time it was back on a firm footing in 1925, the aggressively heroic melodramas of P. J. Bourke and Ira Allen were badly out of touch with the dour post-Civil-War mood, and so the theatre reverted to earlier, more conciliatory Irish plays. In October 1925, for instance, Buckstone's *Green Bushes* (originally staged in 1845) was back, and in January and February of 1928 there were productions of *Arrah-na-Pogue* and *The Colleen Bawn*. On the evening of 17 June 1928, however, the future of the Queen's became clear when it showed its first film, *Old San Francisco*, with an accompanying musical revue. The theatre continued to stage its Christmas pantomime for another twenty-three years, but otherwise from 1928 onwards it staged almost exclusively revue (which had replaced music hall) and a combination of films and stage acts known as 'cine-variety'.

Along with a changed political climate and the encroachments of cinema, the Queen's was registering a change that had taken place in the touring world. A decade earlier, the Theatre Royal and Gaiety had begun to shift the balance of their offerings towards musical and variety acts, and by the 1920s they had added guest appearances by film stars such as Charlie Chaplin or Western star Tom Mix. This may not have left much room for theatre, but it did allow the old patent houses to thrive, so much so that in 1935 the Theatre Royal was rebuilt, with an extensive wintergarden and a 4,000-seat auditorium (claimed to have been the largest in Europe). At that point, both the new Theatre Royal and the Gaiety were managed by the Elliman family, who took over the Queen's in 1936; by the mid-1940s they would control most of Ireland's cinema business, as managing directors of Odeon (Ireland) Ltd, Irish Cinemas Ltd, and Amalgamated Cinemas (Ireland) Ltd. Hence, throughout the 1930s, there was a steady consolidation of one end of the Irish entertainment market, and a consequent homogenisation of what was on offer.

As touring companies everywhere were unpacking their trunks for the final time, Anew McMaster, who had toured Ireland as an actor in the O'Brien-Ireland fit-up company from 1910 to 1914, decided to form a touring company of his own to bring Shakespeare to Ireland. On 7 June 1925, a pile of trunks marked 'McMaster Intimate Theatre Company' embarked from London's Euston Station, and over that summer the company played Wicklow, Arklow, Enniscorthy, Wexford, swinging west to Mallow, Youghal and Cobh in August, before looping back via Clonmel to end up in Waterford on 28 September. Not only was it going against the grain to establish a Shakespearean touring company in 1925, Mac (as he was known) set up a circuit that ignored the usual Belfast/Dublin/Cork touring axis. In their thirty-five years of touring, the McMaster Company played only thirteen weeks in Dublin, and at one point went more than six years between performances in the capital. On the few occasions that he did play Dublin, usually in the Theatre Royal, Mac always tried to upgrade his company with a star performance, with Sir Frank Benson joining him in December 1928, followed in 1929 by the early Abbey actress, Sara Allgood.

On the road, the McMaster Company were as much like a travelling circus as a theatre, with McMaster once parading through the streets of Athlone in his full ecclesiastical regalia from a play called *The Cardinal* to perform a mock excommunication on those who had not attended his performance the night before. They rolled through the south and southwest, and later developed a west coast and midland circuit that took in Tuam, Swinford, Westport, Castlebar, Athlone, Cavan and many other towns and villages. In their wake, they established for the first time (apart from the erratic perambulations of the fit-up companies) a professional theatrical life outside of the major centres. 'We'd find digs', recalled one company member, 'wash basin and jug, tea, black pudding and off to the hall, set up a stage on trestle tables, a few rostrum, a few drapes, costumes out of the hampers, set up shop, and at night play, not always but mostly, to a packed house.'[12] As fewer and fewer companies went on tour, Mac increasingly had the pick of young performers who wanted to learn their trade, so that over the years small Irish towns saw a line-up that in retrospect reads like an Equity *Who's Who*: Harold Pinter, Milo O'Shea, Patrick Magee, T. P. McKenna, Coralie Carmichael and Kenneth Haigh (the first Jimmy Porter in *Look Back in Anger*).

In the best actor-manager tradition, however, the productions always revolved around Mac. 'It was consistent with him', Pinter would later recall, 'that after many months of coasting through Shylock he suddenly lashed fullfired into the role at an obscure matinée in a onehorse village; a frightening performance. Afterwards he said to me: What did I do? Did you notice? . . . He never did it again. Not quite like that. Who saw it?'[13] The short answer is that over the years thousands saw McMaster and his company at a time when amateur theatre companies were springing up at an astounding rate all over the country; and it can be little coincidence that towns which were to establish amateur companies of the highest calibre – Tuam, Ennis, Gorey, to take only three examples – were all regular stops on the McMaster circuit.

In another entirely unexpected way the McMaster Company was to have a profound effect on twentieth-century Irish theatre. Among those who braved boarding houses with 'Sacred Heart pictures and fleas in the beds' to join Mac's third Irish tour was a promising young English actor, who met up with the company in Enniscorthy on 17 June 1927. ' "Ah, here we are", said Mac in the voice he quite genuinely imagined to be his only audible one', introducing the new arrival to his brother-in-law, Micheál Mac Líammóir. 'This is our new Iago, Micheál, Mr Hilton Edwards.'[14] Within six months of this meeting, while touring with Mac, Hilton Edwards and Micheál Mac Líammóir had a meeting with Líam Ó Bríain of University College, Galway, who was trying to establish an Irish-language theatre in the city. By June 1928, Edwards and McMaster had been hired (even though Edwards knew no Irish) as directors of An Taibhdhearc, the country's first Irish-language theatre. An Taibhdhearc opened in Galway's Middle Street on 28 August with *Diarmuid agus Gráinne*, written and designed by Mac Líammóir. Although it began with an original production, in its early days An Taibhdhearc relied largely on translations. However, within a decade it was nurturing a whole new generation of Irish-language playwrights, including Máiréad Ní Ghráda.

Meanwhile, having developed a taste for theatre-founding, Edwards and Mac Líammóir began almost simultaneously assembling the money and personnel to start an English-language theatre in Dublin, and by October 1928 they had found a name, the Gate Theatre (originally intended to indicate a vague affiliation with Peter Godfrey's Gate Theatre in London's Covent Garden) and a venue in the Abbey's little-used second theatre, the Peacock. The Peacock had a stage, as Mac Líammóir later wrote, 'on which you could hardly swing a cat, so we decided we might as well throw discretion to the winds and be bold and daring for once, and we opened one night with *Peer Gynt*'.[15] Cat-swinging was certainly to be discouraged in the Peacock, which had a performance space only 21 feet (6.3 metres) across and 16 feet (4.8 metres) deep, raised a mere 18 inches (0.5 metres) from the auditorium floor. Nor was it helped by the narrowest of proscenium arches (barely enough to conceal an actor waiting for a cue on the stage left side, which abutted a solid wall) a curiously angled back wall, and the absence of any means of crossing backstage – which meant an actor exiting stage left had to stand, pressed flat in a narrow recess, until the next cue to enter. An auditorium seating only 102 patrons was not going to generate enough box office to allow them to throw money at these obstacles.

Deciding to use the Peacock to play *Peer Gynt*, with its huge cast and multiple set changes, was typical of the bravado Edwards and Mac Líammóir were to bring to the Irish theatre. Also typical was the way they went about solving the considerable staging challenge they set themselves. Mac Líammóir, in between running An Taibhdhearc and producing his first play, drew a series of sketches based around a pair of triangular step units on castors, which could be rolled together to form a pyramidal mountain, separated to form a gorge, and placed side by side to form a hut. Edwards, meanwhile, created the dazzling blue of a receding sky by painting the back wall of the Peacock a neutral grey, and lighting it with eight 500-watt lanterns, creating an illusion of depth, and silhouetting Mac Líammóir's stylised mountain / gorge / cabin unit. This may have left an acting area only about four feet deep, but it was still more visually inventive than anything Seaghan Barlow had hammered together at the Abbey for quite some time. 'These very limitations', wrote Edwards in retrospect, 'often proved an advantage in deciding automatically many of those points over which a producer with unlimited facilities is inclined to vacillate.'[16] Three elements of this original production – simple, flexible geometric sets, strong colours in the lighting and lavish costumes – were to establish a template for future productions. From the very outset, the Gate had a modernist appreciation of design, which the Abbey clearly lacked. At the same time, Edwards and Mac Líammóir never lost a more traditional sense of what it meant to work in the theatre, learned in London's West End and on tour with Mac; they respected craftsmanship, showmanship, and business acumen as much as artistry, and this became clear when their repertoire picked up the society comedy *Berkeley Square* (1930), a stage version of *Wuthering Heights* (1934), and some Shakespeare, including an extremely popular *Hamlet* (1932). From the beginning, the Gate made it clear that it was not yet another 'little theatre', doomed to artistic martyrdom and financial oblivion. 'Now that the little theatres of the world have done their best and are dropping into bankruptcy', claimed the Gate's journal, *Motley* in 1933, 'and the commercial theatre has done its worst, and is making a belated search for fresh plays, the Gate retains its balance and is going straight ahead.'[17]

In many ways, the Gate ethos is summed up in the theatre, located in the Rotunda Buildings on Parnell Square, to which they moved in February 1930. The conversion carried out by architect Michael Scott produced the first modernist theatre auditorium in Ireland, unlike all earlier Irish theatres, including the Abbey, in that the entire Gate audience sat in long rows on the same raked level, with no boxes or galleries. At the same time, the auditorium's ornate plasterwork and proscenium arch gesture towards an earlier theatre culture. Within that arch, production photographs from the Gate's early years indicate a design sense which owed as much to German expressionist cinema as to Mac's touring sets, with the 1934 production of Ferenc Molnár's *Liliom*, for instance, made up of a few simple stylised objects (a telephone pole, a miniature railway viaduct, a sign) all at oblique angles, set against a black backcloth. By the end of the first few seasons, the Gate would use this scenographic style to present Eugene O'Neill's *The Hairy Ape*, Karel Capek's *R.U.R.*, two plays by Evreinov, and Strindberg's *Simoom.*

The Gate's decision to stage this modernist repertoire had as much to do with an existing audience demand as with its founders' tastes. After the 1916 Rising had decimated the personnel of Edward Martyn's Theatre of Ireland, the survivors spent the next few years struggling to extend the horizons of Irish audiences. By their final production, in November 1920 (an unusual double bill of *The Changeling* and Chekhov's *The Jubilee*) their place had already been taken by the Dublin Drama League, who mounted their first production, Srgjan Tucic's *The Liberators*, on 9 February 1919. The Dublin Drama League was effectively a quiet *coup* from above by Yeats and Lennox Robinson, rebelling against the dominance of rural comedies in the Abbey's repertoire. Using the Abbey stage on Sunday and Monday evenings (when there were no scheduled performances), the League worked with Abbey actors such as F. J. McCormick, Gabriel Fallon and Barry Fitzgerald (supplemented by amateurs) and in effect became a sort of phantom image of what the Abbey might have been – a democratically run, flexible organisation presenting the best of European modernist theatre to a select audience. They staged Strindberg's *The Spook Sonata* in April 1925, more than a year before its London début, and over the next decade the League would present sixty-six plays from fifteen countries, 'introducing to Dublin', as one participant put it, 'all the *avant-garde* plays of the time'.[18]

In a sense, the Drama League filled a gap created by the departure of the touring companies, and so it should come as little surprise to find it mirrored on the northern and southern ends of the Belfast/Dublin/Cork axis. In Belfast, the Northern Drama League, founded in 1923, was presenting a similar range of plays (Strindberg, Chekhov, Evreinov) supplemented with truly unexpected works (Beaumont and Fletcher's *Knight of the Burning Pestle* in November 1925, for instance). At the other end of the island, in Cork, Frank O'Connor founded the Cork Drama League in 1927, producing a repertoire similar to its Dublin and Belfast counterparts, concentrating on Chekhov and Ibsen, but also staging Corkery's *The Yellow Bittern* and works by Cork writers. Between them, the Drama Leagues provided Edwards and Mac Líammóir with an audience, a repertoire, and actors who could perform it – including Shelah Richards, Meriel Moore and Betty Chancellor, Gate actresses who were all League alumni. Consequently, as Lennox Robinson put it, 'When the Drama League saw that modern European plays were going to be produced by the Gate in Dublin, we decided that the League's main work was done, and dissolved it.'[19]

Among those to come from outside the Abbey to the Dublin Drama League was Denis Johnston, who acted in plays by Strindberg and Pirandello, directed Ernst Toller's *Hoppla!*, and later became involved with the Northern Drama League. In 1926 he began writing a play he called 'Shadowdance', which was rejected by the Abbey with the words 'The Old Lady Says "No!" ' scrawled on it, but accompanied by an offer of £50 from Yeats towards its staging. Johnston slyly retitled it *The Old Lady Says 'No!'*, and gave it to the Gate, who premièred it on 3 July 1929. For the play's first audience, there must have been a momentary sense of disorientation when the curtains first parted on that summer's evening, as if by some accident they had been ferried across the Liffey to the Queen's of a decade earlier. The play's opening scene is a virtuoso pastiche of a Robert Emmet play, such as Boucicault's *Robert Emmet* (1884) – *albeit* a bit purpler than the norm in that it is made up entirely of lines taken from nineteenth-century Irish poets such as Samuel Ferguson, Aubrey de Vere and James Clarence Mangan. Then, as happens in Pirandello's *Henry IV*, which was on the London stage as Johnston was writing his play, and had been staged by the Dublin Drama League on 10 August 1924, the actor playing Emmet (referred to as 'The Speaker') is accidentally hit on the head and awakens on the stage believing that he really is Emmet.

At that point, a chorus of shadowy Forms appear – a moment preserved in an existing production photograph, which shows Mac

Líammóir's Speaker in heavy makeup, stage right, looking like a Queen's actor who has momentarily forgotten his lines, while stage left an orchestrated mass of dark pointing figures, lit only from above, move in from the darkness. The moment is a potent one. Confused and anachronistic, the Romantic hero (like Davoren in *Shadow of a Gunman*) is made redundant by the cultural disarmament of the post-Civil-War era. So too are the cultural forms of that earlier era, standing accused by the dark shadows of a modernity with which the play is only half in love. And, above all, it is a director's moment, its effect relying less on the script than on lighting, design and the orchestration of bodies.

Unlike any previous professional Irish theatre, the Gate was a director's theatre. Although it nurtured a handful of young playwrights over its first few decades (as well as Johnston, there was David Sears, Mary Manning and Mac Líammóir himself) it achieved much greater successes, both commercially and theatrically, with productions of earlier plays – particularly those of Oscar Wilde. Twenty-eight years after his death, Wilde found himself very much alive on the Dublin stage. Although he had appeared personally at the Gaiety Theatre at the height of his fame in the mid-1880s, only two touring productions of his plays reached Dublin after his rapid plummet into notoriety in 1895 (the year in which *The Importance of Being Earnest* was first staged). Hearing of Wilde's death in November 1900, Holloway noted in his diary: 'A few years ago had the world at his feet, he was nonetheless wiped off the memory of everyone, & his name only thought of with loathing.'[20] Consequently, when the Dublin Drama League staged Wilde's *A Florentine Tragedy* in January 1922, it was in some respects just as daring a choice as the Schnitzler play with which it shared the bill. Equally, however, it was a signal that Wilde was coming in from the cold, and this was confirmed when the Abbey mounted its first Wilde production, *The Importance of Being Earnest*, on 6 November 1926. Neither of these productions, however, was to have the impact of the Edwards / Mac Líammóir production of *Salomé*, staged in December 1928.

The 1928 *Salomé* was a defining moment for the Gate. It is tempting to speculate that Micheál Mac Líammóir (a gay Englishman who had reinvented himself as an Irishman) saw in Wilde (a gay Irishman who had reinvented himself as an Englishman) something of an inverted mirror image; and, indeed, both were to prove the truth of one of Wilde's paradoxes, that 'It is only by contact with the art of foreign nations that the art of a country gains that individual and separate life that we call nationality.'[21] It would be closer to the point, however, to think of Wilde as modernist ahead of his time, as several recent critics have urged.[22] This was understood in theatrical terms by Edwards and Mac Líammóir, who, recognising a kindred mixture of traditional theatre craft, camp extravagance and knowing self-theorisation, adopted him as a posthumous writer-in-residence. The Gate went on to stage *Lady Windermere's Fan* (1931), *An Ideal Husband* (1932), *The Importance of Being Earnest* (1933), and, when they ran out of viable Wilde plays, a stage version of *The Portrait of Dorian Gray* (1945), and Mac Líammóir's hugely successful one-man Wilde show, *The Importance of Being Oscar* (1960) – all of which were revived frequently, with *Earnest* becoming one of their most successful productions ever, restaged in 1935, 1936, 1938, toured through Egypt in 1937, and then brought back again in 1971. Steven Berkoff was brought in to direct a new *Salomé* in 1988, and this production was revived in the year 2000.

When Edwards and Mac Líammóir announced that they were to produce that first *Salomé* in December 1928, everyone knew that it was the play the Lord Chamberlain's Office had refused to license in 1892 (on the basis of a sixteenth-century ordinance prohibiting the stage representation of Biblical matter). Like the Abbey production of *Blanco Posnet* in 1909, which had made a point about the relative values of English and Irish freedom, staging the banned *Salomé* in 1928 was an intervention in the on-going debate about censorship – only this time the positions of England and Ireland were reversed. If *Blanco Posnet* showed up the 'imbecility and mischievousness' of English censorship by demonstrating that a colonised Ireland was freer than a sovereign England, the Gate *Salomé* reversed the equation, asking if the Irish Free State were really 'free' after all.

The context for this intervention was the Censorship of Publications Bill, then before the Dáil. As *Salomé* was in rehearsal, the *Irish Statesman* carried a series of articles by George Russell, Yeats and Shaw, attacking the Bill. Yeats approached the issue in his increasingly gnomic public manner, by adopting one of Wilde's aphorisms. 'There is such a thing as immoral painting and immoral literature', he declared. 'They are bad paintings and bad literature.' Shaw, still the scourge of the censor twenty years after *Blanco Posnet*, announced that 'the moment we got rid of tyranny we rushed to enslave ourselves', before launching into a mischievously paradoxical argument, maintaining that the most sensual aspect of Irish culture was the iconography of the Catholic Church, 'all those figures of the dead Christ . . . the Catherines and Margarets with their long tresses, teaching the young to associate loveliness with

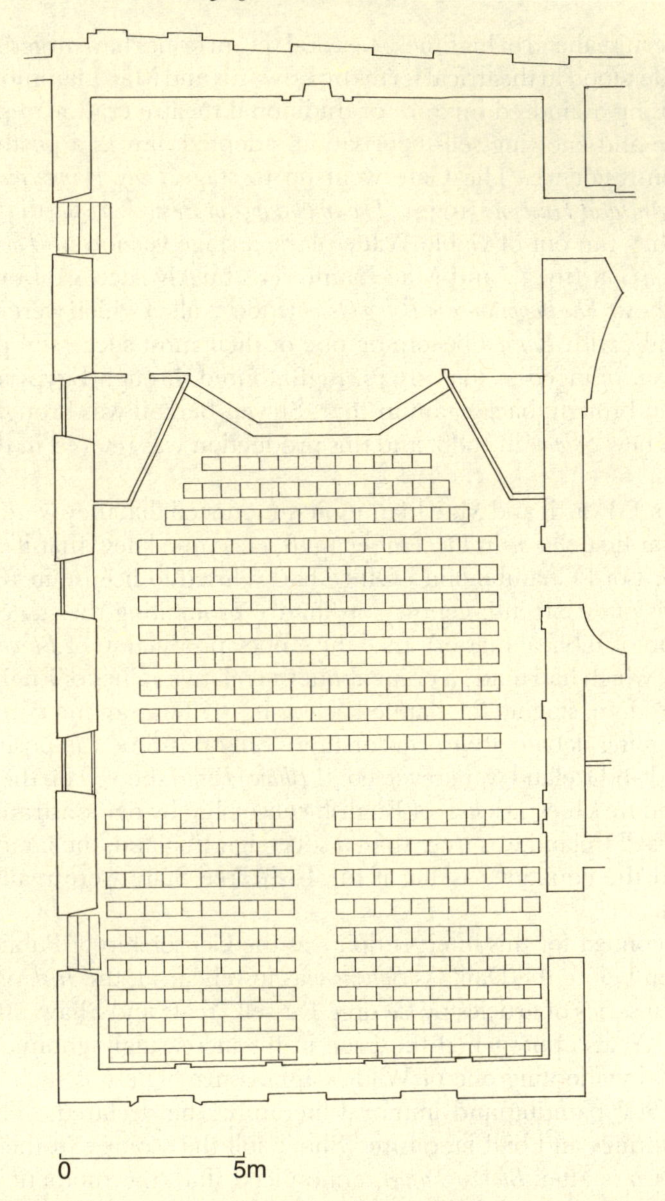

Plan 4. When the Gate Theatre, designed by Michael Scott, opened in February 1930, it was the first modern fan-shaped auditorium on the island. Although Hilton Edwards and Micheál Mac Líammóir created many innovative set designs on the stage, it suffers from the lack of a fly system and limited wing space. This drawing is based on a 1955 survey, courtesy of Scott Tallon Walker, Architects.

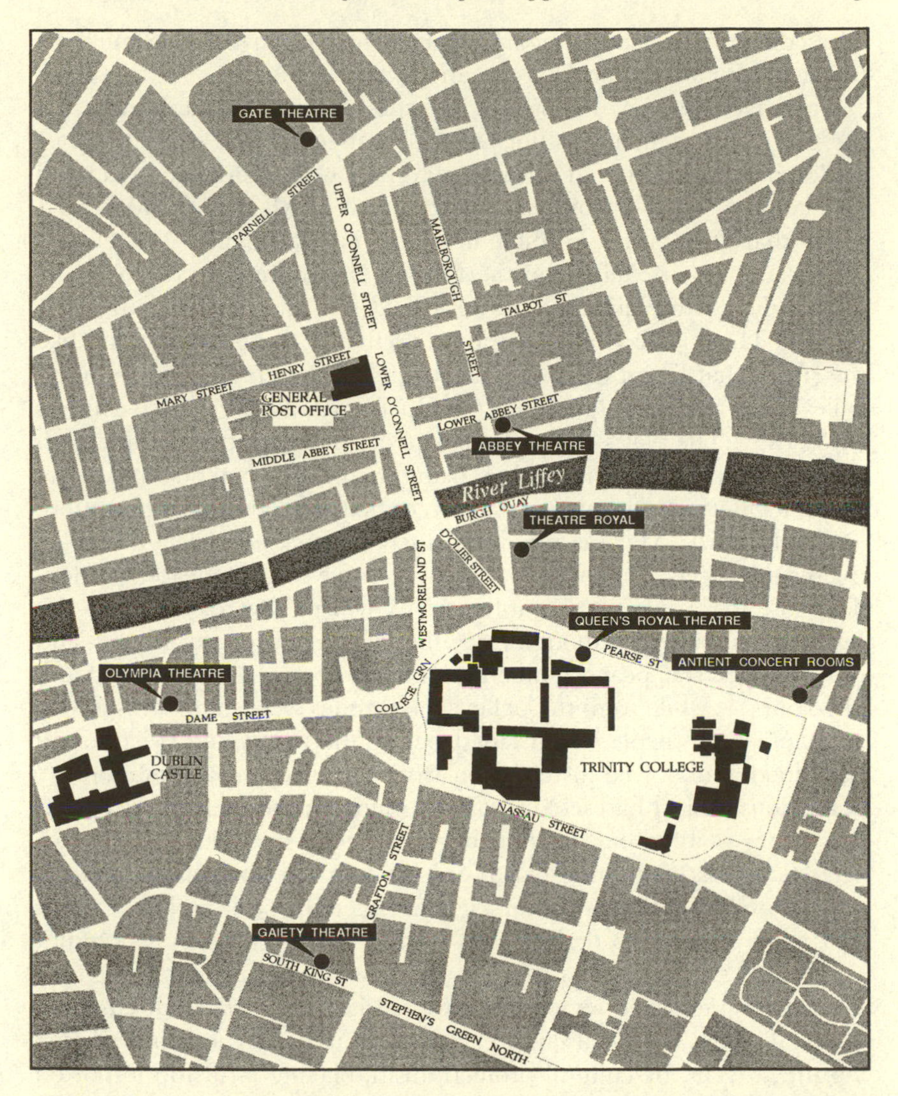

Map 4. Major theatres in Dublin, *c.* 1930. Like the city itself, the theatrical centre of Dublin shifted to the east in the two hundred years after 1730. When the Abbey, and later the Gate, took up premises on what was at that time the unfashionable north side of the River Liffey, the city's theatrical geography was re-aligned yet again.

blessedness'.[23] In a sense, *Salomé* was the contribution to the debate from the absent contemporary of Yeats and Shaw: Wilde.

Indeed, *Salomé* may well provide the subtext for Shaw's argument, for the play's real scandal was not just that it used Biblical subject matter (Wilde had pointed out at the time that the law had not been enforced in relation to Saint-Saëns' *Samson and Delilah* or Massenet's *Hérodias*),[24] it was that *Salomé* used the Bible in such an extravagantly sensual way. 'Jokanaan', Salomé tells John the Baptist, 'I am amorous of thy body! Thy body is white like the lilies of a field that the mower hath never mowed. Thy body is white like the snows that lie on the mountains, like the snows that lie on the mountain of Judea and come down into the valleys. The roses in the garden of the Queen of Arabia are not so white as thy body.'[25] The play's technique is one of excess, heaping image upon image, metaphor upon metaphor, using five or six when one makes the point, hypnotising the audience into a trance of languorous exhaustion.

The Edwards–Mac Líammóir production of *Salomé* used light to stage the script's excesses in a way that would not have been possible in 1892. The costumes were a 'venomous green', while Edwards describes the set as 'matt black picked out in metallic silver against a sky of jade, and lit with a peculiar peacock-blue-green flood obtained by an admixture of colours . . . while from the palace the thrones were faintly flushed by a smouldering purple which faded before the moon and became red like blood and glowed in reflection from the silver ornamentations'.[26] A religious subject had seldom so fully inundated the senses (except, as Shaw slyly pointed out, in stained glass windows). 'Wilde's monstrous orchid', as Mac Líammóir called *Salomé*, did more than throw down a gauntlet to Ireland's new censors; it challenged the basic preconceptions that made censorship desirable in the first place. 'We are at present', wrote Fr R. S. Devane in the Jesuit journal *Studies* in 1927, 'engaged in an heroic effort to revive our national language, national customs, national values, national culture.'[27] This could only be achieved, the argument went, by cultural protectionism, placing tariffs on imported publications; it was but a short step to the censorship of anything not 'national'. At the root of support for the Censorship Bill, therefore, was a sense of operating within narrow margins, as the dark shadows of global modernity plotted to disorient the fixed certainties of national identity.

As possible futures seemed to be shutting down, Ireland found an image of itself in rural plays where the plot typically hinges around a situation in which characters have very few choices, usually narrowed down to marriage (comedy), emigration (serious drama) or death (tragedy). The dominant production style at the Abbey reinforced this sense of limitation by confining the actors within a box-set that varied little from one rural play to the next, and drew on a limited palette of earth tones, lit, as always, with an amber wash. To all of this restraint, the overwrought sensuality of the Gate *Salomé* was an affront, and all the more so because it showed what could be done with such obviously limited means. Crammed on the tiny Peacock stage, what Mac Líammóir euphemistically called the 'sartorial economies' of the production were among its most erotic features, 'with the entire cast stripped almost naked. This we did partly because it was the obvious thing to do and partly for reasons of economy'.[28] From the very beginning, the Gate thus challenged the notion that the power of self-transformation could be limited by a simple lack of resources.

The trick was to be iconoclastic and entertaining at the same time, as the Gate showed with their next Wilde production, *The Importance of Being Earnest*, in October 1933. This 'trivial comedy for serious people', as Wilde had subtitled it, was perfectly suited to the developing Gate production style. The 1890s costumes, which had looked more or less normal at the time of the original production, blazed out from the stage as fantastic concoctions of ruffles and satin by the austere standards of 1933 fashions. Edwards and Mac Líammóir framed these unreal creations against a simple, stylised set that made only the most parodic gestures towards realism, and adopted a playing style to match. By emphasising its own artificiality, the Gate production simultaneously preserved the pleasures of the play's triviality, and underscored the seriousness of its games with truth and appearance.

At a time when the prevailing aesthetic in the Irish theatre proclaimed that the truth was what you saw, *The Importance of Being Earnest* begins with a character named Jack who pretends to be called Ernest ('My name is Ernest in town and Jack in the country') but who at the end of the play turns out to be named Ernest after all, having been lost by his original parents, and adopted. The plot, of course, is an entirely conventional society comedy (the misplaced orphan who discovers that he really has the aristocratic background required to marry the heroine); however, Wilde's dialogue changes it into something altogether more subversive. 'It is a terrible thing for a man', says Jack/Earnest in the play's closing moments, 'to find out suddenly that all his life he has been speaking nothing but the truth.'[29] In a culture trying to cling to what it had thought had been the truth, *The Importance of Being Earnest* questioned truth itself – *albeit* with a light enough touch to carry off the performance.

With productions such as *Salomé* and *The Importance of Being Earnest*, the Gate achieved a commercial and critical success the Abbey directors quickly came to envy. As early as 1929, they had hired Denis Johnston to direct a production of *King Lear* with an abstract, modernist set, and in 1934 they brought in an English director, Bladon Peake, and a designer, James Bould; when Peake and Bould left a year later, they were replaced by another young English director, Hugh Hunt, and the designer Tanya Moiseiwitsch, who struggled to inject new life into the Abbey's tired set designs for the four years she was associated with the theatre. And yet, within the theatre there was resistance to these innovations. Mesmerised by a fantasy of its own origins, the Abbey (like the country at large), had a fundamentalist wing quick to sniff out heresy or innovation. 'The great fundamental fact in the Theatre', announced the Abbey actor-turned-critic Gabriel Fallon in 1936, 'are the three A's – the Author, the Actor and the Audience. The three A's *are* the Theatre' – leaving little room for the director or the designer. 'In the Fays' time', he sniffed, 'it was not fashionable to talk about "production".'[30]

Politically, however, the Abbey was in no position to reinvent itself in the 1930s. When the directors had thrown in their lot with the Free State government in 1922, courting government ministers such as Ernest Blythe and Kevin O'Higgins, they had been pursuing a simple survival strategy as much as anything else. When a government subsidy was announced in 1925, it seemed as if this strategy had paid off. With the coming to power of Fianna Fáil under Eamon de Valera in 1932, however, the Abbey found itself on the wrong side of the political fence. With many of the same people who had opposed *The Plough and the Stars* in 1926 now in government, its annual subsidy was cut to £750 shortly after de Valera took office. That same year, Lady Gregory died. 'All is changed', Yeats wrote in 'Coole Park and Ballylee, 1931', 'that high horse riderless'. Yeats had been behind the hiring of Peake and Hunt, but lacked Lady Gregory's diplomatic skills, and throughout the mid-1930s the Abbey boardroom became the scene of almost continuous firings, hirings and resignations.

Ironically, Yeats was then entering into his maturity as a playwright, and needed a theatre with the sort of directorial and design skills more in evidence at the Gate than at the Abbey. Yeats' position in the world of Irish theatre after he received the Nobel Prize in 1923 was unique; on the one hand, he was the undisputed elder statesman of Irish letters, the 'smiling public man' as he describes himself in 'Among School Children'. Meeting him for the first time later that same year, Micheál Mac

Líammóir (never easily intimidated) recalls feeling 'suddenly shyer than I had felt since my first rehearsal when I was ten'. He was ushered into the Abbey Green Room where Yeats sat beside Lady Gregory, 'who had the air of watching a sacred snake to whom she was high priestess'. And yet, for all his aura of power, many of Yeats' plays after 1910 were only ever produced privately, and some were not produced at all. He was, for many years, the great unproduced Irish playwright.

This pattern changed somewhat in the late 1920s, when Yeats' translations of Sophocles' *Oedipus the King* and *Oedipus at Colonus* (1927) surprised sceptical Abbey audiences with their theatrical power. For the next decade, the Abbey continued to stage his plays, challenging the house style by bringing in choreographer Ninette de Valois and composer George Antheil for the 1929 production of the 'ballet-play', *Fighting the Waves*: 'My greatest success on the stage since *Kathleen-ni-Houlihan*' according to Yeats; 'In the balcony, people started to leave' recorded Joseph Holloway.[31] From that point on, Yeats' private search for a form began to coalesce in a type of theatre which can only be described as Yeatsian, in plays such as *The Resurrection* (1934), *The King of the Great Clock Tower* (1934; staged by the Gate in 1942), and ultimately in *Purgatory* (1938), the last of his plays to be premièred in Yeats' lifetime. Here, in a design by the poet's daughter, Anne Yeats, with 'just a bare whitish tree in the middle of the stage and a backcloth with a window cut out of it', an old man and a boy occupy a stage world in which the living mingle with the dead, the real with the symbolic, in a moment of revelation that will be acted – like theatrical performance itself – 'not once but many times'. The result is a rare work of distilled theatrical power, and one of the best short plays ever written.

'My play has been a sensational success as far as the audience went', Yeats wrote to a friend. 'The trouble is outside. The press or the clerics get to work . . . This time the trouble is theological.'[32] Indeed, the trouble in Ireland had been theological for some time, and it was getting worse. In spite of the best efforts of Yeats, Shaw and Wilde's ghost, the Censorship of Publications Act became law in 1929, and while it did not cover stage performances, the theatres were unwilling to goad the new moral watchdogs. So, in 1935, when the Abbey directors decided to stage Sean O'Casey's *The Silver Tassie*, they were accused of 'indecency' and 'blasphemy', and informed that it would not be tolerated. For their part, the Abbey directors were partly trying to compensate for having rejected their most profitable writer's epic play in 1928 amid some very public acrimony. Equally, they were trying to show that they could cope with the expressionist second act, set on a symbol-strewn First World War battlefield, with a statue of the Virgin Mary and a life-size crucifix hanging over the figure of a soldier, strapped cruciform to a gunwheel. 'There's a Gawd knocking abaht somewhere', as one of the soldiers puts it. The *Irish Catholic* responded on 7 September 1935, by calling for a law banning all of O'Casey's plays, and the Abbey's only Catholic director, Brinsley MacNamara, resigned in protest. It was clearly not the time for a fight, and the play was withdrawn after a brief run.

In its own ramshackle way, however, the Abbey was sturdy enough by the mid-1930s to weather such storms. So too was the Gate, improbably ruled over by a gay couple, Edwards and Mac Líammóir, at a time when Catholic Ireland could hardly bear the thought of heterosexual sex, let alone any other kind. However, the swelling tide of heresophobia was capable of sweeping away less sturdy edifices. In 1934, in the town of Birr, County Offaly, for instance, a group of local citizens founded the Birr Little Theatre. With their own money, they built a good basic performance space, not much smaller than the Peacock stage, 19 feet deep (5.7 metres) with a 15-foot wide (4.5 metres) proscenium opening and upstage well for lighting the cyclorama. Ambitious from the start, productions in the Birr Little Theatre's first few years included T. C. Murray's *Autumn Fire* and Eugene O'Neill's *The Emperor Jones*. For one production, they engaged Ria Mooney from the Abbey and commissioned designs from Micheál Mac Líammóir. Then, in December of 1938, the Birr Little Theatre announced that it was to perform *Shadow and Substance* by Paul Vincent Carroll.

Carroll's play is very much a critique of Irish Catholicism from within, dealing with a cultured, continentally educated priest, Canon Skerritt, who is forced by his zealous curates into a confrontation with a local schoolteacher, named O'Flingsley, who has written a book claiming 'that Ireland has dangerously materialized the outlook of the Church, and its profound spiritual essence has been stolen'.[33] Caught in the middle of this power struggle is Canon Skerritt's housekeeper, Bridget, who sees visions of her namesake, St Bridget, and who, with a tragic inevitability signalled early in the play, is accidentally killed when a reactionary mob attack O'Flingsley's house. *Shadow and Substance* may have been critical of Irish Catholicism, but only within its own deeply conservative limits. There was thus shock in Birr when, on the night before *Shadow and Substance* was to open, the actors received an objection from a local Catholic vigilance society. The play was cancelled; the Theatre lost money, and over the next two years performed only two plays, whereas previously they had been doing between three and five per year. 'It was if someone had died on us', one of the actors later wrote.[34]

The production history of *Shadow and Substance* in the late 1930s tells us much about the state of theatre in Ireland at the time. In the same year that it was banned in Birr, *Shadow and Substance* won the Drama Critics Circle award in New York for best foreign play, showing that the trans-Atlantic sea-lane to success was still open. Before that, however, Carroll's play had premièred at the Abbey, which, in spite of its woes, continued to be flooded with as many as three hundred new plays every year. Some were from writers who had established reputations in prose or poetry (Francis Stuart, Myles na gCopaleen and Austin Clarke, for instance); others were from aspiring playwrights who would sink without a trace. Contained within this deluge was much dross, but equally there were plays of intelligent power, like *Shadow and Substance.* Throughout it all, the Abbey consolidated what had been its greatest strength since 1904: the ability to absorb talent from all over the island.

It is possible to imagine an Abbey script-reader in those years, wading through heaps of predictable, poorly written pages, and then coming upon Teresa Deevy's *The Reapers* (1930), followed up in 1931 with *A Disciple.* By the time she wrote *The King of Spain's Daughter* in 1935, it was clear that she had forged a distinctive theatrical voice. *The King of Spain's Daughter* is a one-act play, set on a stage dominated by a 'Road Closed' sign. The play's main character, Annie, is offered a choice between factory work and a loveless marriage, and in this sense of limited options the play resembles much Irish drama of the period. However, Annie maintains a secret freedom that she hides not only from the male characters in the play, but from the audience as well. It is strongly suggested, for instance, that she is having sexual relations with at least two men other than Jim Harris, who wants to marry her. 'Why do you go with Roddy and Jack?' Jim demands of her, but Annie seems insulated from what she may have done the previous night, uninterested and unable to remember. With equal detachment and privacy, she chooses to marry Harris when she sees his savings book. In a curtain line the stage directions describe as 'quiet, exultant', she says: 'He put by two shillin's for two hundred weeks. I think he is a man that – supposin' he was jealous – might cut your throat!'[35] The play is a comedy, Deevy insists in an unpublished letter, because Annie 'marries Jim, quite reconciled at the last as she has found passion in his persistent affection & so can visualise herself as the heroine of a possible tragedy!'[36] Like the heroine of Deevy's full-length play, *Katie Roche* (1936), Annie copes with the steady erosion of her hopes by secretly fantasising a cruelty more spectacular than anything she actually suffers.

In the late 1930s and early 1940s, however, Deevy's work could not compete with the popularity of what was known as 'the Abbey Play', of which George Shiels', *Professor Tim* (1925), is a prime example. Still capable of filling the house for a two-month run in 1944, and notching up 247 productions by 1963. *Professor Tim* takes over the old Boucicauldian melodrama of reconciliation, placing it in a recognisable (but not harshly realistic) rural twentieth-century Irish landscape. The play revolves around two families of prosperous farmers and their neighbour, Hugh O'Cahan, a typical stage Anglo-Irishman, a lovable rogue with a stable full of horses and a rickety mansion full of dotty, but loyal, servants. Holding the plot together is the joker-figure, like the Conn or Myles of melodrama, in this case the eponymous Professor Tim, played by Queen's alumnus F. J. McCormick in the original production. Professor Tim is a returned wanderer who pretends to be a drunken wastrel, but is finally revealed as a wealthy and respected professor capable of winding up the plot to everyone's satisfaction, allowing the girl from the farmhouse to marry the impoverished aristocrat from the big house, in a variation on a plot that went back at least as far as John O'Keeffe's *The Poor Soldier*.

In the three decades after its first production in 1925, *Professor Tim* became one of the inescapable landmarks in the Irish theatre landscape. The Abbey premièred a new Shiels play every year from 1927 to 1948 (with the exceptions of 1928 and 1943). Shiels thus joined Brinsley MacNamara, Rutherford Mayne, Lennox Robinson, T. C. Murray, and later Louis D'Alton as a core group of writers who not only kept the Abbey financially afloat, but also provided the main repertoire for a plethora of small amateur theatre companies then springing up all over the country in a quiet cultural revolution. 'It gave me real pleasure to think that my plays, apart from their merits, had helped to get things going in the provinces', wrote Shiels in 1946.[37] Just as the early Abbey plays were so influential because they were so simple, a play like *Professor Tim* contains nothing to daunt an enthusiastic amateur: it requires only a couple of basic sets, no special staging effects, no virtuoso acting skills, and can be played in an Irish actor's own accent. Even the frequent shoddiness of Abbey productions in those years sometimes encouraged non-professionals to think that they could do a better job.

The transformation of so many Irish people from audience into actors in the decades after Independence is one of the most remarkable and largely unrecorded stories of recent Irish social history. Of course, going back to the eighteenth century, members of the aristocracy, such as Richard Martin of Galway, had staged amateur theatrical productions; similarly, there was a long tradition of plays such as *The Battle of Aughrim* being produced in barns, particularly in rural Ulster. However, the real emergence of amateur drama did not take place until the final years of the nineteenth century, which saw the frenzied formation of cultural societies of all kinds – from Gaelic League branches to 1798 commemoration committees. In the radicalisation of cultural politics that took place in the years leading up to 1916, few of these early organisations were primarily concerned with producing plays. Most either evolved into more strictly political groups or simply disappeared before 1920. The few that did survive were usually outside the ambit of nationalist politics, like the Dublin-based British Empire Shakespeare Society, founded in 1907. It hung on to its anachronistic name until it was reborn as the Dublin Shakespeare Society in July of 1933.

By the mid-1930s, changes were taking place in rural Irish society that would redraw the country's theatrical map. The automobile was opening up the countryside, making the old rail routes less important, while a rural and small town middle class, made up of teachers, clergy, doctors, and shopkeepers were consolidating their roles as community leaders. A generation earlier, their efforts had been channelled into the maelstrom of nationalist politics; however, by the time Fianna Fáil entered into electoral politics in 1927, the Irish political landscape was beginning to settle into a reasonably stable shape, and people began to direct their organisational skills in other directions. Some turned to the Gaelic Athletic Association, some to lay religious confraternities (like that which had opposed *Shadow and Substance* in Birr); but others were forming amateur theatre companies. Indeed, many of the same social changes (and, indeed, many of the same individuals) responsible for the repressive religiosity of the period were also responsible for the growth of amateur theatre.

By 1932, there were enough amateur companies around the island to form a national Amateur Dramatic Association. The following year in Kerry, for instance, the Tralee Theatre Society was founded, followed shortly afterwards by a group in Listowel, and by 1943 there was an annual amateur drama festival being held in Killarney. In 1944, after a similar flourishing of small companies, a new festival was launched at the opposite end of the country, in Bundoran, County Donegal, followed the next year by a festival in Bray, just outside Dublin. In that same year, an

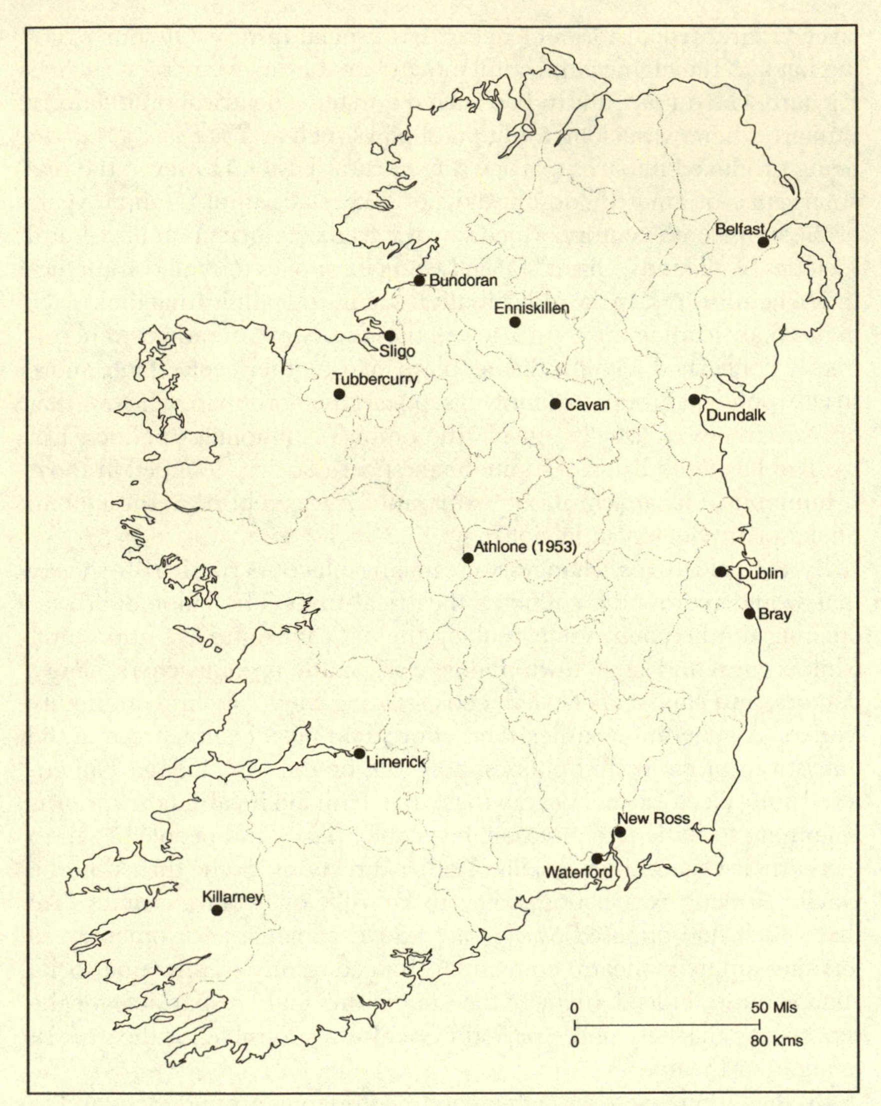

Map 5. Sites of amateur drama festivals, 1946. As amateur theatre companies shot up around Ireland in the 1930s and 1940s, they transformed the geography of the Irish theatre, which had been concentrated along the eastern and southern coasts for two centuries. By 1946, there were thirteen annual festivals, spread throughout the island, with a notable cluster in the north-west.

amateur company in Omagh acquired a transmitter to broadcast radio plays to the local area. By 1946, there were annual festivals in Belfast, Cavan, Enniskillen, Limerick, New Ross, Sligo, Tubbercurry, Waterford and the Father Mathew Festival in Dublin. Six years later, discussions were under way that would lead to the creation of the All-Ireland Drama Festival in Athlone, first held in 1953.

'The main hope of Irish Drama', wrote Roger McHugh in *The Bell* in 1947, 'lies in the amateur little-theatre groups of Ireland.'[38] Indeed, from the mid-1930s, onwards the amateur movement provided much of Ireland's missing theatre infrastructure. The McMaster Company, for instance, began using the network of performance spaces maintained by amateur companies. The same is true of the Longford Players, who (in addition to playing at the Gate Theatre) from 1936 onwards supplemented the nation's theatrical diet with touring productions of Pirandello, Denis Johnston, and Shaw, as well as presenting Christine Longford's own plays. At the same time, in the absence of any professional actor or technical training programme, the amateur companies at least offered something like an informal apprenticeship. The same was true for playwrights. The Abbey still continued to receive several hundred unsolicited scripts every year; yet, with a policy of long runs and revivals, it would only stage sixty-two new plays in the decade 1940–50 (down from 104 in the previous decade). The amateur movement, therefore, allowed both established and novice playwrights a chance to see their work staged, and more than one company was set up with the express purpose of providing a local writer with an outlet.

Equally importantly, the amateur companies provided an important source of income for professional playwrights. Amateur productions earned for playwrights between three and five guineas per night in royalties – 'exactly the same rate of pay', St John Ervine complained in 1958, 'as was paid more than sixty years ago'.[39] This may not have been a fortune in itself. However, a writer like Shiels had more than twenty plays available for production, and there were well over a hundred companies around the country ready to stage one of them for a four or five night run each year. Cumulatively, amateur royalties could add up to the living that Abbey productions alone could not provide. Hence, while Paul Vincent Carroll left the country to earn a living by writing for film and radio, and even O'Casey was saved from penury only by writing autobiographies and selling the film rights to his early plays, George Shiels and T. C. Murray were able to remain in Ireland largely due to the royalties from amateur productions.

The links between the amateur and professional theatres were particularly important – and particularly tangled – in Northern Ireland. 'In any given Dramatic Society up North', wrote Michael Farrell (from a distinctively Dublin perspective), 'the members will almost certainly belong exclusively to one church.'[40] This gave rise to plays designed for specific denominational groups, such as Patricia O'Connor's *Select Vestry* (1946), set in the home of a Church of Ireland clergyman, or its Catholic counterpart, Joseph Tomelty's *Is the Priest At Home?* (1954), in which a Catholic priest, after struggling to balance the many demands of his parishioners, admits that while 'they tell you that the country's priest-ridden . . . it's the other way around, the priest is people-ridden'. While the religious affiliations of Ulster plays from this period are always clearly signposted, most contain a mandatory gesture of conciliation, and a few – such as Louis J. Walsh's *The Pope in Killymuck* – carried off this balancing act so well that they could play to audiences from both sides of the community. Walsh's play in particular was a local phenomenon, filling the Belfast Empire Theatre for a three-week run every year from 1926 until the late 1940s.

The real problem in Northern Ireland was the absence of a permanent theatre company to provide a focus for this activity in the way that the Abbey did south of the Border. The Ulster Literary Theatre, originally established as a Northern Abbey, might have filled this role, but, as St John Ervine put it, 'It suffered from the fact that it was a society for *occasional* productions and that it had no theatre of its own.' The Opera House, in which the Ulster Literary Theatre staged its productions, was simply too big for a small group of committed amateurs, and in 1934 it hosted the company's last performance. Meanwhile, the Belfast Repertory Theatre had been established in 1929 as a professional Ulster company, taking up residence in the smaller Belfast Empire Theatre. The company's aesthetic is summed up in their logo, which featured the Red Hand of Ulster juxtaposed with a Chaplinesque figure lit by footlights – a combination of regional identity and traditional theatre values.

On 13 October 1932, it looked as if the Belfast Repertory Theatre had found a resident playwright when it staged *Workers* by Thomas Carnduff. An unemployed shipyard worker, Carnduff became something of a celebrity, writing a second play, *Machinery* (1933), before critics began to note the creaking narrative apparatus of his plots when he wrote a full-blooded historical melodrama, *Castlereagh*, in 1935. However, those first two plays, set in the Belfast shipyards, showed one of the roads not taken in Irish theatre. Unlike O'Casey (to whom he was inevitably compared) Carnduff was not simply an urban writer; at a time when Irish theatre had a rural fixation, he was an industrial writer. 'The giant gantries have always stirred me', he told a reporter, 'and the great liners seem to me the most beautiful symbols of man's creative genius.'[41] While fascinated by the power of machinery, his plays are equally aware of its dehumanising power. 'Do ye mind the time Jimmie Paterson was killed', asks a character in *Machinery*. 'Ten ton of metal was squeezing him tae death in a wee space like that (*Places his fingers about three inches apart*) and we could do nothing but luk at him dying.'[42] Lacking its own theatre building, however, the Belfast Repertory Theatre folded, and Carnduff never had the chance to develop; had he done so, Ulster theatre might have found a distinguishing feature other than its obsessive concern with sectarianism.

Meanwhile, there were other, short-lived, attempts to found a professional theatre in Belfast, each of which left its residue in the form of personnel who could act, direct, and produce plays, until in the winter of 1939–40 three amateur companies – the rump of the Ulster Literary Theatre, the Jewish Institute Dramatic Society, and the Northern Irish Players – came together to form the Ulster Group Theatre. 'I have always seen very vividly', wrote George Shiels to a friend, 'what an Ulster Theatre might be, and on various occasions my hope revived, only to be quenched again by some idiot, or set of idiots, talking in terms of "Charlie's Aunt".'[43] This time, however, it was to be different. In 1944, the newly formed Council for the Encouragement of Music and the Arts (Northern Ireland) – or CEMA – sponsored a Group tour of the smaller centres in the Province. Over two September nights in 1944, for instance, more than a thousand people turned out in Ballymena to see *A Doll's House* paired with St John Ervine's *Friends and Relations*; and, noted CEMA's annual report, 'there were many who preferred the Ibsen piece'.[44] The same tour took in Armagh, Ballymoney, Portadown and half a dozen other towns, establishing a circuit that would later support CEMA's own resident company, headed by Louis D'Alton.

Yet, while there were stirrings of theatrical activity all over the island by 1950, no one could miss the sour tone of dissatisfaction that pervades the period. Writing in *Envoy*, Thomas Hogan complained that 'downright excruciatingly dull and vapid badness is, I regret to say, apparently Dublin's main theatrical dish – like soggy cabbage in Dublin's restaurants'.[45] Earlier, on 7 November 1947, a young poet, Valentin Iremonger, stood up in the stalls during a production of *The Plough and the Stars* and declared: 'When Yeats died, he left behind him to the Irish nation as a legacy his beloved Abbey theatre. Today, eight years later, under the utter incompetence of the present directorate's artistic policy, there is nothing left of that fine glory.'[46] By 'the present directorate', Iremonger meant, of course, Ernest Blythe, who (following the short interregnum of F. R. Higgins) had taken over the Abbey after the death of Yeats. 'I could see that to Blythe design meant something which could be added or taken away *ad lib*', wrote Liam O'Laoghaire, who spent a brief spell at the Abbey in 1946, 'just as acting was so much tricks to be performed.'[47]

While Blythe may not have been wholly to blame, things certainly were falling apart. The company who had first staged O'Casey's Dublin plays began to drift away, Barry Fitzgerald to Hollywood in 1936, followed a few years later by his brother, Arthur Shields. Shelah Richards and Ria Mooney were freelancing, and the Abbey's most highly acclaimed actor, F. J. McCormick, died in April 1947, the same year in which the leading players of a younger generation, Cyril Cusack and Siobhán McKenna, started independent careers. For many, the image of the Abbey in the late 1940s was summed up in the annual Irish-language Christmas pantomime, in which Abbey actors did comic turns and sang Irish versions of popular songs like 'Chatanooga Choo Choo'. It was a long way from 'a Theatre where beautiful emotion and profound thought might have their three hours' traffic'.

There was a final indignity yet to come. Two men standing on the corner of Abbey Street at one o'clock on the morning of Wednesday, 18 July 1951, noticed flames coming from the upper windows of the theatre. Within minutes, there were flames shooting up through the roof, and by two o'clock the backstage, props and scenery rooms, most of the wardrobe and many of the offices had been destroyed, and the auditorium roof had collapsed. By morning, the Abbey was a smouldering ruin.

A night at the theatre 6

Waiting for Godot by Samuel Beckett
Pike Theatre
Friday, 28 October 1955

A country road. A tree. Evening.

'Nothing to be done.'

Or, as the line was spoken when *Waiting for Godot* opened in Dublin's Pike Theatre on 28 October 1955:

'It's no good.'[1]

In the years since that first Irish production, Samuel Beckett (and later his estate) would become legendary for zealously safeguarding the author's texts from any directorial meddling.[2] However, when director Alan Simpson received his copy of the then-unpublished *Waiting for Godot* in late 1953, there was nothing in the heavily annotated typescript (a carbon copy of the version sent to Grove Press in New York) to indicate that this was anything but a work in progress. 'I have translated it myself into English, as literally as I could', Beckett told him, 'and am now revising this translation for American publication in the Spring.'[3] Consequently, when Simpson put the play into rehearsal, he saw no reason not to continue what he considered to be an ongoing process of revision.

'When I first received the script from Sam Beckett', Simpson later recalled, 'my immediate reaction was that the two tramps should be played as two Dublin characters.' It seemed to Simpson that Beckett's own changes in the typescript indicated the author was striving for a more colloquial English – specifically Hiberno-English – equivalent for the play's original French. For instance, in the typed version of the Grove script, Estragon says: 'Yesterday evening we spent talking about nothing in particular' – which Beckett had amended by crossing out the word 'talking' (*bavarder* in French), replacing it with 'blathering'. Noting this, and other 'Dublinisms' (such as 'Estragon's referring to Godot as "your man" '), Simpson made further changes: Vladimir's comment 'we'd be ballocksed' became 'bandjacksed' [*sic*]; Estragon's suggestion that they give Lucky 'a good beating' became 'what if we wired into him'; and the idea that 'It'd be amusing' to find new names for Pozzo, became 'It'd be gas'[4] – all common Dublin usages.

As Alan Simpson was giving his copy of *Waiting for Godot* a Dublin flavour in the early months of 1954, he was responding to the new problem of marketing the *avant garde* to a mainstream theatre audience. At the beginning of the twentieth century, news of experimental writers such as Strindberg or Chekhov trickled slowly through the theatrical world, and productions outside of the writer's home country usually did not follow until decades after their première. Fifty years later, however, a transformed telecommunications network was once again redrawing the map of the theatre world. So, when *En Attendant Godot* opened at the 230-seat Théâtre de Babylone on 3 January 1953, audience protests and spirited defences by Jean Anouilh and Alain Robbe-Grillet quickly turned an exclusively Parisian phenomenon into an event reported on in London, Dublin, New York and around the world. Before the play even had a chance to move to a larger venue in Paris, it had acquired one of the ingredients of commercial success: the patina of fame. The ability to shock and scandalise may have been the hallmark of an authentic modernist masterpiece; paradoxically, it was equally a key to commercial success.

The speed with which *En Attendant Godot* went from a script that no one wanted to the object of an international bidding war explains how it ended up at the Pike Theatre. When Simpson first contacted Beckett about the possibility of staging *Godot* at the Pike in the autumn of 1953, Beckett – who had spent more than two years finding someone to stage his play in Paris – thought (not without reason) that the Pike would be a sort of Théâtre de Babylone *sur Liffey*. The Pike was a converted coach-house on Herbert Lane, just off Upper Mount Street on the city's South side, away from the traditional theatre districts of the city centre, but at the heart of a hard-drinking bohemian culture of Ireland in the 1950s, which revolved around nearby literary haunts such as Parson's Bookshop and Doheny and Nesbitt's pub. Simpson (whose day job was in the engineering corps of the Irish Defence Forces) and his wife, Carolyn Swift, had designed the building themselves. They covered in an open yard to make the small auditorium, seating only fifty-five patrons, and used the coach-house itself as a stage and backstage area, cutting through the ceiling of the two-storey building to construct a small fly system. The auditorium was decorated with Regency-stripe wallpaper, gilt and plaster cupids, producing an effect which Swift has described as 'the weird cross between Covent Garden Opera House and a doll's house'[5]–just the setting for a play in which the hollow echoes of music-hall's successor, variety, can be heard.

Beckett seemed to think this tiny theatre was as good a place as any for *Godot*'s English-language première. 'I don't think it can do any good in London', he wrote from Paris to his friend Thomas MacGreevy. 'But then I didn't think it could do any good here.'[6] Provided Simpson could overcome the difficulties arising from 'certain crudities of language', Beckett wrote: 'There should be no difficulty about permission, from us here and from whoever acquires the English rights.'[7] He was wrong. The English producer and director Donald Albery, who had bought the rights to *Waiting for Godot*, was planning a gala London opening, hoping to cast Alec Guinness and Sir Ralph Richardson in the lead roles. He had no intention of being pre-empted by an unknown group of Dubliners. Consequently, Albery continued to try to block the Pike production even after his own plans fell through, and the first London production took place at the private Arts Club on 3 August 1955 (without either Guinness or Richardson).

This put Beckett in a very awkward situation. 'Though I am not, I hope, a gentleman', he wrote to Simpson in May 1955, 'there is not and there has not at any time been any question of my going back on my agreement with you, and you may rest assured that I shall not authorize any theatre other than yours to present *Godot* in English in Ireland.'[8] The impasse was only broken after Simpson went through the fine print of Albery's contract and realised that it conferred performance rights only within North America and the British Commonwealth – from which Éire had conveniently absented itself in 1949, when it became a republic. Simpson and Swift thus announced their production for October 1955, and Albery was not notified until after the opening.

Although it delayed the Dublin opening of *Godot*, the difficulty over rights was, of course, more grist for the publicity mill. Consequently, there was a palpable sense of anticipation in the Pike Theatre on Friday, 28 October 1955, when the curtains parted to show an almost empty stage. 'A country road. A tree. Evening.' The tree, Simpson insisted, must be no more than a branch; if it was too sturdy, he argued, the possibility that the tramps might hang themselves would be too real. The rest of the stage contained only a simple backcloth and wings, painted in roughly horizontal 'daubs of green, black and brown paint, very vaguely suggestive of Irish bogland and gloomy sky'[9] – once again emphasising Simpson's Irish interpretation. Against such visual austerity, the performers became the production's real focus, although only the most basic blocking was possible when four actors and a tree were crammed into the Pike's 12-foot (3.6 metre) square acting space.

The Pike's size may have imposed limitations on the actors, but it created possibilities in the lighting design. No seat in the theatre was more than four rows from the stage, so seeing the actors was never a problem. This allowed Simpson to use almost exclusively directional toplights and sidelights, with very little spill, and only minimal front lighting was necessary to make the actors' faces visible. So, towards the end of each act, as the day ended, Simpson brought down his front lights, creating a backlighting effect in which 'the tree and the tramps were dimly and impressively lit, in contrast to the negative dreariness of the preceding sections'[10] – an effect, coincidentally, not unlike the silhouetted figures in the Caspar David Friedrich painting, *Zwei Männer betrachten den Mond (Two Men Contemplating the Moon)*, which Beckett would later claim was 'the source' for *Waiting for Godot.*[11]

The first Irish audience of *Waiting for Godot* were thus almost within touching distance of the two figures who stood before them, sharply outlined with light. Simpson dressed his two tramps, Vladimir and Estragon, played by Dermot Kelly and Austin Byrne, respectively, in frayed, oversized black suits and bowler hats, differentiating them by giving Kelly a tie and Byrne a neckcloth. The baggy suits suggested the play's debt to variety; equally, they were part of Simpson's overall conception that Vladimir and Estragon should be played as two down-at-heels Dubliners, talking endlessly. 'How time flies when we're having a bit of gas', says Vladimir, in another of Simpson's Dublinised lines, delivered in what *The Stage* called an 'authentic O'Casey voice'.[12] Beckett's friend Con Leventhal, although voicing some reservations about loss of the play's 'universal' meaning, thought the accents worked. 'It sounded strange at first', he noted, 'and the laughs seemed to come more from the intonation than the text, but the added humour helped the audience to bear the more searing portions of the play.'[13] It was not simply that Dublin accents were comic *per se*; they evoked a particular type of comic routine whose tenets Beckett had identified many years before in Sean O'Casey's work. 'Mr O'Casey is a master of knockabout in this very serious and honourable sense', Beckett had written in 1934: 'that he discerns the principle of disintegration in even the most complacent solidities, and activates it to their explosion'.[14]

It was not until Pozzo and Lucky staggered on to the stage about a third of the way through the opening act that the politics of Simpson's interpretation became evident. 'Because of my own Irishness', wrote

Simpson, 'I saw Pozzo as an Anglo-Irish or English gentleman, whose excellent manners and superficially elaborate concern for others conceals an arrogant and selfish nature.' To this end, he cast Nigel Fitzgerald (an Irish actor from Anew McMaster's company with 'a rich, fruity Anglo-Irish voice') as Pozzo. Fitzgerald had been educated at an English public school and had served in the British Army, and his Pozzo was dressed as 'a Somerville and Ross Anglo-Irish squire',[15] in a tweed jacket and cape, bowler hat, waistcoat, bow-tie and severe military moustache.

Similarly, Donal Donnelly's Lucky was dressed like an Irish servant from a Boucicault play, in a torn and misshapen dark red velvet footman's jacket with gold frogging, navy satin knee-breeches, striped wastcoat, but no stockings. On an almost monochrome set, playing opposite actors dressed in blacks and browns, this red, white and blue Lucky, with his shock of long white hair and stark greyish-white make-up – applied much more heavily than was necessary in such a small theatre – dominated the stage visually, even as he stood (his great monologue aside) in complete silence. Dressed in livery (like Jean Martin's Lucky in Paris, but unlike Timothy Bateson's in London, who wore a dirty peacoat), Donnelly's character reminded the audience that, no matter what else was taking place on stage, the play dealt with power and suffering. 'The relationship established between the tramps and Pozzo', claimed Simpson, 'is thus comparable to that between the native Irish and an Anglo-Irish or English landowner.' 'So you were waiting?' Pozzo demands of Vladimir. 'Here? On my land?'[16]

Pushed too far, Simpson's reading of *Godot* could have been crudely reductive; however, having sketched in a rough Irish framework, he left it at that, refusing to interpret the play any further. 'Leave all that to the newspapermen', he would tell his cast. 'They get paid for it. You get paid for acting.'[17] Dermot Kelly, who played Vladimir, took this advice to heart, spreading the rumour that his contract forbade him from disclosing the play's meaning. For the most part, this approach seems to have worked, with one major exception: Lucky's long speech in the first act, his 'think', which Simpson considered to be purely 'words of gibberish'. In the *Godot* typescript Beckett sent to Simpson, Lucky's speech is the most heavily edited part of the play, suggesting that it gave Beckett the most trouble in translation. This is not surprising, for in many ways Lucky's 'think' crystallises the epistemological balancing act of the play as a whole. It must intimate the possibility of meaning ('Given the existence . . . of a personal God . . . who . . . loves us dearly with some exceptions for reasons unknown . . .'), without ever confirming or fulfilling that possibility.

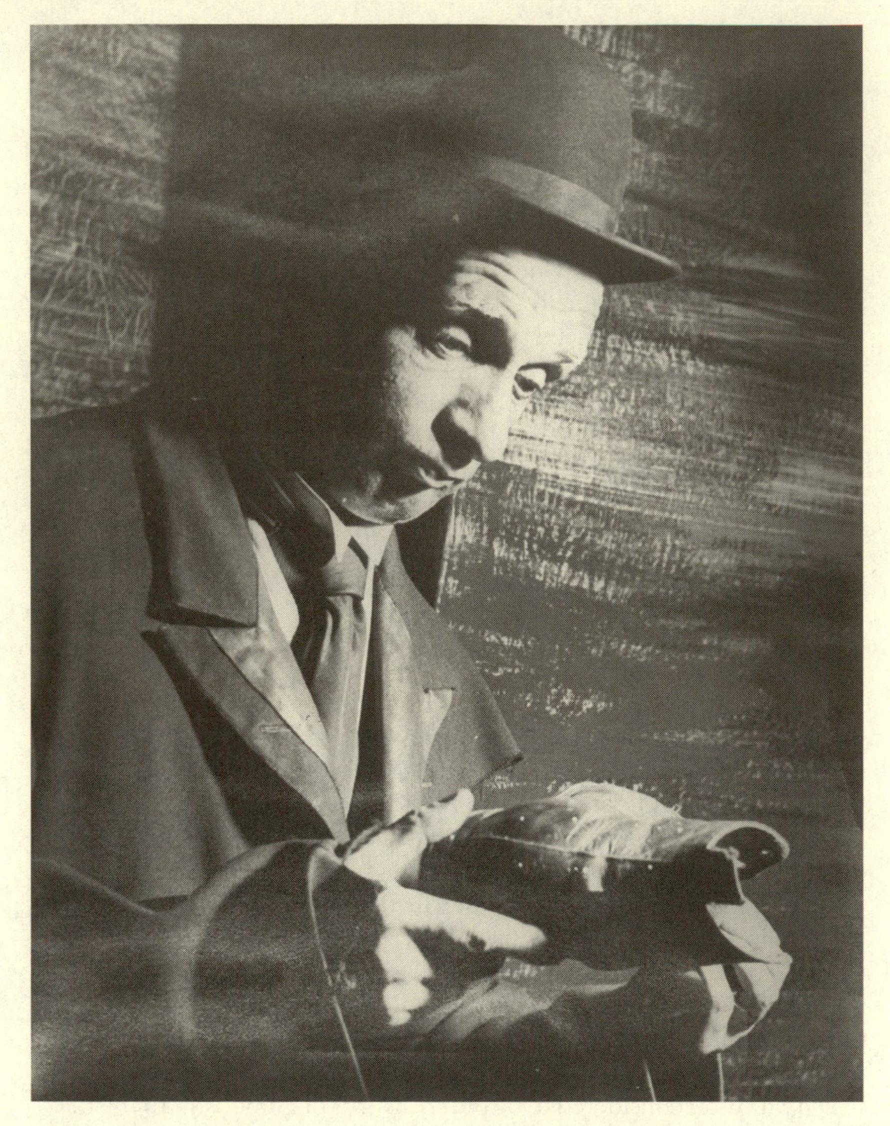

Photograph 5. 'Thanks for the letter and photographs', Samuel Beckett wrote to director Alan Simpson after the first Irish production of *Waiting for Godot* in 1955. 'I like particularly that of Vladimir [actor Dermot Kelly] looking at the boot as if it were an early 17th century skull.'

In this regard, Con Leventhal, who was probably the only member of the Pike audience to have seen the Paris and London productions of the play, noted that Lucky's speech in the Dublin production suffered by comparison. Jean Martin in Paris and Timothy Bateson in London had both delivered the speech 'as though it had the background of sense evident in the text'; Donnelly, on the other hand, 'smothered his words in the hysteria of his delivery', which the *Irish Times* complained was delivered in a 'parrot-like tempo'.[18] While Leventhal may have been the only person able to compare the Dublin *Godot* to the two earlier productions, most of the audience who filed down Herbert Lane in October of 1955 had the advantage of having followed the play's already considerable trail of controversy. Indeed, Kenneth Tynan's famous remark – 'it will be a conversational necessity for many years to have seen *Waiting for Godot*' – was helpfully repeated by the *Irish Times* in the same week the Dublin production opened.[19] In particular, there had been extensive coverage of the English Lord Chamberlain's Office balking at the play's 'crudities', which Beckett had adamantly refused to amend, and the *Pike Newsletter* played up this *risqué* reputation, warning its patrons: 'Many will find its philosophy and parts of its dialogue repellent.'[20] Although he had no qualms about making changes elsewhere in the script, Simpson was proud of having retained passages that had to be cut from the London production. In performance, he even accentuated potentially offensive lines. For instance, when Pozzo threatens to kick Lucky out 'on his arse', Simpson had Lucky begin to cry on the offending word, 'arse'. At a time when O'Casey's *Plough and the Stars* was still being performed by the Abbey in a bowdlerised version that left out words such as 'bitch' and 'snotty', Dubliners were studiously unscandalised by *Godot*. 'Few are shocked nowadays', observed Leventhal, 'by the traditional (mainly oral) terminology for certain physiological functions.'

Similarly, Dublin reviewers had learned from the edifying spectacle of their London counterparts stumbling around in search of a definitive interpretation for the play. For instance, as late as February 1956, G. S. Fraser, writing in *The Times Literary Supplement*, was trying to convince readers that the play was 'a modern morality play on permanent Christian themes'. By contrast, a review in the *Irish Independent* published the morning after the Dublin première was more circumspect about the play's potential allegory. 'The questions are posed', wrote its reviewer, 'and there is no answer but the one which each member of the audience chooses.' In a more extended discussion in the *Irish Times* a few weeks later, John J. O'Meara compared Beckett to Aristophanes, suggesting that the plot (or absence of a plot) in *Waiting for Godot* was irrelevant. 'The interest is primarily in the comment', he concluded, 'and the comment itself need not be consistent, full, or even always relevant.'[21]

Perhaps the best critique of *Waiting for Godot* during its Dublin run was the profile of Samuel Beckett published by Michael George in the *Irish Tatler and Sketch* in February 1956. 'There is a fundamental difference between nought, a definite entity, and nothing, an abstract conception', he wrote. 'Thus in life there is the ever-present sense of not-knowing, a feeling that is keener, more real and more terrible than the mere absence of knowledge.' Beckett, he goes on to argue, was the only artist who had made a serious attempt to 'give artistic expression to this profound frustration and not-knowingness – something larger than pessimism which implies some knowledge, and something deeper than nihilism, which itself becomes a philosophy'. As his argument develops, George produces a reading of *Waiting for Godot* that anticipates by two decades a post-modern understanding of the play. 'The fundamental difficulty is one of communication, to find some means whereby the unknowable can at least be established . . . The more consciously the form is developed, as in Kafka, the more is the content, the emotional unknowingness, falsified; conversely, the more precarious the form – the nearer it approaches to disintegration, the truer is the emotional content.' This, George concluded, explains why *Waiting for Godot*'s apparent inconsequentiality appears to bear so much consequence, and why, in its long silences, when it threatens to 'dissolve before our eyes' it seems to say the most.[22]

The Dublin response to *Waiting for Godot* belies the image of Ireland in the 1950s as an intellectually timid cultural wasteland. Apart from voices like George, Leventhal (and later Alec Reid) who were capable of formulating an informed response to the wider context of Beckett's work, Irish audiences were drawn to the play by more than characters who spoke like 'O'Casey's Joxer tempered by Myles na gCopaleen's "Dubalin" man'. Ever since Juno had pleaded at the end of *Juno and the Paycock* to 'take away our hearts o' stone, and give us hearts o' flesh', post-Independence Irish theatre had been sceptical of idealism. For instance, while *Godot* was still playing at the Pike in November 1955, the Abbey premièred Walter Macken's *Twilight of the Warrior*, a naturalistic family drama about a veteran of the Irish War of Independence who finds that he can not adapt to post-war life. 'You live on', he says at one point. 'You have won what you fought for; your vision is on fire; you have the indelible picture in your mind of what it will be like when the sweat and dirt and bleeding and hunger is over. You have won. So, what happens? It's not the same.'[23] In terms of its theatrical form, *Waiting for Godot* could not be more different from *Twilight of the Warrior*; in terms of its refusal to imagine a perfect world after 'the sweat and dirt and bleeding and hunger', the two plays are strikingly similar. Indeed, Vladimir's half-remembered maxim that 'hope deferred maketh the something sick' might stand as an epitaph for the Ireland of the 1950s.

Consequently, while the swell of pre-production publicity brought in the initial Dublin audiences, the sustained, and increasingly complex, level of critical response kept them coming. Numbers quickly swelled from forty-six on the first night to full houses up until Christmas 1955, with sixty-seven patrons packing the fifty-five-seat auditorium on one particularly crowded night in November. The increasingly crotchety Liam O'Flaherty may have denounced the play as 'tripe', but by early 1956, *Waiting for Godot* was still running at the Pike, notching up its one-hundredth performance on 22 February, thereby surpassing Louis D'Alton's *This Other Eden* as the longest continuous run in Irish theatre history to that point. That same month, Faber and Faber published the English text of *Godot*, sparking a fresh round of critical debate, which would establish some of the basic points for discussion of the play in the years ahead.

For instance, Vivian Mercier, writing in the *Irish Times* on 18 February 1956, coined the most quotable one-line account of *Waiting for Godot*: 'A play in which nothing happens, *twice*.' Mercier was lastingly influenced by Simpson's Irish interpretation of *Godot*, and in his 1956 essay he outlines the basic tenets of an argument he would develop over two decades in *The Irish Comic Tradition* (1962) and *Beckett / Beckett* (1977): that *Godot* is part of a specifically Irish iconoclastic tradition in both languages, which laughs at despair. 'There is no object so sacred or intimate that an Irishman will not turn it to ridicule', wrote Mercier in 1956. Meanwhile, Con Leventhal had little hesitation in hailing *Waiting for Godot* as 'possibly the most important drama this century', seeing the play in terms that evoke Beckett's later *Breath*, as a 'vision of mankind in perpetual expectation, desperately endeavouring to fill the hiatus between birth and death'.[24]

Meanwhile, even as the play continued to generate intellectual debate, it became a part of Irish popular culture. The pantomime actor, Jimmy O'Dea, introduced Godot into his variety routines, and a cartoon in one of the Irish daily papers showed a puzzled policeman explaining to his colleague that a suspicious-looking vagrant claimed to be 'waiting for Godot'. Capitalising on this continuing wave of success, the Pike company took up residence in the much larger Gate Theatre during the week of 17 March, before taking the show around the touring circuit, playing Dundalk, Navan, Drogheda, Cork, Clonmel, and Waterford and finishing up in Carlow Town Hall on 15 April 1956, four days before the play's New York début. Although it was not obvious at the time, when 'perhaps the most important play of the century' played the Carlow Town Hall before it opened on Broadway, it was an early ripple in a wave of change that would transform the relationship between centre and periphery in the theatre world.

The other sign that things were changing could be read in the Pike's account books, which show that the *Godot* tour brought in more than £2,553 at the box office (the equivalent of almost £52,500 in the year 2000).[25] 'Are Dublin audiences interested in intellectual plays?' asked the caption beneath a picture of a beaming Alan Simpson in the *Irish Times* on 18 January 1956. The answer was obviously 'yes'. Not only was *Waiting for Godot* to teach more than one future generation of Irish playwrights the possibilities of theatrical form; its commercial success taught Irish producers that controversial, puzzling, and even offensive plays could make money. In a sense, the Pike Theatre production of *Waiting for Godot* heralded the arrival in Ireland of that oxymoronic beast, a mainstream *avant-garde*.

CHAPTER 7

Phoenix flames, 1951–1972

It was not an auspicious beginning.

Ireland's great cultural festival, An Tóstal, was to open at midnight on 4 April 1953, with the lighting of an eternal flame in the middle of Dublin's O'Connell Bridge. By eleven o'clock, the streets of the city centre were so full of people that police gave up trying to direct traffic. By eleven thirty, a group of young men (who had obviously assumed 'festival' was a synonym for 'drink') started to tear down the hoardings from around the 'Bowl of Light' – which turned out to be a plastic flame poking up through a hideous metal dish. For the next hour, the assembled crowds had 'a grand-stand view of a clash between the police and a band of young hooligans. Flowers, shrubs, and earth from the flower beds at the O'Connell monument were thrown at the police' and windows were smashed. 'I trust', said President Sean T. O'Kelly, ceremonially lighting the plastic 'flame' the next morning, 'that when visitors to An Tóstal leave our shores they will have formed a truer conception of the Irish Nation, and of the progress made in the cultural, social, and economic spheres in the relatively short time since we won our national independence in this part of the country.'[1]

The history of Ireland in the 1950s is so full of false starts and stops that it is difficult to point to the moment at which the country settled into the accelerated modernisation of its late twentieth-century life. Economic historians usually take as a starting point the Industrial Development Act of 1958, and the publication of T. K. Whitaker's *Economic Development* later that year; political historians often prefer to wait until Séan Lemass took over as Taoiseach in 1959. In the cultural sphere, the formation of the Arts Council in the Republic in 1951 is certainly a landmark; equally, however, the Tóstal festival of 1953 – for all its elements of rowdy farce – is as good a starting point as any for charting the break-up of the spiralling entropy that had existed since the mid-1920s. As critic Anthony Cronin had written in *The Bell* earlier that year: 'We must look outward again or die, if only of boredom.'

Sponsored by Bord Fáilte (the Irish tourist authority), An Tóstal was an early attempt to break an enclosed economic cycle by attracting foreign capital into the country through tourism. In this alone it is important, for it marks the beginning of a new way of thinking about Irish culture. Earlier government-sponsored cultural events had been motivated by the doctrine that Irish culture was, like the Irish language, 'the soil of a people's genius, and a mark and guard of nationality' (as Thomas Davis had put it in the 1840s); by contrast, the 1953 Tóstal festival was part of a dawning recognition that culture could be more than just the spirit of a nation; it could also be its bankroll. In this new dispensation, culture was part of a tourist industry that would magically transform the scars of underdevelopment – stunted industrialisation and a population thinned by emigration – into an unspoilt countryside where a nostalgic diaspora could spend their dollars.

From the beginning, theatre was central to this new economic understanding of Irish culture. So, when Brendan Smith suggested to Bord Fáilte late in 1956 that a theatre festival might attract more tourists than a drunken brawl around a plastic torch, policy-makers paid attention. By April 1957 An Tóstal had spawned the Dublin Theatre Festival, which remains the pivotal event of the professional theatre calendar. As was the case in other areas of trade, it quickly became apparent that, when it came to theatre, making Ireland into an exporter (insofar as tourism is an 'invisible export') also meant turning the country back into an importer. 'The original idea', recalled Smith, 'was to have a festival that would be, roughly speaking, given over to about two-thirds Irish contributions – in terms of writing, acting, and directing – and one-third foreign contributions.'[2] Consequently, while the Theatre Festival was originally marketed as a tourist promotion showcasing the best of home-produced theatre, it would also provide the sort of stimulus from world theatre that the big touring companies had brought to Ireland in the vibrant years before the First World War.

Of course, this was still a few years down the road in 1953; much more immediately, the 1953 Tóstal festival consolidated the structure of the amateur theatre community. When the Cultural Director of An Tóstal, Cecil ffrench-Salkfield, began talking to groups of amateurs late in 1952 with a view to establishing a national amateur theatre festival, he quickly found that he was pushing at an open door. By the early

1950s, the competitive festival circuit had evolved well beyond the point of handing a trophy to the most popular play at the end of a week. For instance, the Western Drama Festival, first held in Tubbercurry in 1944, offered prizes in five categories judged according to strict criteria by adjudicators from the professional theatre – and Tubbercurry was only one of a network of such festivals throughout the country, cutting across the Border and opening up parts of the country ignored by the traditional theatre geography.

When the first All-Ireland Drama Finals were held in Athlone in 1953, all of this disparate activity was given a competitive focus, investing the theatre with the same passionate local rivalries that had installed the Gaelic Athletic Association as a populist pillar of Irish society. While there was some criticism that competition encouraged groups to stage what were considered 'festival plays' rather than take chances, this was never more than partly true, if only because it was not always possible to predict a winner. For instance, Yeats' *Dreaming of the Bones* won the verse category in the first All-Ireland and the best actress award went for a performance of Antigone. In any case, the adjudication process compensated for the negative effects of competition by opening formal channels between the amateur and professional theatre, both raising the standards of amateur productions and easing the transition to professional status for talented amateurs, whether actors, writers or directors.

As the amateur theatre movement became more highly organised, it helped playwrights to reach audiences the Irish theatre had hitherto ignored. This was particularly true of M. J. Molloy. His early plays were all produced professionally by the Abbey: *The Old Road* (1943), *The King of Friday's Men* (1948), and *The Wood of the Whispering* (1953). However, his plays of rural depopulation had their greatest impact on the audiences watching amateur productions in small communities like those represented on the stage. *The Wood of the Whispering*, for instance, strips away the nostalgic sheen of the folk tale to concentrate on a group of grotesque characters, the human flotsam stranded by the ebbing tide of emigration. With only a minimal plot holding the play together, these characters parade through the encampment of Sanbatch Daly, 'in his middle sixties, lanky, haggard and worn by privation and adversity'. 'How could you abide this country', asks one of the characters. 'What's in it but poverty and bad wages and slavery with no cinema within ten miles?' 'Even the dead themselves aren't half or quarter as plentiful as they used to be in midnight', admits Sanbatch. 'Tis near a week now since a gang of ghosts stretched their fingers at me.' The rural Ireland of Molloy's theatre was a place of failure, thinned by emigration in a sort of reverse eugenics so that only the mad and impotent remained.

'For forty years Ireland has been free', Molloy wrote in his introduction to a 1961 edition of the play, 'and for forty years it has wandered in the desert under the leadership of men who freed their nation, but who could never free their own minds and souls from the ill-effects of having been born in slavery.' This was hardly the Ireland striding forward 'in the cultural, social, and economic spheres' invoked by President O'Kelly when he switched on the Tóstal flame a few months after *The Wood of the Whispering* opened. Nor was it the bucolic rural Ireland that John Ford's *The Quiet Man* (released the previous year) was selling to the Irish diaspora. With as many as 50,000 people leaving the country every year in the early 1950s, *The Wood of the Whispering* was a play for those left behind, watching productions played by amateurs in countless church halls around the country, usually with a diesel-powered electric generator providing a basso accompaniment from the darkness beyond. In these communities, the theatre, like everything else, had to struggle against a falling population. Manuscript copies of Molloy's play passed among groups in villages like Inchovea, County Clare, and Killeedy, County Limerick, where the play had its first productions outside of Dublin. By the time the script was published in 1961, both of these drama groups were gone, their members having emigrated. 'Leave this country', warns Sanbatch near the end of the play. 'Soon the crows'll be flying between every two rafters in this village.'[3]

The excitement generated by these amateur productions was in sharp contrast to the boredom of which Abbey audiences so often complained. This contrast was seldom more evident than in Walsh's Ballroom, Listowel, County Kerry, on the night of 2 February 1959, when the Listowel Drama Group presented the first production of John B. Keane's *Sive*. Although the Abbey had rejected *Sive*, it created a sensation in Listowel, and began gathering force as it moved around the festival circuit of the Southwest. On 17 March 1959, when the play was booked into the 200-seat Playhouse Theatre in Limerick, Gardaí had to be brought in to prevent a riot among the more than 300 people on the streets outside who could not get tickets, and much of the performance was lost in bursts of spontaneous applause and cheering. Not since the heady days of the Queen's had the enthusiasm of Irish theatre audiences spilled so visibly on to the streets. The following month, *Sive* became the first original production to win an All-Ireland trophy, defeating a production of *The*

Wood of the Whispering and assuring its status among amateur companies. Waiting backstage in Athlone, Brendan Carroll, the play's original director, would later write that the atmosphere 'reminded him of the hours before an All-Ireland football final at Croke Park'.[4]

Sive's popularity reveals the fissures in the pious puritanism usually attributed to rural Ireland in the 1950s, for the play crackles with sexual undertones as it deals with an illegitimate young woman, Sive, who is to be forced into an arranged marriage with an older, wealthy farmer. This is not to say that Keane was not sometimes accused of writing pornography. 'If we entered a pub after the show', Keane later recalled, 'some annoyed party was bound to approach us.' 'Have you read the play', Keane would ask. 'No, I couldn't read such a filthy thing!' 'But how do you know it's filthy, if you haven't seen it or read it?' 'I don't have to! 'Tis all about bastards, isn't it?'[5] This play 'all about bastards' touched other nerves as well. Sive, a young woman attending school, aspires to small-town respectability; sharing her world are her parents, her pipe-smoking grandmother, and the matchmaker Thomaseen, who are all part of an older Ireland of struggling small farmers, 'pulling bogdeal out of the ground with a jinnet'; their world, in turn, is disrupted by a group of travelling 'tinkers', carrying with them memories of a fragmented folk culture. *Sive* reminds its audience that the archaic and the modern co-exist in the same moment in the Ireland of 1959, resulting in a clash of values that would be one of the defining features of Irish culture over the next couple of decades.

In 1959 – the same year that *Sive* won the All-Ireland – a member of the amateur Tuam Theatre Guild submitted the manuscript of a one-act play to the Festival's new play competition, winning the fifteen-guinea prize. Tom Murphy's *On the Outside*, which was first produced in Cork by an amateur company, is set outside a rural dance-hall, where Joe and Frank, two 'townies' without the price of admittance, listen to the dancers in growing frustration. Like Sive's family, they are 'on the outside' in more ways than one, caught, as one of them puts it, in the bottom of 'a huge tank with walls running up, straight up . . . splashing around in their Friday night vomit, clawing at the sides all around'.[6] The following year, Murphy won the All-Ireland script competition again, this time with a full-length play called *The Iron Men*. Adjudicator Godfrey Quigley passed the script to Joan Littlewood, who in 1961 staged it with Patrick Magee at the Theatre Royal, Stratford East, as *A Whistle in the Dark*.

For a play to go directly from Athlone to London (by-passing Dublin) was, of course, an affront to the established way of doing things. But then,

A Whistle in the Dark is an appropriate play to have moved the periphery to the centre in such an unprecedented way, for once again Murphy is writing about people 'on the outside' of the emerging new Ireland. In this case, the play focuses on a working-class Mayo family who have emigrated to Coventry, where Michael Carney has tried to set up an orderly, modern life for himself and his English wife. However, Michael finds he cannot escape from his brutal brothers, Harry and Iggy, a pimp and an extortionist respectively, or from their violent father, Dada, who arrives from Mayo with yet another brother, Des. Like *Sive*, *A Whistle in the Dark* is a play about a society in transition, where an older culture based on family pride clashes with the modern values of individualism and self-improvement. 'We can drink out of saucers', Michael says only half-jokingly to his wife, as the house becomes more and more chaotic. 'And we'll get a little pig, a bonham, to run around as a house pet.'[7] By the time the play was produced, first in London, and later at the Olympia Theatre in Dublin on 13 March 1962, Ireland was well into its first Economic Programme, and the 'pigs in the kitchen' image cut sharply against the prevailing ethos. 'It is a mournful thought', wrote the *Evening Herald*, when the play finally transferred to Dublin, 'that this was the picture of the Irish race that was paraded for three months last year to the wondering gaze of London theatregoers.'[8]

The degree to which *A Whistle in the Dark* registered the strains in Irish society was less controversial for its original audiences, however, than the stage impact of its violence. For the play's London audience in particular, *A Whistle in the Dark* was part of a new aggressiveness in the theatre, felt in plays as otherwise dissimilar as John Osborne's *Look Back in Anger* (1956) and Pinter's *The Birthday Party* (1958). Unlike the traditional play structure, in which violence erupts suddenly, usually in a moment of revelation, these plays keep up a sustained level of verbal violence, which masks more than it reveals. In *A Whistle in the Dark*, the characters struggle for dominance relentlessly and pointlessly, from the opening moment, when one of Michael's brothers throws a cup against the wall, to the shocking final scene, in which Michael is goaded into killing his youngest brother, Des, while Dada yells: 'Into it! Go on! Dirt! Dirt! Filth! Dirt! Muck and trash!'[9] The *doyen* of the London critics, Kenneth Tynan, set the tone for *A Whistle in the Dark*'s subsequent reception when he called it 'arguably the most uninhibited display of brutality that the London theatre has ever witnessed'. 'Murphy comes near to convincing us', wrote *The Times*, 'that the whole world consists of stupid fighting animals.'[10]

A Whistle in the Dark ends with Dada standing alone and isolated, denying his responsibility for having driven one son to kill another. 'I had nothing to do with – Not my fault' – before pleading for understanding: 'Must have some kind of pride. Wha'? I tried, I did my best . . . I tried, I did my best . . . Tried . . . Did my best . . . ' while the curtain falls slowly over him. This moment is uncannily similar to the final scene of Walter Macken's *Twilight of the Warrior* (first produced by the Abbey at the Queen's in 1955) except that in Macken's case the bullying father figure, Dacey Adam, is a hero of the War of Independence, who finds that the Ireland of the 1950s has no place for him. Played in the original production by Ray McAnally, an actor with a powerful physical presence, Adam is onstage throughout the play, struggling continuously with his wife, his daughter and her fiancé. 'You see', his son explains, 'he fought for things that could only turn out to be half what he wanted them to be. That's why he is still fighting.' Like Dada in *A Whistle in the Dark*, Dacey dies isolated, his violence now lacking a context in a room filled with 1950s formica and chrome furniture. 'Oh, I am heartily sorry – because – and I'm . . . '[11]

Both of these plays touch directly on one of the central problems of Irish theatre in the 1950s. 'The two pillars upon which the achievement of the Abbey Theatre rested were the dramatic treatment of legend and of contemporary life', wrote Roger McHugh in 1951. 'The former was popular enough when people could identify the legends somehow with our struggle against England; after the heroes had appeared on both sides in the Civil War, they became suspect.'[12] 'The nationalist impulses which led to the foundation of the Abbey Theatre are no longer with us', agreed Gabriel Fallon in 1955, 'and seemingly we have nothing to take their place.'[13] For Macken, Murphy, Keane and Molloy, values suddenly drained of their context were beginning to form the basis for a new type of dramatic conflict, even for tragedy. For other writers of the period, however, the evaporation of the values that had made heroism possible was the stuff of farcical comedy.

For instance, John McCann's trilogy – *Twenty Years A-Wooing* (1954), *Give Me a Bed of Roses* (1957) and *Put a Beggar on Horseback* (1961) – were as beloved by audiences as they were reviled by critics, with John Jordan calling them 'witless, meretricious, and fundamentally dishonest entertainments'.[14] Like Louis D'Alton's comedies of the 1940s, *The Money Doesn't Matter* (1941) and *They Got What They Wanted* (1947), McCann's plays form part of a genre which goes back at least as far as Farquhar, creating an entirely conventional dramatic world in which a true hero is not one who dies a glorious death, or suffers for an abstract principle; he is the one who ends up with the money. Such plays may seem completely apolitical; however, it was to become increasingly clear that the director of Abbey, Ernest Blythe, saw them as important weapons in the National Theatre's mission to defuse the unexploded mines of Ireland's recent history.

As early as 1922, when he was Minister for Finance, Blythe had argued in an influential memo that 'There is no prospect of bringing about the unification of Ireland within any reasonable period of time by attacking the North-East, its forces, or Government.'[15] His political writings of the 1950s and early 1960s make it clear that as the decades passed, he became ever more closely wedded to the belief that Partition would be ended only when Northern Protestants ceased to feel threatened by the Republic. Time and time again, Blythe condemned the 'over-tense feeling that had previously frustrated all attempts to examine the problem of Partition coolly and with an eye to the future'. 'It is sometimes asked', Blythe wrote in 1963, 'if in the future the Abbey will be able, in any way, to match the service it gave to the nation in former days when it helped to raise the fighting spirit of the people' – to which he answers very clearly: 'yes'. However, instead of raising 'the fighting spirit of the people', the theatre's new role would be to disarm that same 'fighting spirit' now that its time was perceived to be past.

According to Blythe, the theatrical form best suited to the task of demilitarising public opinion was comedy, and in this regard Louis D'Alton's *This Other Eden* emerges as one of the paradigmatic Irish plays of the 1950s. 'Those who saw and laughed at Louis D'Alton's *This Other Eden*', claimed Blythe, 'will not again come under the influence of the doctrinaire views which used to impede, if not prevent, full consideration of the practical issues arising from the existence of the Border.'[16] Premièred by the Abbey company at the Queen's on 1 June 1953, shortly after the first Tóstal festival, *This Other Eden* consciously echoes *John Bull's Other Island*. D'Alton's central character is an Englishman, Crispin, who has arrived in a small Irish town to purchase some property, just as a memorial is being unveiled to a local IRA commander who died in the War of Independence. It soon becomes clear that, like Shaw's Broadbent, Crispin's capacity for effusive sentimentality does not fully mask a clear-eyed pragmatism which makes him a foil for the Irish characters, who are almost all in some way maimed by their inability to escape ideals of the past. 'It is my firm conviction', Crispin tells Devereaux (an embittered revolutionary veteran) and Conor (an austere young republican), 'that neither of you would know Zion if you saw it. You, Devereaux, would refuse to believe in it, and you, Conor, would insist it was still around the corner. Only I know that it is here and now, and that we must make the best of it.'[17]

When it opened in 1953, *This Other Eden* ran for over a hundred nights, the longest continuous run in Irish theatre history to that point; and yet, Irish society was changing so quickly that, in spite of a solid 1959 film version, it had all but faded from the repertoire by the end of the decade. The problem, as Thomas Kilroy suggested in his seminal 1959 essay, 'Groundwork for an Irish Theatre', was that 'during the last twenty years few Irish dramatists have been in any way exciting technically'.[18] As a generalisation, this was not entirely true, although it did apply to the larger theatres; meanwhile, real changes were bubbling up not just from rural amateurs, but also from smaller Dublin theatres. 'The real prodigy of the Dublin theatre world today,' Ulick O'Connor told BBC listeners on 19 April 1956, 'is what I have named the basement-theatre movement. This movement is partly professional, but there are just enough amateurs in it to keep the spirit of dedication alive.'[19]

While 'basement-theatre' was technically a bit of a misnomer, the most challenging Irish theatre in the 1950s was certainly to be found in the most unexpected places. In Belfast, Mary O'Malley's Lyric Theatre (founded 1951) staged plays in a converted loft above her home on Derryvolgie Avenue. Initially, the Lyric staged primarily verse drama, with a particular affinity for the plays of Yeats and Austin Clarke, picking up where Clarke's own Dublin theatre group of that name had left off after the Abbey fire. An Chlub Drámaíochta, with funding from Gael Linn, came closest to occupying a true basement in Amharclann an Damer, beneath a Unitarian Church on St Stephen's Green, where they staged an increasingly challenging Irish-language repertoire. The only one of these small theatres to be located in anything like a traditional theatre neighbourhood was the 37 Club, which operated in a small performance space above a shop on Dublin's O'Connell Street, where on the night of the 1953 Tóstal riot they presented Maurice Meldon's astonishing *Aisling*, a bilingual pastiche of Shaw, O'Casey, Synge, Lady Gregory, Christine Longford, Chekhov, Ibsen, Strindberg and Eugene O'Neill, ending with the heroine, Cathleen, auctioned off by a County Council as 'a relic of the foreign occupation'.[20]

In that same year, 1953, Anew McMaster's touring company – still going strong – spawned yet another theatre, when two of its members, Carolyn Swift and Alan Simpson, opened the Pike Theatre in Dublin's

Herbert Lane. In a remarkable flurry of activity, this tiny, fifty-five-seat theatre staged the Irish premières of Brendan Behan's *The Quare Fellow*, and Samuel Beckett's *Waiting for Godot* in a period of just over twelve months, beginning on 19 November 1954. The Pike was an ideal venue for both plays, and particularly for *The Quare Fellow*, a play about the claustrophobia of prison life in the hours before an execution. Commenting on 'the blurred edges of characterisation and motivation' in Behan's play, the *Irish Times* noted: 'It produces in retrospect something horribly true to life in its apparent pointlessness.'[21] Simpson would later recall how, with a cast of more than twenty characters on a stage twelve feet (3.6 metres) square, and up to a dozen audience members standing behind the theatre's four rows of seats, the performance recreated the oppressive closeness of prison life.

'Remember me to the new O'Casey', Samuel Beckett wrote to Alan Simpson, shortly after *The Quare Fellow* opened on 19 November 1954. The comparisons with O'Casey were unavoidable – given an extra push by an only partly inebriated Behan who met calls of 'author, author' on the play's opening night by singing O'Casey's 'Red Roses For Me'. However, in taking over from music hall and variety the joker's licence to mock the dignity of church and state (which naturalistic theatre often presented as given), Behan was less the heir of the Sean O'Casey with which most theatregoers were familiar – the O'Casey of the Dublin trilogy – than he was the contemporary of the late O'Casey, who was writing plays like *The Bishop's Bonfire* (1955). Indeed, when *The Bishop's Bonfire* opened in Dublin early in 1955 (shortly after *The Quare Fellow* finished its run) it was lambasted by the *Irish Times* as 'a disappointing combination of variety sketch and horse opera',[22] while other critics hailed the originality of its theatrical form.

Although *The Quare Fellow* marches relentlessly through the minutes towards the execution, it is made up of a series of what are essentially comic routines, such as the one in which an old prisoner, Dunlavin, eulogises the pleasures of smoking prison mattress stuffing wrapped in pages from the Bible. What begins as a comic monologue takes a distinctly O'Caseyesque turn when it takes a swipe at the lack of change Irish independence has brought for those on the margins of society. 'When the Free State came in', says Dunlavin, 'we were afraid of our life they were going to change the mattresses for feather beds . . . But sure, thanks to God, the Free State didn't change anything more than the badges on the warders' caps.'[23] Simpson and Swift – who had been staging satirical cabaret late at night in the Pike – recognised the politicised variety show that lurked beneath *The Quare Fellow*'s naturalistic exterior, even negotiating with variety artist Noel Purcell to play the role of Dunlavin as part of a plan to transfer the play to the Gaiety.

Even though Behan gave his next play, *An Giall*, to An Damer, and later to Joan Littlewood, who transformed it into *The Hostage*, it was not the defection of their star playwright that cut short the Pike's short, but remarkable, life. It was a condom. On 12 May 1957, the Pike staged the Irish première of Tennessee Williams' *The Rose Tattoo*, and Simpson was promptly prosecuted for obscenity because of a scene in which a character drops a condom on the stage (even though, in the Pike's production, the condom had been mimed). Not dropping a non-existent condom might seem like a minor offence; however, Catholic social teaching was so deeply engrained in Irish law that it took a year's gruelling trek through the courts (in the course of which Alan Simpson was imprisoned for a short period) before the Pike was finally exonerated in June 1958. Even so, the court costs were enough to sink the theatre.

It may have been a pyrrhic victory, but it was still a victory. In his ruling on *The Rose Tattoo* case, Justice O'Flynn stated that Simpson was not guilty of 'exploiting a filthy business', and, more importantly, that the State had been wrong to arrest Simpson in the first place. 'I can only infer', commented O'Flynn, 'that by arresting the accused, the object would be achieved of closing down the play.'[24] The O'Flynn judgement meant that a play could not be closed on a charge of obscenity until that charge had first been proven in court – by which time, in the normal course of events, the play would have come to the end of its run anyway.

The *Rose Tattoo* judgement came just a month after the 1958 Dublin Theatre Festival was ingloriously aborted when Archbishop John Charles McQuaid refused to offer up a Votive Mass for An Tóstal (of which the Theatre Festival was part) on the basis that it contained two works presumed to be anti-clerical, Sean O'Casey's *The Drums of Father Ned*, and *Bloomsday*, Alan McCelland's dramatisation of Joyce's *Ulysses*. 'The various pious organizations got busy protesting against any work by these two writers', O'Casey wrote to a friend, explaining why he subsequently forbade all professional productions of his work in the Republic of Ireland. Hearing of the Archbishop's decision, Samuel Beckett wrote in a fury to Alan Simpson, who was planning a production of *Endgame*: 'As long as such conditions prevail in Ireland I do not wish my work to be performed there, either in festivals or outside them. If no protest is heard they will prevail for ever. This is the strongest I can make . . . My best wishes to you both and long flame to the Pike in that hideous gale.' Although David Kelly circumvented Beckett's ban, staging the Irish première of *Krapp's*

Last Tape in the seventy-eight-seat Trinity Players' Theatre on 30 March 1959, Beckett's decision held until May 1960, when he decided it was time 'I fell off my high Éire moke',[25] allowing Irish productions of his plays to resume.

Meanwhile, similar battles were being fought in Northern Ireland. The Committee for the Encouragement of Music and the Arts steadily increased their funding for Ulster theatre throughout the early 1950s, until the Ulster Group Theatre had become effectively CEMA's resident company. This allowed the Group to tour more widely than their earlier, semi-professional status would have permitted; at the same time, however, the original directors of the theatre were gradually replaced by managers with more overt political agendas, so that by 1958 the Chairman of the Group's Board of Directors was J. Ritchie McKee, a Belfast estate agent whose brother was the Unionist Lord Mayor of Belfast. 'Plays with sectarian themes', McKee's brother had warned, 'make it difficult for Lord Mayors who are anxious to give money to the arts.'[26] Unfortunately for McKee 'plays with sectarian themes' had long been a defining feature of Ulster dramaturgy.

McKee was still smarting from a controversy over a particularly violent play about sectarianism, Gerard McLarnon's *The Bonefire*, when Sam Thompson presented the Group's artistic director, James Ellis, with the script of *Over the Bridge* in 1958. The Group's governing body rejected the play. 'The Ulster public is fed up with religious and political controversies', declared McKee, announcing that the Group would not perform the play. 'We have no censorship in the North', Thompson told a reporter. 'When they ban a play they tell you it's postponed.'[27] There then followed a very public row, in which Ellis and Thompson withdrew from the Group, forming their own Ulster Bridge Productions, which opened Thompson's play at the Empire Theatre on 26 January 1960. It played for more than six weeks, and was seen by more than 42,000 people, more than any single run in Belfast's theatre history to that point.

Thompson's principled stand on his play would become a point of reference for future generations of Ulster playwrights. At the same time, what is perhaps most remarkable about *Over the Bridge* as a play is how little of an advance it makes over St John Ervine's *Mixed Marriage*, staged almost fifty years earlier. Set in the Belfast shipyards (with the final act in a workman's home), *Over the Bridge* deals with a Protestant worker, Davy Mitchell, who defies a mob to protect a Catholic colleague. In both plays, however, sectarianism is not something that can be analysed, for it is presented only as a beast heard howling offstage (apart from a brief appearance by the oily mob leader in Thompson's play). In *Mixed Marriage* it 'runs like lightning', while in *Over the Bridge* it is 'a disease' with 'a nasty habit of spreading'[28] – both metaphors suggesting that it is a force of nature, unstoppable and at best treatable only after it has struck. Only in its staging did *Over the Bridge* show real signs of innovation, with giant gantries and bridges permanently spanning the top of the stage behind the proscenium, while below two revolves turned to produce an office, workshop exterior, and Mitchell's kitchen. And yet, as Stewart Parker later noted, 'it was and is almost impossible to think of Thompson's work in aesthetic terms, to divorce it from its social and historical context.'[29]

The confrontations generated by *The Rose Tattoo* and *Over the Bridge* showed that Ireland's various theocracies were still powerful enough to fight and win local battles; meanwhile, larger shifts in the tectonic plates of culture were underway that would soon make these battles seem quaintly redundant. The first signs of this change were innocent enough. As early as 1951, when Louis Elliman had leased the Queen's to the Abbey, he had sensed that audiences for variety were declining, and in 1953, when the Olympia was taken over by the partnership of Stanley Illsley and Leo McCabe, they too announced that they would move away from variety to concentrate on straight theatre, motivated in part by a controversial production of Paul Vincent Carroll's *The Strings are False*, which broke all box-office records for the theatre. Throughout the 1950s, an increasingly subsidised English theatre began to include Dublin once again in a limited touring circuit, giving audiences an opportunity to see actors such as John Gielgud, Paul Scofield, and Tyrone Power. The Gaiety, too, registered the declining taste for variety, continuing to stage opera and ballet, and acting as a base for the Edwards–Mac Líammóir company, who staged more productions at the Gaiety than at the Gate Theatre in the decade 1950 to 1960. The only major Dublin theatre to continue as a variety house in the mid-1950s was the Theatre Royal, and it too would close by 1962, more than 140 years after the first theatre of that name had been built on the Hawkins Street site.

Just as melodrama had been absorbed by cinema, variety was becoming the domain of television. Broadcasting had begun in Northern Ireland in 1955, the East coast of the Republic could receive BBC by the late 1950s, and Radio Telefís Éireann began broadcasting on 31 December 1961. The first director of Drama for the new station was Hilton Edwards, and he was soon joined by Carolyn Swift. Over the coming years, television would provide Irish actors (and some playwrights) with a more or less steady income, making a career in theatre far more feasible than it had been in the past. What is more, television began to expose Irish audiences to a global media in which sexuality and politics could be discussed with growing frankness in some contexts; at the same time, television's own self-imposed censorship of such frankness in the area of drama seemed to open up a kind of licence in the live theatre. Simultaneously, television brought the visual language of the screen into people's homes, renewing the challenge to theatre designers that had been issued, and then largely forgotten, after the initial impact of cinema in the decade or so after 1910.

When all of these forces were combined with an expanding economy and the gradual retirement from the seats of power of the generation of 1916, there was a dawning realisation that 'that hideous gale' was beginning to blow itself out. The success of *Waiting for Godot*, *The Quare Fellow* and *A Whistle in the Dark* had proven that challenging, even shocking, theatre could be commercially viable and critically respected. For the first time in decades, Irish writers were gaining international reputations for acting like live rebels, not for venerating dead ones, whether by writing a play in which nothing happens twice (like Beckett) or by getting drunk and saying 'fuck' on BBC television (like Behan). Innovative theatre was moving out of the basements into the mainstream, transferring, like *An Giall*, from the damp confines of the Damer Hall to Stratford East in a matter of months. At the dawn of a decade that would make a fetish of rebellion, being an Irish rebel (*albeit* of a particular variety) was suddenly fashionable.

So, just as T. K. Whitaker's programme for opening up the Irish economy gradually overtook Éamon de Valera's long-held policy of economic self-sufficiency, the Irish theatre once again rejoined the wider theatre world. In April 1959, as de Valera wound up his final days as Taoiseach, Dubliners had a choice of Brecht's *Mother Courage* at the Gate, or an influential production of Eugene O'Neill's *Long Day's Journey into Night* at the Abbey. Meanwhile, the Dublin Theatre Festival was emerging as an important locus of change, bringing in productions that would not usually tour, and showcasing the new sense of possibility in Irish theatre. The 1962 Festival, for instance, saw the première of Hugh Leonard's *Stephen D.*, an adaptation of Joyce's *Portrait of the Artist*, which deliberately poses a series of complex staging problems, requiring rapid changes of place and time and a narrator who later becomes a character. The following year, 1963, Hilton Edwards directed Sam Thompson's *The Evangelist* in a production in which Ray McAnally, in the title role, preached directly to the audience from a ramp running into the auditorium. It was the highlight of a Festival responsible for selling more than 70,000 theatre tickets, attracting 2,500 visitors to Dublin and adding £125,000 to the local economy.

In an essay published in 1964, entitled 'Ireland: The End of an Era?', sociologist David Thornley had written: 'In so far as any conclusive picture can be drawn, the period in which we are now living in Ireland seems to me a transitional one, a valley between two generations',[30] and the Dublin Theatre Festival that year made it clear that this was certainly true of the Irish theatre. On 18 September 1964, Sean O'Casey died, predeceased six months earlier by 'the new O'Casey', Brendan Behan. Meanwhile, Leonard, Keane and Murphy had established themselves as the vanguard of a new generation. 'We are, I believe', wrote the *Irish Times* on 24 September 'on the verge of a complete change of tone and outlook in Irish writing.'[31] On 2 September Eugene McCabe's *King of the Castle*, directed by Godfrey Quigley, had opened at the Gaiety; it would be followed by Brian Friel's *Philadelphia, Here I Come!*, directed by Hilton Edwards, which opened on 28 September. On both nights, the sets confronting the Gaiety audiences looked familiar: a farmyard in McCabe's play, and the kitchen of a country shop in Friel's. What was to happen in those sets, however, was a repudiation of much of what had taken place on Irish stages for the previous half century.

King of the Castle deals with a recognisable figure in Irish drama, going back to Bat Morrissey in T. C. Murray's *Birthright*: a small farmer who has struggled against poverty and bad soil to achieve a measure of hard-won prosperity. Scober MacAdam in *King of the Castle*, however, is sexually impotent, and the play hinges around his attempt to pay a younger man, Lynch, to impregnate his wife, Tressa. 'I was hired to thresh corn', Lynch tells her, 'not dog a bitch in heat', at which she 'suddenly slaps and claws at Lynch', biting him before they go off behind a stack of bales to have sex.[32] 'McCabe expects his play to shock and dismay many of its patrons', reported the *Irish Times*, while McCabe himself described it as 'ugly' and 'unlikeable'. And yet, although *King of the Castle* helped to re-establish the commercial and aesthetic value of shock, it was the formal challenge of Friel's *Philadelphia, Here I Come!* that was to have the more permanent impact. Indeed, a sixteen-year old Joe Dowling (who fifteen years later would be Artistic Director of the Abbey), attended every night of that initial run, mesmerised by what he saw.

Philadelphia, Here I Come! uses the familiar *mise en scène* of a Donegal shop from which a young man is preparing to emigrate, but splits its protagonist, Gar O'Donnell, into two characters, one private and the other public. This simple device allows the play to address the basic theatrical problem that Friel would explore throughout the rest of his long career: 'the conflict between the world of the flesh and the world of the spirit, or, if you dislike the terms, the world of the physical and the world of cerebral'.[33] In the theatre, one of the basic, irreducible elements of performance is the presence of a living actor playing a character who is physically present before an audience. Most theatre, particularly naturalistic theatre, works from the assumption that 'the cerebral world' – the hopes, memories and dreams of that character – can be communicated by the physical presence. *Philadelphia, Here I Come!* splits its protagonist, Gar O'Donnell, into two characters: Public Gar and Private Gar. In so doing, it splits the 'physical' from the 'cerebral' (to use Friel's terms), so that while each continues to exist, they are separated by a gulf, thereby questioning one of the central assumptions of naturalistic theatre and the whole empiricist worldview that supports it.

Almost at the same moment that Friel was writing *Philadelphia, Here I Come!*, in the autumn of 1963, Samuel Beckett's *Happy Days* was playing at the Eblana Theatre, in the basement of Dublin's central bus station, as part of the Theatre Festival. Meanwhile in France, Beckett himself was struggling with a play he called 'Kilcool,' working on the manuscript first in Paris, and later in his small country house at Ussy-sur-Marne. 'Woman's face alone in constant light. Nothing but fixed lit face and light', reads the opening stage direction: '– come now to Kilcoole this ruin is Kilcoole from those other times other times'. As he pushed further with 'Kilcool', leaving behind its Irish setting (Kilcoole is just south of Dublin), he began to question the relationship between the figure who was speaking, and the self about whom she was speaking. 'There is no me and there is no one else', he writes on a fresh page in the exercise book. 'There is no one at all, there was never any me at all . . . My I's are nothing and my mes are nothing and my my's are nothing and so for all the other pronouns.'[34] Beckett could not, of course, go much further than that, and the manuscript was abandoned not long after, remaining unpublished, although he was to pick it up again later when writing *Play* and *Not I*.[35] The exploration of dramatic character had already gone as far as possible in a farmhouse in Ussy-sur-Marne by December 1963. Indeed, there is a sense in which we can see Friel's *Philadelphia, Here I Come!* as the domesticated contemporary of the abandoned 'Kilcool'.

The more Irish writers and directors pushed the possibilities of dramatic form, the more forlornly antique the island's theatrical infrastructure appeared. There were, quite simply, no major twentieth-century theatre buildings in the country as late as 1965. Of the large professional theatres, only the Gate had a modern, fan-shaped auditorium of the type pioneered at Bayreuth in 1876, and even this was housed in an eighteenth-century building with pathetically small backstage facilities. The Abbey, meanwhile, were at the Queen's trying to present Brecht on a stage designed for Boucicault. These were frustrating years for the Abbey company, knowing that as they struggled in seemingly interminable exile, architect Michael Scott and his colleagues were caught up in a series of bureaucratic wrangles, but nonetheless were continuing to produce innovative designs demonstrating a restless, utopian rethinking of theatrical space.

Robin Walker, who had trained with Le Corbusier and Mies Van der Rohe, created the most remarkable of these plans for the new Abbey. Walker designed a theatre that would have extended from the current Abbey site to the River Liffey. It contained two stages, back to back, with a screen between them. The screen would have been removable, revealing a massive acting space over which two audiences faced one another. It is possible to fantasise that this theatre, had it been built, would have given rise to plays written specifically for it, emblematic of an increasingly fractured Irish society, in which parts of a performance would be shared by both audiences, and parts would be seen by only one group or the other. 'But', recalled Scott, 'Blythe, being a politician, was afraid of his life that the government wouldn't give the money for the Abbey', and was reluctant to ask for more. So, when the new Abbey, like a large, tardy Phoenix, finally emerged from behind the hoardings on the site of its burned predecessor in the summer of 1966, a headline in the *Irish Times* hailed it as a 'A Miracle of Compression'. Michael Scott later put it more frankly when he complained: 'There is nowhere to park, there is no graciousness about it, it's crushed, the public areas are too small and the stage is not deep enough.'[36]

The 1966 Abbey, designed by Michael Scott and Ronald Tallon, can stand as an image of much that was taking place in Irish culture in the mid-1960s. Ernest Blythe had insisted that the new Abbey must occupy the site of the old Mechanics Institute, thereby confining a building intended to house two theatres, seating 785 patrons between them, into a 0.3-acre (0.12 hectare) site. Within this straightjacket of tradition, Scott built a pure modernist cube, presenting windowless brick façades to Marlborough and Abbey Streets (later broken by a glass addition to the main foyer). Like so many Irish public buildings of the period, Scott's Abbey is a concrete renunciation of tradition, a structure strenuously

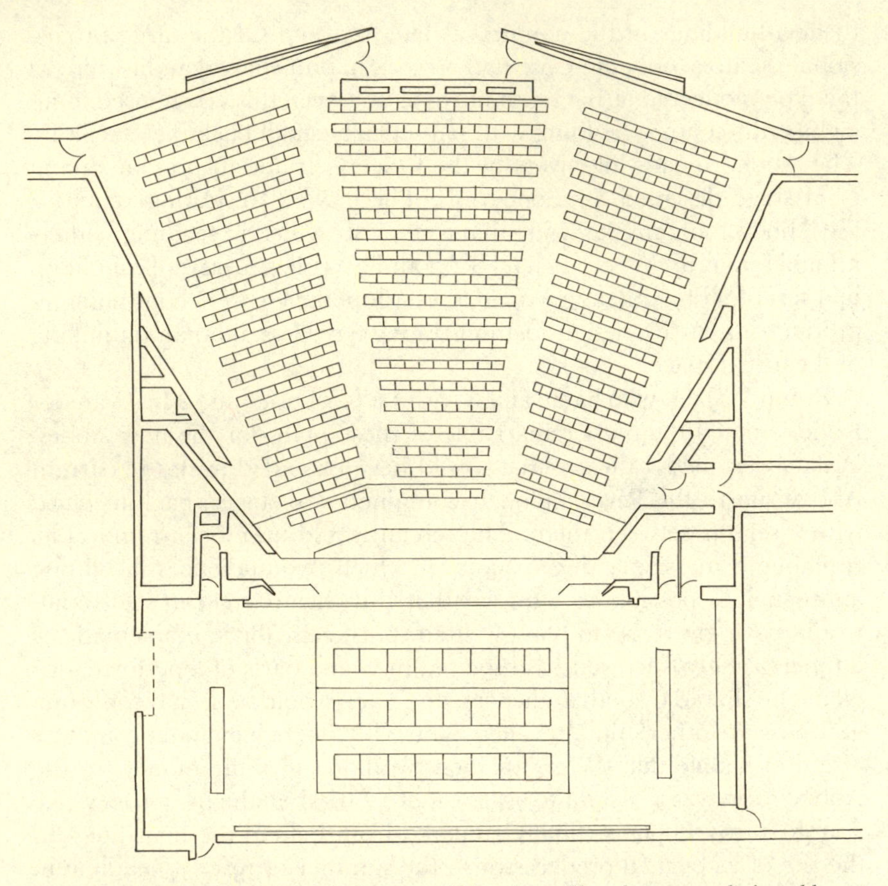

Plan 5. Unlike the claustrophobic 1904 Abbey, its 1966 replacement, designed by Michael Scott and Ronald Tallon, has no sense of enclosure, with its extendable forestage, hydraulic stage lifts, fly system, and ample offstage space.

unimpressed by past glories. Unlike the horseshoe auditoria to which the Abbey had played previously, the 1966 Abbey has an unadorned fan-shaped 628-seat house in the purest modernist tradition, focusing all the room's energies on the stage, forcing its audience to give the performance their full attention. Such an auditorium tells its audience that what is happening on the stage is important and serious. Similarly, while the stage has a proscenium arch, its width (72 feet (21.5 metres), with movable false proscenium) makes it difficult to create the sense of claustrophobic enclosure and limited possibility required by so much of the theatre's traditional repertoire, particularly O'Casey's tenement plays and Synge's *Playboy* or *Shadow of the Glen*. On the other hand, the new stage is equipped with a forestage that can be extended by 14 feet (4.2 metres), three large and flexible hydraulic traps, thirty counter-weighted flies, acoustic baffles, and a full lighting rig, allowing types of performance not possible earlier in the company's history. Tucked into the basement of the building, a second theatre the 157-seat, Peacock, pushes the Abbey even further away from its past. It is designed so that it can be used either as a small proscenium stage facing a raked auditorium, or converted into a sunken three-quarters thrust performance space.

'An old theatre', writes theatre architect Iain Mackintosh, 'may be a sacred place and the ghosts of past productions are a reality and, if friendly, are a benign presence.'[37] Joseph Holloway's Abbey had so many ghosts that they often blocked the stage, their bony fingers wagging accusingly; the Queen's too had its share of ghosts, but they were not Abbey ghosts. Scott's 1966 Abbey, by contrast, was such a pure space that it was necessary to perform an act of conjuration to prove that the old Abbey spirits still existed. So, when the first audience filed into the theatre on the night of 18 July 1966, they saw a show entitled *Recall the Years*, which began with actors playing Yeats, Lady Gregory and Edward Martyn evocatively (but inaccurately) meeting in Coole Park, before being introduced to living ghosts such as the Abbey carpenter Seaghan Barlow and the actress Maire Ni Shiubhlaigh, who were trotted out to meet, once again, their dead contemporaries. These now elderly men and women must have looked like Yeats' 'souls in Purgatory', who 'come back / To habitations and familiar spots . . . . Re-live their transgressions, and that not once / But many times'. And yet, like the presence of an aging de Valera at the ceremonies marking the fiftieth anniversary of the 1916 Rising earlier that year, their anachronistic appearance at the opening of the new Abbey was as much an exorcism as a séance, a laying to rest of troublesome ghosts rather than their conjuration.

'The new facilities are going to make it easier for us to devise new and exciting productions', Tomás Mac Anna told the *Irish Times* on 18 July 1966. 'The main thing about moving into a new theatre is this: that you have an opportunity of breaking with a certain tradition of writing.'[38] While the new Abbey would continue to honour its own past (its first show after *Recall the Years* was *The Plough and the Stars*), the new theatre was to open up new possibilities for Irish writers, accelerating the flow of talent from the smaller art theatres to the mainstream. Although the critic Fergus Linehan had predicted in 1965 that the new Peacock would be devoted to 'Yeats's poetic plays, for the benefit mainly of the American tourist market',[39] when the new second stage opened in July of 1967, it was only a few months before the first Beckett production took place, a showing of *Film* paired with *Play* (one of the texts born of the 'Kilcool' manuscript), followed in 1968 by a production of *Come and Go*. By 1969, the year in which Beckett was awarded the Nobel Prize, the Abbey's main stage would mount its first *Waiting for Godot*, with Peter O'Toole's Vladimir, 'bubbling and soft-shoe shuffling in indefatigable Micawberish optimism between the abysses of despair . . . protecting the incurable carping pessimism of Donal McCann's Estragon in beautifully balanced and timed counterpoint'.[40]

At the same time, the new Peacock signalled its intention to promote Irish-language writing by opening with an Irish play (a stage version of Flann O'Brien's *An Béal Bocht*), even though its stage would eventually be dominated by English-language theatre. In the late 1960s, however, it provided a venue for more than one generation of Irish-language writers, at a period when Amharclann An Damer was staging plays such as Eoghan Ó Tuairisc's *Lá Fhéile Míchíl* (1964), as well as two of the most important Irish-language productions of the 1960s: Máiréad Ní Ghráda's *An Triail* (1964) and Críostóir Ó Floinn's *Cóta Bán Chríost* (1969). Ní Ghráda had been writing plays since the 1930s, while Ó Tuairsc and Ó Floinn had written for the Abbey's Irish-language pantomimes in the 1950s (a tradition that mercifully vanished with the new building). The plays written by these Irish-language writers in the mid-1960s registered the same willingness to tackle hitherto taboo subjects evident in English-language counterparts like Eugene McCabe. Indeed, *An Triail* can be placed with *King of the Castle* and *Philadelphia, Here I Come!*, with which it featured at the 1964 Dublin Theatre Festival, while *Cóta Bán Chríost* later cost its author his job when it came under attack from the Church. 'That decade of the Sixties was the most productive in the century as far as drama in Irish was concerned', Ó Floinn later wrote.[41] Indeed, at one point in 1968, Ó Floinn had three plays running simultaneously: *Is É A Dúirt Polonius* in the Peacock, *Cóta Bán Chríost* at An Taibhdhearc, and *Aggiornamento*, a comic satire about the effect of the Second Vatican Council on a small Irish town, playing in An Damer.

Asked what he would like to see in the new Abbey in 1966, Barry Cassin had responded that he would 'like to see a Brecht'. When Tomás Mac Anna staged *Galileo* during the Abbey's final year at the Queen's in September 1965, it was only the third professional production of the writer's plays in Ireland, and it had a stunning effect on audiences. 'I remember Micheál Ó hAonghusa as Galileo', recalled one playgoer, 'his shirt open to the waist, his belly out; it was in-your-face theatre.'[42] In Ireland, as elsewhere, Brecht was one of the great talking points of the theatre in the 1960s, and by March 1968 his influence on Irish writing became evident when Tom Murphy's *Famine* opened at the Peacock. Set during the Famine of the 1840s, *Famine* is clearly Brechtian in its use of projected (usually ironic) titles above each scene, its episodic structure, and, as Fintan O'Toole has argued, in its insistence on the link 'between material and economic conditions on one hand, and the intimate life of the mind'.[43] The play works with dramatic conventions familiar to the audience, but juxtaposes them with situations to which they are no longer adequate. For instance, Scene Four is labelled 'The Love Scene', and it is set in a moonlit wood, where a young man and a young woman, Liam and Maeve, meet; downstage, out of sight of the characters, but in full view of the audience, are the corpses of a young mother and her two children, dead of starvation.

When *Famine* opened on 18 March 1968, there were student riots in Paris and protests against the Vietnam War in the United States. In Ireland, the Censorship of Publications Act had been eased in the Republic, and Taoiseach Jack Lynch and Northern Ireland Prime Minister Terence O'Neill were holding meetings that seemed to promise a thaw in the paralysing stalemate of Partition. And then – suddenly, it seemed to those watching from outside Northern Ireland – the Province was in flames. Working-class Catholic homes were being burnt out, and there were clashes between civil rights protestors and police. By the summer of 1969 there were areas of Northern Ireland in an open state of civil war, with the Bogside area of Derry declaring itself off-limits to the police. By 14 August the British Army were on the streets of Belfast and Derry.

'When the North blew up in '68', the critic Seamus Deane later recalled, 'I think everybody who had grown up in it thought: "Now we can interpret it in the light of this flame-thrower." If you had been beaten up by the police in the past, that was no big deal. But then you saw the police being televised battling people in '68, and this was suddenly a political matter – a matter of history now – then you began to make connections.'[44] If the eruption of violence gave the working classes of Northern Ireland a context in which to understand the slow burn of their history, in the Republic, particularly among the urban middle classes who dominated the professional theatre, both as artists and as audience, there was a feeling of disorientation. In a sense, the demilitarisation of mindsets in the Republic, to which Ernest Blythe had contributed so powerfully in the 1940s and 1950s, had done its work.

Indeed, the Abbey's earliest attempt to deal with the eruption of violence in Northern Ireland went badly wrong. On the evening of 16 September 1970, press, politicians (including all of the opposition MPs from Stormont) and other public figures gathered around the low thrust stage of the Peacock Theatre for a satirical revue, *A State of Chassis*, written by Tomás Mac Anna and John D. Stewart. It was composed of short sketches and songs all dealing with Northern Ireland, interspersed with recorded voices of Northern politicians. 'Who are these people?' the voice of the Unionist MP William Craig boomed through the auditorium. 'They call themselves the "People's Democracy" but in reality are the hard core Communists, Marxists and followers of Mao Tse Tung' – whereupon an actress playing the nationalist MP Bernadette Devlin, stood up and sang:

> I'll tell me ma when I get home
> The prods won't leave the tagues alone
> They pulled my hair and stole my comb
> And left me whingin' on my own . . . [45]

Just before the first intermission, a man stood up from the audience, and clambered on to the Peacock's stage. 'The caricature of Bernadette Devlin on this stage for your delectation is a disgrace', declared an apoplectic Eamonn McCann, chairman of the Derry Labour Party, 'I object to this production.' Some of McCann's supporters in the audience cheered him, but there were also calls from the audience: 'Go to hell', and 'Throw him out.' A couple of men attacked McCann when he began handing out leaflets, before he was finally escorted from the hall by Mac Anna.

The response to McCann's disruption of *A State of Chassis* revealed the gulf between liberals in the South and working-class republicans in the North. Seamus Kelly, the *Irish Times* drama critic, called McCann's protest 'an ignorant interruption as bigoted and humourless as anything that one might expect from the Paisleyites',[46] while the moderate nationalist MP, John Hume, who was present in the audience, politely but firmly told reporters that he did not like the revue, leaving no doubt that he felt it trivialised a dangerous situation. At that point, after a decade of economic programmes and quick-march modernisation, culture in the Republic – and theatre in particular – was ill-equipped to deal with the civil war then erupting on a part of the island which the Republic's

Constitution still claimed as 'the national territory'. Very quickly, the euphoric sense of experimentation that had made the Theatre Festivals of the early 1960s so exciting gave way to a darker, more anxious sense of freefall.

On 15 March 1971 – a little more than a month after the IRA killed the first British soldier in Northern Ireland – two plays opened on the same night in Dublin which crystallised the spiralling sense of things falling apart: Tom Murphy's *The Morning After Optimism* at the Abbey; and Hugh Leonard's *The Patrick Pearse Motel* at the Gaiety. In some respects, the two plays could not have been more different. Murphy's play had been written almost a decade earlier, during a frantic two-week burst in September 1962, and is not obviously the work of the same author who had written the naturalistic tragedy, *A Whistle in the Dark*. In that first production, designer Bronwen Casson created a stage full of 'wreathlike forests rising forever like straw against a murky blue-green mystery with a cottage at once romantic and brassy set in the middle'. In this nightmarish fairytale world a pimp, a prostitute, a poet and an orphan act out a series of scenes that look like allegories, but yield no obvious interpretation. Leonard's play, on the other hand, was set in the recognisable environs of 'a suburb in Dublin's vodka-and-bitter-lemon belt', and was structurally a conventional farce in the mode of Georges Feydeau, a point Leonard acknowledged with characteristic candour in a programme note.

In spite of major stylistic differences between the two plays, both register a situation in which characters scramble around with no underlying sense of right or wrong to guide them, and this can be alternately funny and shocking, sometimes both. For his part, Leonard recognised that an ethical vacuum lies at the heart of the bedroom farce, and it is no coincidence that in 1969 there had been two major farces on the London stage: Feydeau's *Cat Among the Pigeons* and Joe Orton's *What the Butler Saw*. 'What a bigot you are in this day and age', says the British character in Leonard's play. 'After all, it's the same God we all disbelieve in, isn't it?' *The Patrick Pearse Motel* thus finds a metaphor for the new Ireland – at least, the urban middle-class Dublin part of it – in the eponymous motel with its 'Famine room restaurant' ('best steaks in Ireland'), bedrooms named for Irish patriots, and an aging 1916 veteran named 'Hoolihan' as a caretaker. 'The rubbidge Pearse used to come out with', scoffs Hoolihan. ' "Never tell a lie. Strength in our hands, truth on our lips, and cleanness in our hearts". Jasus, what sort of way is that to run a country?'[47]

In *The Morning After Optimism*, the pimp, James, describes what sounds like the starting premise of *The Patrick Pearse Motel*. 'The permissive society?' he asks. 'I was a member, when that club was exclusive, when 'twas dangerous to be in it, when the tension was there. And I might have got lost, but they threw open the doors, didn't they? The amateurs came in to desecrate with innocence.' In a world in which there are no ideals to which James and the prostitute Rosie can aspire, those who continue to hold ideals – the poet Edmund and the innocent orphan Anastasia – live on as a reproach. 'If we can't get to their ridiculous level', James tells Rosie, 'they must be brought to ours.' In the play's final, shocking moments, James and Rosie kill Edmund and Anastasia. 'We done it, James', says Rosie. 'What have we done?' With the 1960s over, this was indeed the question. By 1971, Ireland was, as James puts it, 'done with the innocent shit'.[48]

A night at the theatre 7

Translations by Brian Friel
The Guildhall, Derry
Tuesday, 23 September 1980

It was raining lightly in Derry on the evening of 23 September 1980, and Cyril Cusack, dressed formally in black tie, was in the back of a taxi on his way to join the opening-night audience for Brian Friel's *Translations*. 'I'm taking Cyril Cusack to the Guildhall', the driver radioed his controller. 'Ask him if he remembers', came back the reply, 'acting here at the Carlisle Road Opera House in 1917.' Earlier that same evening, in another taxi, Brian Friel had also been on his way to the Guildhall, when the driver glanced back and recognised his old school teacher, known to his students as 'Scobie Friel'. For Cusack, the night was a return to the past; for the rest of the Irish theatre community who gathered in Derry that night, it was a venture into new territory; however, for Brian Friel and the Field Day Theatre Company, it was a kind of homecoming.

Derry had long been on the periphery of Ireland's theatrical geography. In 1741, when the Smock Alley company first blazed a northern touring route, Derry marked the north-western limit of their itinerary. For the rest of the eighteenth century, the city had a lively, if sporadic, theatrical life, and the theatre built in Artillery Lane in 1789 (replacing an earlier building) was described as being 'equal in elegance to any house in the Kingdom'.[1] A century later, however, the touring map had been redrawn, and as the major English and Irish companies stayed close to the Belfast–Dublin–Cork axis, Derry was left to the vagaries of small fit-up companies, like the one which carried Cusack to the city in 1917. After the demise of the fit-ups, CEMA-sponsored tours passed through in the 1940s, but it was not until the formation of one of Ireland's best amateur companies, the '71 Players (who brought Friel's *Freedom of the City* to the All-Ireland Finals in 1976) that theatre became part of the texture of the city's life again. Even so, when the cast of *Translations* sat down in the Guildhall for a preliminary read-through on 12 August 1980, it was the first time in almost two centuries that a professional company had rehearsed a play in Derry.

As new plays opened in Dublin and Belfast, but never in Derry, fresh scars were added to the city's already wounded sense of having been shunted to the periphery. In spite of its hallowed place in Irish Protestant iconography, when the island was partitioned in 1920 Derry found itself on the margins of the new Northern Ireland state to the east, while at the same time cut off from part of its natural hinterland across the border to the west. This double sense of division and marginalisation became particularly acute in the mid-1960s, when policy-makers in Belfast chose the small town of Coleraine over Derry as the site for a new university. For a brief period, moderate nationalists and unionists in the city joined forces in an unsuccessful effort to bring the institution to Derry, and the memory of that lost opportunity still rankled fifteen years later. *Translations* need not have been performed on a makeshift stage, argued one reviewer, had it not been for 'the insult of the decision to site the second university at Coleraine'.[2]

While the university debate had shown that the sense of being suspended between two states could open up possibilities, it was equally true that the old divisions cut deeply in Derry. The Civil Rights campaigns of the late 1960s, agitating for better housing and fairer electoral divisions, were fought more fiercely in Derry than almost anywhere else in the Province. After the Civil Rights movement fragmented in the early 1970s, the Provisional IRA became an established force in the city's Bogside area, and not long afterward the steel-clad Army observation towers on the city's seventeenth-century walls became part of the city's architecture. Indeed, in the week in which *Translations* opened, the Province's simmering civil war entered one of its tensest periods, as talks with Republican prisoners collapsed; within a month, some of the prisoners would begin a hunger strike in which ten would die. That same week, 900 people lost their jobs in Derry, as a DuPont chemical plant and a shirt factory closed, adding to the 13,000 job losses in the Province over the previous nine months.

In spite of these problems, Derry was the obvious place to stage *Translations*. Looking out of the Guildhall's windows during rehearsals, the cast could see the hills of the Inishowen peninsula where the play is set, across the border in the Irish Republic. Moreover, when staging a play so concerned with place names, there could be few better choices than Derry – or, as the unionist community call it, Londonderry. 'Derry', from the Irish *doire* (meaning 'place of the oaks') was the original name, until in 1613 the city was granted to a consortium of London companies, who changed the name to Londonderry. However, in 1973, electoral reforms gave the city's Catholic population a majority on the City Council, and in 1978 – just as Friel was beginning to sift through the ideas that would become *Translations* – they rechristened themselves *Derry* City Council. Refusing to recognise the change, the British government still called the city *Londonderry*, as did most unionists. And yet, while London / Derry's name remained contentious, local unionist and nationalist politicians had worked out a power-sharing arrangement on the Council, and it was a unionist Lord Mayor, Marlene Jefferson, who helped to make it possible for *Translations* to be staged in the Guildhall.

While all of these factors would be at work in the reception of *Translations* on its opening night, the decision to stage the play in Derry came partly at the urging of the play's director, Art O Briain, who had been involved in community theatre in the city;[3] equally, it was the product of Brian Friel sharing with actor Stephen Rea a sense of dissatisfaction with the existing theatre structures. In some respects, the fact that Derry was more or less a clean slate, in terms of professional theatre, was part of its attraction. When Friel finished writing *Translations* on 5 November 1979, he could have handed it to the Abbey, or looked for a venue in New York, where his previous play, *Faith Healer*, had opened. However, Friel wanted greater control over the staging of his plays, telling Ciaran Carty in the *Sunday Independent* he was 'very doubtful about the whole idea of a director interpreting a play in any kind of way that's distinctive to him'.[4] Similarly, Rea could have remained in London, where he had an established acting career at the National Theatre. However, he too was chaffing at the limitations imposed by success. 'Friel and I often talked of our notion of theatre in Ireland', Rea told an interviewer in October 1980. 'You know, an Irishman in English theatre is very conscious of belonging to a sub-culture rather than a culture proper. I felt less expressed in terms of England than I did over here, but not in the narrow national way.'[5]

A few years earlier, these aspirations might have come to nothing. There had been almost no Arts Council money for new theatre companies throughout the 1970s, but by early 1980 cultural policy was edging towards the idea of decentralisation. Consequently, when Friel and Rea decided to stage *Translations* themselves, the Northern Ireland Arts Council told them that they would be eligible for funding if they were members of an existing regional company – whereupon they formed a company called Field Day, a play on their combined names: Friel / Rea. The Northern Ireland Arts Council gave them £40,000, while the Arts Council in the Republic later added £10,000. Meanwhile, Derry City offered them use of the Victorian Guildhall, and voted out of their own funds an additional £13,000 with which to build a lighting rig and construct a stage. By 6 June 1980, Friel, Rea, and Derry's Lord Mayor Marlene Jefferson were able to announce the date of the opening.

At that point, the play had already been cast in a way that would give the production its shape. The plot of *Translations* is both simple and conventional, a cross-cultural romantic triangle that ends in tragedy. It is set in 1833 on the Irish-speaking Inishowen peninsula of Donegal, in a hedge school run by a polyglot master, Hugh O'Donnell, and his son Manus. A British Army Ordnance Survey team arrive, accompanied by Manus's brother, Owen, to begin triangulation work for what will become the standard map of the whole island. An attraction quickly develops between one of the school's adult students, Maire, who had been betrothed to Manus, and an English officer, Lieutenant Yolland. Yolland then disappears, and the play ends with Yolland's superior officer, Captain Lancey, threatening to destroy the entire parish unless he is found, driving Manus into hiding.

Described in these terms, *Translations* sounds like a naturalistic play with a triangular love story plot. However, of the three characters at the centre of this story, in the Field Day production only Manus was played by a well-known actor, Mick Lally, while the roles of Maire and Yolland were filled by two relatively unknown performers, Nuala Hayes and Shaun Scott. By contrast, Stephen Rea cast himself as Owen, and chose Ray McAnally as the schoolmaster, Hugh. Owen and Hugh may be background characters in the love story, but they are at the crux of the meeting between two cultures – Owen as the translator accompanying the Ordnance Survey, and Hugh as the play's linguistic philosopher. In a sense therefore, the casting of the first *Translations* recognised that it is a love story in which the foreground and background have been reversed.

While Rea played Owen with the kind of economy of gesture that would characterise his later film work, McAnally's performance was at the heart of the Derry *Translations*. His film career went back to *Shake Hands with the Devil* in 1959, and his stage work began with the Abbey's days in the Queen's, when he played the lead in Walter Macken's *Twilight of a Warrior*. 'Watching this actor at work is sheer joy', wrote Gus Smith reviewing the play. McAnally was at his best playing characters who are self-consciously playing a part. The title role in Sam Thompson's *The Evangelist* gave him one such role in 1961; Commandant Frank Butler, who he played in the first production of Friel's *Living Quarters* in 1977 was another; and so, of course, is Hugh in *Translations*. While such roles are easily overplayed, McAnally's Hugh 'verged on slow motion', so that 'with a mere flicker of his eyes, or movement of his hand he conveyed a world of meaning'. Dressed, unlike any of the other characters, in a flowing knee-length greatcoat, he 'dominated the stage each time he appeared', in spite of the fact that his character – like Stephen Rea's Owen – has almost no influence on the development of the plot.[6]

Weighting the play towards Hugh creates a palpable sense of loss in the play's final moments. With Owen torn between two sets of responsibilities, Manus on the run, and the hedge school dispersed, Hugh stands alone on the stage at the curtain with Maire and the 'infant prodigy', Jimmy Jack, an aging, gently-mad scholar who dreams of wedding the Greek goddess, Pallas Athene. In later productions, Jimmy Jack would often be played as a wizened old man; in Derry, however, Roy Hanlon's Jimmy Jack was a heavy-set, bearded figure, whose strong physical resemblance to McAnally's Hugh (also bearded) made him into a kind of admonitory *doppelganger*. 'It is not the literal past, the "facts" of history, that shape us, but images of the past embodied in language', Hugh tells Owen in the play's closing scene. 'James has ceased to make that discrimination.' In the diminuendo slide to the curtain, Hugh and Jimmy Jack merge, their erudition turning them into helpless prisoners of 'a linguistic contour which no longer matches the landscape of fact'.[7]

Apart from his commanding stage presence, McAnally had another great advantage in playing Hugh: he was born in Moville, just up the banks of Lough Foyle from Derry on the Donegal side. When Friel and Rea cast him in *Translations*, McAnally had just finished directing a young Ballymena actor, Liam Neeson, in a Dublin production of John Steinbeck's *Of Mice and Men*, and Neeson followed the older actor to Derry to play Doalty. Selecting a predominantly Ulster cast was a conscious decision, with Brenda Scallon (from Enniskillen, County Fermanagh) playing Bridget, and Ann Hasson (from Derry) as the mute Sarah. In performance, there was no mistaking the cast's origins, as their native Ulster accents, nurtured by six weeks' rehearsal in Derry, were allowed to come through strongly – so much so that one Dublin-based critic thought they 'may have to be toned down when the play comes south'.[8] In particular, Liam Neeson gave such free rein to his Northern vowels that some Southern critics could not understand him. By contrast, Captain Lancey, 'the perfect colonial servant' who threatens to destroy the parish at the end of the play, was played by an English actor, David Heap.

Translations is, of course, a play about 'the meeting of two cultures, and specifically of two languages', as Friel told the *Derry People*.[9] On the stage, this was clearly underlined in the contrast between the clean lines and primary colours of the British army uniforms, and the rumpled layers and mottled earth tones worn by the Irish characters. However, *Translations* is also about a collision between the values of a local community and a centralised state. The need to change place names arises not so much from a will to dominate on the part of the Ordnance Survey cartographers, as from the need for uniformity throughout the entire island. By contrast, when a name is used locally, it need only correspond to the communal lore out of which it arises. 'Look at that crossroads, Tobair Vree', Owen tells Yolland. 'Why do we call it Tobair Vree? . . . Tobair means a well . . . Because a hundred and fifty years ago there used to be a well there . . . and an old man called Brian, whose face was disfigured by an enormous growth, got it into his head that the water in the well was blessed; and every day for seven months he went there and bathed his face in it. But the growth didn't go away; and one morning Brian was found drowned in that well.'[10]

Staging *Translations* in Derry thus generated the kind of local, community passion usually associated with the amateur theatre (and, indeed, amateur companies would quickly make the play a staple of the festival circuit). Considered in the context of some of the concerns about the nature of language in *Translations*, this can be seen as part of the production's meaning, rather than simply a strategy to generate press interest and fill seats. 'The play has a great deal of political resonance', Stephen Rea told the *Derry Journal*. 'If we put it on in a place like Dublin's Abbey Theatre, its energy would be contained within the theatre and its clientele. But its energy is bound to spread much more profoundly through a place like Derry.'[11] Performing *Translations* with a largely Ulster cast in a building only a few miles from its Donegal setting allowed the audience to feel the same kind of local pride that the play itself sets against any kind of centralising, standardising authority, be it imperial or national. Like the character of Hugh, the audience's experience of the Derry production drew heavily on what he calls 'the *desiderium nostorum* – the need for our own'.[12]

This feeling was powerfully vindicated on 23 September 1980, when Derry became the cultural centre of Ireland for the night. Joining Cyril Cusack, Friel and local politicians on their way to the Guildhall for the première were two future Nobel Laureates, Seamus Heaney and John Hume, as well as the Abbey's Artistic Director, Joe Dowling, Colm O'Briain and Michael Longley from the two Arts Councils, Tom Murphy, Seamus Deane, and reporters from all of the major Irish and British newspapers, including Eamonn McCann, who had been behind the protest over *A State of Chassis* in 1970. Also in the audience was the Catholic Bishop of Derry, Most Rev. Dr Edward Daly, a founder of the '71 Players. 'I have always emphasized the importance of culture as an antidote to violence', Bishop Daly told a reporter. '*Translations* could not have come at a better time.'[13]

When this audience first took their seats, there was initially little to suggest that they were about to watch what Friel would later describe as 'a three-act naturalistic play'.[14] Consolata Boyle's design was not a conventional naturalistic box set, in that it lacked side flats, and the stage was a seven-sided thrust with 1:16 rake, lacking the proscenium arch usually associated with naturalism. Along the back of the stage, she built a simple wall of unfinished, vertical wooden boards, angled along the top so as to create a false perspective. In this wall were two unframed doors, one stage right, and one opening to a small platform, just left of centre at the set's highest point (rising to about 12 feet (3.6 metres)) reached by six stairs. There was almost no stage furniture, apart from a table down left, and a few very low scattered stools, so that the set's most prominent feature was the large, open playing space, projecting out towards the audience – ideal for an actor like McAnally.

'The play has to do with language', Friel wrote in his diary as he was working on *Translations*, 'and only with language.'[15] Just as casting decisions pushed the two characters most intimately associated with language – Owen and Hugh – to the fore, so too did the thrust stage emphasise the play's linguistic focus (even if the Guildhall's high ceilings were an acoustic nightmare). In order to emphasise this point, the love scene between Yolland and Maire was the only scene in the play to be played completely downstage, creating a moment in which the two characters are alone, surrounded by a void of darkness. As they reach out to each other from their linguistically separate worlds, the play's most important theatrical device – that characters speaking English are accepted by the audience as speaking Irish – is at its most self-exposed. In a sense, this was the point towards which the entire production moved. Everything afterwards was, in a sense, an extended coda, and was played as such – so much so that some reviewers criticised Art O Briain's direction for allowing too much of a falling off in the final act.

In his diary, however, Friel also wrote 'it is a political play – how can that be avoided?'[16] Towering above Consolata Boyle's set on that opening night was the Guildhall's mighty pipe organ (which was left unmasked) framed by neo-Gothic oak panels and coats of arms. More than any other building in Derry, the Guildhall was a symbol of unionist power. Indeed, in his play set in the aftermath of a Civil Rights march seven years earlier, *The Freedom of the City*, Friel had used the building in precisely this way, an irony not lost on anyone who attended the opening night of *Translations*. '*Translations* deals powerfully with a number of themes of particular interest to Republicans', wrote the Sinn Féin weekly, *An Phoblacht*: 'language and identity, the meaning of education and its relation to political reality, colonial conquest through cultural imperialism'.[17] At the same time, it was possible for the unionist Lord Mayor of Derry to lead a standing ovation on the opening night.

The Derry production of *Translations* was clearly designed to provoke debate, and in this it succeeded. While the show was still on its Irish tour, and on the eve of the IRA Hunger Strikes, Seamus Heaney set the agenda for much that would follow when he wrote in *The Times Literary Supplement* in October 1980 that the play forced us to examine 'the need we have to create enabling myths of ourselves and the danger we run if we too credulously trust to the sufficiency of these myths'.[18] A few years later, in a public debate held in January 1983, the historian J. H. Andrews, whose study of the Ordnance Survey, *A Paper Landscape*, suggested the mapping metaphor in *Translations*, took Friel gently to task for what the playwright admitted were 'tiny bruises inflicted on history in the play'. The debate's moderator, Kevin Barry, developed this exchange into a wider discussion on *Translations* as a 'collision between fiction and history that re-interprets the past in such a way as to project an imagined and persuasive future'.[19]

The philosopher Richard Kearney developed these ideas a few months later, taking as his starting point the quotation from Heidegger that had prefaced the programmes for *Translations* sold during the performance: 'Man behaves as if he were the master of language, whereas in fact it is language which remains his mistress. When this relationship of dominance is inverted, man has recourse to strange contrivances.' Kearney argued that in *Translations*, Friel moved beyond an understanding of language as a system of naming (or of history as a record of the past) to a search for 'a new vocabulary, a new mode of communication which will acknowledge and perhaps ultimately mediate between the sundered cultural identities of this island'. The possibility of finding a language that would both acknowledge and move beyond Ireland's cultural divisions came to be associated with the concept of an imaginary 'Fifth Province' (Ireland was historically divided into four Provinces) 'to which cultural and artistic loyalty can be offered'.[20]

By the time the idea of a 'Fifth Province' was being floated, Field Day had an impressive Board of Directors, which in addition to Friel and Rea included Seamus Heaney, Seamus Deane, Tom Paulin and the musician David Hammond. And yet, as Heaney later acknowledged, the project which Field Day would become had arisen out of the excitement felt during that first production of *Translations*. The play, Heaney claimed, generated 'a feeling that dramatic form had allowed inchoate recognitions, both cultural and historical, to be clarified and comprehended'.[21] 'For people like ourselves, living close to such a fluid situation', Friel told an interviewer shortly after the opening night, 'definitions of identity have to be developed and analysed much more frequently. We've got to keep questioning until we find some kind of portmanteau term or until we find some kind of generosity that can embrace the whole island.'[22] Of course, there is no better, nor more fluid, place to develop and to analyse identity than the theatre, where actors transform themselves every night. Standing on the stage of the Guildhall to acknowledge the audience's applause on that September night in 1980, Friel may well have glimpsed his Fifth Province, a mirage both as transient and as important as an audience assembled in a specific place, at a specific time, to watch a play.

CHAPTER 8

Babel, 1972–2000

On 22 January 1972, Taoiseach Jack Lynch signed the Treaty of Accession which brought Ireland into the European Economic Community. It should have been 'the fulfilment of Ireland's historical and economic destiny', as he told the *Irish Times*. And yet, the Ireland that was taking its place among the nations of Europe was ailing economically and mired in escalating political violence. On the week that Lynch signed the Treaty, there were more than 122,000 people unemployed on the island; eight days later, British Army Paratroopers opened fire on civil rights demonstrators in Derry, killing thirteen of them. 'The events of Bloody Sunday ripped Ireland apart', playwright Frank McGuinness later recalled. 'My adolescence ended that day.' John Hume spoke for many when he told a reporter that the shootings had 'left this city numb with shock, horror, revulsion and bitterness'.[1] In Derry that evening, soldiers still patrolled the Rossville Flats area where the shooting had taken place; in Dublin, audiences were watching Boucicault's *Arrah-na-Pogue* at the Abbey and Anouilh's *Time Remembered* at the Gate, while in Belfast, they were watching *John Bull's Other Island* at the Lyric.

By 1972, the Irish theatre was strangely out of date. The 1960s had brought more sweeping changes than the previous three decades combined: there were new theatres, taboos had been broken, and a new generation of writers, directors and actors no longer saw their rightful place within the three walls of a farmhouse kitchen. Part of the problem was the velocity of change in the theatre elsewhere. When Jerzy Grotowski's *Akropolis* played the Edinburgh Festival in 1968, for instance, the Abbey's production of *King of the Castle* no longer looked daring. At the same time, a rapidly mutating Irish society was leaving its interpreters behind, and there is a strong sense in the early 1970s of a culture scrambling to chart the trajectory of its own tailspin. Writing in *The Times Literary Supplement* less than two months after Bloody Sunday, Brian Friel dismissed the relevance to the Irish situation of 'Artaud, Peter Brook,

Roger Planchon, Brecht, theatre of the absurd, happenings, theatre of fact, etc.' 'Matter', he wrote, 'is our concern, not form.' Friel went on to argue: 'It requires no great gift of prophecy to foresee that the revolt in Northern Ireland is going to spread to the Republic; and if you believe that art is an instrument of the revolutionary process, then you can look forward to a spate of committed plays.'[2]

As a prophecy of the direction Irish theatre would take in the 1970s, this was accurate, but only partly so, even in relation to Friel's own work. If one were to concentrate on the work of the Project Arts Centre in Dublin, for instance, or John Arden and Margaretta D'Arcy's twenty-six-hour long *Non-Stop Connolly Show* (1975) or on Friel's own *Freedom of the City*, it would be possible to argue that the Irish theatre in the 1970s was radically politicised. However, a look at the repertoire of the major theatres shows them working with more or less the same canon pioneered in Ireland by the Gate and the Abbey in the 1930s: Chekhov, late Ibsen, Wilde, O'Neill, Synge, O'Casey, and, of course, Shaw. Watching a revival of Shaw's *Heartbreak House* at the Gate in 1971, one of the original Gate actresses, Betty Chancellor, is reported to have remarked that it was 'exactly the same Gate show' as the one in which she had acted in 1933.[3] In addition, there were dutiful productions of Yeats and a surprisingly eclectic selection of Beckett (given the stamp of respectability by his 1969 Nobel Prize) but theatre history prior to 1900 had been stripped down to Shakespeare, Goldsmith, R.B. Sheridan, with the irrepressible Boucicault making a comeback after a couple of decades' well-earned rest. And, of course, ballasting the whole edifice were the Christmas pantomimes, which continued to fill the big nineteenth-century theatres every year as they had for over a century.

If the Irish theatre found itself out of step, the causes were to a large extent institutional. In 1973, a new Arts Act went into effect in the Republic, making long-overdue changes in the Arts Council, which had been formed in 1951. And yet, there were still only three subsidised theatres on the island: the Abbey (including the Peacock), which received £150,000 per annum; the Gate, which received £58,000, and the Lyric, which received £40,000 per year from the Northern Ireland Arts Council. While this represented a higher *per capita* spending on theatre than was the case in England, state funding did not come close to meeting the running costs of even these subsidised theatres, and so they were compelled to keep a steady eye on the box office. Otherwise, the Arts Council in the Republic was spending only a little over £10,000 annually on theatre, leaving no funding whatsoever for young, alternative companies.

At the same time, the subsidised theatres had good reason to be wary of the hand that fed them in the early 1970s. In October 1971, the Fianna Fáil Minister for Posts and Telegraphs, Gerard Collins, responded to the escalating cycle of violence in Northern Ireland by forbidding RTÉ (the state broadcasting system) from transmitting anything that promoted the aims of organisations advocating violence. When the IRA Chief of Staff was interviewed on radio the following year, Collins promptly sacked the entire broadcasting authority. While the Broadcasting Act did not extend to the theatre, no one was under any illusions as to what would happen if the subsidised theatres were to flaunt their exemption too openly, adding to the institutionalised inertia.

The situation of the Lyric Theatre in Belfast was particularly precarious. From the beginning, its founder Mary O'Malley had conscientiously steered the Lyric down a narrow, rocky path of liberal, non-partisan engagement. This meant that while the Lyric never avoided controversial plays, it also stumbled endlessly into apparently innocuous questions that exploded like hidden landmines. Do you sing 'God Save the Queen' before performances? Do you close for the National Day of Mourning called for the victims of Bloody Sunday? How do you respond when, as happened in 1974, you arrive at the opening night of *Jesus Christ Superstar* to find the theatre surrounded by members of Ian Paisley's Free Presbyterian Church, praying for God's judgement on a 'diabolically inspired and iniquitously blasphemous production'?[4] At every step of the way, the Lyric risked alienating audiences, government funding bodies, and private sponsors from all sides of the community.

All of these incidents, however, paled beside the events of the afternoon of 4 September 1973. A small group of actors was rehearsing a new play in the Lyric, while Patrick Galvin's *Nightfall to Belfast* was due to continue its run in the evening. Galvin's play dealt directly with the conflict, and includes characters who address the audience directly with testimonies of brutality. 'The door was smashed in', begins one statement. 'A soldier pushed me out of bed and I landed, face down on the floor. I was kept there for half an hour. I was naked. A soldier kept his foot on my back.'[5] As the rehearsal was taking place, a car drove across the city from Protestant East Belfast, and was abandoned outside the theatre. A British Army patrol, pulling up behind it, found that the car contained a 300 pound bomb, which, had it not been defused, would have blown the front off the building. *Nightfall to Belfast* continued its run, and the theatre gingerly picked its way along a hazard-strewn path, even refusing to close the following year when the Ulster Workers' Strike cut off electricity supplies and barricaded roads. For a few days in May 1974, the actors presented Yeats' *Purgatory* by storm lantern in an auditorium warmed by portable gas heaters, closing only after a performance during which the cast and crew outnumbered the audience.

Between trying to remain financially afloat, uncensored and alive, the subsidised theatres were in one sense ill-equipped to respond to what was happening around them. At the same time – the fiasco of the Abbey's *A State of Chassis* notwithstanding – the Irish theatre could draw on a long tradition of plays dealing with political violence. One result was that Sean O'Casey became the most frequently produced playwright in the Irish professional theatre during the 1970s, with the Abbey and the Lyric staging eighteen of his plays in the decade. Moreover, the example of his Dublin trilogy was at that point inextricably intertwined with a distinctive Ulster Protestant tradition of the 'Troubles play'.[6] Although this line predates O'Casey, beginning with St John Ervine's *Mixed Marriage* in 1911, it had absorbed O'Casey, developing through plays such as John Coulter's *The Drums Are Out* (1948) and Sam Thompson's *Over the Bridge* (1960). Hence, when the British Army rolled on to the streets of Northern Ireland in 1969, there was a dramatic model for writing about the situation waiting to be used. And this is precisely what happened in the first Northern play to deal with the post-1969 violence, John Boyd's *The Flats*, staged at the Lyric in March 1971.

'I was walking along the streets near the centre of the city one afternoon', Boyd later recalled, 'when I stopped, and stood for a long time studying Unity Flats', the Catholic enclave in which his play is set. 'I began to wonder about the lives of the people inside. And that was the germ: one family, one day, one death.'[7] If we allow 'family' to include surrogate families (like the tightly knit groups of workers who populate the pubs and workplaces of the Belfast tradition of industrial plays going back to Thomas Carnduff in the 1930s); and if we allow some latitude in the neo-classical unity of 'one day', then we can take Boyd's formula as defining the Irish Troubles play: 'one family, one day, one death'.

This formula is more than simply a recipe for a plot; in performance it divides the stage space. The world of the family is the world we see onstage; it is almost always an interior, often a family kitchen (as in *The Flats*). This onstage world is a place of debate, open to at least one character from an opposing tradition. *The Flats*, for instance, is set in a Catholic working-class home in Belfast; however, there is a Protestant neighbour, Monica, who is very much part of the extended family. In some Troubles plays, like Ervine's *Mixed Marriage*, the relationship with the outsider is romantic, in what Christopher Murray has called 'the *Romeo and Juliet* typos' (the Shakespearean original of which both the Gate and the Lyric staged, in 1971 and 1972, respectively). While television dramas about the Northern situation were particularly fond of this plot, it was also used on stage, in John Wilson Haire's *Bloom of the Diamond Stone*, for instance, staged at the Abbey on 9 October 1973, and it persisted into the 1980s in Graham Reid's *Remembrance* (1984) and Christina Reid's *Did You Hear the One About the Irishman . . . ?* (1985).

The cross-community relationships in these plays create the impression that divisions in the world outside are being bridged on the stage, whereas, in fact, the real conflict in the Troubles play is between the onstage world of the family, and the unseen offstage world, a realm of mindless violence where death can come from an anonymous mob or a hidden sniper. 'There was a near riot outside our window last night', says a character in *The Flats*, 'a screamin' mob of wild protestants were out for blood.' The Troubles play moves towards the inevitable collision of the onstage and offstage worlds, as a vulnerable family member (usually female and often the outsider) rushes into the wings in the final moments to be killed, her body carried back on to the stage for the final fade to black. 'She's dead . . . Monica's dead . . . Who done it? Who shot 'er?'[8]

The pleasures of the classic Troubles play are those of Aristotelian tragedy, where the visible world of the stage provides the frame for an offstage presence of some force too vast or amorphous to be seen. However, when that offstage world swells into a timeless, unappeasable horde of sectarian Bacchants, the effect is not unlike that of the broadcasting bans: it makes political violence appear mindless and unmotivated because it is unrepresentable. Consequently, as Seamus Deane argued in a 1973 article, 'The medium through which politics is viewed is the one in which politics does not operate, the apolitical family unit. Thus, the complexities of the political situation are, of their nature, inaccessible to the play.'[9] This in turn meant that while the Irish tradition provided playwrights with a model that all too readily accommodated the conflict, the dark logic of terror remained, for the most part, beyond the glare of the stage lights.

In many ways, therefore, the importance of the classic Troubles play is that it provides a set of rules to be broken in the search for a more meaningful response to an increasingly extreme reality. And this is precisely what happened less than two years after the première of *The Flats*, when Brian Friel's *The Freedom of the City* opened at the Abbey on 20 February 1973. In later years, the play would figure prominently in studies of Friel's work, and in 1989 Ulick O'Connor would use it as the centrepiece of his argument that Friel was a true *écrivain engagé*, 'our one major writer who has consistently addressed himself to the root of the problem of contemporary Ireland'. At the time, however, critical response was muted and uncertain, and even though it played to 86 per cent capacity houses for its first twenty-three performances, the Abbey would not restage the play for twenty-six years.[10]

The Freedom of the City begins with three characters from working-class Catholic Derry – Michael, Lily and Skinner – lying 'grotesquely' dead on the stage. Then, in a replay of one of the most famous media images of Bloody Sunday, a priest rushes forward, waving a white handkerchief above his head, while a photographer crouches to photograph the tableaux. Framed by testimony from a police witness and a sociologist, the three characters, whom we saw dead in the opening moments of the play appear on the stage, very much alive, taking refuge from the soldiers in Derry's Guildhall. As we watch the final few hours of these characters' lives, we are offered analyses of the situation by the sociologist, a balladeer, a priest, and a television reporter, all producing their own versions of the deaths of Lily, Michael and Skinner. Even the characters themselves offer their own, competing analyses at the beginning of act II, stepping forward in character to describe, 'calmly and without emotion', their last thoughts 'as everything melted and fused in a great roaring heat'.

In spite of its mixed reception at the time, *The Freedom of the City* is something of a template for more than one strand of Irish theatre in the 1970s. Although the generic Troubles play would be written with slight twists for two decades, from Graham Reid's *Dorothy* (1981) to Christina Reid's *Joyriders* in 1986 and Gary Mitchell's *In a Little World of Our Own* in 1997, Friel's play explodes its form in 1973 by collapsing the basic onstage / offstage opposition on which it is based. The Mayor's parlour in which the makeshift family unit of Lily, Michael and Skinner live out their last hours is a parodic version of the conventional besieged family home. Indeed, Lily comments that if it were hers, she would cover up the oak panels 'with a nice pink gloss that you could wash the dirt off', and 'put a nice flight of them brass ducks up along that wall'. However, unlike characters in most Troubles plays, who endlessly debate their situation, the three characters in *Freedom of the City* fail to understand up until the moment of their death what the audience already knows, and what the voices of authority understand with clear, merciless logic: 'that a price would be exacted . . . and the poor are always overcharged'.[11] In short, even though it is chronologically one of the earliest Troubles plays to deal with the post-1969 conflict, *The Freedom of the City* is also the genre's end, its fullest working out and its critique.

The critical response to *Freedom of the City* was slow in developing momentum largely because the type of formally experimental committed theatre it represented had a difficult time finding a place in the subsidised theatres, and in the absence of subsidies for new theatre companies, there was little scope for the emergence of new alternative theatre companies. Among the few places to provide scope for an alternative was the Project Arts Centre, which could be hired for a percentage of the box-office takings. Founded as an artists' cooperative in 1967, the Project was based in a leaking warehouse in Dublin's Temple Bar, which at the time was 'an area of shabby decay . . . full of relics of once-flourishing little businesses'.[12] Here two brothers – Jim and Peter Sheridan – staged plays like Jim Sheridan's *Mobile Homes* (1976) dealing with low-income families on a mobile-home site, and Peter Sheridan's *The Liberty Suit* (1977), set in a juvenile prison. 'The question for the "alternative" is how far it can accept the complexities of reality', wrote Peter Sheridan in 1978, 'merge this with its dramatic method, and infer, without recourse to polemics, a political way forward.'[13]

For many directors and writers, finding a way forward in terms of stagecraft was impeded by a lack of basic skills. As the Lyric's founder, Mary O'Malley, lamented in 1973, there were still no formal training facilities on the island for actors, directors, designers or technicians. At the Abbey there were sporadic attempts to set up a theatre school, and from 1967 onwards the tiny Focus theatre in Dublin, headed by Deirdre O'Connell, struggled heroically against an almost complete absence of resources to train some of the leading Irish actors of the late twentieth century in the techniques of Stanislavski. However, most theatre professionals followed an informal apprenticeship, usually with amateur companies. This, combined with the continued dominance of a basically naturalistic tradition, meant that there was no shortage of theatre people capable of staging 'a local dialect play in a realistic setting'. However, argued O'Malley, 'When one moves toward poetic, classical, ritualistic or expressionistic modes, the inadequacy of our present training facilities is immediately exposed. There are relatively few players well trained in speech and movement, and casting problems restrict play selection.'[14]

This is not to say that there was not room to work within conventional dramatic forms. For instance, Hugh Leonard's three major plays of the 1970s – *Da* (1973), *Time Was* (1976) and *A Life* (1979) – emerge not only as hugely entertaining pieces of theatre (the New York production of *Da* in 1978 was to win a Tony Award for best play) but also as important social commentaries on a society that, in spite of a slowing of the economic growth of the 1960s, was continuing to become more dominated by the values of an urban middle class. 'They're so common', says one character of her neighbours in *Time Was*: 'Nouveau riche, do you mean?' 'No, no . . . Nouveau middle-class.' In these suburban settings, Leonard charts a culture that is tearing away from its past, alternately seduced and fearful of the pleasures of nostalgia.

Leonard finds an image of this situation in a simple theatrical device, the presence on stage of characters belonging to the play's fictional past. In *Da*, for instance, Leonard's quasi-autobiographical Charlie carries on a series of conversations with his dead father, who for the audience is a live presence. In *A Life*, events separated by forty years cut across each other on the same stage; while rounding out a sort of trilogy, *Time Was* is about an evening's suburban socialising, which goes badly wrong when figures from the past (including characters from old movies) begin showing up unexpectedly. Comic as these situations may be, there is a telling comment in the surreal premise of *Time Was*: 'So many people are longing for the simplicity of bygone days that Time has been ruptured. . . . people who can't cope with the present, who want no part of it, are disappearing back into the past.'

The confidence with which Leonard was able to write about people like those in *Time Was* who 'always get up early on Sundays' so as to 'be sure to miss Mass from principle and not laziness'[15] suggests that if the Irish theatre's inherited forms and audience caused it to stumble when confronting the causes of political violence, it provided a prescient view of cracks that were just beginning to appear in the edifice of the Catholic ethos which had dominated so much of the island for so long. Irish Mass attendance rates in the mid-1970s were much as they had been for a century, and in many ways the edifice of the Church was as sturdy as ever; in retrospect, however, it would become obvious that the radical decline in the Church's power in the 1990s was already underway in the mid-1970s. And it was at that point that three plays appeared – like a trilogy by different hands – which were to prefigure what lay ahead: Tom Murphy's *The Sanctuary Lamp* (1976), Thomas Kilroy's *Talbot's Box* (1977) and Brian Friel's *Faith Healer* (1979). All three attempt to reconfigure Christian (and, more specifically, Catholic) faith outside of the limits of institutionalised religion; and all three do so by creating theatrical forms whose breaks with stage realism signal a wider change in society as whole.

The Sanctuary Lamp grew out of a period when Murphy, although protesting that he was 'not a Catholic and that he would not wish his Catholic background on anyone',[16] worked as one of two lay members of the International Commission on the Use of English in the Liturgy, charged with creating the English version of the Latin liturgy to be used by millions of Catholics around the world. Set in an empty church, shot through with shafts of darkness in Bronwen Casson's 1976 design, 'you have the three people knocking at the door', Murphy explained, 'and this feeling of being lost, adrift, cut off from something – call it God or Nature, whatever'. As realistic as this setting may seem, Murphy was moving towards a style which would blend the dreamlike, densely symbolic world of *The Morning After Optimism* with the brutal realism of *A Whistle in the Dark*; hence, when asked about the play, he explained: 'They are locked inside this metaphorical monster that is a church and what does the church stand for? Stability, civilisation.'[17]

Thomas Kilroy was equally unwilling to concede that *Talbot's Box* was purely a play about belief. *Talbot's Box* was the first play to realise the potential of a writer who had been an astute commentator on Irish theatre since the late 1950s. On the surface, it appeared to be concerned primarily with questions of faith. Its main character, Matt Talbot, was a real historical figure, a Dublin working man who, when he died in 1925, was found to have lived a life of extreme self-imposed religious penance, binding his body with chains and scapulars, undergoing lengthy fasts, and attending three Masses every morning before going to work. And yet, Kilroy would later claim that his play was about 'the essentially irreducible division between such extreme individualism and the claim of relationship, of community, society'.

In the original production at the Peacock on 13 October 1977, director Patrick Mason and designer Wendy Shea found a visual metaphor for this gulf between 'extreme individualism' and 'community' in the box of the play's title, a huge structure out of which all the materials for the play emerge after the curtain rises. Within the box are five actors, four of whom take on a variety of roles, usually overplayed with an edge of self-caricature; and a fifth, John Molloy, who played Matt Talbot with seamless realism. By juxtaposing these two theatrical styles, Kilroy stages both Talbot's strength and his inaccessibility. The other characters can transform themselves whenever they pick up a new prop, making them free, but depthless; by contrast, the realistically acted Talbot can never be other than what he is, and in this lie both his limitations and his strength, a paradox given force in performance by the continual presence of his almost naked body, bound with ropes and chains. In the play's final moments, the box closes on him, leaving the four actors 'looking in through the cracks in the walls from which bright light comes which illuminates their faces'.[18]

The Sanctuary Lamp and *Talbot's Box* could easily be read as the theatrical products of a modernising urban society pulling away from a more traditional rural hinterland. At the same time, the Tuam Theatre Guild staged both plays in Murphy's hometown shortly after their Dublin premières, receiving warm receptions in the very heart of the West of Ireland that was supposed to be the bastion of traditional values. Moreover, it would be a mistake to see a country in which there would be very few professed atheists or agnostics even in the final years of the twentieth century as simply marching down the straight road to secularism. Instead, these are the plays of a society in which structures of belief – and not exclusively religious structures – are fragmenting as the sanction of a central authority collapses. In its absence, truth disperses into contradictory and irresolvable versions, which exist side by side with each other. 'The questionings, the questionings', muses Frank, the faith healer in Brian Friel's play of that name. '*Am I endowed with a unique and awesome gift?* – my God, yes, I'm afraid so. And I suppose the other extreme was *Am I a con man?* – which of course was nonsense, I think.'[19]

Frank asks these questions on an almost bare stage during the first of four monologues which make up *Faith Healer*; in the second and third monologues, Grace, his partner, and Teddy, his manager, tell their versions of Frank's story, before Frank returns again in the final section. Apart from a few fleeting moments of corroboration, the stories all contradict each other. Moreover, no two characters ever share the stage, so there is no external viewpoint from which the audience might say: 'I saw that, it's true.' As in *Philadelphia, Here I Come!*, where Gar and his father share differing memories of Gar's childhood, or as in *The Freedom of the City* where competing versions of the shootings emerge, *Faith Healer* opens up a gap between the past and its remembrance. In *Faith Healer*, however, the form is purified, becoming a metaphor for theatre itself, where truth exists only in the present moment. As such, the play takes a further step in the investigation of the fate of truth in a land where the markers of communal memory have dwindled to a few random place names or anecdotes.

While these plays speak of a culture beginning to disperse in a Babel of voices, the channelling of all government subsidies for the theatre into the Abbey, Gate and Lyric perpetuated a centralised theatre culture

Photograph 6(a) 'Rawness and attack' were the words Fintan O'Toole used to describe Druid Theatre Company's 1982 production of Synge's *Playboy of the Western World* (with Maeliosa Stafford, Mick Lally and Marie Mullen).

Photograph 6(b) The demure Maire O'Neill as Pegeen Mike, in a publicity still from the Abbey's original production of the same play in 1907 – in sharp contrast to the 1982 production.

that owed more to the eighteenth than to the late twentieth century. Meanwhile, hundreds of well-established amateur companies and festivals continued to thrive around the country, their repertoire often more adventurous than their professional counterparts, with Peter Weiss's *Marat/Sade* winning the All-Ireland Finals in 1972. The Arts Council in Dublin made a partial move towards decentralisation in 1974 when it established the Irish Theatre Company, a state-funded touring group. And yet, in spite of the quality of the ITC's work, by 1981 it was acknowledged that hauling light and sound rigs around the country could no longer be justified by the argument that smaller Irish towns and cities lacked the expertise and the audiences to support their own theatres. There were, quite simply, too many small groups spread throughout the island who wanted only the tiniest subsidies to turn professional. When that support came, it would bring about a seismic shift that would utterly transform the geography of the Irish theatre.

One of the first rumblings of this change was heard in Galway in 1975, when director Garry Hynes and actress Marie Mullen joined with Mick Lally, a part-time actor with An Taibhdhearc, to form a company to produce Synge's *Playboy of the Western World* for the summer tourist season. Calling their company Druid (after a character in the *Asterix the Gaul* comics) they knew that there was no money available from the Arts Council, so they turned to the Irish tourist board, Bord Fáilte, who gave them £350. By 1979, they would have their own theatre, a 102-seater with a three-quarter arena stage in Galway's Chapel Lane (later renamed Druid Lane). Within a few years they were on the road. In 1982 they played Synge's *Playboy of the Western World* to more than 22,000 people, playing to one hundred per cent capacity houses in theatres ranging from the 1,500-seat Olympia Theatre in Dublin to the 150-seat hall on the Aran Island of Inis Meáin, becoming the first company to perform Synge's work on the island. By the end of the 1980s, Druid would be joined in Galway by Macnas, who specialised in large-scale outdoor spectacles, and there would be strong regional companies, almost all of which toured, in Waterford (Red Kettle), Cork (Meridian and Graffiti), Limerick (Island), Clonmel (Gallowglass), Derry (Field Day) and Ennis (Theatre Omnibus); by the end of the 1990s, there would be further subsidised companies in Kilkenny (Barnstorm and Bickerstaffe), Portstewart (Big Telly), Sligo (Blue Raincoat), Cork (Corcadorca), Drogheda (Upstate), and a further sixteen non-subsidised professional companies outside of Dublin and Belfast.

Before Garry Hynes and Marie Mullen invited Mick Lally to join them, they had been members of the Drama Society of University College Galway, where they were both students. Although there had been university drama societies since the turn of the century, often more willing and able to take risks than their professional counterparts, their members seldom turned professional. In the days when the universities were still the preserve of a small, elite minority destined for the professions, theatre was simply another trapping of student life, like rugby or rowing, to be discarded on graduation day. By the mid-1970s, however, the numbers in third-level education had burgeoned, and a new generation of university graduates was emerging into an economy in deep recession. For someone talented, educated and facing an uncertain job market, a career in the theatre seemed as good a prospect as anything else on offer. Consequently, entire companies like Druid, and later Rough Magic (formed in 1984 by former student actors, mostly from Trinity) began to make the transition from student to professional.

For these companies, nurtured in the experimentation of student theatre, a wide knowledge of contemporary European and American theatre was not a new discovery; it was a baseline. Garry Hynes, for instance, first attracted attention as a student director when she brought *Elizabeth One*, a play written for La Mama Experimental Theatre Club, to the All-Ireland Finals in Athlone. Druid's subsequent reputation would be for producing plays by Irish writers, but in its early years they were just as likely to be performing Dario Fo, Sam Shepard, or Edward Albee. Similarly, Rough Magic was initially formed to produce the work of contemporary British and American playwrights, staging plays by David Mamet and Caryl Churchill, before it too began to focus on Irish plays, not least those of its co-founder, Declan Hughes. During the same period, the phrase 'new Irish theatre' increasingly meant writers like Frank McGuinness, Thomas Kilroy or Stewart Parker, directed by Hynes, Joe Dowling, Ben Barnes or Patrick Mason – all of whom had university backgrounds. A degree in history or literature does not necessarily make a great director or writer; it does, however, generate a different sense of tradition than that which comes from an apprenticeship in repertory theatre. The universities in turn responded to this new situation, with Trinity establishing a School of Drama and Theatre Studies in 1984, followed within a decade by other third-level institutions. The foundation in 1986 of an actor training institute, The Gaiety School of Acting, further professionalised the Irish theatre.

One mark of the change that was taking place in the Irish theatre from the early 1980s onwards was the ability to absorb plays from other traditions. Brian Friel, for instance, would produce four versions of Russian plays: *Three Sisters* (1981), *Fathers and Sons* (1987), *A Month in the Country* (1992) and *Uncle Vanya* (1998). Similarly, Thomas Kilroy would put *The Seagull* (1981) in an Irish setting, while his 1989 version of Ibsen's *Ghosts* moves the setting forward to the late eighties. Frank McGuinness would write translations of Ibsen's *Rosmersholm* (1987), *Peer Gynt* (1988), *Hedda Gabler* (1994), and *A Doll's House* (1994), as well as Chekhov's *Three Sisters* (1990) and *Uncle Vanya* (1995), Lorca's *Yerma* (1987), Brecht's *Threepenny Opera* (1991) and *Caucasian Chalk Circle* (1997), and Ramón Maria del Valle-Inclán's *Barbaric Comedies* (2000). His version of Sophocles' *Electra* (1997) would join a long list of Irish versions of classical Greek theatre, including no fewer than three *Antigone*s produced in 1984, and Seamus Heaney's influential version of *Philoctetes*, produced by Field Day as *The Cure at Troy* in 1990.

'I'm not sure why I find late nineteenth-century Russians so sympathetic', Friel would write. 'Maybe because the characters in the plays behave as if their old certainties were as sustaining as ever – even though they know in their hearts that their society is in melt-down and the future has neither a welcome nor even an accommodation for them.'[20] This sense that 'old certainties' were dissolving began to take a definite shape in the larger Irish cultural sphere in the early 1980s. Like its predecessors, the new Irish cultural debate's starting point was the economic and political failure of Ireland, North and South. In earlier decades, almost all such arguments reverted to one of two positions: either tradition (whether it be Republican, Unionist, socialist, Catholic or Protestant) had been betrayed, or else it had been so slavishly served that Ireland had reneged on its share of modernity. 'The more intractable the problem seems', wrote Seamus Deane in 1982, 'the more we consign it to the realm of the irrational, the purblind, the atavistic. In its place, we find many longing for a truly *modern* state, pluralistic, peaceful, democratic, free of the Original Sin of the past.'[21]

Deane was part of a group of critics who began to suggest that the problem was neither tradition nor modernity *per se*, but rather the inability to see these two terms as other than locked in mortal combat. Was it possible, people began to ask, that what passes for tradition might be an aspect of modernity – or that some as yet unknown formation might supplant them both? Soon, this deconstructive style of thinking was extending to the other seemingly inescapable oppositions: Catholic/

Protestant, Republican/Unionist, Irish/English, rural/urban. At the forefront of this debate was a new journal, *The Crane Bag* (1977–85) and the series of pamphlets launched by Field Day in September 1983. Critics including Deane, Declan Kiberd, Luke Gibbons and Terence Brown, poets Seamus Heaney and Tom Paulin, and philosopher Richard Kearney joined historians like Roy Foster in a series of re-interpretations of Irish history and contemporary society, from which new constellations of thought began to emerge.

From the Field Day camp, the concept of an imaginary 'Fifth Province' entered the Irish vocabulary, an imaginary place somewhere beyond (and yet inextricably part of) the historical four provinces of Ireland. Placing the Irish theatre of the early twentieth century in this new formation, Declan Kiberd wrote in his 1984 Field Day pamphlet, *Anglo-Irish Attitudes*: 'In all the plays discussed, opposites turn out to be doubles; clichés employed at the start by one side are appropriated by the other.'[22] Indeed, the involvement of Field Day in the theoretical end of the debate ensured that the theatre was never far from its centre, and in 1986 Thomas Kilroy gave it a theatrical form. His Field Day play *Double Cross* featured Stephen Rea as both William Joyce, an Irishman who made propaganda broadcasts from Nazi Germany during the Second World War, and Brendan Bracken, an Irishman who was Churchill's Minister of Information from 1941 to 1945. 'I was drawn to the stories of these two men', Kilroy wrote, 'out of an interest in doubleness or doubling, that is, in the way things repeat themselves in life or attract their opposites.'[23] With Rea as Joyce acting opposite video footage of himself as Bracken (and *vice versa*), *Double Cross* creates a stage world in which the old oppositions that had structured Irish cultural debate for so long collapse into a hall of mirrors

The launch of the journal *Theatre Ireland* (1982–93) in the midst of this ferment made sure that Field Day did not have the running to itself, as did the appearance in its first issue of a young reviewer named Fintan O'Toole, who would become the most influential Irish theatre critic of his generation. In this new atmosphere, with the past no longer pinned securely in place and now offering 'a creative freedom not possible in the drab givenness of the present',[24] earlier plays which had either disappeared, or had faded into the haze of their own reputations, suddenly re-emerged with stark clarity. Druid's productions of M. J. Molloy's *Wood of the Whispering* (1983), Tom Murphy's *Famine* (1984) and Synge's *Playboy of the Western World* (staged in three different versions, in 1975, 1977 and 1982) were received almost as if they were new plays.

'Pegeen starts scraping the left-overs into a bin', wrote David Nowlan of the play. 'Christy, after a few minutes acquaintance, is picking his dirty feet. The Widow Quin has a seedy sexuality which makes her a convincing threat to Pegeen's hatchet-faced, thin-lipped determination . . . Overall, this is the definitive *Playboy*.' 'The kind of harsh, physical and direct style of performance developed in Garry Hynes' work as a director', argued Fintan O'Toole, 'has in itself become a comment on the social realities of modern Ireland.'[25] Similarly, at the Gate theatre, saved from terminal decline after the deaths of Mac Líammóir and Edwards (in 1978 and 1982 respectively) by manager Michael Colgan, director Joe Dowling had a major critical success with his 1986 production of *Juno and the Paycock*. Dowling shifted the play's balance towards the character of Joxer, thereby 'divesting it of every shred of sentimentality, turning the warm glow of Juno's resigned, proud survival to the gnawing chill of poverty in the bones.'[26]

These revisionist readings of older plays were a part of a growing restlessness in Irish theatre culture in the early 1980s. So, when Kazimierz Braun and the Contemporary Theatre of Wrocław visited the Dublin Theatre Festival in 1981 and 1982, they brought a welcome whiff of heresy into a theatre culture where the playwright had reigned supreme for almost a century. For Braun, 'the script was simply an outline for the production'[27] and his productions helped to nurture an audience for a type of theatre not dominated by the spoken word. Playwright Tom Mac Intyre sensed this change in direction, and in the spring of 1983 he began a series of collaborations with director Patrick Mason, actor Tom Hickey, and designer Bronwen Casson. Since the late 1970s, Mac Intyre had been working in the United States and Paris with a company called Calck Hook, a New-York-based collective, made up of musicians, actors, and dancers, including Wendy Shankin, an associate of Meredith Monk. Developing Calck Hook's approach of treating the spoken word as only one theatrical language among many, Mac Intyre, Mason and Hickey began developing a performance based on Patrick Kavanagh's 1942 poem, *The Great Hunger*, which charts the stunted emotional life of a small midlands farmer, Patrick Maguire, a man who is 'not so sure now if his mother was right / When she praised the man who made a field his bride'.[28]

The Great Hunger has little plot as such; instead, it stages a series of scenes linked by a tightly interwoven language of phrases, movement, and objects. The first rehearsal script was produced only after Hickey and Mason had commented on an earlier draft, and it contains suggestions for 'movement images', which were to be repeated in shifting contexts: 'flinging-the-stone – the boredom of that'; 'turn-over-the-weedy-clod – the clay / pursuit of that'.[29] These movements, some of which are simply marked 'explore in rehearsal', were to be developed further in performance by Hickey, a tall, thin actor with a talent for what he once described as 'physical bizarreness'. Later in the process, when designer Bronwen Casson became involved, stage objects introduced another theatrical language, most memorably the wooden monolith with a basilisk stare that dominated the stage, described in the script simply as 'The Mother'.

In many ways, *The Great Hunger* was the inescapable production of the 1980s. Audience response was initially slow after the opening on 9 May 1983, but it built steadily, and the play was restaged for the 1986 Edinburgh Festival, before being taken to New York and Paris. In 1988, it was chosen by the Soviet Ministry of Culture to travel to Moscow to join a production of John B. Keane's *The Field* as part of the Irish trade delegation accompanying Aer Rianta, the Irish company who had been awarded a contract to provide duty free services for Aeroflot. There, in the Moscow Art Theatre, audiences watched Patrick Maguire, a small farmer bound to family, church and the land, 'cut off from the outside world, finding consolation thin as gruel in cigarettes, pints of porter and cards in the pub', as John Barber put it in *The Daily Telegraph*. Muscovites thus saw a play whose subject was the oppressive insularity of Irish rural life; however, its form – breaking gestures and words into free-floating signifiers – was the product of the American and Polish avant-gardes, and its performance marked the establishment of a beach-head for free market capitalism in the Soviet Union.

It was at this point that commentators like Desmond Bell began to ask if Ireland, 'largely untouched by the high tide of European modernism and cultural internationalism, had passed effortlessly into a post-modern malaise'.[30] In some respects, the pieces of 'traditional' Ireland still seemed firmly in place. The decade had begun with Pope John Paul II saying Mass for over a million people in Dublin's Phoenix Park; referenda on abortion (1983) and divorce (1986) had both been defeated, the Evangelical churches of Ulster were as sturdy as ever, and neither Republican nor Unionist paramilitaries showed much recognition of the new post-nationalist Ireland of young Europeans. At the same time, no one could ignore the way in which Ireland had become integrated into the vertiginous swirl of a global media culture in which images of 'tradition' were endlessly relativised and recycled. As the edifice of traditional Ireland shattered almost imperceptibly, the Irish theatre once again found itself at the cutting edge of the new cultural formation. In the early 1970s, the Irish theatre had seemed to lag behind the world around it; by the early 1980s, it had moved beyond an increasingly tired set of conflicts, which it was now able to look back upon with irony, anger, sometimes even compassion and forgiveness.

Tom Murphy's work had been moving in this direction since at least *The Sanctuary Lamp*, and in the early 1980s he wrote two plays which (as much as *The Great Hunger*), defined this new situation: *The Gigli Concert* and *Bailegangaire*. *The Gigli Concert* brought Tom Hickey, Patrick Mason and Bronwen Casson back together in the Abbey in September 1983, only a few months after the première of *The Great Hunger*. Joining them was veteran actor Godfrey Quigley, playing a character called only 'Irish Man', a successful builder haunted by a nameless anger and equally by the desire to sing with the voice of the operatic tenor Beniamino Gigli. Over the course of the play, the Irish Man transfers both his anger and his longing to a quack therapist, JPW King (played by Hickey) who, while attempting to overdose on vodka and sleeping pills in the penultimate scene, suddenly, inexplicably, sings with the voice of Gigli. In an otherwise naturalistic production, this is a stunning moment of magic, a gesture beyond the limited possibilities of the play's world. 'Do not mind the pig-sty, Benimillo', JPW tells the voice of Gigli at the curtain. 'Mankind still has a delicate ear.'[31] For Lynda Henderson, editor of *Theatre Ireland*, this was perhaps the most important theatrical moment of the decade. 'In *The Gigli Concert*,' she wrote, 'Murphy celebrates the triumph of man, any man, everyman, over the circumstances which demean him. For Murphy, none of us is fallen.'[32]

The Gigli Concert is part of a theatre of exorcism that emerged in the 1980s, where the past is conjured up, neither to be mocked nor to open old wounds, but so that it might be accepted and healed. Murphy continued moving in this direction with his next play, *Bailegangaire*, staged by Druid with an elderly Siobhán McKenna playing the lead, Mommo, with such authority that the play has seldom been remounted. From her bed centre stage in a small West of Ireland cottage, the aging, senile Mommo tells the story – with torturous stops, starts and rewinds – of how Bailegangaire (Irish for 'the town without laughter') came by its name. Ultimately, her apparently mythic story of past tragedy winds its way into the present in which she is speaking, and we realise that the characters in her tale are the living beings on the stage before us. Only then, when the story is concluded, does the crying which echoes throughout the play become 'infused with a sound like the laughter of relief'.[33] Opening on

5 December 1985, just three weeks after the signing of the Anglo-Irish Agreement enshrined in law the need for 'genuine reconciliation and dialogue' and 'mutual recognition and acceptance of each other's rights' in the Northern conflict, *Bailegangaire*, like *The Gigli Concert*, reminded audiences that reconciliation, dialogue and acceptance – if they were to be more than banal liberal platitudes – carried their own costs.

'It was hard for me', Frank McGuinness told an interviewer when asked about his 1985 play, *Observe the Sons of Ulster Marching Towards the Somme*, 'coming from a Catholic, Donegal background and all *that* means, to understand that things were being done not solely for reasons of aggression and repression but because they had very powerful historical roots.'[34] An enormous red and white Ulster flag dominated Patrick Mason's production of the play in the Peacock, hanging over characters from the almost exclusively Protestant 36th Ulster Division, 6,000 of whose members had been massacred at the Battle of the Somme in 1916. Later readings of the play would elaborate the playwright's own sense of discovery to the point at which *Observe the Sons* would be hailed as the first theatrical uttering of 'voiceless' Ulster unionist culture – which, of course, is nonsense, given the existence of an Ulster Protestant theatre tradition extending from eighteenth-century productions of *The Battle of Aughrim*, through countless amateur productions in Orange Halls, to more interrogatory works by writers like Stewart Parker and Graham Reid in the late 1970s and 1980s. Instead, *Observe the Sons* is a harsh lesson about accepting difference rather than trying to obliterate it. For the playwright and his original Dublin audience, this involved acceptance of Unionist history and tradition; within the play itself, it required that the main character, Pyper, accept the other characters' naive belief in God and Ulster, while they, in turn, must accept his gay sexuality.

Observe the Sons opens with Pyper, an old man lying on a hospital bed, grappling the ghosts of his dead comrades. 'Why does this persist?' he pleads with them. 'What more have we to tell each other?' 'Plays and ghosts have a lot in common', Stewart Parker commented a few years later. 'The energy which flows from some intense moment of conflict in a particular time and place seems to activate them both.' His 1987 play, *Pentecost*, gives this idea theatrical form. Directed by the ubiquitous Patrick Mason for Field Day in 1987, it returns to the Ulster Workers' Strike of 1974 for what initially looks like a conventional Troubles play, as a Belfast terrace house provides refuge from the anarchy on the streets outside for a mixed group of characters (including the ghost of the house's previous owner). However, as events develop, it becomes clear that the barricades on the streets outside are less of an obstacle to the future than the characters' own pasts, and the play moves towards a moment of ritualistic absolution, in which characters seek forgiveness from each other and the past, from 'our innocent dead. They're not our masters, they're only our creditors, for the life they never knew'.[35]

Frank McGuinness' *Carthaginians* was to have been staged by Field Day as a companion piece to *Pentecost*, and while this did not happen (McGuinness believed that staging two full-length plays would stretch the company too far[36]) the two plays share the same cultural moment. When *Carthaginians* did open in the Peacock the following year, the curtain rose on a Derry cemetery in which a group of characters, including a drag queen named Dido, perpetually mourn the dead of Bloody Sunday, 'waiting for them to rise'. The play acknowledges and rejects the inherited forms of the Troubles play when the characters stage Dido's play *The Burning Balaclava*, parodying a whole tradition that threatened to turn real grief into a melodrama of reconciliation. 'Son, son, where were you when my Sacred Heart was riddled with bullets?' 'I was having a quick pint with the girlfriend, ma.' Having reached an accommodation with its own theatrical past, *Carthaginians* (like *Pentecost*) moves towards a moment of ritualistic stillness, as characters set out the terms on which they can live with the past. 'Forgive the dead.' 'Forgive the dying.' 'Forgive yourself.' . . . 'Bury the dead.' 'Raise the dying.' 'Wash the living' – at which point the stage becomes saturated with beams of golden light, accompanied by faint birdsong.[37] In performance, Dido is the key to *Carthaginians*, his queer sexuality breaking down the old oppositions the play excavates; the same is true of Pyper in *Observe the Sons*, and, more obliquely, of the compassion shared by the three men – one Irish, one English, and one American – who are bonded by their captivity as hostages in Lebanon in McGuinness' most successful play of the 1990s, *Someone Who'll Watch Over Me* (1992).

In September 1994, while Patrick Mason was rehearsing a new production of *Observe the Sons* for the Abbey's main stage, the IRA suddenly, unexpectedly, declared the cease-fire. The main Loyalist paramilitaries, who had always claimed they were simply defending their communities from republican attacks, followed suit a few weeks later. When *Observe the Sons* had first been staged, critics had talked blithely about the need to accept unionist culture; suddenly, with the guns silent, it was time to begin accepting. As a character puts it in Christina Reid's *Clowns* (1996), 'the day them clowns in the IRA declared their cease-fire, they killed off half the Irish jokes'.[38] At around the same time, even more Irish jokes became obsolete when the endemically dysfunctional Irish economy unexpectedly began outperforming many of its European counterparts. Within a few years, job shortages became labour shortages, and a nation of emigrants became a destination for immigrants. This is not to say that there was no more poverty or crime in what became known as 'the Celtic Tiger', nor even that the island was now one big, happy community; it did mean, however, that Ireland's problems increasingly looked like those of other post-industrial Western democracies. As the old grey certainties of Irish culture faded into the past, new questions became visible. 'Gradually', wrote Fintan O'Toole, 'there ceased to be dramatic conflicts between tradition and modernity in Ireland. What we got instead were fragments, isolated pieces of a whole story that no one really knows.'[39]

The Irish theatre world was also becoming more diverse, and this in turn meant that no one theatre needed to feel full responsibility for representing the entire island. The plays Jim and Peter Sheridan had staged at the Project in the late 1970s, for instance, addressing social problems such as juvenile crime or housing shortages, would give way to the work of the Passion Machine Company of the late 1980s, whose vigorous, often comic, plays of urban life would attract a young, predominantly working-class audience who for the most part did not attend the other theatres. The same period saw the emergence of community theatre, which shifted its emphasis from the performance of the finished work before an audience to the production of the work by a community drawing on shared experiences. The first indications of this sort of work would come from groups like the Turf Lodge Fellowship Community Theatre, founded by Martin Lynch in Belfast in 1976. By the early 1980s, community theatre had become part of a wider community arts movement, centred primarily (but not exclusively) in the major urban centres of Dublin and Belfast; by the end of the decade, it would have spread throughout the island.

Paradoxically, the emergence of community theatre marks the dissolution of a wider sense of national community in Ireland. When the Abbey had been founded in the early years of the twentieth century, it was as a theatre to reflect the life of the entire country. The community arts movement challenged the idea that one theatre might represent the whole island, pushing the wider concept of representation to the breaking point by blurring the lines between artist and audience. Those who were represented were now the same people who were doing the representing. As theatre-in-education companies, and youth theatres came into being at around the same time (often in conjunction with community arts projects) there were further tacit acknowledgements of the divisions in what was once imagined as a single national community, and this subdivision of audiences would continue with the emergence in the 1980s of women's companies, gay and lesbian theatre, and theatre for (and by) the disabled, all of which introduced new voices to Irish stages.

Among the most important of these voices was first heard in Belfast on 15 May 1983 (in the same week that *The Great Hunger* opened in Dublin) when five actresses calling themselves Charabanc first presented a co-operatively written play, *Lay Up Your Ends*, dealing with a 1911 strike by women working in Belfast's linen mills. The group had originally come together, because 'in the first five years of my professional life', recalled founding member Eleanor Methven, 'I played nothing but Noras and Cathleens. . . . When Charabanc started, it was from a very pragmatic base. We didn't think of it in feminist terms – it was an unconscious feminism, if you like.'[40] By the time their tour ended on 22 October 1983, they would have played to more than 13,000 people.

On 9 November 1983, the first Charabanc tour had just ended, *The Gigli Concert* was still playing in the Abbey, and the Lyric premièred *Tea in a China Cup* by Christina Reid. Reid's play refocuses the basic form of the Troubles play by concentrating on the lives of a Protestant mother and daughter, Sarah and Beth. Usually in a Troubles play, the obligatory offstage riot claims its sacrificial female victim; in *Tea in a China Cup*, however, Sarah refuses to give up her home, insisting that its seemingly inconsequential details – tea cups, framed photos, curtains – are 'her life'. For Reid, political violence is just one aspect of a hostile world, so that, in Sarah's case, 'the Troubles couldn't shift her, but undetected cancer did within a year'.[41] Charabanc would disband in 1995, having produced eighteen new plays, but at that point there would be a whole new generation of women working in the Irish theatre, including former Charabanc member Maire Jones, who would take inspiration from work done in the early 1980s. Critics might still ask: 'where are our major Irish women playwrights'[42] – but there would be more and more answers.

Plays of the 1980s in which the past is a living presence, such as *Tea in a China Cup* (or *Observe the Sons* or *Pentecost*), signal one of the major concerns of Irish theatre in the 1990s. Indeed, there is a sense in which the last decade of the century opened with its defining play when on 24 April 1990, Patrick Mason directed Brian Friel's *Dancing at Lughnasa* at the Abbey. 'When I cast my mind back to that summer of 1936', begins the play's narrator, Michael, 'different kinds of memories offer themselves to me': memories of August days when he lived with his mother and four aunts, dancing to céilí music from their new radio, and awaiting the return of a revered uncle, an African missionary. Set between the fighting of the 1920s and the economic changes of the 1950s, it might seem that all the elements are in place here for a fantasised traditional Ireland of close families, shining the beacon of faith around the world while comely maidens dance at the crossroads.

And yet, the family unit in *Dancing at Lughnasa* is made up of five unmarried women, one with an illegitimate child; the missionary uncle (played with angular puzzlement by Barry McGovern) returns from Africa 'shrunken and jaundiced with malaria', 'unable to remember even the simplest words'; in the end, only the music remains, so that 'when I remember it', Michael tells us, 'I think of it as dancing . . . dancing as if language no longer existed because words were no longer necessary.'[43] In other words, in *Dancing at Lughnasa*, we do not simply see a traditional world breaking up; the seeds of its dissolution are already there, even when it is at its most idyllic. In performance, this is all the more evident as we watch an adult narrate a play about his own childhood, constantly reminding us that characters we see before us, alive and present on the stage, are part of a past that is already dead before the curtain rises.

Of course, Friel had mapped this theatrical territory before; both *Freedom of the City* and *Faith Healer* work with the paradox of characters who are present (because in performance all theatrical characters exist in the present) and yet are part of the past. In 1994, he would return to it again with *Molly Sweeney*, a play made up of a series of past-tense monologues in which a blind woman, whose sight had been briefly restored and then lost, speaks from a darkened present about a fleetingly illuminated past. However, whereas in the plays of the 1970s the lost past had been looked back upon with anger, grief and bafflement, *Dancing at Lughnasa* and *Molly Sweeney* are plays at peace with the past, their dominant tone regret rather than grief, nostalgia rather than anger. Indeed, Joe Vanek's set for the original 1990 Abbey production of *Dancing at Lughnasa* filled the upstage area with angled rows of wheat, illuminated in the final scene with a 'very soft, golden light'. If proof were needed that it was possible to see an Ireland of cramped lives, pitiful exile, and various forms of blindness as part of the past, it was there in the sepia glow Vanek's set cast around the summer of 1936.

As Irish plays in 1990s increasingly conjured up images from the middle decades of the twentieth century, so too did the theatrical forms of those years once again became available to directors and writers as a part of a palette of styles. In the 1960s and 1970s, Irish playwrights who wanted to be innovative had felt obliged to challenge the conventions of stage realism; by the early 1990s, however, it was once again possible to see realism as one legitimate style among many. Tom Mac Intyre, for instance, went from work like *The Great Hunger* in the early 1980s to the more naturalistic *Kitty O'Shea* in 1990. Similarly, Marina Carr first came to prominence for *A Low in the Dark* in 1989, which features a female character named Curtains, who is, literally, 'covered from head to toe in curtains'. Then, while reading Ibsen and American novelist Flannery O'Connor, Carr wrote *The Mai* (1994), a play reminiscent of *Hedda Gabler*, in that its main character is a woman with the strength to build a home and a life for her daughters, but who ultimately commits suicide because she is unable to relinquish the belief that her selfish, philandering husband 'is utterly mine and I am utterly his'.[44] Where *A Low in the Dark* was radical in both its feminist politics and its form, *The Mai* showed an awareness that the theatrical forms of early modernism still retained their oblique power.

As prominent playwrights like Carr retreated from more overt forms of politics, it did not pass without comment in 1990 that Friel chose to stage *Dancing at Lughnasa* – not an obviously political play – with the Abbey, and not with Field Day, the company he had helped to found a decade earlier. In a sense, the fate overtaking Field Day was emblematic of what was elsewhere happening in Irish culture. Its directors were dispersing to high-profile positions in the United States and England, with Seamus Heaney on course for a Nobel Prize in Literature, and Stephen Rea consolidating his acting career in Hollywood. What had started out as a local, regionally based touring company, had become part of a new, transnational diaspora, still rooted in Irish concerns and images, but as likely to be found in London or Los Angeles as in Dublin or Derry. As Irish studies became increasingly well established as an academic discipline – not only in Ireland, but also elsewhere in Europe, in North America and in Australia – more books and articles would be published on Irish theatre and drama in the 1990s than in any other previous decade. Moreover, debate was now being carried on with unprecedented theoretical sophistication, aided in no small part by a productive cross-fertilisation with post-colonial theory that began in the late 1980s. Instead of looking like a small, stunted European anomaly, Ireland in the 1990s looked like the paradigm of a certain form of postmodernity, where the local has global significance, and where relations between margins and centres are in constant flux.

In this new ex-centric order of things, Irish theatre in the final decades of the twentieth century became more international than at any point since the end of the nineteenth century. During the 1970s, when Irish film-making had been almost non-existent, most Irish actors had to choose between working in Ireland or working in film. However, when Stephen Rea took the lead in Neil Jordan's *Angel* in 1982 – the film which marks the re-emergence of the Irish film industry – he was still very much a part of Field Day, and over the next two decades would alternate between Irish projects (on both stage and screen) and more mainstream film work. Similarly, touring outside of Ireland had been rare in the 1970s; however, by the mid-1980s *The Great Hunger*, Joe Dowling's *Juno and the Paycock* and Charabanc would all travel the world, as would Barry McGovern's one-man Beckett show *I'll Go On*, with its stark, angular set by artist Robert Ballagh. Ballagh also designed the production of *Endgame* that formed part of the Gate's Beckett Festival in October 1991, where for the first time all nineteen of Beckett's plays were staged together, before going on to play New York's Lincoln Centre in 1996. By the end of the 1990s, thirty-two of Ireland's subsidised companies would have toured internationally in the previous decade.

Not only were Irish productions being seen abroad; they increasingly originated outside of Ireland, as the pull of the London theatre (which had always been strong for actors, directors and designers) drew Irish writers into its gravitational field. In July 1987, Friel's *Fathers and Sons* opened at the National Theatre in London, which three months earlier had commissioned Frank McGuinness to translate Ibsen's *Rosmersholm*. In September 1989, McGuinness' *Mary and Lizzie* would open in London, as would *Mutabilitie*, which Trevor Nunn directed in the Cottesloe Theatre in 1997. *Mutabilitie* is McGuinness' most ambitious work to date, a powerful, sprawling piece of theatre, which imagines Shakespeare arriving in Edmund Spenser's County Cork estate at the beginning of the seventeenth century; however, it would have to wait three years for an Irish production. Similarly, in 1993 Rough Magic would première *New Morning*, by one of its founders, Declan Hughes, at the Bush Theatre, a hundred-seat theatre located above a London pub. The Bush was already very much a part of Irish theatre geography, if only because it had commissioned an acclaimed trilogy of plays from Wexford writer Billy Roche: *A Handful of Stars* (1988), *Poor Beast in the Rain* (1989) and *Belfry* (1991). It would later stage the first production of Conor McPherson's *This Lime Tree Bower* (1995) and commission him to write *St Nicholas* (1997), by which time he had attracted the attention of the

Royal Court, for whom he wrote *The Weir*, which opened on 4 July 1997.

A survey of *Irish Times* readers in the year 2000 would rank *The Weir* as one of the top ten best Irish plays of the twentieth century. In some respects, this tells us where the mainstream of the Irish theatre had moved by the century's end. At first glance, *The Weir* might not seem out of place in the Abbey of the 1940s, as the play opens in a pub in rural Leitrim where three bachelors are sharing the day's frugal gossip, later joined by a neighbour and a woman who has moved to the area from Dublin after the death of her child. It quickly becomes apparent, however, that the pub in *The Weir* is like a trace of an older theatrical style, more an occasion for telling deeply private tales of haunting than a real place. All of McPherson's earlier plays had been made up of monologues, and by the time he wrote *The Weir* it was evident that he found this form best suited to a fragmented society, where stories are no longer common property. So, all that the characters in *The Weir* can share is the recognition that each is alone with a story of ghostly contact. These stories cut across the differences in class, gender and geography that in earlier Irish plays would have provided the dramatic conflict. In a sense, the real ghost in *The Weir* is the ghost of an earlier, communal, theatrical form.

Indeed, from Friel's *Faith Healer*, through the long opening section of *Observe the Sons of Ulster*, to the retrospective narrators in *Dancing at Lughnasa* and *The Mai*, the Irish theatre in the closing decades of the twentieth century has been increasingly filled with monologues delivered to spectres of the past. Carr was to follow *The Mai* with *Portia Coughlan* (1996), *By the Bog of Cats* (1998) and *On Raftery's Hill* (2000), all of which revolve around characters for whom a world of ghosts is more compelling than the reality around them. 'I must not speak to shadows', Thomas Dunne, the main character in Sebastian Barry's *The Steward of Christendom*, tells himself as his bare room fills with ghosts. When *The Steward of Christendom* opened at London's Royal Court in March 1995, much of its success was attributed to Donal McCann's performance as Thomas Dunne, a retired chief superintendent with the Dublin Metropolitan Police, an Irish Catholic who had proudly served Queen Victoria, 'the very flower and protector of Christendom', but who as an old man in the county home in 1932 must admit that he is 'part of a vanished world and I don't know what has been put in its place'. With 'all the long traditions . . . broken up and flung out, like so many morning eggs on to the dung heap', Dunne's private world in 1932 parallels that of the audience in the 1990s, a place of discontinuities and broken traditions, where even the linearity of past and present cannot be assumed. And so, when the play reaches its final monologue (delivered by McCann with extraordinarily moving simplicity), in which Thomas tells his dead, ghostly son a simple tale of 'the mercy of fathers',[45] *The Steward of Christendom* seems to sum up more than a decade of trying to forgive (and ask forgiveness of) a past whose only remnants are ghosts.

In *The Weir*, *The Steward of Christendom*, as well as in Barry's earlier play, *The Prayers of Sherkin* (1990) there is a longing to recover lost communal stories. 'Community', asks a character in Jim Nolan's evocatively titled *The Salvage Shop*, 'did it mean so little to you?'[46] At the same time, the Irish theatre is part of a world in which film, television and popular music are all more immediately accessible than Synge or O'Casey. So, Billy Roche, for instance, would claim that his trilogy of determinedly realistic plays of small town Wexford is 'a tribute' to Hollywood films like '*Rebel Without a Cause*... and *The Last Picture Show*',[47] just as Declan Hughes would structure his 1991 play, *Digging for Fire*, around 1980s pop songs, later claiming that reading *New Musical Express* magazine had a greater role in shaping his emerging theatre sensibilities than watching Irish plays. Similarly, Barry's *White Woman Street*, first staged at the Bush Theatre in 1992, is set in an imaginary Wild West, complete with campfires and horses, and Stewart Parker was at work on a Western at the time of his death in 1988.

'I can name every single play I've ever seen even now', Martin McDonagh would claim in 1997, 'because there's only about 19 or 20, and two of those are my own.' For someone who 'always thought that theatre was the least interesting of the art forms', McDonagh has been outstandingly successful.[48] Although Druid dutifully premièred each of the plays in his Leenane Trilogy – *The Beauty Queen of Leenane* (1996), *A Skull in Connemara* and *The Lonesome West* (both 1997) – at their new theatre in Galway, each was a co-production with the Royal Court, where they transferred within a couple of weeks. The plays were later taken to Broadway, where they won a number of Tony Awards. Like *The Weir* (which played the Royal Court two weeks before the trilogy's London opening) McDonagh's plays create a theatrical world – each is set in a farmhouse kitchen in the west of Ireland – which looks like it might have come from any one of dozens of Irish plays from the middle decades of the twentieth century (plays which McDonagh claims never to have seen) or from a film like *The Quiet Man*. For this reason, they have sometimes been seen as parodies of 'the naïve drama of a past which really must be left behind', a view which has been criticised by Vic Merriman on the grounds that it allows audiences from a 'comfortable echelon' to laugh at those left behind by the economic boom.[49]

However, the experience of watching McDonagh's *Leenane Trilogy* is more complicated and contradictory than this. The plays are, in a sense, copies that have forgotten their originals, or, as Fintan O'Toole puts it, 'plays that are both pre-modern and post-modern . . . where the fifties are laid over the nineties, giving the play's apparent realism the ghostly, dizzying feel of a superimposed photograph.'[50] Hence, while the three plays weave together a detailed, interlocking fictional world, the characters in that world lack the communal values that gave earlier Irish drama its structure. In each play, a character (allegedly) kills a family member, while the priest, Father Welsh (or is it Walsh? – there is a running joke that no one can remember his name) wanders aimlessly through the *Trilogy*, admitting: 'God has no jurisdiction in this town.' By creating an image that audiences are invited to see as 'traditional', and then removing from it the last vestige of 'traditional' values, the plays stage the contradictions of a society that continues to nurse images of itself in which it no longer believes. It is no coincidence that one of the main industries in McDonagh's Leenane is selling faked souvenirs of *The Quiet Man* to 'eejit Yanks'.[51]

To focus on the major international success of productions such as Druid's *Leenane Trilogy*, however, would be to miss the sheer diversity and vitality of the Irish theatre in the closing years of the twentieth century, which is unmatched in a history going back more than four hundred years. When the new Abbey opened in 1966, it marked the belated beginning of a building boom in Irish theatre, and there are now more than fifty professionally run venues around the country (not to mention the hundreds of amateur halls, many of which are equipped to a professional standard). Performance spaces now extended from the 80-seat Crypt Theatre in the basement of Dublin Castle (not far from where *Gorboduc* was staged in 1601) through medium-sized venues like the 290-seat Ardhowen Theatre in Enniskillen, to the surviving Victorian theatres, like the 1001-seat Grand Opera House in Belfast. Indeed, in spring of the year 2000, the government of the Republic announced that it was earmarking £50 million for a new Abbey theatre. Consequently, Ireland at the end of the twentieth century has an unprecedented range of venues, making possible a variety of theatrical forms impossible earlier in its history. Not surprisingly, theatre audiences have increased along with the number of theatres, with more than thirty per cent of the Irish population attending a professional play at least once a year in the late

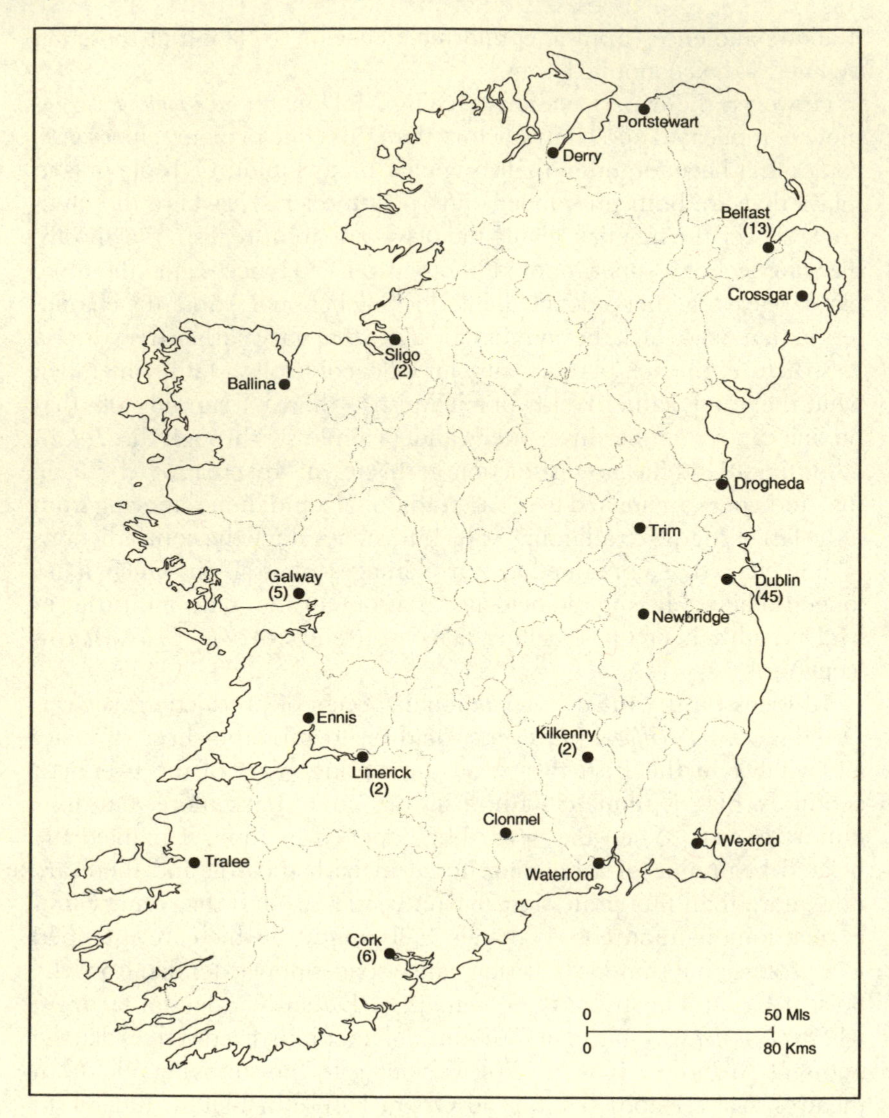

Map 6 Location of professional companies (including children's and theatre – in educational companies), 1998. In the early 1980s, Arts Councils North and South began funding regional companies, finally breaking up the Belfast – Dublin – Cork axis that had defined the geography of Irish theatre since the 1730s. In most cases, new professional companies developed in communities in which strong amateur theatre cultures had been established in the 1930s or 1940s.

1990s, and the gap steadily closing between the numbers of urban and rural playgoers. This in turn has stimulated an already vibrant amateur scene, which in the year 2000 hosted thirty-eight competitive festivals.

To a large extent, the growth in theatre audiences has been the product of a steady increase in state funding for the theatre, which in the Republic in 1998 totalled almost £8 million. At the same time, spreading this money among the more than forty companies who now receive funding (to which can be added almost fifty non-subsidised companies) means that Irish theatre is now more fragmented and makes fewer claims to represent an entire nation than ever before. Some companies, such as Red Kettle in Waterford, have a regional focus (which does not, however, prevent them from touring nationally and internationally); others concentrate on particular types of theatre, such as Macnas, who specialise in outdoor spectacles, or Theatre of Fire, who work exclusively with fireworks; others, again, have a particular aesthetic, such as the Focus or Bloodstone, both of which are Stanislavski theatres, or Pale Mother, a Brechtian company. Some companies, including Muted Cupid and Room B Productions, focus on gay and lesbian audiences, and as Ireland becomes more ethnically diverse, we can expect to see a rise in the number of companies like the Indo-Irish Theatre Combine. There are two subsidised Irish-language companies, Aisling Ghéar and Amharclann de hÍde, based in Belfast and Dublin, respectively. Meanwhile, the number of theatre-in-education companies is rising, and there are both new and established youth companies and children's theatre companies, the latter given added impetus when, in 1995, Europe's first children's cultural centre, The Ark, opened in the vibrant Temple Bar district of Dublin, just around the corner from the new Project Theatre, which re-opened in the year 2000.

In short, at the end of four hundred years of Irish theatre history, there is no such thing as *the* Irish theatre; there are Irish *theatres*, whose forms continue to multiply as they leave behind the fantasy of a single unifying image, origin or destiny.

Conclusion. A millennial flourish

24 March 1999. In The Mint, a small black box studio above a pub on Dublin's North Side, an audience sits facing an enormous black cube. Suddenly, there is a rush of sound, and the sides of the cube fall away, revealing a figure lying on the floor, an angled mirror suspended above her head. The figure (actress Olwen Fouere) is androgynous, barely human; attached to her fingers, her arms, legs, even her face, are a jumble of electrodes, hooking her to a computer. She tries to speak. There is only guttural sound. She moves a finger, triggering a note from the computer, which becomes a part of composer Roger Doyle's electro-acoustic score. She struggles to speak again, eventually producing individual words, 'channel . . . channel . . . system', and finally a sentence: 'The point of system contact is centred behind the free will', which the computer system picks up, breaks down, and echoes in new syntaxes, new permutations. 'The point of system contact is made thereby utilising the vocal chords, facial expression, legs, etcetera' – prompting the room to fill with a deafening wall of sound, out of which emerges a new voice, hoarse, animalistic, reduced to single words again, speaking as if possessed: 'Body. Body. Desire. Body'.[1]

The performance is Operating Theatre's *Angel / Babel*. In one possible telling of the tale, it could be a terminus, a millennial flourish with which to conclude a history of the Irish theatre at the end of the twentieth century. Throughout the centuries, the single irreducible element of theatrical performances has always been the living presence of a human being before an audience, allowing her body – 'vocal chords, facial expression, legs, etcetera' – to become the conduit through which other beings, human or otherwise, come into existence. In this regard, *Angel / Babel* is a pure piece of theatre, a performance whose subject is the nature of theatrical performance itself. At the same time, the Angel / Babel figure is beyond gender, beyond nationality, even beyond human agency, as the tiniest flicker of her finger prompts the computer to generate its own

Photograph 7. Olwen Fouere in Operating Theatre's *Angel / Babel* (1999), suspended between human and machine. Sensors attached to her body triggered sounds from a computer. This photo was taken during rehearsals; weeks spent rehearsing suspended from the ceiling took their toll, and she was forced to perform the play lying flat on her back.

random selection of words and sounds, independent of her will. Outside of history and at the margins of the human, there is a sense in which *Angel / Babel* takes theatrical performance as far as it can go.

In another version of the story, *Angel / Babel* is not an end. Indeed, it could not be an end, if only because the theatre is not evolving towards an end point. Theatre transforms itself continually, sometimes reinventing itself with unexpected suddenness, sometimes remaining apparently static for decades; theatrical forms borrow from each other, from other art forms, and from new technologies; archaic forms are resurrected and made new, while once-vibrant forms reveal their conventionality, grow stale and wither. 'I would take no year I ever heard of in exchange for the present', exclaimed an Irish journalist excited by the flowering of small theatre groups in 1905. Forty-five years later, the situation would be utterly changed. 'Downright excruciating dull and vapid badness is, I regret to say, apparently Dublin's main theatrical dish', complained a critic in 1950, 'like soggy cabbage in Dublin's restaurants.'[2] Sometimes the apparent centre of the culture, at other times almost irrelevant, the theatre does not develop; it responds, moment by moment, with whatever resources available, to the continual challenge the audience carries with it into the auditorium from the world outside.

Ever since Lord Mountjoy and Neale Moore watched *Gorboduc* in Dublin Castle in the months before the Battle of Kinsale in 1601, Irish audiences have brought into the theatre a concern with what it means to be Irish (or to be in Ireland, which is not necessarily the same thing). And yet, the theatre's relationship to an Irish identity has never been simple for a number of reasons. Foremost of these is the nature of theatre itself, which does not lend itself (in the same way, for instance, that the printed word does) to that trick of uniting individuals who are geographically distant from one another in what is the basic premise of a national consciousness. A theatrical performance happens in a particular place at a particular time; it may try to be national, but its basic form is local.

James Shirley was looking for an image of the Earl of Strafford's Ireland in *St Patrick for Ireland*, just as the Volunteers of the 1780s attended *Douglas* as a way of nurturing an emerging nationalist consciousness; later, Abbey plays like *Cathleen ni Houlihan* would be such self-conscious icons of nationality that there would be a temptation to see everything that happened on Irish stages in the twentieth century as the incarnated face of the nation's spirit. Each of these performances, however, could only reach a small number of people at any one moment, and they could only be national – in the sense of creating a bond of solidarity among otherwise distant people – at one remove, as performances were commented on in reviews, or as scripts were printed and read as drama. The closest the theatre could come to being national was through touring.

It is no coincidence that a touring circuit first developed in Ireland at around the same time as the first political theatre riots, just as the seeds of modern nationalism were beginning to germinate. Indeed, the spread of Irish theatre culture from Dublin to Cork, Belfast, and Limerick in the 1730s was part of an expanding national consciousness that would blossom into a fully fledged nationalism by the end of the eighteenth century. However, even as tours by Dublin-based companies were creating a sense of a shared national culture, they were sowing the seeds of regional theatre cultures, evident in lost plays such as John O'Keeffe's *Harlequin in Derry* or *Tony Lumpkin's Ramble Thro' Cork* in the 1770s. Similarly, the Ulster Literary Theatre in the first decade of the twentieth century would begin as part of a national theatre movement, but would quickly orientate itself towards its particular local, regional audience. From the early 1930s onwards, the same would be true of the hundreds of amateur companies founded all over the island, and of writers such as John B. Keane or M. J. Molloy, who wrote for them. After 1980, when there was a conscious effort to foster regional theatres through subsidy, regional difference would be inscribed on the institutional structure of the Irish theatre.

If touring was instrumental in producing both national and regional theatres in Ireland, it was also responsible, paradoxically, for helping to breach national and regional boundaries. Once a production is on the road, it is just as easy for a Galway-based company to play London as Dublin; similarly, it is easier for a Belfast touring house to bring in a show from Glasgow than from Cork. Although critics like to think of theatres in national terms, in practice theatre companies have seldom respected national borders, going wherever they could find audiences. Indeed, linguistic boundaries are more of an obstacle to a tour itinerary than the lines statesmen draw on maps, and this helps to explain why, with a professional theatre culture traditionally clustered along the east coast and the greatest concentration of Irish-speakers on the western seaboard, Irish-language theatre has always fought an uphill battle for existence.

In fact, as much as the Irish theatre imagined itself as national, it has always been at its most vibrant when it has been most international. In the rollercoaster years of the 1740s and 1750s, Thomas Sheridan, Charles Macklin and their contemporaries moved freely back and forth across the Irish Sea, as did the actors who played Hawkins Street in the 1820s. In the first decade of the twentieth century, many in the early Abbey saw themselves as crusaders in a purifying nativist movement, drawing on Irish folklore and mythology, but from the beginning their work owed just as much to the dramaturgy of Ibsen and Maeterlinck, the acting of Coquelin, and the rich mix of repertoire available in the big touring houses; by 1903, the Abbey too had joined the touring circuit, and by 1911 they were playing Broadway. Similarly, in the closing decades of the twentieth century, major Irish plays from Tom Murphy's *A Whistle in the Dark* to Conor McPherson's *The Weir* were as likely to open in London as in Dublin, as the channels between the two theatre cultures become increasingly permeable, linked in turn with that of New York.

This does not mean, however, that theatre has not been an important part of Irish culture: quite the contrary. Since at least the eighteenth century, theatre has more often than not been at the centre of Irish culture, in spite of the fact that the island has only a comparatively modest cluster of cities, and its cultural life has often found itself mesmerised by an ancient past in which theatre played only a minor part. Part of the explanation for this phenomenon must lie in the proximity to London, which since 1600 has been one of the centres of the English-language theatre world. London is close enough to provide a constant stimulus and a reliable outlet for talented Irish theatre practitioners; equally, it is distant enough for the strong but constantly shifting sense of Irish cultural difference to trigger a continual process of self-definition. In moments of pressure, this tension spurred Thomas Sheridan to write *The Brave Irishman*, Shaw to write *John Bull's Other Island*, and Stephen Rea to return from London to Ireland in 1980 to form Field Day, telling a Dublin newspaper that he felt 'less expressed in England than I did over here, but not in a narrow national way'.[3]

Over the past four centuries, the Irish theatre has nurtured the dream that a human figure present before an audience could be inhabited by those identities – local, regional, and national – that are always threatening to collapse under pressure from the very forces that feed the theatre with new forms and new ideas. At moments, that dream has been fulfilled, and an audience has seen itself in Katherine Philips' *Pompey*, Boucicault's *Shaughraun*, or staring through Maud Gonne's eyes as Cathleen ni Houlihan; at other moments, there has been the thrill of recognition in simply hearing an Ulster or a Kerry accent on the stage. At the beginning of the twenty-first century, the Irish theatre still feeds on these dreams and conflicts, even as their configurations change.

At the same time, the theatre in Ireland is now in a position to become self-perpetuating, for if theatre history teaches us anything, it is that theatre is born of a strong theatre culture, regardless of the social and political climate (although a strong economic base certainly helps). There are now more theatre buildings, more people involved in creating theatre, better training and a greater variety of performance to be seen than ever before. This is the most obvious manifestation of a healthy theatre culture; equally, there is its hidden side explored in this book, an awareness of the ghosts of Ireland's theatre history, continually challenging performers in the present to do something so remarkable that the past will have to be re-imagined yet again.

Biographical glossary

NUIM	National University of Ireland, Maynooth
QUB	Queen's University, Belfast
TCD	Trinity College, Dublin
UCC	University College, Cork
UCD	University College, Dublin
UCG	University College, Galway
UU	University of Ulster

Ashbury, Joseph (1638–1720); b. London; came to Ireland as a Royalist soldier, helping to capture Dublin Castle for Charles II; received a commission in the King's Horse Guard; actor at Smock Alley from 1662; manager and Master of the Revels (1676–1720). Initiated Smock Alley tours to Oxford, Edinburgh and Kilkenny.

Banim, John (1798–1842); b. Kilkenny; trained as a painter, he wrote a long poem, *The Celt's Paradise* (1821), and two tragedies, including *Damon and Pythias* (1821; with Sheil); found success writing fiction, including his epic novel *The Boyne Water* (1826). Died of spinal tuberculosis.

Barry, Sebastian (1955–); b. Dublin; educated TCD; three critically acclaimed novels and two poetry collections (1982–7) led to his election to Aosdána in 1989. His first successful play, *Boss Grady's Boys* (1988), won the Stewart Parker Award; *The Steward of Christendom* won the London Critics' Circle Award (1995).

Barry, Spranger (1719–77); b. Dublin; originally a silversmith; stage début in Smock Alley (1744), appearing at Drury Lane (1746) opposite Macklin in *Othello*. Alternated parts with Garrick throughout the 1750s; built Crow Street Theatre (1759) and Theatre Royal, Cork (1760), where his productions featured lavish spectacles. Buried Westminster Abbey.

Beckett, Samuel Barclay (1906–89); b. Dublin; educated TCD; lived primarily in Paris after 1928; wrote novels and poems throughout the 1930s and 1940s, including *Molloy*, *Malone Dies* and *The Unnameable* (1947–51); joined French Resistance, 1941–2; achieved fame with *Waiting for Godot* (1953), thereafter writing increasingly shorter works. Nobel Prize for literature, 1969.

Behan, Brendan (Breandán Ó Beacháin) (1923–64); b. Dublin; part of a talented extended family including P. J. Bourke; imprisoned for IRA bombing campaign, 1939; a popular wit and raconteur, he gained fame with *The Quare Fellow* (1954) and an English reworking of *An Giall*, *The Hostage* (both 1958). His early death was alcohol-related.

Blythe, Ernest (Earnán de Blaghd) (1889–1975); b. Mageragall, Co. Antrim; joined Gaelic League and IRB while working in Dublin; imprisoned, 1916; TD for North Monaghan (1918–33), supporting Treaty; successively Minster for Commerce, Finance and Posts and Telegraphs; senator (1933–6); manager of Abbey (1941–67); a committed Irish language revivalist throughout his life.

Boucicault, Dionysius Lardner (1820–90); b. Dublin; acted as Lee Moreton until success of *London Assurance* (1841) took him to New York. As well as writing more than 200 plays, he acted for many years with his common-law wife, Agnes Robertson, and was an innovative stage designer and manager. Married Louise Thorndyke, 1888.

Bourke, Patrick J. (1883–1932); b. Dublin; began acting at the Queen's and in smaller venues around Dublin *c.* 1903; later formed a company to perform his plays, including *In Dark and Evil Days* (1914); wrote the first full-length Irish feature film, *Ireland a Nation* (1913). Later opened theatrical supply firm.

Boyd, John (1912–); b. Belfast; born into a working-class Protestant family; educated QUB and TCD; co-founded magazine *Lagan*, 1943; producer, BBC Northern Ireland, 1947; became associated with Lyric Theatre, 1971, editing its journal, *Threshold*. Wrote his first play, *Assassin* (1969), followed by a number of plays dealing with sectarianism.

Boyle, Roger, Lord Broghill, first Earl of Orrery (1621–79), b. Lismore; son of Richard Boyle, Earl of Cork; initially a supporter of Charles I; joined with Cromwell, 1649, later switching allegiance back to Charles II. Powerful statesman, influential controversialist and soldier; playwright and author of *Treatise on the Art of War* (1677).

Carnduff, Thomas (1886–1956); b. Belfast; soldier in the First World War and gun-runner for Ulster Volunteer Force; worked in Belfast shipyards, binman and finally caretaker of Linenhall Library. A collection of poetry, *Songs from the Shipyard* (1924) was followed by plays, including *Workers* (1932); Master, Belfast Lodge, Independent Orange Order.

Carr, Marina (1964–); b. Dublin; raised in County Offaly; educated UCD; Carr began writing while in university; her early, experimental plays gave way to a more naturalistic style in plays with midland settings, including *The Mai* (1994), and *On Raftery's Hill* (2000). Member of Aosdána.

Carroll, Paul Vincent (1900–68); b. Dundalk, Co. Louth; educated St Patrick's College, Drumcondra; moved to Glasgow, 1920; early plays premièred by the Abbey include *Things that Are Caesar's* (1932); *The White Steed* opened in New York (1939); later screenplays for film and television include Alexander Korda's *Saints and Sinners* (1949).

Colgan, Michael (1950–); b. Dublin; educated TCD; directed plays at the Abbey (1974–7), before moving into arts administration as manager of Dublin Theatre Festival (1978–84); artistic director, Gate Theatre (1984–);

Honorary LL.D, TCD (2000); member of Irish Arts Council (1987–94); one of Ireland's most respected arts administrators.

Corkery, Daniel (1878–1964); b. Cork; born into a family of carpenters and trade unionists; trained as a teacher and joined Gaelic League; co-founded Cork Dramatic Society (1908); wrote plays, short stories, journalism, and books, including *Synge and Anglo-Irish Literature* (1947); Professor of English, UCC until 1947; Fianna Fáil senator, 1951–4.

Cusack, Cyril (1910–93); b. Kenya; educated UCD; toured with a fit-up company as a child; an influential actor, producer, and director from late 1930s onwards, his wry acting style was ideally suited to his playing of Conn in *The Shaughraun* (Abbey 1968). His daughters (Niamh, Sorcha and Sinead) are accomplished actresses.

D'Alton, Louis Lynch (1900–51); b. Dublin; son of touring actor-manager; an early play, *Rags and Sticks* (1938), examines the decline of a touring company; managed small Irish touring companies from the late 1920s onwards. A successful playwright throughout the 1940s, his greatest success was the posthumous *This Other Eden* (1953).

Deevy, Teresa (1903–63); b. Waterford; became deaf in early adulthood; began writing for the Abbey with *The Reapers* (1930), but turned to writing radio plays after rejection of *Wife to James Whelan* (written 1937; staged 1956). Lived a quiet, retired life; her work began to be reappraised in the 1980s.

Dowling, Joe (1948–); b. Dublin; educated UCD; began acting with the Abbey, 1967, but quickly turned to directing. Artistic Director, Irish Theatre Company, 1976–8; Artistic Director, Abbey, 1978–85. Founded the Gaiety School of Acting, 1986. Became Artistic Director of the Guthrie Theatre, Minneapolis, 1993. Honorary D. Litt., NUIM, 2001.

Edwards, Hilton (1903–1982); b. London; acted in Old Vic before joining McMaster touring company; with his partner, Micheál Mac Líammóir co-founded An Taibhdhearc and Gate Theatre (both 1928); directed and/or acted in more than 400 productions; honorary doctorates from UCD and TCD. His acting can be seen in *The Quare Fellow* (1962).

Ervine, St John Greer (born John Irvine) (1883–1971); b. Belfast; after his first play, *Mixed Marriage* (1911), became manager of the Abbey, but his unionist politics alienated the actors; he quit in 1916 and joined the Dublin Fusiliers, losing a leg in the First World War, wrote plays, political journalism, and biography until the late 1950s.

Falconer, Edmund (born O'Rourke) (1814–79); b. Limerick; manager of Lyceum Theatre, London (1858–9 and 1861–2), introducing a Shakespearean repertoire; played Danny Mann in *Colleen Bawn*. Wrote *Peep O' Day* (1861), *Galway-go-bragh* and *The O'Flahertys* (both 1867). Joint Lessee of Drury Lane (1862–6); acted in New York (1867–70), before returning to London.

Farquhar, George (1678–1707); b. Derry; educated TCD, acted at Smock Alley, but left after wounding a fellow actor. Wrote *Love and A Bottle* (1699), followed by seven plays in seven years, ending with *The Beaux Stratagem* (1707). He died in poverty, hoping for an army commission, although his plays were frequently staged after his death.

Fay, Frank (1871–1931) b. Dublin; brother of W. G. Fay; drama critic for *United Irishman* (1899–1902); an amateur actor, he joined the Irish National Dramatic Society, which provided the Irish Literary Theatre with its original company. Left Abbey in 1908, acting in England and America; returned to Dublin as an acting coach.

Fay, George William (1872–1947); b. Dublin; electrician and part-time professional actor; founded amateur Irish National Dramatic Society, 1902; later merged with Irish Literary Theatre; played original Christy Mahon in Synge's *Playboy*; left Abbey in 1908, but continued his film and theatre career; final film appearance in *Odd Man Out* (1947).

Fitzgerald, Barry (born William Joseph Shields) (1888–1961); b. Dublin; while working as a civil servant, began acting at the Abbey (1916–29) and Queen's (*c.* 1916–19); praise for performances in O'Casey's plays led to freelance American tour, 1929; went to Hollywood, 1937; Oscar for *Going My Way* (1944). His brother, Arthur Shields, had a similar career.

Friel, Brian (1929–); b. Omagh, Co. Tyrone; educated St Columb's College, Derry; began writing short stories and plays in 1950s; worked full-time as a teacher until 1960; achieved international fame with *Philadelphia, Here I Come!* (1964). Has continued to write critically acclaimed, popular plays, including *Dancing at Lughnasa* (1990).

Gregory, Isabella Augusta (née Persse) (1852–1932); b. Roxborough, Co. Galway; m. Sir William Gregory, 1880; wrote anti-Home Rule pamphlet, 1893, but supported cultural nationalism by 1901. Met W. B. Yeats, 1894, with whom she co-founded Abbey theatre. An accomplished folklorist, theatre manager and playwright, her home at Coole Park was a centre for the Irish literary revival.

Head, Richard (?1637–?1686); b. Carrickfergus; educated New Inn Hall, Oxford; after being ruined by gambling, wrote part of *The English Rogue* (1665), a rambling picaresque narrative, partly set in Ireland, where he may have been a bookseller. Wrote *Hic et Ubique: or, the Humors of Dublin* (1663); drowned at sea.

Hickey, Tom (b. 1948–); b. Naas, Co. Kildare; began as an amateur with the Moate Club, Naas; trained with Focus Theatre, achieving national recognition with *The Riordans* television serial. He has brought his distinctive physical style to the premières of plays including *The Gigli Concert* (1983) and *On Raftery's Hill* (2000).

Holloway, Joseph (1861–1844); b. Dublin; architect with T. T. O'Callaghan, (1880–96), and in private practice (1896 – *c.* 1914); Governor of National Gallery of Ireland, and deputy film censor. A diary of his almost nightly visits to the theatre between June 1888, and March 1944, amounts to more than twenty-five million words.

Horniman, Annie Elizabeth Fredericka (1860–1937); b. London; educated Slade School; member of occult Order of the Golden Dawn; a believer in subsidised theatre, she funded Avenue Theatre, London (1894), Abbey (1904–10) and Gaiety Theatre, Manchester (1908–17), where she established a repertory company; a founder of English repertory movement.

Hyde, Douglas (1860–1945); b. Frenchpark, Co. Roscommon; educated TCD; an accomplished linguist, his *Love Songs of Connaught* (1893) and *Literary History of Ireland* (1899) were influential in the Gaelic revival; first President, Gaelic League (1893); first Professor of Modern Irish, UCD (1905); Senator (1925–6) and first President of Ireland (1938).

Hynes, Garry (1953–) b. Galway; educated UCG; co-founder and artistic director of Druid (1975–91; 1995–); Artistic Director, Abbey (1991–4). Productions of plays such *Bailegangaire* (1985) have placed her among the most respected directors of her generation; Honorary LL.D, UCG; Tony Award for directing (1998).

Johnston, Denis (1901–84); b. Dublin; educated Edinburgh, Cambridge and Harvard; called to the bar, 1925; directed for Dublin Drama League; wrote *The Old Lady Says 'No!'* (1929); joined BBC, 1938; among the first journalists to enter Second World War concentration camps; BBC Director of Programmes (1948); playwright, essayist and lecturer; OBE, 1948.

Keane, John B (1928–); b. Listowel, Co. Kerry; began managing a pub in Listowel, 1954; his first play, *Sive* (1959), won All-Ireland Festival; thereafter wrote a series of successful plays, including *The Field* (1965) and *Big Maggie* (1969), frequently revived. Popular author of satirical essays, short stories and a novel.

Kilroy, Tom (1934–); b. Callan, Co. Kilkenny; educated, UCD; Professor of English, UCG, 1978–89; director of Field Day, 1988; began writing for the theatre with an historical play, *The O'Neill* (1969), followed by distinguished series of plays at roughly five-year intervals. Much respected for his critical essays on Irish theatre.

Knowles, James Sheridan (1784–1862); b. Cork; second cousin to R. B. Sheridan; wrote first play at age sixteen, joining Edmund Kean as a child actor; acted with Crow Street company (1808). Macready had a success with his *Virginius* (1820), as did Knowles himself with *The Hunchback* (1832). Became a Baptist pastor, 1844.

Leonard, Hugh (born John Keyes Byrne) (1926–); b. Dublin; joined Civil Service, 1945, and wrote for amateur companies until the Abbey staged *The Big Birthday* (1954); continued to write prolifically for both television and stage, his *Da* (1973) was a major Broadway success; also a popular journalist, reviewer and memoirist.

Mac Intyre, Tom (1931–); b. Cavan; educated UCD; taught at Clongowes Wood College (1958–65); an idiosyncratic and distinctive author of poetry, fiction and drama; achieved recognition for *The Great Hunger* (1983); difficulty in finding performers capable of staging his work helped turn him towards more conventional theatrical forms after 1990.

Macken, Walter (1916–67); b. Galway; began acting with An Taibhdhearc (1933), for whom he wrote *Oidhreacht na Mara*; joined the Abbey as actor and playwright, where his work includes *Home is the Hero* (1952); published eleven novels. His acting can be seen on film in *The Quare Fellow* (1962).

Macklin, Charles (born McLoughlin) (?1697–1797); b. Culduff, Co. Donegal; a travelling actor early in life, his natural style of acting was not appreciated until he played Shylock, 1741. He acted in Smock Alley and Crow Street, and managed a theatre in Capel Street (1763–70); plays include *Love à la Mode* (1759). Final performance, 1788.

Mac Líammóir, Micheál (born Alfred Wilmore) (1899–1978); b. London; child actor in London; joined McMaster touring company; with his partner, Hilton Edwards, co-founded An Taibhdhearc and Gate Theatre (both 1928); acted, directed and designed until mid-1970s; wrote ten plays and nine books; Honorary LL.D, TCD, 1962. His acting can be seen in Orson Welles' *Othello* (1952).

Martyn, Edward (1859–1923); b. Tulira, Co. Galway; raised in an aristocratic Catholic family, he showed a taste all his life for visionary religious art. Co-founded Irish Literary Theatre, and Theatre of Ireland (1906); President of Sinn Féin (1904–8). Plays include *The Heather Field* (1899); involvement with theatre ceased after 1914.

Mason, Patrick (1951–); b. London; educated London University; lecturer in Performance Studies, University of Manchester; began directing at the Abbey, 1977; directed for Irish Theatre Company, Gate, Bristol Old Vic, Guthrie Theatre, Minneapolis, and elsewhere; Tony Award for *Dancing at Lughnasa* (1992). Artistic Director, Abbey (1994–9).

Maturin, Charles Robert (1782–1824); b. Dublin, educated TCD; Episcopalian curate of Loughrea and St Peter's Dublin. His novel *The Wild Irish Boy* (1812) would be influential, and his play *Bertram* was staged at Byron's recommendation in Drury Lane, 1816; after writing two unsuccessful tragedies, returned to fiction with *Melmoth* (1820).

McAnally, Ray (1926–89); b. Moville, Co. Donegal; a leading Abbey actor during the 1950s; rose to international attention with the film *Shake Hands with the Devil* (1959); his career reached a second peak in the 1980s, with numerous stage and television roles, and a leading role in *The Mission* (1986).

McCabe, Eugene (1930–); b. Glasgow; moved to Ireland, 1939; educated UCC; began farming in County Monaghan, 1964; continued to farm after success of *King of the Castle* (1964; filmed 1977); has subsequently written plays, novels, children's literature and screenplays for film and television.

McDonagh, Martin (1971–); b. London; born of Irish parents who spent their summers in County Galway; his first play, *The Beauty Queen of Leenane* (1996) won four Tony Awards (1998); it is part of the Leenane Trilogy, completed by *A Skull in Connemara* and *The Lonesome West* (both 1997).

McGuinness, Frank (1953–); b. Buncrana, Co. Donegal; educated UCD; lectured UU (1977–9), UCD (1979–80; 1997–present), Maynooth (1984–1997); *Observe the Sons of Ulster* (1985) established his reputation as an uncompromising, yet versatile and prolific writer; *Someone Who'll Watch Over Me* (1992) was a Broadway success; his translation of *A Doll's House* (1997) won a Tony Award.

McKenna, Siobhán (1923–86); b. Belfast; educated UCG; began acting with An Taibhdhearc (1940), joined the Abbey, 1944; rose to international fame with title role in Shaw's *St Joan* (London, 1954); toured widely in the 1970s with her one-woman show, *Here Are Ladies*; later roles include Mommo in Murphy's *Bailegangaire* (1985).

McMaster, Anew (1891–1962); b. Birkenhead; established his acting reputation in West End; toured Australia, 1921; formed his own Shakespearean touring company, 1925, playing throughout Ireland; also acted in Stratford-upon-Avon, Chicago, Australia and throughout Europe; a mentor to many leading actors and last of the actor-managers. Brother-in-law of Michéal Mac Líammóir.

McPherson, Conor (1971–); b. Dublin; educated UCD; co-founded Fly by Night Theatre Company, and began writing and directing short monologues while at university; Royal Court production of *The Weir* won an Olivier Award (1998); directed and wrote screenplay for *Saltwater* (2000).

Molloy, Michael Joseph (1917–94); b. Milltown, Co. Galway; began writing about the dying folk culture of his home with *The Old Road* (1943), followed by *The King of Friday's Men* (1948) and other plays; after returning to farming in the 1950s, his later plays were premièred by amateur companies.

Moore, George (1852–1933); b. Ballyglass, Co. Mayo; born into a Catholic aristocratic family; moved to Paris, 1873, becoming a Zolaesque novelist. Briefly involved with Irish Literary Theatre and Gaelic League *c.* 1900, amusing accounts of which can be found in his autobiography, *Hail and Farewell* (1911, 1912 and 1914).

Mossop, Henry (?1729–?1774); b. Tuam; educated TCD; stage debut, Smock Alley, 1749; was in the company that played *Mahomet*, 1754. Successful at Drury Lane throughout late 1750s; he returned to Dublin to manage Smock Alley (1761–71), and Crow Street (1768–71); arrested in London for gambling debts, 1771; died of starvation.

Murphy, Thomas (1935–); b. Tuam, Co. Galway; worked initially as a metalwork teacher; acted and wrote for amateur Tuam Theatre Guild; after West End success of *A Whistle in the Dark* (1960) became a full-time writer; plays like *Famine* (1968), *Bailegangaire* (1985) and *The House* (2000) have earned him widespread critical respect.

Murray, Thomas Cornelius (1873–1959); b. Macroom, Co. Cork; trained as a teacher, and taught in Cork and Dublin, where he was headmaster of Inchicore Model School. His first success was *Birthright* (1910); wrote twelve more plays, several still popular in the 1960s. Retired from teaching, 1932; President, Irish Playwrights Association.

Ní Ghráda, Máiréad (1899–1971); b. Co. Clare; educated UCD; member of Cumann na mBan; secretary to Ernest Blythe during first Dáil; broadcaster, short-story writer, novelist, and author of textbooks; wrote her first play, *An Uacht* in 1935, but her greatest success was not until *An Triail* (1964).

O'Casey, Sean (born John Casey) (1880–1964); b. Dublin; born into a poor, working-class family; involved in trade union politics during Dublin Lock-Out, 1913; his trilogy of Dublin plays, (1923–6) established his international reputation; he moved to England, 1926, continuing to write plays, essays and his *Autobiographies* until late 1950s.

Ó Floinn, Críostóir (1927–); b. Limerick; educated TCD; Irish-language novelist, poet, and playwright, who gained recognition and a degree of notoriety with *Cóta Bán Chríost* (1966). His memoirs, *Consplawkus*, provide a witty account of the Abbey in the 1960s.

O'Grady, Hubert (1841–99); b. Limerick; trained as an upholsterer. Acted in 1876–7 revival of Boucicault's *The Shaughraun*, after which he formed his own Irish National Company, touring England, Scotland and Ireland, performing his political melodramas, including *Eviction* (1879) and *The Famine* (1886). Died while on tour.

O'Keeffe, John (1747–1833); b. Dublin into a Catholic family; acted in Mossop's company (1763–75) but retired due to blindness; first playwriting success with *Tony Lumpkin in Town* (1778); wrote more than thirty-five farces, comedies and operettas, some of which held the stage for many years. Given a royal pension, 1820.

Ogilby, John (1600–76); b. Edinburgh; created first Master of the Revels in Ireland, 1638, but fled to London 1641, becoming a respected print-maker and cartographer. Choreographed coronation procession for Charles II (1661); returned to Dublin to build and manage Smock Alley theatre in 1662; resumed print-making in London, 1669.

Parker, Stewart (1941–88); b. Belfast; born in a Protestant Unionist family; educated QUB; lectured Hamilton College and Cornell; first came to attention with *Spokesong* (1974) as a versatile, experimental, yet popular playwright. Continued to write for stage, radio and television, including a six-part series, *Lost Belongings* (1987). Died of cancer.

Pearse, Patrick Henry (Pádraig Mac Piarais) (1879–1916); b. Dublin; father a stone-mason; joined Gaelic League, 1896, and edited its journal, *An Claidheamh Soluis* (1903–9); playwright, poet, educator and founding member of the Irish Volunteers; commandant-general of Republican forces during Easter Rising, for which he was executed.

Philips, Katherine (née Fowler) (1631–1664); b. London; married James Philips, 1648. Her earliest Cavalier verses were prefixed to Henry Vaughan's *Poems* (1651); moved to Dublin, 1662, founding a Platonic 'Society of Friendship', whose members included leading policy makers. Translated Corneille's *Pompey* (1663); translating *Horace* when she died from smallpox in 1664.

Philips, William (1675–1734); b. Derry; educated TCD; bought a captain's commission, 1698. A Tory supporter of the Earls of Inchiquin and Thomond, he represented Doneraile in the Irish Parliament, 1703–13; suspected of involvement with the failed Jacobite rebellion of 1715. Plays include *St Stephen's Green* (1700) and *Hibernia Freed* (1722).

Rea, Stephen (1943–); b. Belfast; educated QUB; professional career began at the Abbey (1966); moved to London, acting at the National Theatre and Royal Court; returned to Ireland to co-found Field Day, 1979. His role in Neil Jordan's film *Angel* (1982) established his film career and association with Jordan.

Reid, Christina (1942–); b. Belfast into a Protestant family; worked in office jobs, 1957–70, entered QUB as a mature student; began writing in university; writer-in-residence, Lyric (1983–4) and Young Vic (1988–9); achieved prominence with *Tea in a China Cup* (1983) and *Joyriders* (1986), which played New York in 1992. George Devine Award (1986).

Robinson, Esmé Stuart Lennox (1886–1958); b. Douglas, Co. Cork; initially associated with the Cork Dramatic Society; hired to manage the Abbey (1909), with which he would be associated for the rest of his life; achieved international success with *The Whiteheaded Boy* (1916); became an adjudicator for amateur theatre in 1940s.

Scott, Michael (1905–89); b. Drogheda, Co. Louth; acted at the Abbey, touring America in 1928. Set up architectural practice, 1929; designed conversion of Gate Theatre (1929), Irish Pavillion for New York World Fair (1938); collaborated with Ronald Tallon on Abbey Theatre (1966). One of the most important Irish modernist architects.

Shadwell, Charles (?1675–1726); b. London; son of English Poet Laureate and playwright Thomas Shadwell; moved to Dublin as an assurance broker, 1713. A Whig in politics; wrote *The Hasty Wedding* (1716), *The Sham Prince* (1718), and other plays for Smock Alley; also *Rotherick O'Connor* (1720). Supported Swift's 'Drapier's Letters' campaign, 1725.

Shaw, George Bernard (1856–1950); b. Dublin; a self-educated, self-proclaimed social 'downstart', his move to London in 1876 marked the beginning of an astonishingly prolific writing career, producing a steady flow of theatre and music criticism, plays, prefaces, essays, and screenplays until the eve of his ninety-fourth birthday. Nobel Prize for literature, 1925.

Sheil, Richard Lalor (1791–1851); b. Drumdowney, Co. Kilkenny; educated TCD; called to the bar, 1814; lack of clients led him to write *Adelaide* (1814) and three other plays. Joined campaign for Catholic Emancipation; MP successively for Milborne Port, Louth and Tipperary, sitting as a Repealer. Master of the Mint, 1846–50.

Sheridan, Richard Brinsley (1751–1816); b. Dublin; son of Thomas Sheridan; m. Elizabeth Ann Linley, 1773; plays include *The Rivals*, *St Patrick's Day*, *The Duenna* (all 1775) and *The School for Scandal* (1777); manager of Drury Lane (1776–1809). As a Westminster MP (1780–1812), he became an admired orator, holding a number of important ministerial posts.

Sheridan, Thomas (1719–88); b. Quilca, Co. Cavan; son of Thomas Sheridan (the elder), a noted educator; educated TCD; wrote *The Brave Irishman* (1743); manager of Smock Alley, 1743–54; acted until 1777, but spent most of his later years teaching elocution, and publishing works on education and language theory; edited Swift's *Works* (1784).

Shiels, George (1886–1949); b. Ballymoney, Co. Antrim; emigrated to Canada, where he was crippled in a railway accident; returned to Ireland, 1913; wrote as 'George Morshiel' for Ulster Literary Theatre; became very popular Abbey playwright after *Paul Twyning* (1922) and *Professor Tim* (1925); wrote for Ulster Group Theatre after 1944.

Shirley, James (1596–1666); b. London; took Anglican orders, but probably converted to Catholicism *c.* 1624. Wrote for Cockpit and Salisbury Court theatres; author of influential masque *The Triumph of Peace* (1634). Resident playwright in Dublin, 1637–40; returned to England, joining the Royalist Army. Died in Great Fire of London.

Southerne, Thomas (1660–1746); b. Oxmantown, Co. Dublin; educated TCD; entered Middle Temple, 1678; received commission in James II's army after success of *The Disappointment* (1685); returned to playwriting after defeat of James, producing his most popular works, *The Fatal Marriage* (1694) and *Oroonoko* (1696). Died a respected, but unfashionable figure.

Synge, John Millington (1871–1909); b. Rathfarnham, Co. Dublin; educated TCD and Royal Irish Academy of Music; settled in Paris, 1895; first visit to Inis Meáin, 1898, resulted in a volume of prose, *The Aran Islands* (1901); also wrote poetry and the plays on which his reputation rests. Died of Hodgkin's disease.

Thompson, Sam (1916–65); b. Belfast; painter in Belfast shipyards, but fired for trade union activities; began writing for radio in mid-1950s; his play *Over the Bridge* (1960) was considered too controversial by the Ulster Group Theatre; a final television play, *Cemented with Love* (1965), was produced posthumously.

Whitbread, James William (1847–1916); b. England; moved to Dublin *c.* 1884 to lease Queen's Royal Theatre (1884–1907); wrote fifteen Irish plays, including *The Spectre of the Past* (1893) and *Wolfe Tone* (1898). His earlier writing career in the English theatre has not been traced. Retired to Scarborough, where he died.

Wilde, Oscar Fingal O'Flahertie Wills (1854–1900); b. Dublin; educated TCD and Magdalen College, Oxford; influential conversationalist, essayist, poet, novelist and playwright. His life and work defined the aesthetic movement of the 1890s; at the peak of his career, imprisoned for gross indecency arising from a homosexual relationship, 1895–7; died in exile.

Woffington, Peg (?1718–60); b. Dublin; daughter of a bricklayer; professional actress at age twelve. Famed for playing Sir Harry Wildair as a breeches part, Smock Alley (1740) and Covent Garden (1741). Beautiful and deep-voiced, she was a leading comic actress, frequently appearing with Garrick and Sheridan. Final stage appearance, 1757.

Yeats, William Butler (1865–1939); b. Dublin; son of John Butler Yeats; established his reputation as a poet with *The Celtic Twilight* (1893); continued to publish poetry, plays, essays, and occult works throughout his life. Co-founder of Abbey Theatre; Nobel Prize for literature, 1923; most important Irish poet of the twentieth century.

Notes

1 PLAYING COURT, 1601–1692

1 Russell A. Fraser and Norman Rabkin (eds.), *Drama of the English Renaissance*, 2 vols. (New York, 1976), vol. I, pp. 82, 100.
2 See Alan J. Fletcher, *Drama, Performance and Polity in Pre-Cromwellian Ireland* (Cork, 2000), pp. 9–60, 226.
3 Fynes Moryson, *An Itinerary*, 4 vols. (Glasgow, 1907–8), vol. III, pp. 282, 85.
4 W. S. Clark, *The Early Irish Stage: The Beginnings to 1720* (Oxford, 1955), p. 27. See also Raymond Gillespie, 'Dublin 1600–1700: A City and its Hinterland', in Peter Clark and Bernard Lepetit (eds.), *Capital Cities and their Hinterlands in Early Modern Europe* (Aldershot and Brookfield, Vt., 1996), p. 86.
5 Allan H. Stevenson, 'James Shirley and the Actors at the First Irish Theatre', *Modern Philology* (Nov. 1942), p. 151; Fletcher, *Drama, Performance and Polity*, pp. 270–1; Sandra Burner, *James Shirley: A Study of Literary Coteries and Patronage in Seventeenth-Century England* (New York, 1988), p. 113.
6 Fletcher, *Drama, Performance and Polity*, p. 263.
7 Clark, *Early Irish Stage*, p. 29; personal comment, Linzi Simpson, June 2000.
8 Thomas Wilkes, *A General View of the Stage* (London and Dublin, 1759), p. 306.
9 Keith Sturgess, *Jacobean Private Theatre* (London and New York, 1987), p. 40.
10 James Shirley, *Poems* (London, 1646), p. 154.
11 John H. Astington, 'The *Messalina* Stage and Salisbury Court Plays', *Theatre Journal* 43 (1991), p. 146.
12 Henry Burnell, *Landgartha* (Dublin, 1641), pp. 70, 36; the prologue to *The General* is by Shirley, *Poems*, p. 495.
13 William Knowler (ed.), *The Earl of Strafforde's Letters and Dispatches*, 2 vols. (Dublin, 1760), vol. I, pp. 28, 96.
14 James Shirley, *The Dramatic Works and Poems of James Shirley*, W. Gifford and A. Dyce (eds.), 4 vols. (London 1833), vol. IV, p. 492.
15 *Ibid.*, pp. 365, 373.
16 *Ibid.*, pp. 388, 443.
17 Burnell, *Landgartha*, pp. 8, 67, 71.
18 *Ibid.*, p. 36.
19 I am indebted to Ray Gillespie for his thoughts on this play. See Raymond Gillespie, 'Political Ideas and Their Social Contexts in Seventeenth-Century

Ireland', in Jane H. Ohlmeyer (ed.), *Political Thought in Seventeenth-Century Ireland: Kingdom or Colony* (Cambridge, 2000), pp. 121–2.

20 *The Plott and Progresse of the Irish Rebellion Wherein Is Discovered the Machavilian Policie of the Earle of Straford, Sir George Radcliffe and Others* (London, 1644), p. 7.

21 Cited in Clark, *Early Irish Stage*, pp. 29, 180.

22 *Ibid.*, pp. 10, 20–21.

23 Henry Burkhead, *A Tragedy of Cola's Furie, OR, Lirenda's Miserie* (Kilkenny, 1646), pp. 2–3.

24 For a convincing identification of all major characters in the play, see Patricia Coughlan, '"Enter Revenge": Henry Burkhead and *Cola's Furie*', *Theatre Research International*, 15:1 (Spring 1990), pp. 6–8.

25 Burkhead, *Cola's Furie*, pp. 33, 15.

26 *Ibid.*, pp. 48, 43.

27 Cited in Roy Foster, *Modern Ireland 1600–1972* (London and New York, 1988), p. 96.

28 'Smock Alley Epilogues and Prologues', Ms. English 674 f.21. By permission of the Houghton Library, Harvard University.

29 John Ogilby, *The Entertainment of His Most Excellent Majestie Charles II, in His Passage through the City of London to His Coronation* (London, 1662), p. 136.

30 Cited in Clark, *Early Irish Stage*, p. 182.

31 *Ibid.*, pp. 54–5; Linzi Simpson, *Smock Alley: The Evolution of a Building* (Dublin, 1996), pp. 52–7.

32 Katherine Philips, *The Collected Works of Katherine Philips, The Matchless Orinda*, Patrick Thomas (ed.), 3 vols. (Stump Cross, 1990–3), vol. II, p. 54.

33 Patrick Adair, *A True Narrative of the Rise and Progress of the Presbyterian Church in Ireland* (Belfast, 1866), p. 290.

34 Cited in Gillespie, 'Dublin 1600–1700', p. 88.

35 Thomas Morrice, *A Collection of the State Letters of the Right Honourable Roger Boyle, The First Earl of Orrery, Lord President of Munster in Ireland* (London, 1742), p. 38. See also Nancy Klein Maguire, 'Regicide and Reparation: The Autobiographical Drama of Roger Boyle, Earl of Orrery', *ELR*, 21:2 (Spring 1991), p. 265.

36 Roger Boyle, *The Dramatic Works of Roger Boyle,* W. S. Clark (ed.), 2 vols. (Cambridge, Mass., 1937), vol. I, pp. 135, 111.

37 Orrery to Ormond, (20 June 1662), in Morrice, *State Letters*, p. 63.

38 Richard Head, *The English Rogue Described, in the Life of Meriton Latroon*, 2 vols. (London, 1665), vol. I, p. xii.

39 Richard Head, *Hic et Ubique; or, the Humors of Dublin* (London, 1663), pp. 23, 18, 7.

40 Fraser and Rabkin (eds.), *Drama of the English Renaissance*, vol. II, p. 228.

41 Cited in Clark, *Early Irish Stage*, p. 69; Adair, *Presbyterian Church*, pp. 303–4.

42 'Smock Alley Prologues', f. 21.

43 Thomas Southerne, *The Works of Thomas Southerne*, E. Jordan and H. Love (eds.), 2 vols. (Oxford, 1988), vol. I, p. 153.

44 'Smock Alley Prologues', f. 4, f. 33.

A NIGHT AT THE THEATRE I

1 Philips, *Works*, vol. II, p. 47.
2 Katherine Philips, *Poems by the Most Deservedly Admired Mrs Katherine Philips, The Matchless Orinda. To which is Added Monsieur Corneille's Pompey and Horace, Tragedies* (London, 1667).
3 Katherine Philips, *Pompey. A Tragedy* (Dublin, 1663), p. ii.
4 Philips, *Poems*, n.p.
5 Philips, *Pompey*, p. ii.
6 Philips, *Poems*, n.p.
7 Philips, *Works*, vol. II, p. 75.
8 Philips, *Pompey*, p. 1.
9 *Ibid.*, pp. 2, 7, 23.
10 Philips, *Works*, vol. I, p. 75.
11 Philips, *Pompey*, pp. 15, 80, 81.

2 STAGE RIGHTS, 1691–1782

1 Samuel Garth, *The Prologue that Was Spoken at the Queen's Theatre in Dublin* (Dublin, 1712), n.p; *Lloyd's Newsletter* (8 Nov. 1712).
2 William Carleton, *The Life of William Carleton*, D. J. O'Donoghue (ed.), 2 vols. (London, 1896), vol. I, p. 28.
3 Robert Ashton, *The Battle of Aughrim: Or, the Fall of Monsieur St Ruth* (Dublin, 1728), p. 5.
4 John Michelburne, *Ireland Preserv'd; or, The Siege of London-Derry* (Belfast, 1744), p. 42.
5 John Locke, *Two Treatises of Government*, P. Laslett, (ed.) (Cambridge, 1963), p. 437.
6 William Molyneaux, *The Case of Ireland's Being Bound by Acts of Parliament in England, Stated*, in Seamus Deane (ed.), *Field Day Anthology of Irish Writing*, 3 vols. (Derry, 1991), vol. I, p. 872.
7 Cited in Clark, *Early Irish Stage*, p. 181.
8 John Dunton, *The Dublin Scuffle* (London, 1699), p. 339.
9 John C. Greene and Gladys Clark, *The Dublin Stage, 1720–1745* (Bethlehem, 1993), pp. 44–6.
10 George Farquhar, *The Works of George Farquhar*, Shirley Strum Kenny (ed.), 2 vols. (Oxford, 1988), vol. II, pp. 82, 380, 370.
11 *Ibid.*, vol. I, pp. 304, 197.
12 Shirley Strum Kenny, 'Farquhar, Wilks, and Wildair; or, the Metamorphosis of the "Fine Gentleman"', *Philological Quarterly*, 57:1 (Winter 1978), p. 50.
13 Greene and Clark, *Dublin Stage*, p. 45.
14 Charles Shadwell, *Rotherick O'Connor, King of Connaught, or the Distress'd Princess* (Dublin, 1720), pp. 267, 283.
15 William Philips, *Hibernia Freed: A Tragedy* (Dublin, 1722), p. 3. See also Joep Leerssen, *Mere Irish and Fíor-Ghael: Studies in the Idea of Irish Nationality, its*

Development and Literary Expression Prior to the Nineteenth Century (Cork, 1996), p. 326.

16 Shadwell, *Rotherick O'Connor*, p. 291.
17 Philips, *Hibernia Freed*, pp. 60–1.
18 G. C. Duggan, *The Stage Irishman* (Dublin, 1937), pp. 242–55. See also Leerssen, *Mere Irish*, pp. 77–202.
19 Farquhar, *Works*, vol. 1, pp. 5–6.
20 William Philips, *St Stephen's Green*, Christopher Murray (ed.) (Portlaoise, 1980), p. 103.
21 Charles Shadwell, *The Works of Mr Charles Shadwell*, 2 vols. (Dublin, 1720) vol. 1, p. 234.
22 Leerssen, *Mere Irish*, p. 116.
23 Thomas Sheridan, *The Brave Irishman; or, Captain O'Blunder: A Farce* (Belfast, 1761), pp. 11, 23.
24 Thomas Sheridan, *A Course of Lectures on Elocution* (London, 1762), pp. 175, 261. See Conrad Brunström, 'Thomas Sheridan and the Evil Ends of Writing', *New Hibernia Review*, 3:4 (Winter, 1999), pp. 130–42.
25 Esther K. Sheldon, *Thomas Sheridan of Smock Alley* (Princeton, 1967), p. 84.
26 Benjamin Victor, *The History of the Theatres of London and Dublin*, 2 vols. (London, 1761), vol. 1, pp. 97–8.
27 *The Gentleman* (Dublin 1747), pp. 8–9.
28 Thomas Sheridan, *An Humble Appeal to the Publick* (Dublin, 1758), p. 323.
29 Thomas Sheridan, *A Full Vindication of the Conduct of the Manager of the Theatre-Royal* (Dublin, 1747), pp. 12, 6.
30 Sheridan, *Humble Appeal*, p. 34.
31 George Stayley, *The Rival Theatres: Or, A Play-House to be Let* (Dublin, 1759) p. 8.
32 Sheridan, *Humble Appeal*, p. 86.
33 David Thomas (ed.), *Restoration and Georgian England, 1660–1788. Theatre in Europe: A Documentary History* (Cambridge, 1989), pp. 319–20.
34 *Dublin Journal* (25–7 Feb. 1772).
35 Jesse Foot, *The Life of Arthur Murphy, Esq.* (London, 1811) p. 34.
36 James T. Kirkman, *Memoirs of the Life of Charles Macklin, Esq.*, 2 vols. (London, 1799), vol. 1, p. 2.
37 William Appleton, *Charles Macklin* (Cambridge, Mass., 1960), pp. 120–1, 141.
38 Charles Macklin, *The True-Born Irishman, or the Irish Fine Lady* (Dublin, 1783), p. 8.
39 Charles Macklin, *Four Plays*, J. O. Bartley (ed.) (Hamden, Conn., 1968), pp. 58–9.
40 Christopher Wheatley, *Beneath Iërne's Banners: Irish Protestant Drama of the Restoration and Eighteenth Century* (South Bend, 1999), p. 169.
41 Leerssen, *Mere Irish*, pp. 150, 361.
42 Macklin, *True-Born Irishman*, p. 47.
43 Sheridan, *Humble Appeal*, p. 208.

44 Gorges Edmond Howard, *The Miscellaneous Works in Verse and Prose*, 2 vols. (Dublin, 1782), vol. I, p. 248; vol. II, p. 294.
45 Kirkman, *Memoirs*, vol. II, pp. 50–1.
46 Richard Brinsley Sheridan, *The Dramatic Works of Richard Brinsley Sheridan*, Cecil Price (ed.), 2 vols. (Oxford, 1973), vol. I, pp. 47, 49, 71. See Fintan O'Toole, *A Traitor's Kiss: The Life of Richard Brinsley Sheridan* (London, 1997) pp. 164–170, and Joep Leerssen, *Mere Irish*, pp. 144–8.
47 Sheridan, *Dramatic Works*, vol. I, p. 192.

A NIGHT AT THE THEATRE 2

1 Except where noted otherwise, accounts of the *Mahomet* riot have been taken from the following sources: Sheridan, *Humble Appeal*; Sheridan, *A Vindication*; and Victor, *The History of the Theatres*, vol II.
2 *An Address from the Independent Freeholders of the P—v—ce of M—ns—r, to Sir R— C— Baronet, With a Collection of Forty-Eight Original Patriot Toasts, Drank at a Select Assembly of Free-holders at Corke, the First of this Instant January, 1754* (London, 1754), p. 10.
3 Alicia LeFanu, *Memoirs of the Life and Writings of Mrs Frances Sheridan* (London, 1824), p. 53.
4 Voltaire, *Mahomet: The Impostor*, Dorothy Miller (trans.) (Dublin, n.d.), p. 25.
5 *A Grand Debate Between the Court and Country at the Theatre-Royal, in Smock-Alley* ([Dublin], 1754), p. 6.
6 *An Address from the Independent Electors of the Antient, Loyal and ever Memorable Town of Inniskillen . . . And 40 original Patriot Inniskillen Toasts* (Belfast, 1754), p. 28.
7 Voltaire, *Mahomet*, p. 8.
8 *Remarks on Two Letters Signed Theatricus and Hibernicus* (Dublin, 1754), p. 5.

3 'OUR NATIONAL THEATRE', 1782–1871

1 Lady Sydney Morgan, *Lady Morgan's Memoirs: Autobiography, Diaries and Correspondence*, 2 vols. (London, 1862), vol. II, pp. 23–4.
2 *Hibernian Journal* (24 Dec. 1784).
3 James Kelly, 'Parliamentary Reform in Irish Politics', in David Dickson, Dáire Keogh and Kevin Whelan (eds.), *The United Irishmen: Republicanism, Radicalism and Rebellion* (Dublin, 1993), p. 78.
4 W. S. Clark, *The Irish Stage in the Country Towns* (Oxford, 1965), p. 11.
5 John Home, *Douglas: A Tragedy* (Newry, 1786), pp. 38, 62.
6 Mary O'Brien, *The Fallen Patriot: A Comedy in Five Acts* (Dublin, 1794), p. 5.
7 *Freeman's Journal*, (24–8 Dec. 1784).
8 *Reasons for a Parliamentary Regulation of the Irish Stage* (Dublin, [*c.* 1786]), p. 1.
9 Clark, *Irish Stage in the Country Towns*, pp. 230, 103.
10 John O'Keeffe *Recollections of the Life of John O'Keeffe*, 2 vols. (London 1826), vol. I, p. 241; vol. II, p. 48; vol. I, pp. 119–20.

11 John O'Keeffe, *The Dramatic Works of John O'Keeffe, Esq.*, 2 vols. (London 1798), vol. I, p. 273.
12 Clark, *Country Towns*, p. 211; Charles Benson, '"Wild Oats" in New Ross: Theatre in an Irish Country Town, 1789–95', *Longroom* (Spring–Autumn, 1981), p. 15.
13 See: Karen J. Harvey and Kevin B. Pry, 'John O'Keeffe as an Irish Playwright Within the Theatrical, Social and Economic Context of his Time', *Éire/Ireland* 22:1 (Spring, 1987), pp. 19–43.
14 O'Keeffe, *Dramatic Works*, vol. II, pp. 153, 190.
15 T.C.D. [John Wilson Croker], *Familiar Epistles to Frederick Jones, Esq. on the Present State of the Irish Stage*, 3rd edn (Dublin, 1805), p. 30; Frederick Jones, *An Answer to Familiar Epistles to Frederick J—s, Esq.* (Dublin, 1804), pp. 22–3.
16 Anon., 'Journal: Sept. 19, 1800 to May 9, 1803', RIA Ms. 24.K.15, p. 65.
17 John Wilson Croker [attrib.], *The Amazoniad: Or, Figure and Fashion.* 2nd edn (Dublin 1806), p. 55.
18 *Theatrical Observer* (19 Jan. 1921).
19 *The Stage* (9 April 1821); *The Theatrical Observer* (8 Feb. 1821); *The Drama* (30 November 1821).
20 *The History of the Theatre Royal, Dublin, From its Foundation in 1821 to the Present Time* (Dublin, 1870), p. 147.
21 *Theatrical Observer* (7 March 1821).
22 *The Drama* (2 Jan. 1822).
23 Michael R. Booth, *Theatre in the Victorian Age* (Cambridge, 1991), p. 143.
24 Richard Lalor Sheil, *Adelaide: Or, The Emigrants* (Dublin, 1814), p. v.
25 John Banim, *Damon and Pythias* (London, 1821), p. 26.
26 Richard Lalor Sheil, *The Speeches of the Right Honourable Richard Lalor Sheil*, 2nd edn (Dublin, 1859), p. 397.
27 Charles Robert Maturin, *Bertram: Or, the Castle of St Aldobrand* (London, 1816), p. 26.
28 James Sheridan Knowles, *Brian Boroimhe: The King of Munster* (New York, 1828), pp. 26, 27, 40.
29 *Theatrical Observer* (28 April 1821); *The Stage* (28 April 1821).
30 Gerald D. Parker, '"I Am Going to America": James Sheridan Knowles' *Virginius* and the Politics of "Liberty"', *Theatre Research International* 17:1 (Spring, 1982), p. 15.
31 James Sheridan Knowles, *The 'Rock of Rome': Or, the Arch Heresy* (London, 1849), p. 243.
32 James Sheridan Knowles, 'Brian Boroimhe: The King of Munster', Prompt Book, Lafayette Theatre, New York (17 March 1870); Harvard Theatre Collection, Houghton Library, TS 2084.25.
33 *The Catholic Telegraph* (30 March 1861); (6 April 1861).
34 *The World* (19 Sept. 1890).
35 Dion Boucicault, *The Colleen Bawn*, Prompt Book, provenance unknown (*c.* 1860); Harvard Theatre Collection, Houghton Library, TS 3121.50, p. 1
36 Richard Fawkes, *Dion Boucicault: A Biography* (London, 1979), pp. 81–2.

37 Edmond Falconer, *Peep O' Day; or Savoureen Deelish*, Prompt Book, Barney Williams' Broadway Theatre, New York (17 Jan. 1868); Harvard Theatre Collection, Houghton Library TS 2512 50, p. 2.

38 *Ibid.*, pp. 25–6.

39 Dion Boucicault, *Arrah-na-Pogue; or, The Wicklow Wedding*, Prompt Book, Theatre Royal, Dublin (June 1864), Harvard Theatre Collection, Houghton Library TS 3055 45, p. 43.

A NIGHT AT THE THEATRE 3

1 Most of the material in this chapter is taken from testimony at the two trials and Parliamentary enquiry that followed the events of 14 December 1822. This testimony was widely published at the time. Four main sources are used here: *The Only Accurate and Impartial Report of the Trials of James Forbes, Henry Handwich, William Graham, Mathew Handwich, George Graham, and William Brownlow*, 2nd edn (Dublin, 1823); *A Report of the Speech of the Attorney General upon the Trial of James Forbes and Others* (Dublin, 1823); *House of Commons: Minutes of Evidence Taken Before the Committee of the Whole House* (Dublin, 1823); *The Williamites' Magazine; or Protestants' Advocate for Civil and Religious Liberty* (February–March, 1823).

2 Harcourt Lees, *An Address to the Orangemen of Ireland Relative to the Late Riot at the Theatre Royal, Hawkins Street* (Dublin, 1823), pp. 8–9.

3 Daniel O'Connell *The Correspondence of Daniel O'Connell*, Maurice R. O'Connell (ed.), 8 vols. (Dublin, 1972–80), vol. II, pp. 413, 427.

4 *Wilson's Dublin Directory for the Year 1823* (Dublin, 1823), p. 232.

5 *Williamite Scrap Book*, no. 1 (Dublin, 1823).

6 *Letters of 'An Old Juror' on the Late Ex-Officio Proceedings in the Court of King's Bench* (Dublin, 1823), p. 18.

4 'THAT CAPRICIOUS SPIRIT', 1871–1904

1 *Dublin Evening Mail* (1 Sept. 1871).

2 Joseph Holloway, *Souvenir of the Twenty-Fifth Anniversary of the Opening of the Gaiety Theatre, 27th November, 1871* (Dublin, 1896), p. 11.

3 Maire Nic Shiubhlaigh, *The Splendid Years* (Dublin, 1955), p. 7.

4 Dion Boucicault, *The Shaughraun*, in *Selected Plays of Dion Boucicault*, Andrew Parkin (ed.) (Gerrards Cross, 1987), p. 284.

5 Dion Boucicault, 'The Future American Drama', *The Arena*, 12 (November 1890), 647–8. See also: John P. Harrington, '"Rude Involvement": Boucicault, Dramatic Tradition, and Contemporary Politics', *Éire/Ireland*, 30:2 (Summer 1995), pp. 89–103.

6 Cheryl Herr (ed.), *For The Land They Loved: Irish Political Melodramas, 1890–1925* (Syracuse, 1991), p. 6.

7 Joseph Holloway, 'Diaries', NLI Ms. 1795, p. 98; NLI Ms. 1801, pp. 162–3.

8 *Ibid.*, NLI Ms 1797, pp. 397, 399.

9 Hubert O'Grady, *The Famine*, in Stephen Watt (ed.), *Journal of Irish Studies*, 14:1 (Winter 1985), p. 43.
10 Holloway, 'Diaries', NLI Ms. 1801, p. 162.
11 J. W. Whitbread, *'Wolfe Tone'*, in Herr (ed.), *For the Land They Loved*, p. 257.
12 Holloway, 'Diaries', NLI Ms 1796 (ii), p. 675.
13 *United Irishman* (4 March 1899).
14 St John Ervine, *The Theatre in My Time* (London, 1933), pp. 14–15.
15 Thomas Carnduff, 'I Remember', *The Bell*, 5:4 (Dec. 1943), pp. 279–80.
16 Lady Gregory, *Our Irish Theatre: A Chapter of Autobiography* (Gerrards Cross, 1972), p. 19.
17 W. B. Yeats, *The Collected Letters of W. B. Yeats*, John Kelly and Eric Domville (eds.), vol. I (Oxford, 1986), pp. 384, 386.
18 Local Government Act, 1898 (61 and 62 Vict.); chap. 37; section 89 (1 and 2).
19 Gregory, *Our Irish Theatre*, p. 20.
20 *The Complete Letters of J. M. Synge*, Ann Saddlemyer (ed.), 2 vols. (Oxford, 1983), vol. I, p. 74.
21 *Beltaine* (May 1899).
22 *Samhain* (October 1901).
23 Gregory, *Our Irish Theatre*, pp. 267, 269.
24 O'Grady, *Famine*, 49.
25 W. B. Yeats, *The Variorum Edition of the Plays of W. B. Yeats*, Russell K. Alspach (ed.) (London, 1966), p. 176.
26 Holloway, 'Diaries', NLI Ms 1798, p. 339.
27 Joseph Holloway, 'Irish Drama in Modern Dublin', *Irish Playgoer* (12 April 1900), p. 13.
28 George Moore and Edward Martyn, *Selected Plays of George Moore and Edward Martyn*, David B. Eakin and Michael Case (eds.) (Gerrards Cross, 1995), p. 220.
29 Cited in Hugh Hunt, *The Abbey: Ireland's National Theatre 1904–1979* (Dublin, 1979), p. 29.
30 *United Irishman* (26 Oct. 1901).
31 Joseph Holloway, 'The Art of Gazing into Space As Witnessed in *The Bending of the Bough*', *Irish Playgoer* (1 March 1900), p. 3.
32 *Samhain* (Oct. 1902).
33 Nic Shiubhlaigh, *Splendid Years*, p. 9.
34 W. B. Yeats, *The Collected Letters of W. B. Yeats*, John Kelly and Ronald Suchard (eds.), vol. III, (Oxford, 1994), p. 185.
35 Certificate of copyright registration; Harvard Theatre Collection, Houghton Library, bms Thr 24, (218).
36 Robert Hogan and Michael J. O'Neill (eds.), *Joseph Holloway's Irish Theatre: A Selection from his Unpublished Journal, 'Impressions of an Irish Playgoer'* (Carbondale, London and Amsterdam, 1967), p. 17.
37 J. M. Synge, *Collected Works*, Ann Saddlemyer (ed.), 4 vols. (London, 1968), vol. III, p. 57. See Nicholas Grene, *The Politics of Irish Drama: Plays in Context from Boucicault to Friel* (Cambridge, 1999), pp. 72–6.

38 Hogan and O'Neill (eds.), *Holloway*, p. 27; *The Leader* (17 Oct. 1903).
39 *United Irishman* (24 Oct. 1903); (10 Oct. 1903); (17 Oct. 1903).
40 Yeats, *Collected Letters*, vol. III, p. 450.
41 *United Irishman* (19 Dec. 1903).
42 Annie Horniman to George Roberts (1 Jan. 1904); Harvard Theatre Collection, Houghton Library, bms Thr 24 (98).
43 Yeats, *Collected Letters*, vol. III, p. 563.
44 Annie Horniman to George Roberts (12 May 1904); Harvard Theatre Collection, Houghton Library, bms Thr 24 (109).
45 Yeats, *Collected Letters*, vol. III, p. 573; Annie Horniman to George Roberts (28 Nov. 1904), Harvard Theatre Collection, Houghton Library, bms Thr 24 (114); *Universe* (14 Jan. 1905).
46 *United Irishman* (10 Oct. 1903).

A NIGHT AT THE THEATRE 4

1 Ann Saddlemyer (ed.), *Theatre Business: The Correspondence of the First Abbey Theatre Directors* (Gerrards Cross, 1982), p. 205.
2 Robert Hogan and James Kilroy (eds.), *The Abbey Theatre: The Years of Synge 1905–1909, The Modern Irish Drama*, vol. III (Dublin 1978), p. 123.
3 Saddlemyer (ed.), *Theatre Business*, p. 205.
4 *The Arrow* (24 November 1906).
5 Hogan and O'Neill (eds.), *Holloway*, p. 82.
6 R. F. Foster, *W.B. Yeats: A Life*, vol. I: *The Apprentice Mage* (Oxford and New York, 1997), p. 360.
7 Yeats, *Collected Letters*, vol. III, p. 642.
8 Hogan and Kilroy (eds.), *Years of Synge*, pp. 32–3.
9 Gregory, *Our Irish Theatre*, p. 68.
10 Saddlemyer (ed.), *Theatre Business*, p. 214.
11 Foster, *W.B. Yeats*, p. 365.
12 Saddlemyer (ed.), *Theatre Business*, p. 213.
13 Hogan and Kilroy (eds.), *Years of Synge*, p. 52.
14 *The Abbey Row* (Dublin, 1907), p. 10.

5 NOT UNDERSTANDING THE CLOCK, 1904–1921

1 *To-Day* (4 January 1904).
2 *An Claidheamh Soluis* (16 June 1906).
3 W. B. Yeats, *Explorations* (London, 1962), p. 252.
4 *United Irishman* (26 April 1902).
5 *Daily Express* (16 March 1903).
6 Cited in Hunt, *Abbey Theatre*, p. 45.
7 Eye-level in theatre architecture is considered to be horizontal plus 5 degrees. See Iain Mackintosh, *Architecture, Actor and Audience* (London and New York, 1993), p. 135.

8 Stephen Gwynn to George Roberts (15 Feb. 1904), Harvard Theatre Collection, Houghton Library, bms Thr 23 (44).
9 Lady Gregory to Thomas Keohler (30 Jan. 1905), Harvard Theatre Collection, Houghton Library, bms Thr 24 (18).
10 Terence Brown, *The Life of W.B. Yeats* (Dublin, 1999), p. 161
11 George Bernard Shaw, 'Preface to *The Shewing Up of Blanco Posnet*' in *The Bodley Head Bernard Shaw*, 7 vols. (London, 1971), vol. III, p. 698.
12 *Bodley Head Shaw*, vol. II, p. 808.
13 *Bodley Head Shaw*, vol. III, p. 774.
14 *An Claidheamh Soluis* (20 Aug. 1909).
15 Robert Hogan, Richard Burham and Daniel P. Poteet (eds.), *The Rise of the Realists, The Modern Irish Drama*, vol. IV (Dublin, 1979), p. 21.
16 Abbey Theatre Account Books, Harvard Theatre Collection, Houghton Library, bms Thr 24 (217); Abbey Theatre Account Books, NLI Ms. 19,849.
17 Cited in Liam Miller, *The Noble Drama of W. B. Yeats* (Dublin, 1977), p. 148.
18 John P. Harrington, *The Irish Play on the New York Stage 1874–1966* (Lexington, 1997), pp. 70–1.
19 W. B. Yeats, 'The Abbey Theatre', Theatre Programme, Abbey Theatre (4 Sept. 1908).
20 Maurice Bourgeois to W. A. Henderson, (24 June 1912), Abbey Scrapbooks, vol. 7 (Jan. to June, 1912), NLI Ms. P8132.
21 Lennox Robinson, *Curtain Up: An Autobiography* (London, 1942), p. 16; Ervine, *Theatre in my Time*, p. 94.
22 Donald Campbell, *Playing for Scotland: A History of the Scottish Stage 1715–1965* (Edinburgh, 1996), p. 92.
23 Sam Hannah Bell, *The Theatre in Ulster* (Dublin, 1972), p. 2.
24 *Uladh* (Nov. 1904).
25 Lewis Purcell, *The Enthusiast*, *Uladh* (May 1905), 33.
26 Bell, *Theatre in Ulster*, p. 25.
27 St John Ervine, *Selected Plays*, John Cronin (ed.) (Gerrards Cross, 1988), pp. 50, 54; see: Joe Cleary, 'Domestic Troubles: Tragedy and the Northern Ireland Conflict', *South Atlantic Quarterly*, 98:3 (Summer 1999), pp. 507–11; see also Christopher Murray, *Twentieth-Century Irish Drama: Mirror Up to Nation* (Manchester, 1997), p. 192.
28 Robinson, *Curtain Up*, p. 18.
29 Patrick Maume, *Life that is Exile: Daniel Corkery and the Search for Irish Ireland* (Belfast, 1993), pp. 20–1.
30 Terence MacSwiney, *The Revolutionist* (Dublin and London, 1914), p. 5.
31 T. C. Murray, *Selected Plays*, Richard Allen Cave (ed.) (Gerrards Cross, 1998), p. 35.
32 Lennox Robinson, *Selected Plays*, Christopher Murray (ed.) (Gerrards Cross, 1982), p. 56.
33 Maume, *Corkery*, p. 37.
34 W. I. Thompson, *The Imagination of an Insurrection* (New York, 1967), p. 118.
35 Hogan and O'Neill (eds.), *Holloway*, p. 178.

36 Lady Gregory, *Seventy Years: Being the Autobiography of Lady Gregory*, Colin Smythe (ed.) (Gerrards Cross, 1972), p. 549.
37 Herr (ed.), *For the Land They Loved*, p. 308
38 Joseph Holloway, 'Diaries', NLI Ms. 1823, P. 961.
39 Luke Gibbons, John Hill and Kevin Rockett, *Cinema and Ireland* (Syracuse, 1988), pp. 12–15.
40 *Weekly Freeman's Journal* (15 October 1910).
41 John Stokes, 'Prodigals and Proligates', *New Theatre Quarterly* (Feb. 1999), pp. 27–9.
42 Hogan and O'Neill (eds.), *Holloway*, p. 188.
43 *Bodley Head Shaw*, vol. II, pp. 905, 925.
44 Yeats, *Explorations*, p. 254.
45 Cited in Brown, *Life of W. B. Yeats*, p. 242
46 Yeats, *Plays*, pp. 773–4, 775.
47 Yeats, *Explorations*, p. 244.
48 Lady Gregory, *Collected Plays*, Ann Saddlemyer (ed.), 4 vols. (Gerrards Cross, 1979), vol. I, p. 63.
49 *Irish Times* (11 March 1907).
50 Gregory, *Collected Plays*, vol. III, pp. 266–7.
51 Lady Gregory, *Journals*, vol. I, Daniel J. Murphy (ed.) (Gerrards Cross, 1978), p. 224.
52 Hogan and O'Neill (eds.), *Holloway*, p. 209.

A NIGHT AT THE THEATRE 5

1 W. B. Yeats to Sean O'Casey (1 Aug. 1925), NLI Ms. 27, 027 (8).
2 Robert Hogan (ed.), *The Years of O'Casey 1921–1926*, *The Modern Irish Drama*, vol. VI (Dublin, 1992), p. 277.
3 Sean O'Casey, *The Letters of Sean O'Casey*, vol. I: *1910–1941*, David Krause (ed.) (Washington, 1975), p. 144.
4 Sean O'Casey, *Three Plays* (London, 1980), p. 179.
5 O'Casey, *Letters*, vol. I, pp. 146–7.
6 Hogan and O'Neill (eds.), *Holloway*, p. 246.
7 *An Phoblacht* (15 January 1926).
8 O'Casey, *Letters*, vol. I, p. 285.
9 Hogan (ed.), *Years of O'Casey*, pp. 251, 294.
10 Cumann na mBan Minute Book (19 Dec. 1925 to 4 Nov. 1926), Sighle Humphreys Papers, UCD Ms. P106/1107. Entries for 19 Dec. 1925; 26 Dec. 1925; 28 Jan. 1926.
11 Sean O'Casey, *Autobiographies*, 2 vols. (New York, 1984), vol. II, p. 149.
12 O'Casey, *Three Plays*, p. 162.
13 O'Casey, *Autobiographies*, vol. II, p. 149.
14 Hunt, *Abbey Theatre*, pp. 128–9.
15 *Irish Independent* (12 Feb. 1926).
16 Rosamund Jacobs Papers, NLI, Ms. 32,582 (51), p. 34.

17 Hogan and O'Neill (eds.), *Holloway*, pp. 256, 258.
18 Jacobs Papers, p. 42.
19 *An Phoblacht* (19 February 1926).
20 Jacobs Papers, p. 41.
21 *Catholic Bulletin* (March 1926).
22 *Voice of Labour* (20 February 1926).

6 AFTERMATH, 1922–1951

1 Richard Allen Cave, 'Introduction', *Selected Plays of T.C. Murray* (Gerrards Cross, 1998), p. xvi.
2 Terence Brown, *Ireland: A Social and Cultural History, 1922–1985* (London, 1981), p. 13.
3 *United Irishman* (12 April 1902).
4 Hogan and O'Neill (eds.), *Holloway*, p. 212.
5 O'Casey, *Three Plays*, p. 110.
6 Denis Johnston, 'Plays of the Quarter', *The Bell*, 2:1 (April 1942), p. 90.
7 Gregory, *Journals*, vol. I, p. 445.
8 Robert Hogan (ed.), *Feathers from a Green Crow* (London, 1963), p. 293.
9 O'Casey, *Autobiographies*, vol. II, p. 100.
10 O'Casey, *Three Plays*, pp. 72–3.
11 Stephen Watt, *Joyce, O'Casey and the Irish Popular Theatre* (Syracuse, 1991), pp. 176–84.
12 Harold Pinter, *Mac* (London, 1968), p. 17.
13 Pinter, *Mac*, p. 13.
14 Micheál Mac Líammóir, *All for Hecuba* (London, 1946), p. 27.
15 Micheál Mac Líammóir, *Enter a Goldfish* (London, 1977), p. 190.
16 Bulmer Hobson (ed.), *The Gate Theatre, Dublin* (Dublin, 1934), p. 22.
17 *Motley*, 2:2 (Feb. 1933).
18 Brenna Katz Clarke and Harold Ferrar, *The Dublin Drama League, 1918–1941* (Dublin, 1979), p. 14.
19 *Irish Times* (13 January 1936).
20 Joseph Holloway, 'Diaries', NLI Ms. 1798, p. 462.
21 Oscar Wilde, *The Works of Oscar Wilde* (Leicester, 1987), p. 972.
22 See Richard Pine, *The Thief of Reason: Oscar Wilde and Modern Ireland* (Dublin, 1995), pp. 381–404; also Norbert Kohl, *Oscar Wilde: The Works of a Conformist Rebel* (Cambridge, 1989), p. 318.
23 Julia Carlson (ed.), *Banned in Ireland: Censorship and the Irish Writer* (London, 1990), pp. 132–3, 135.
24 Richard Ellmann, *Oscar Wilde* (Harmondsworth, 1987), p. 351.
25 Wilde, *Works*, pp. 544–5.
26 Hobson (ed.), *Gate*, p. 26.
27 R. S. Devane, 'Suggested Tariff on Imported Newspapers and Magazines', *Studies*, 16:63 (December 1927), p. 552.
28 Mac Líammóir, *All for Hecuba*, p. 71.

29 Wilde, *Works*, pp. 325, 369.
30 *Irish Monthly* 44:762 (Dec. 1936), p. 836 and 66:779 (May 1938), p. 342.
31 Miller, *Noble Drama*, p. 284; Robert Hogan and Michael J. O'Neill, *Joseph Holloway's Irish Theatre*, vol. 1 : *1926–1931* (Dixon, California, 1968), p. 51.
32 W. B. Yeats, *The Letters of W. B. Yeats*, Allan Wade (ed.) (London, 1954), p. 913.
33 Paul Vincent Carroll, *Shadow and Substance* (New York, 1937), p. 91.
34 *The Bell*, 1:2 (Nov. 1940), p. 82.
35 Teresa Deevy, 'The King of Spain's Daughter', Abbey Theatre Collection, NLI Ms. 29,171, p. 17.
36 Teresa Deevy to Matthew O'Mahony (n.d.), O'Mahony Papers, NLI Ms. 24,900.
37 George Shiels to Matthew O'Mahony (8 March 1946), O'Mahony Papers.
38 *The Bell*, 15:2 (Nov. 1947), p. 63.
39 St John Ervine to Matthew O'Mahony (17 Oct. 1958), O'Mahony Papers.
40 *The Bell*, 9:1 (Oct. 1944), p. 68.
41 *Irish News and Belfast Morning News* (11 May 1932).
42 Thomas Carnduff, 'Machinery', Linenhall Library Ts., p. 6. By permission of Noel Carnduff.
43 Ophelia Byrne, *The Stage in Ulster from the Eighteenth Century* (Belfast, 1997), p. 45.
44 CEMA, *Annual Report 1944–5* (Belfast, 1945), p. 7.
45 *Envoy*, I:4 (March 1950), p. 78.
46 Hunt, *Abbey Theatre*, p. 173.
47 *The Bell*, 15:4 (January 1948), p. 29.

A NIGHT AT THE THEATRE 6

1 Samuel Beckett, 'Waiting for Godot', TCD Ms 10730a/1, p. 1.
2 For the justness of this reputation see: Jonathan Kalb, *Beckett in Performance* (Cambridge, 1989), pp. 149–54, and James Knowlson, *Damned to Fame: A Life of Samuel Beckett* (London, 1996), pp. 691–6.
3 Samuel Beckett to Alan Simpson (17 Nov. 1953); Pike Theatre Collection, TCD Ms. 10730.
4 Alan Simpson, *Beckett and Behan and a Theatre in Dublin* (London, 1978), pp. 121, 123; Samuel Beckett, 'Waiting for Godot', Pike Theatre Collection, TCD Ms. 10730, 78, 83; Alan Simpson to John Axon (18 July 1956), Pike Theatre Collection, TCD Ms. 10813/398/102.
5 Carolyn Swift, *Stage by Stage* (Dublin, 1985), p. 107.
6 Samuel Beckett to Thomas MacGreevy (14 Dec. 1953); MacGreevy Papers, TCD Ms. 10402.
7 Beckett to Simpson (17 Nov. 1953), Pike Theatre Collection, TCD Ms. 10730.
8 Beckett to Simpson (May 1955), Pike Theatre Collection, TCD Ms. 10730.
9 Simpson, *Beckett and Behan*, pp. 131–2.
10 *Ibid.*, p. 134.
11 Knowlson, *Damned to Fame*, p. 378.

12 *The Stage* (3 Nov. 1955).
13 *Dublin Magazine* (Jan./March 1956).
14 Samuel Beckett, 'The Essential and the Incidental', *Disjecta,* Ruby Cohn (ed.) (London, 1983), p. 82.
15 Simpson, *Beckett and Behan*, p. 124
16 *Ibid.*, pp. 124–5; Samuel Beckett, *Waiting for Godot* (New York, 1956), p. 16.
17 Simpson, *Beckett and Behan*, p. 129.
18 *Irish Times* (29 Oct. 1955).
19 *Irish Times* (20 Nov. 1955).
20 *Pike Theatre Club Newsletter*, no. 11 (n.d.), Pike Theatre Collection, TCD Ms.10813/383/11.
21 *Times Literary Supplement* (10 Feb. 1956); *Irish Independent* (29 Oct. 1955); *Irish Times* (14 Nov. 1955).
22 Michael George, 'Profile: Samuel Beckett', *Irish Tatler and Sketch* (Feb. 1956); cf. 'The postmodern would be that which, in the modern, puts forward the unpresentable in presentation itself . . . that which searches for new presentations, not in order to enjoy them but in order to impart a stronger sense of the unpresentable', Jean-François Lyotard, *The Postmodern Condition* (Minneapolis, 1984), p. 81.
23 Walter Macken, *Twilight of the Warrior* (London 1956), p. 57.
24 *Irish Times* (18 Feb. 1956); *Dublin Magazine* (Jan./March 1956).
25 Pike Theatre, Royalty Statement for *Waiting for Godot* to 17 June 1956, Pike Theatre Collection, TCD Ms. 10730.

7 PHOENIX FLAMES, 1951–1972

1 *Irish Times* (6 April 1953).
2 *Irish Times* (24 Sept. 1964).
3 M. J. Molloy, *Selected Plays* Robert O'Driscoll (ed.) (Gerrard's Cross, 1998), pp. 129, 136, 111, 169.
4 Gus Smith, *Festival Glory in Athlone* (Dublin, 1977), p. 32.
5 John B. Keane, *Self-Portrait* (Cork, 1964), p. 92
6 Tom Murphy, *Plays: 4* (London, 1989), p. 180.
7 Murphy, *Plays: 4*, p. 7.
8 Fintan O'Toole, *Tom Murphy: The Politics of Magic* (Dublin and London, 1994), p. 12.
9 Murphy, *Plays: 4*, p. 86.
10 O'Toole, *Politics of Magic*, p. 11; *The Times* (12 Sept. 1961).
11 Macken, *Twilight*, p. 48.
12 Roger McHugh, 'Tradition and the Future of Irish Drama', *Studies* (Winter 1951), p. 471.
13 Gabriel Fallon, 'The Future of the Irish Theatre', *Studies* (Spring 1955), p. 99.
14 John Jordan, 'Comic Strip at the Abbey', *Hibernia* (May 1961), p. 23.

15 Blythe Papers, UCD P24/70.
16 Ernest Blythe, *The Abbey Theatre* (Dublin, 1963), pp. 22–3.
17 Louis D'Alton, *This Other Eden* (Dublin, 1954), pp. 8, 90.
18 Thomas Kilroy, 'Groundwork for an Irish Theatre', *Studies* (Summer 1959), p. 195.
19 Ulick O'Connor, 'Dublin: Decline and Fall', *The Listener* (19 April 1956), p. 446.
20 Maurice Meldon, *Aisling: A Dream Analysis* (Dublin, 1959), p. 75.
21 *Irish Times* (20 Nov. 1954).
22 *Irish Times* (1 March 1955).
23 Brendan Behan, *Two Plays* (New York, 1964), p. 21.
24 Swift, *Stage by Stage*, p. 300.
25 Samuel Beckett to Carolyn Swift (27 Feb. 1958); and Samuel Beckett to Alan Simpson (7 May 1960), Pike Theatre Collection, TCD Ms. 10730.
26 John Keyes, 'Introduction', *Over the Bridge and Other Plays*, by Sam Thompson, John Keyes (ed.) (Belfast, 1997), p. 11.
27 *Belfast News-Letter* (15 March 1960).
28 Ervine, *Selected Plays*, p. 54; Thompson, *Over the Bridge*, p. 23.
29 Keyes, 'Introduction', *Over the Bridge*, p. 12.
30 David Thornley, 'Ireland: The End of An Era?' *Studies* (Spring 1964), p. 15.
31 *Irish Times* (24 Sept. 1964).
32 Eugene McCabe, *King of the Castle* (Oldcastle, County Meath, 1997), p. 69.
33 Brian Friel, 'The Theatre of Hope and Despair', *Everyman* (1968), p. 21.
34 Samuel Beckett, 'Kilcool', Samuel Beckett Collection, TCD Ms. 4664.
35 For Beckett's uses of the Kilcool manuscript, see: S. E. Gontarski, *The Intent of Undoing in Samuel Beckett's Dramatic Texts* (Bloomington, 1985), pp. 131–49.
36 Michael Scott, *Michael Scott, Architect in (Casual) Conversation with Dorothy Walker* (Kinsale, 1995), p. 166.
37 Mackintosh, *Architecture, Actor and Audience*, p. 84.
38 *Irish Times* (18 July 1966).
39 *Irish Times* (22 Sept. 1965).
40 Christopher Murray, 'Beckett Productions in Ireland: A Survey', *Irish University Review*, 14:1 (Spring 1984), p. 115.
41 Cristóir Ó Floinn, *Consplawkus: A Writer's Life* (Cork, 1999), p. 296.
42 John Devitt, personal comment (3 Sept. 1999).
43 O'Toole, *Politics of Magic*, p. 112.
44 Seamus Deane, interview with the author (March, 1986).
45 Tomás Mac Anna and John D. Stewart, 'A State of Chassis', Abbey Theatre Collection, NLI Ms. 29, 578 (D), p. 14.
46 *Irish Times* (17 Sept. 1970).
47 Hugh Leonard, *Selected Plays*, S. F. Gallagher (ed.) (Gerrards Cross, 1992), pp. 159, 140.
48 Tom Murphy, *Plays: 3* (London, 1994), pp. 17, 77, 50.

A NIGHT AT THE THEATRE 7

1 *Londonderry Journal* (22 May 1789), in Clark, *Country Towns*, p. 206.
2 *Belfast Telegraph* (2 Oct. 1980); Marilyn Richtarik, *Acting Between the Lines: The Field Day Theatre Company and Irish Cultural Politics, 1980–1984* (Oxford, 1995), pp. 15–18.
3 Marilyn Richtarik to the author (June 2000).
4 *Sunday Independent* (5 Oct. 1980).
5 *Irish Times* (10 Oct. 1980).
6 *Irish Press* (13 Jan. 1981); *Sunday Independent* (12 Oct. 1980); *Belfast Telegraph* (24 Sept. 1980).
7 Brian Friel, *Selected Plays* (London, 1984), p. 419.
8 *Evening Herald* (24 Sept. 1980).
9 *Derry People* (27 Sept. 1980).
10 Friel, *Selected Plays*, p. 420.
11 *Derry Journal* (23 Sept. 1980).
12 Friel, *Selected Plays*, p. 445.
13 *Derry Journal* (26 Sept. 1980).
14 *Irish Times* (15 Jan. 1981).
15 Brian Friel, *Essays, Diaries, Interviews: 1964–1999*, Christopher Murray (ed.), (London, 1999), p. 75.
16 Friel, *Essays, Diaries, Interviews*, p. 74.
17 *An Phoblacht* (11 Oct. 1980).
18 Seamus Heaney, '. . . English and Irish', *Times Literary Supplement* (24 Oct. 1980), p. 1199.
19 J. H. Andrews, Kevin Barry and Brian Friel, 'Translations and a Paper Landscape', *Crane Bag*, 7,2 (1983), pp. 120, 123.
20 Richard Kearney, 'Language Play: Brian Friel and Ireland's Verbal Theatre', *Studies* (Spring 1983), p. 27.
21 Richtarik, *Acting Between the Lines*, p. 65.
22 *Sunday Independent* (5 Oct. 1980).

8 BABEL, 1972–2000

1 Frank McGuinness, *Plays: 1* (London, 1996), p. xi.; *Irish Times* (31 Jan. 1972).
2 Friel, *Essays, Diaries, Interviews*, pp. 55–6.
3 Christopher Fitz-Simon, *The Boys: A Biography of Micheál Mac Líammóir and Hilton Edwards* (London, 1994), p. 291.
4 Conor O'Malley, *A Poet's Theatre* (Dublin, 1988), p. 65.
5 O'Malley, *Poet's Theatre*, p. 61.
6 See Murray, *Twentieth-Century Irish Drama*, pp. 190–1.
7 John Boyd, *Collected Plays I* (Dundonald, 1981), p. ix.
8 Boyd, *Plays I*, pp. 7, 85.
9 Seamus Deane, *Celtic Revivals* (London and Boston, 1985), p. 111.
10 Ulick O'Connor, *Brian Friel: Crisis and Commitment: The Writer and Northern*

Ireland (Dublin, 1989), p. 7. Box-office figures for *Freedom of the City* are courtesy of Mairead Delaney, Abbey Theatre Archivist.

11 Friel, *Selected Plays*, pp. 150, 121.
12 *Irish Times* (26 Sept. 1983).
13 Peter Sheridan, 'The Theatre and Politics', *Crane Bag Book of Irish Studies* (Dublin, 1982), p. 75.
14 Mary O'Malley, 'Foreword', *Threshold* (Spring 1973), 1–2.
15 Hugh Leonard, *Da/A Life/Time Was* (Harmondsworth, 1981), pp. 184, 206, 196.
16 O'Toole, *Politics of Magic*, p. 185.
17 *Irish Times* (10 Oct. 1975).
18 Tom Kilroy, *Talbot's Box* (Dublin, 1979), pp. ii, 63.
19 Friel, *Selected Plays*, p. 333.
20 Friel, *Essays, Diaries, Interviews*, p. 179.
21 Seamus Deane, 'The Longing for Modernity,' *Threshold* (Winter 1982), p. 1.
22 Declan Kiberd, *Anglo-Irish Attitudes* (Derry, 1984), p. 93.
23 Thomas Kilroy, *Double Cross* (London, 1986), p. 6.
24 Terence Brown in Richtarik, *Acting Between the Lines*, p. 185.
25 *Irish Times* (28 Sept. 1982); Jerome Hynes (ed.) *Druid: The First Ten Years* (Galway, 1985), p. 48.
26 Fintan O'Toole, 'The Juno Phenomenon', *Theatre Ireland*, 13 (1987), p. 18.
27 *Irish Times* (26 Sept. 1983).
28 Patrick Kavanagh and Tom Mac Intyre, *The Great Hunger: Poem Into Play* (Dublin, 1988), p. 4.
29 Tom Mac Intyre, 'The Great Hunger', Rehearsal Script, Mac Intyre Papers, NLI Ms 33,560/8, p. 31.
30 Desmond Bell, 'Ireland Without Frontiers? The Challenge of the Communications Revolution', *Across the Frontiers: Ireland in the 1990s*, Richard Kearney (ed.) (Dublin, 1988), p. 228.
31 Murphy, *Plays: 3*, p. 240.
32 Lynda Henderson, 'A Fondness for Lament', *Theatre Ireland*, 17 (December 1988/March 1989), p. 19.
33 Murphy, *Bailegangaire* (Dublin, 1986), p. 76.
34 *Irish Times* (7 Feb. 1985).
35 Stewart Parker, *Three Plays for Ireland* (London, 1989), pp. 9, 208.
36 Anthony Roche, *Contemporary Irish Drama: From Beckett to McGuinness* (Dublin, 1994), p. 277.
37 McGuinness, *Plays: 1*, pp. 342, 378–9.
38 Christina Reid, *Plays: 1* (London, 1997), p. 343.
39 *Irish Times* (12 Feb. 2000).
40 Claudia W. Harris, 'Reinventing Women: Charabanc Theatre Company', in Eberhard Bort (ed.), *State of Play: Irish Theatre in the 'Nineties* (Trier, 1996), p. 114.
41 Reid, *Plays: 1*, pp. 57, 59.

42 Victoria White, 'Cathleen ni Houlihan is not a Playwright', *Theatre Ireland*, 30 (Winter 1993), p. 26.
43 Brian Friel, *Plays: 2* (London, 1999), pp. 7, 108.
44 Marina Carr, *The Mai* (Oldcastle, 1995), p. 72.
45 Sebastian Barry, *Plays: 1* (London, 1997), pp. 252, 250, 246, 263, 301.
46 Jim Nolan, *The Salvage Shop* (Oldcastle, 1998), p. 34.
47 Billy Roche, *The Wexford Trilogy* (London, 1992), p. 187.
48 *Irish Times* (26 April 1997).
49 Vic Merriman, 'Decolonisation: The Theatre of Tiger Trash', *Irish University Review*, 29:2 (Autumn/Winter 1999), pp. 315, 317.
50 *Guardian* (2 Dec. 1996).
51 Martin McDonagh, *Plays: 1* (London, 1999), pp. 134, 67.

CONCLUSION. A MILLENNIAL FLOURISH

1 Roger Doyle, *Angel/Babel*, performed by Olwen Fouere of Operating Theatre, The Mint, Dublin (24 March 1999). Video recording of performance courtesy of Roger Doyle.
2 *To-Day* (4 Jan. 1905); *Envoy* (March 1950).
3 *Irish Times* (10 Oct. 1980).

Bibliographic essay

Irish theatre history is a curiously lopsided discipline. There are some areas – Irish theatre architecture, stage design, nineteenth-century repertoire, theatre finance – for which only the scantiest secondary literature exists, even where there is plenty of primary material. Conversely, there are areas – the early Abbey, anything to do with Yeats, Synge, O'Casey or Beckett – for which many primary sources have been published, and for which the secondary literature is correspondingly daunting in quantity and quality. Consequently, what follows makes no claims to exhaustiveness. Instead, it is intended as a guide, through both barrens and thickets.

SEVENTEENTH CENTURY

The starting point for the study of the early modern Irish stage is Alan Fletcher's *Drama, Performance, and Polity in Pre-Cromwellian Ireland* (Toronto and Cork, 2000), a superbly documented account of all forms of performance in Ireland from the seventh century to 1640. Equally foundational and scholarly is W. S. Clark's *The Early Irish Stage: The Beginnings to 1720* (Oxford, 1955); more anecdotal is La Tourette Stockwell, *Dublin Theatres and Theatre Customs (1637–1820)* (Kingsport, Tenn., 1938). Breaking new ground in our understanding of the drama of the period is Christopher Wheatley's *Beneath Iërne's Banners: Irish Protestant Drama of the Restoration and Eighteenth Century* (South Bend, 1999). Wheatley and Kevin J. Donovan are also preparing an edition of early Irish plays from the period, many hitherto available only in rare original editions. Although frustrating at times, Peter Kavanagh's *The Irish Theatre* (Tralee, 1946), attempts to be exhaustive in its list of Irish plays, and is strongest on the late seventeenth and eighteenth centuries. The only book to cover the same period as the current study, Christopher Fitz-Simon's *Irish Theatre* (London, 1983) is the best source of visual material for the study of theatre in Ireland.

Most studies of the first playwright to write for the Irish stage, James Shirley, treat his years in Dublin as a wilderness period, although one exception is Sandra Burner's *James Shirley: A Study of Literary Coteries and Patronage in Seventeenth-Century England* (New York, 1988). The best accounts of Burnell and Burkhead are Catherine M. Shaw, '*Landgartha* and the Irish Dilemma', *Éire/Ireland*, 13:1 (Winter 1978), 26–39 and Patricia Coughlan, ' "Enter Revenge": Henry Burkhead and *Cola's Furie*', *Theatre Research International*, 15:1 (Spring 1990), 1–17. There is a standard edition of Orrery's works edited by the ubiquitous W. S. Clark: *The Dramatic Works of Roger Boyle*, 2 vols. (Cambridge, Mass., 1937), and a growing body of critical writing on Philips, of which the best account of her stage work is: Catherine Cole Mambretti, 'Orinda on the Restoration Stage', *Comparative Literature*, 37:3 (Summer 1985), 233–51. Also see: Nancy Klein Maguire, 'Regicide and Reparation: The Autobiographical Drama of Roger Boyle, Earl of Orrery', *ELR*, 21:2 (Spring 1991), 257–82.

EIGHTEENTH CENTURY

In the eighteenth century, the paper trail for Irish theatre history grows considerably deeper, and there is a large primary archive of pamphlets, scripts and newspaper references, of which there is a good listing in James J. O'Neill, *A Bibliographical Account of Irish Theatrical Literature* (Dublin, 1920). This is the period in which the first Irish theatre historians begin to write. William R. Chetwood's *A General History of the Stage* (London, 1749), Benjamin Victor's *The History of the Theatres of London and Dublin*, 2 vols. (London, 1761) and Robert Hitchcock's *Historical View of the Irish Stage*, 2 vols. (Dublin, 1788–94) are all rich in detail, anecdote, and eyewitness accounts, although their statements of fact often need to be checked.

W. S. Clark's *Early Irish Stage* is as essential here as it is for the earlier period, while his *The Irish Stage in the Country Towns: 1720–1800* (Oxford, 1965) picks up where his earlier work leaves off, *albeit* with a different focus. Clark's work built on the largely unpublished research of his mentor, W. J. Lawrence, deposited in the University of Cincinnati, and in a kind of apostolic succession, Clark's widow, Gladys L. H. Clark and John C. Greene have produced *The Dublin Stage, 1720–1745: A Calendar of Plays, Entertainments, and Afterpieces* (Bethlehem, London and Toronto, 1993), which lists every Dublin performance in a twenty-five year period. Esther K. Sheldon's *Thomas Sheridan of Smock Alley* (Princeton, 1967) provides a vivid account of the years of Sheridan's management to 1758, concluding with a complete listing of plays for the period 1745–58 and a reliable

Sheridan bibliography. Working with a very different set of research tools, Linzi Simpson's archaeological work on Smock Alley, Crow Street and Werburgh Street theatres throws new light on these early theatres: see Linzi Simpson, *Smock Alley Theatre: The Evolution of a Building* (Dublin, 1996).

Given the international reputations of many Irish playwrights in the period, there are now extensive secondary literatures and standard editions for the major authors – *The Works of George Farquhar*, Shirley Strum Kenny (ed.), 2 vols. (Oxford, 1988); *The Dramatic Works of Richard Brinsley Sheridan*, Cecil Price (ed.), 2 vols. (Oxford 1973) – and selections of less well-known writers, such as Arthur Murphy, *Plays by Samuel Foote and Arthur Murphy*, George Taylor (ed.) (Cambridge 1984) and Charles Macklin, *Four Plays by Charles Macklin*, J. O. Bartley (ed.) (Hamden, Conn., 1968). Theatrical memoirs and biography were flourishing forms in this era, and James Thomas Kirkman's *Memoirs of the Life of Charles Macklin*, 2 vols. (London, 1799) is particularly fascinating. More recently, Fintan O'Toole's *A Traitor's Kiss: The Life of Richard Brinsley Sheridan* (London, 1997) is indispensable. Finally, anyone who wishes to understand the development of Irish identity on the stage in the eighteenth-century cannot ignore the chapter entitled 'The Fictional Irishman in English Literature' in Joep Leerssen's *Mere Irish and Fíor-Ghael* (1986; rpt. Cork, 1996).

NINETEENTH CENTURY

The early nineteenth century has long been something of a blind spot for Irish theatre historians, although T. J. Walsh's *Opera in Dublin 1798–1820: Frederick Jones and the Crow Street Theatre* (Oxford, 1993) is a notable exception. Otherwise, anyone interested in early nineteenth-century Irish theatre must be prepared to work with memoirs, pamphlets, and playbills, of which the Harvard Theatre Archive has particularly rich holdings. The theatrical dailies of the early 1820s, such as *The Theatrical Observer*, are a largely untapped source of detail, as are the articles published by the theatre manager J. W. Calcraft in the *Dublin University Magazine* beginning in 1850.

The second half of the nineteenth century has been better served by recent commentators. The opening chapters of Martin Meisel's *Shaw and the Nineteenth-Century Theatre* (New York, 1963) and Stephen Watt's *Joyce, O'Casey and the Irish Popular Theatre* (Syracuse, 1991) both provide a vivid sense of Irish popular theatre in the period, while

Kerry Powell's *Oscar Wilde and the Theatre of the 1890s* (Cambridge, 1990) places Wilde in the context of the English theatre culture of the time. Cheryl Herr has edited a collection of scripts by J. W. Whitbread and P. J. Bourke: *For the Land They Loved: Irish Political Melodramas 1890–1925* (Syracuse, 1991), while Stephen Watt has edited some of Hubert O'Grady's works for a special edition of *The Journal of Irish Literature*, 13:1 and 2 (January to May 1984). There is lively biography of the era's most important figure, *Dion Boucicault* by Richard Fawkes (London, New York and Melbourne, 1979), and an excellent chapter on Boucicault in John P. Harrington's *The Irish Play on the New York Stage, 1874–1966* (Lexington, Ky, 1997). Philip B. Ryan fills in many gaps with *The Lost Theatres of Dublin* (Westbury, 1998), while the popular theatre's most colourful advocate, Séamus de Búrca, has published a history of the Queen's, *The Queen's Royal Theatre Dublin 1829–1969* (Dublin, 1983), the materials for which he donated to the Gilbert Collection in the Dublin City Library. There are further de Búrca deposits in the Dublin Theatre Archive.

TWENTIETH CENTURY TO 1930

When the Irish theatre historian reaches the Irish Literary Renaissance of the 1890s, the challenge is not too little, but too much published commentary. A short bibliographic essay cannot hope to do justice to a period in which the bibliographies for the major figures – Yeats in particular – are book length studies in their own right. In this regard, the standard research tools become a necessity, in particular K. P. S. Jochum, *W.B. Yeats: A Classified Bibliography of Criticism*, 2nd edn (Urbana and Chicago, 1990), which contains sections on the Abbey, Gate and Dublin Drama League. At the risk of making invidious choices, two recent biographies of Yeats make good starting points: Terence Brown, *The Life of W.B. Yeats* (Dublin, 1999) and Roy Foster, *W.B. Yeats: A Life*, vol. I, *The Apprentice Mage* (Oxford, 1997). James W. Flannery's *W.B. Yeats and the Idea of a Theatre* (London, New Haven, 1976) still holds its place, and anyone looking for visual material on Yeats' theatre should see Liam Miller, *The Noble Drama of W.B. Yeats* (Dublin, 1977).

Similarly, recent encyclopedic biographies of Shaw and Synge make good starting points for these writers: Michael Holroyd, *Bernard Shaw*, 4 vols. (London, 1988–92); and W. J. McCormack, *Fool of the Family: A Life of J.M. Synge* (London, 2000), although Declan Kiberd's *Synge and the Irish Language*, 2nd edn (Dublin, 1993) stands up well in the comparatively less populated world of Synge criticism. Although now dated as a guide to recent criticism, E. H. Mikhail's *J.M. Synge: A Bibliography of Criticism* (London, 1975) provides a valuable list of early reviews. When working on O'Casey, the most important research tool is Bernice Schrank's exhaustive *Sean O'Casey: A Research and Production Sourcebook* (Westport, Conn., 1996). There are a number of lively biographies of Sean O'Casey, none yet definitive, against which details in his unreliable, but fascinating, *Autobiographies,* 2 vols. (New York, 1963) should be checked.

Anyone who wants to get a sense of Dublin theatre culture in the early twentieth century must see Joseph Holloway's diaries, which record his almost nightly visits to the theatre from the late 1890s until his death in 1944. The original diary, amounting to over twenty-five million words, is in the National Library of Ireland, while a selection up to 1926 has been edited by Robert Hogan and Michael J. O'Neill as *Joseph Holloway's Irish Theatre* (Carbondale, Ill., 1967), with three shorter volumes covering years 1926–44 (Carbondale, Ill., 1968, 1969 and 1970). Hogan has been the period's indefatigable annalist, editing *The Modern Irish Drama: A Documentary History* in six volumes: *The Irish Literary Theatre 1899–1901* (with James Kilroy) (Dublin, 1975); *Laying the Foundations 1902–1904* (Dublin, 1976); *The Years of Synge 1905–1909* (Dublin, 1978); *The Rise of the Realists 1910–1915* (with Daniel J. Poteet) (Dublin, 1979); *The Art of the Amateur 1916–1920* (with Richard Burnham) (Dublin, 1984) and *The Years of O'Casey 1921–1926* (Dublin, 1992). Bringing together newspaper clippings and other source materials, largely from the Abbey Scrapbooks in the National Library of Ireland, this series is a rich mine of primary material.

Indeed, many of the primary sources relating to the early Abbey have been published, and there are scholarly editions of the collected letters of Yeats, Synge and O'Casey: *The Collected Letters of W.B. Yeats*, vol. 1, John Kelly and Eric Domville (eds.) (Oxford, 1986); vol. 2, Warwick Gould, John Kelly and Deirdre Toomey (eds.) (Oxford, 1997); vol. 3, John Kelly and Ronald Suchard (eds.) (Oxford, 1994); *The Complete Letters of J.M. Synge*, Ann Saddlemyer (ed.), 2 vols. (Oxford, 1983–4) and *The Letters of Sean O'Casey*, David Krause (ed.), 4 vols. (Washington, 1975–1992). The Coole edition of Lady Gregory's work includes her autobiographical writings: *Our Irish Theatre*, *Seventy Years* and two volumes of *Journals* (all Gerrards Cross, 1972, 1974, 1978 and 1987). For a serviceable cross-section of this basic primary material, see Ann Saddlemyer (ed.) *Theatre Business: The Correspondence of the First Abbey Theatre Directors* (Gerrards Cross, 1982). Similarly, editions of plays by the major figures in the Irish Renaissance range from multi-volume definitive editions to inexpensive paperbacks, with some of the more obscure material in *Lost Plays of the Irish Renaissance* Robert Hogan (ed.) (Dixon, California, 1970).

From the beginning, the Abbey had a sense of its own history, and following Peter Kavanagh's bad-tempered *The Story of the Abbey Theatre* (New York, 1950), authorised histories have appeared at roughly twenty-year intervals: Lennox Robinson, *Ireland's Abbey Theatre: A History 1899–1951* (London, 1951); Hugh Hunt, *The Abbey: Ireland's National Theatre 1904–1979* (Dublin, 1979), and Robert Welch, *The Abbey Theatre 1899–1999: Form and Pressure* (Oxford, 1999). Robinson contains full cast lists for most productions, Hunt has an appendix of Abbey premières, while Welch draws on the extensive collection of unpublished plays in the National Library of Ireland and in the Abbey Archive. For a more detailed account of the early Abbey, see Adrian Frazier, *Behind the Scenes: Yeats, Horniman and the Struggle for the Abbey Theatre* (Berkeley, Los Angeles, London, 1990). For a reminder that the Abbey was not the only show in town, see William J. Feeney, *Drama in Hardwicke Street: A History of the Irish Theatre Company* (Madison, 1984) and Brenna Katz Clarke and Harold Ferrar, *The Dublin Drama League, 1918–1941* (Dublin, 1979).

TWENTIETH CENTURY: 1930–2000

It is almost with relief that the Irish theatre historian reaches the 1930s, when the stream of secondary material dwindles. Indeed, there is still no thorough study of the amateur theatre, apart from local histories published by individual companies and festivals. For the professional theatre, there is Robert Hogan's *After the Irish Renaissance* (London, 1968), and Michael J. O'Neill's *The Abbey at the Queen's* (Nepean, Ontario, 1999) provides full cast lists for the period 1951–66. The recovery of Teresa Deevey's critical reputation has been aided by a special issue of the *Irish University Review* (Spring/Summer 1995), edited by Christopher Murray. What commentary does exist for this period has been included in larger surveys, of which Murray's *Twentieth-Century Irish Drama: Mirror Up to Nation* (Manchester, 1997) is more sympathetic than most to the theatre of the 1930s and 1940s. Sam Hanna Bell's *The Theatre in Ulster* (Dublin, 1972) begins with the Ulster Literary Theatre at the turn of the century, but is strong on Ulster theatre at mid-century, for which excellent sources exist in the Linenhall Theatre Archive in Belfast, whose archivist, Ophelia Byrne, has published a very useful short study, *The Stage in Ulster from the Eighteenth Century* (Belfast, 1997). Nonetheless, many key plays of mid-century are unpublished or out of print, although this has been remedied in part by the publisher Colin Smythe, who has printed selected plays by St John Ervine, M. J. Molloy, Lennox Robinson, Micheál Mac Líammóir, Denis Johnston, as well as earlier work by T. C. Murray, Lady Gregory, Douglas Hyde, Edward Marytn, George Moore, and Boucicault.

Otherwise, most studies skip directly from the late Yeats to Samuel Beckett. With Beckett, the best strategy is to begin with James Knowlson's unsurpassed biography, *Damned to Fame: A Life of Samuel Beckett* (London, 1996), before sifting through P. J. Murphy's *Critique of Beckett Criticism* (Columbia, SC, 1994). Beckett in performance is a particularly rich area, ranging from classics like Ruby Cohn's *Just Play: Beckett's Theatre* (Princeton, NJ, 1980) to more specialised studies, including Anna McMullan's *Theatre on Trial: Samuel Beckett's Later Drama* (London and New York, 1993). Anyone wishing to make sense of Beckett as an Irish writer should see Vivian Mercier, *Beckett/Beckett* (Oxford, 1977), John P. Harrington, *The Irish Beckett* (Syracuse, 1991) and Anthony Roche, who makes Beckett and Behan the starting points for his survey, *Contemporary Irish Drama: From Beckett to McGuinness* (Dublin, 1994). For Beckett on the Irish stage, an essential resource is: Christopher Murray, 'Beckett Productions in Ireland: A Survey', *Irish University Review*, 14,1 (Spring 1984) 103–25. For the first Irish *Godot*, see Alan Simpson, *Beckett and Behan and a Theatre in Dublin* (London, 1978), and Caroline Swift's history of the Pike Theatre, *Stage by Stage* (Dublin, 1985), for which the materials have been deposited in Trinity College, Dublin.

Swift's book is one of only a handful of histories of Irish theatres, including Conor O'Malley's history of the Lyric, *A Poet's Theatre* (Dublin, 1988), and Marilyn Richtarik's well researched *Acting Between the Lines: Field Day Theatre Company and Irish Cultural Politics, 1980–84* (Oxford, 1995). For other theatres, the gap is only partly filled by commemorative booklets, such as Jerome Hynes (ed.), *Druid: The First Ten Years* (Galway, 1985), which is now rare, although the National University of Ireland, Galway, holds archive materials for histories of both Druid and An Taibhdhearc. The same would be true of the Gate, were it not for Christopher FitzSimon's double biography of Edwards and Mac Líammóir, *The Boys* (London, 1994), which is effectively a history of the Gate, whose early material is archived in Northwestern University in Illinois. For a list of Gate productions up to 1978, see Peter Luke (ed.), *Enter Certain Players* (Dublin, 1978).

For the best short account of the workings of the Irish theatre world at the end of the twentieth century, see Christopher Murray and

Martin Drury, 'The Theatre System of Ireland' in *Theatre Worlds in Motion: Structures, Politics and Developments in the Countries of Western Europe*, H. Van Maanen and S. E. Wilmer (eds.) (Amsterdam and Atlanta, 1998), while Declan Gorman (ed.), *Dialogues 1996: Proceedings of the Arts Council Theatre Review Consultations* (Dublin 1996) provides an opportunity to hear theatre practitioners speak about their profession. Also good on performance are some of the essays in Eberhard Bort (ed.), *State of Play: Irish Theatre in the 'Nineties* (Trier, 1996), and Eamonn Jordan (ed.), *Theatre Stuff: Critical Essays on Contemporary Irish Drama* (Dublin, 2000). Loughlin Deegan (ed.), *The Irish Theatre Handbook* (Dublin, 1998; updated regularly) is the best source of information on venues and companies. By 2002 there should be an online database of all new Irish work produced between 1950 and 2000. Meanwhile Bernice Schrank and William M. Demastes (eds.), *Irish Playwrights, 1880–1995: A Research and Production Sourcebook* (Westport, Conn., 1997) is the starting point for tracing production histories in the modern period.

Most writing about the Irish theatre in the final decades of the twentieth century has concentrated on dramatic writing. Fintan O'Toole's study of Tom Murphy, *The Politics of Magic*, 2nd edn (Dublin and London, 1994) is excellent, Frank McGuinness' work has been charted in Eamonn Jordan's *The Feast of Famine: The Plays of Frank McGuinness* (Bern and New York, 1997), while Brian Friel has inspired a whole shelf of books, of which Richard Pine's *Brian Friel and Ireland's Drama* (London, 1990) stands out. However, there is a sense in which Friel is his own best interpreter. See *Brian Friel: Essays, Diaries, Interviews: 1964–1999*, Christopher Murray (ed.) (London and New York, 1999).

The expansion of Irish theatre and drama studies has been aided by an increased availability of Irish plays. Irish-based Gallery Press have been publishing individual plays by Murphy, Friel and others since the early 1970s, while Faber have a tradition of publishing Irish playwrights with international reputations, including Samuel Beckett, Brian Friel and Frank McGuinness. Methuen have responded to the increased interaction between Irish and English theatre worlds with collections by Sebastian Barry, Marina Carr, Declan Hughes, Martin McDonagh, and Tom Murphy, while Nick Hern Books have started publishing younger Irish playwrights, including Conor McPherson and Gary Mitchell. See Peggy Butcher, 'Drama Publishing', *Irish Review*, 22 (Summer 1998), pp. 9–15. Keeping pace, surveys of Irish drama have increased in number and critical sophistication. In addition to Murray's *Mirror Up to Nation* and Roche's *Contemporary Irish Drama* (mentioned above), there is Nicholas Grene's *The Politics of Irish Drama* (Cambridge, 2000), Lionel Pilkington's *National Theatres in Irish Politics* (London, 2001), and Shaun Richards' *The Drama of Ireland: An Infinite Rehearsal* (London, 2001), adding to D. E. S. Maxwell's *Modern Irish Drama 1891–1980* (Cambridge, 1984) – to which the current volume was originally intended as a successor.

Index